MCDST Guide to Supporting Users and Troubleshooting Desktop Applications on a Microsoft® Windows® XP Operating System

Ron Carswell

COURSE TECHNOLOGY
CENGAGE Learning™

Australia • Brazil • Japan • Korea • Mexico • Singapore • Spain • United Kingdom • United States

COURSE TECHNOLOGY
CENGAGE Learning™

MCDST Guide to Supporting Users and Troubleshooting Desktop Applications on a Microsoft® Windows® XP Operating System

Ron Carswell

Managing Editor: William Pitkin III

Product Manager: Manya Chylinski

Developmental Editor: Jill Batistick

Production Editor: Pamela Elizian

Manufacturing Coordinator: Trevor Kallop

MQA Technical Leader: John Freitas

Product Marketing Manager: Brian Berkeley

Associate Product Manager: Sarah Santoro

Editorial Assistant: Jenny Smith

Cover Design: Steve Deschene

Text Designer: GEX Publishing Services

Compositor: GEX Publishing Services

© 2009 Course Technology, Cengage Learning

ALL RIGHTS RESERVED. No part of this work covered by the copyright hereon may be reproduced, transmitted, stored, or used in any form or by any means graphic, electronic, or mechanical, including but not limited to photocopying, recording, scanning, digitizing, taping, Web distribution, information networks, or information storage and retrieval systems, except as permitted under Section 107 or 108 of the 1976 United States Copyright Act, without the prior written permission of the publisher.

For product information and technology assistance, contact us at
Cengage Learning Customer & Sales Support, 1-800-354-9706

For permission to use material from this text or product, submit all requests online at **cengage.com/permissions**
Further permission questions can be emailed to
permissionrequest@cengage.com

ISBN-13: 978-1-4239-0321-5

ISBN-10: 1-4239-0321-8

Course Technology
25 Thomson Place
Boston, Massachusetts, 02210
USA

Cengage Learning is a leading provider of customized learning solutions with office locations around the globe, including Singapore, the United Kingdom, Australia, Mexico, Brazil, and Japan. Locate your local office at: **international.cengage.com/region**

Cengage Learning products are represented in Canada by Nelson Education, Ltd.

Visit our corporate website at **cengage.com**

Printed in Canada

3 4 5 6 7 8 9 12 11 10 09

BRIEF
Contents

TABLE OF

Contents

CHAPTER ELEVEN
Resolve Folder and File Issues

CHAPTER TWELVE
Configure Application Security

Introduction

Welcome to *MCDST Guide to Supporting Users and Troubleshooting Desktop Applications on a Microsoft Windows XP Operating System*. This book offers you real-world examples, interactive activities, and many activities that reinforce key concepts and help you prepare for a career as a Microsoft Certified Desktop Support Technician. In addition, this book contains information that meets the objectives for the Microsoft Certified Desktop Support Technician certification exam #70-272, Supporting Users and Troubleshooting Desktop Applications on a Microsoft Windows XP Operating System. This book also features troubleshooting tips for solutions to common problems that you will encounter supporting users using Microsoft Office 2003 applications while running the Microsoft Windows XP operating system in either a home or corporate environment.

This book offers in-depth study of all the functions and features of installing, configuring, and maintaining Microsoft Office 2003 on the Windows XP operating system. They include configuring Internet Explorer and Outlook Express; resolving issues related to customizing and personalizing Office Applications; migrating from Outlook Express to Outlook; identifying and troubleshooting network problems; configuring Office security settings; and monitoring security vulnerabilities and updates. Throughout the book, we provide detailed Activities that let you experience firsthand the processes involved in desktop support. The main part of the chapter ends with a Chapter Summary to help you review what you have learned. We then provide pointed Review Questions to reinforce the concepts introduced in each chapter and to help you prepare for the Microsoft certification exam. Finally, to put a real-world slant on the concepts introduced in each chapter, we provide Case Projects to prepare you for situations that must be managed in a live desktop environment.

Microsoft released the latest service pack for Windows XP, Service Pack 2 (SP2), during the development of this book. In this book, the discussions, activities, and screen shots all reflect the appearance and functionality of the applications and Windows XP prior to SP2. Rewritten versions of activities and projects affected by the SP2 upgrade can be found on *www.course.com*.

Intended Audience

MCDST Guide to Supporting Users and Troubleshooting Desktop Applications on a Microsoft Windows XP Operating System is intended for people getting started in desktop support who have experience with Windows XP and Microsoft Office 2003 applications, in both home and corporate environments. To best understand the material in this book, you should have a working knowledge of operating in a workgroup or Active Directory domain environment.

Chapter Descriptions

There are 13 chapters in this book, as follows:

Chapter 1, "Introduction to Supporting Users," introduces the role of the Desktop Support Technician (DST). This chapter explains the relationships between the DST and other personnel in Information Technology (IT). Because building problem-resolution skills is important to the success of the DST, this chapter introduces the steps in problem-resolution workflow and the tools that the DST will be using on the job. The chapter finishes with a description of the certification exams available to the DST.

Chapter 2, "Overview of Microsoft User Applications," surveys the applications available in Windows XP and Microsoft Office 2003. The chapter concludes with a discussion of the Microsoft Office 2003 editions and Licensing programs.

Chapter 3, "Resolve Issues Related to Operating System Customization," provides the skills to answer your users' questions about customizing the features of Windows XP. More specifically, this chapter covers customization of the Start menu, regional and language settings, accessibility settings, display fonts, and folder settings.

Chapter 4, "Configure User-Related Issues," prepares you to resolve issues related to user configurations. The chapter starts with the necessary skills to access applications on computers with multiple users. Next, you will learn the steps to configure Windows XP to support applications.

Chapter 5, "Configure and Troubleshoot Internet Explorer and Outlook Express," provides the skills to support Internet Explorer. This includes such skills as: setting the security features of Internet Explorer, repairing Internet Explorer when files are damaged, and configuring the Internet Explorer's privacy options. Next, you will learn similar skills for Outlook Express.

Chapter 6, "Installing Office 2003," prepares you to install Microsoft Office 2003. First, you will learn to install Office using various techniques including installation from the Office CD-ROM and from images placed on file servers. Next, you will learn the process to troubleshoot application installation problems.

Chapter 7, "Configuring and Troubleshooting Operating System Features," shares the skills that you will need to assist your users as they use Windows XP and Microsoft Office 2003. The chapter starts with the features related to the Windows XP operating system: back up and restore files, manage performance settings, and configure settings to run older programs. The chapter closes with a section on troubleshooting, which provides skills you will want to add to your troubleshooting toolkit.

Chapter 8, "Resolving Issues Related to Office Application Usage," prepares you to resolve issues related to Microsoft Office 2003 application usage. You will learn the wide range of capabilities that can be tailored to make your users more productive. To support your users who work in multiple languages, you will want to install, configure, and use the Office Proofing Tools. You will learn to assist your users with the Office System Tools, which expand the capabilities of Office 2003.

Chapter 9, "Configure, Customize, and Migrate to Outlook," shows you how to resolve issues related to Microsoft Office Outlook 2003. First, you will learn to configure and customize Outlook features. Next, you will learn to help your users migrate from Outlook Express to Microsoft Office Outlook 2003. Last, you will learn to restore and repair e-mail files.

Chapter 10, "Configure and Troubleshoot Devices and Connectivity for Applications," focuses on identifying and troubleshooting devices in two areas: locally attached devices, including printers, and network connectivity. This chapter will prepare you to identify and troubleshoot devices with tools such as the Device Manager. Prior to resolving problems, you must first learn to describe the functions and capabilities of network components. Then, you will learn the skills to use the various utilities to assist with troubleshooting network connectivity.

Chapter 11, "Resolve Folder and File Issues," teaches you how to configure and troubleshoot access to the files within folders. To assist your users in sharing data with one or more computers in the Small Office Home Office, you must learn to configure and troubleshoot Simple File Sharing. To assist your users in larger networks, you must learn to work with the more advanced methods for securing access. Should your organization decide to manage hard disk space, you must be prepared to answer your users' questions regarding the controlled availability of disk space. If your users have laptop computers and are mobile, you need to be ready to assist them with the use of offline files.

Chapter 12, "Configure Application Security," zeroes in on the critical issue of network security. Network security is a joint, coordinated effort of all the members of IT. You will be prepared with the skills to assist your users with the settings for the Office applications. You will learn to work with security policies from networks from the Small Office Home Office level to larger organizations. You will learn to protect your organization from the consequences of rampant viruses and worms.

Chapter 13, "Manage Office Application Updates and Upgrades," prepares you to assist with upgrades from the Small Office Home Office to larger organizations. You will learn to work with the Office update process and how to prevent exploits from occurring. Last, you will learn the techniques to distribute updates to your users.

Features and Approach

MCDST Guide to Supporting Users and Troubleshooting Desktop Applications on a Microsoft Windows XP Operating System differs from other desktop support books in its unique hands-on approach and its orientation to real-world situations and problem solving. To help you comprehend how the support of Microsoft Office 2003 applications on the Windows XP operating systems is applied in real-world organizations, this book incorporates the following features:

- **Chapter Objectives**—Each chapter begins with a detailed list of the concepts to be mastered. This list gives you a quick reference to the chapter's contents and is a useful study aid.

- **Activities**—Activities are incorporated throughout the text, giving you practice in setting up, managing, and troubleshooting a network system. The Activities give you a strong foundation for carrying out network administration tasks in the real world. Because of the book's progressive nature, completing the Activities in each chapter is essential before moving on to the end-of-chapter materials and subsequent chapters.

- **Chapter Summaries**—Each chapter's text is followed by a summary of the concepts introduced in that chapter. These summaries provide a helpful way to recap and revisit the ideas covered in each chapter.

- **Key Terms**—All of the terms within the chapter that were introduced with boldfaced text are gathered together in the Key Terms list at the end of the chapter. This provides you with a method of checking your understanding of all the terms introduced.

- **Review Questions**—The end-of-chapter assessment begins with a set of Review Questions that reinforces the ideas introduced in each chapter. Answering these questions will ensure that you have mastered the important concepts.

- **Case Projects**—Finally, each chapter closes with a section that proposes certain situations. You are asked to evaluate the situations and decide upon the course of action to be taken to remedy the problems described. This valuable tool will help you sharpen your decision-making and troubleshooting skills, which are important to the DST.

- **Practice Exam**—A 50-question practice exam is included with this book. The questions are modeled after the actual MCDST certification exam and should serve as a test of your knowledge of the material presented in this book.

- **On the CD-ROM**—The CD-ROM includes CoursePrep® test preparation software, which provides more than 300 sample MCSE exam questions mirroring the look and feel of the MCSE exams.

Text and Graphic Conventions

Additional information and exercises have been added to this book to help you better understand what's being discussed in the chapter. Icons throughout the text alert you to these additional materials. The icons used in this book are described below.

Tips offer extra information on resources, how to attack problems, and time-saving shortcuts.

Notes present additional helpful material related to the subject being discussed.

The In the Workplace icon identifies information about supporting users and real-world examples of best practices.

The Caution icon identifies important information about potential mistakes or hazards.

Each Activity in this book is preceded by the Activity icon.

Case Project icons mark the end-of-chapter case projects, which are scenario-based assignments that ask you to independently apply what you have learned in the chapter.

Instructor's Resources

The following supplemental materials are available when this book is used in a classroom setting. All of the supplements available with this book are provided to the instructor on a single CD-ROM.

Electronic Instructor's Manual. The Instructor's Manual that accompanies this textbook includes additional instructional material to assist in class preparation, including suggestions for classroom activities, discussion topics, and additional projects.

Solutions are provided for the end-of-chapter material, including Review Questions, and where applicable, Activities and Case Projects. Solutions to the Practice Exams are also included.

ExamView®. This textbook is accompanied by ExamView, a powerful testing software package that allows instructors to create and administer printed, computer (LAN-based), and Internet exams. ExamView includes hundreds of questions that correspond to the topics covered in this text, enabling students to generate detailed study guides that include page references for further review. The computer-based and Internet testing components allow students to take exams at their computers and also save the instructor time by grading each exam automatically.

PowerPoint presentations. This book comes with Microsoft PowerPoint slides for each chapter. These are included as a teaching aid for classroom presentation, to make available to students on the network for chapter review, or to be printed for classroom distribution. Instructors, please feel at liberty to add your own slides for additional topics you introduce to the class.

Figure files. All of the figures and tables in the book are reproduced on the Instructor's Resource CD, in bitmap format. Similar to the PowerPoint presentations, these are included as a teaching aid for classroom presentation, to make available to students for review, or to be printed for classroom distribution.

Minimum Lab Requirements

Recommended network:

The recommended network consists of two instructor computers (Instructor01 and Instructor02). The students will have access to multiple computers labeled Student01–Student16. The total configuration is shown in the following figure:

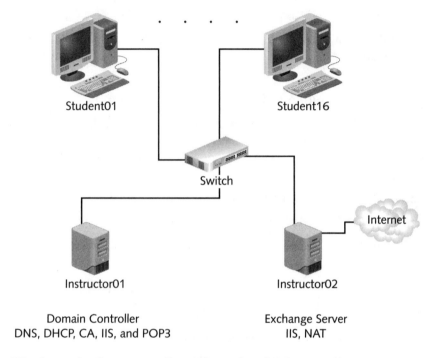

Domain Controller
DNS, DHCP, CA, IIS, and POP3

Exchange Server
IIS, NAT

Hardware/software configurations for the Instructor computers:

Instructor01 is a domain controller with Domain Name System (DNS), Dynamic Host Configuration Protocol (DHCP), Certification Authority (CA), Internet Information Service (IIS), and Post Office Protocol 3 (POP3) installed. The operating system is Microsoft Windows Server 2003. The required hardware configuration follows:

- Pentium 133 MHz (550 Mhz or higher is recommended)
- 128MB RAM (256 MB RAM is recommended)
- 2 GB of free space (4 GB of free space is recommended)
- CD–ROM, floppy disk
- One network interface card networked to other computers in the classroom

Instructor02 is a member server with Microsoft Exchange 2003 Standard, Internet Information Server (IIS), and Routing and Remote Access Network Address Translation (NAT). The operating system is Microsoft Windows Server 2003. The required hardware configuration follows:

- Pentium 133 MHz (550 Mhz or higher is recommended)
- 256MB RAM (512 MB RAM is recommended)
- 4 GB of free space (8 GB of free space is recommended)
- CD-ROM, floppy disk Two network interface cards: the first interface is networked to other computers in the classroom; the second interface is networked to the Internet

Hardware/software configurations for the Student computers:

The Student01—Student16 computers are domain members with Microsoft Windows XP Professional installed. Microsoft Office 2003 will be installed and uninstalled in Chapter 2. Microsoft Office 2003 will be installed again in Chapter 6. The Student computers need the following:

- Pentium 233 MHz (550 Mhz or higher is recommended)
- 128 MB RAM (256 MB RAM is recommended)
- 2 GB of free space (4 GB of free space is recommended)
- CD-ROM, floppy disk
- One network interface card networked to other computers in the classroom

Use the following instructions to set up the Studentxx computers:

1. Name student computers **Student01–Student16**.
2. Set the local administrator password to **Password1**.
3. Create a local user named **Student** during installation and set the password to **Password1**.
4. Join the **classroom.net** domain.

Active Directory Users and Computers setup instructions:

1. Create an OU called **Students** and create 16 user accounts named **user01–user16**. Provide a first name of **First**, **Second**, etc., with the last name of **User**. Make the password **Password1** and select **Allow Password Change**.
2. Create a global group called **Students Global Group** that contains the 16 user accounts located in the Students OU.
3. Create a folder on instructor01 called **users**. Share with **Full control**. Set NTFS permissions for users to **Modify**.

4. Create an OU called **Roaming** and create 16 User accounts named **roam01–roam16**. Provide a first name of **First**, **Second**, etc., with the last name of **Roaming**. Add a profile entry of **\\instructor01\users\%username%** prior to copying the user accounts. Use the password **Password1**.

5. Create an OU called **Student Computers**, then move the **Student01–Student16** computers to this OU.

6. Create a GPO linked to the Student Computers. From Computer Configuration, select **Administrative Templates**, **Remote Assistance**, **Enable Solicited Remote Assistance**, then select **Allow helpers to remotely control the computer**.

POP3 e-mail setup instructions:

1. Install e-mail Services using Add/Remove Windows Components.

2. From Administrative Tools, start the POP3 Service.

3. Open Server Properties, then uncheck the **Always create an associated user for new mailboxes** check box.

4. Open New Domain, then type **classroom.net**.

5. Setup e-mail accounts to match User01–User16.

CA setup instructions:

1. From Windows components, install IIS.

2. From Windows components, install Certificate Services.

3. Select Enterprise root CA. Enter **Classroom** as the Common name.

4. Respond **yes** to each prompt during configuration.

ACKNOWLEDGMENTS

This text is a product of the talents of many individuals. First, I wish to say thanks to the staff at Course Technology. More specifically, I would like to thank my Project Manager, Manya Chylinsky, for her patience and help. This is my third book with my Development Editor, Jill Batistick. Jill has provided the inspiration to mold my thoughts clearly and concisely.

I would also like to thank my wife, Coleen, for the numerous hours devoted to proofing the text and testing each lab activity. Her insight, from a student perspective, enhanced the quality of this text.

Last, I would like to thank the following reviewers for their help in pulling this book together: C. Alex Herron, Project TRAIN IT; Vy Nguyen, Okaloosa-Walton College, Eglin Air Force Base; Glen Porter, Regis University, SPS Graduate Program, Colorado, Westwood College of Technology, Colorado; and Diane Roselli, Harrisburg Area Community College.

ABOUT THE AUTHOR

Ron has more than 20 years of computer experience with both small and large organizations. Ron holds a bachelor's degree in business administration from the University of Texas and a master's degree in business administration from Baylor University. He has received the A+, N+, CTT+, MCSA, MCSE, CCNA, and MCDST certifications. He is currently an assistant professor at San Antonio College, where he instructs in A+, N+, MCSA, CCNA, and MCDST certification courses.

1

INTRODUCTION TO SUPPORTING USERS

After reading this chapter and completing the exercises, you will be able to:

♦ Describe the job role of the desktop support technician

♦ Describe the relationship of the desktop support technician to other Information Technology areas

♦ Describe the steps in the problem resolution workflow and the use of problem tracking software

♦ Explain the importance of the operating system version and computer configuration on troubleshooting

♦ Use Computer Management to troubleshoot problems

♦ Use the Remote Assistant to resolve operating system/application problems

♦ Describe certifications for the desktop support technician

As you know, Microsoft has created a certification for the **Microsoft Certified Desktop Support Technician (MCDST)**. To support the user community, the desktop support technician (DST) calls upon a wide range of personal and technical skills. The successful DST must provide these skills to resolve user problems. The variety of hardware and software deployed in the modern organization demands that the DST continue to update these skills.

This chapter begins with an overview of the role of the DST, a member of a large department that provides the computing needs of the organization. The success of this department is dependent upon an understanding of the roles played by the teams within Information Technology (IT). Next, the importance of problem tracking and the use of problem-tracking software are outlined.

As the DST must resolve problems related to various operating systems and computer applications, he must be keenly aware of the operating system idiosyncrasies. The environment in which the computer functions dictates the actions that the DST may take to troubleshoot problems. Microsoft provides a number of tools for the DST to use in problem resolution. This chapter includes an introduction to a number of tools you will want to include in your tool kit. One important tool permits a DST to view a user's desktop remotely while chatting with the user.

Certification is often a job requirement for the DST. This chapter concludes with an overview of the Microsoft Certified Desktop Support Technician certification. Additional certification alternatives are suggested.

JOB ROLE OF THE DESKTOP SUPPORT TECHNICIAN

The DST is responsible for providing support to users of desktop computers. The term **desktop** is short for "desktop computer." A personal computer, on the desktop or placed next to the desk, qualifies as a desktop. In reality, the typical DST is required to support more than desktops. Many users travel with their laptop computers and depend on a wide range of peripheral equipment, including printers and scanners.

IN THE WORKPLACE
While Microsoft selected the term **desktop support technician**, many other names exist for the "personal computer guy." Most organizations cannot function without their PC Support Technician, Computer Support Analyst, Help Desk Technician, IT Support Specialist, and other personal computer experts.

Users depend on the DST to maintain the functional reliability of their desktop computers. Many skills are required to successfully troubleshoot desktop environments running on the Microsoft Windows operating system. (For the exam, you will be tested on Microsoft Windows XP.) Also required are the skills to troubleshoot the applications, such as Microsoft Office, that are used in the daily work of your organization. (You will be tested on Microsoft Office 2003.)

To be successful on the job, you should understand the nature of the career that you selected. In the following sections, you will be introduced to the skills that the DST needs to be successful.

Nature of the Job

You will be required to provide support when your users have problems. If your users did not have problems, there would be no need for the DST. You are at your best when you successfully resolve the latest crisis, disaster, or calamity!

For your users, these events can be stressful. Your user may be working on a rush project and her desktop is not able to perform the tasks that are required to complete the project, making her angry or upset. Having to wait for the resolution of her problem adds to this anxiety. To be successful as a DST, you must be able to reduce the tension in the air!

Exhibits People Skills

The successful DST is a "people person." The DST is required to interact effectively with various types of people. Just as in society, people can be warm and friendly or cold and difficult. To successfully operate in your environment, the following must be true:

- You must possess excellent communication skills, both oral and written.

- You must exhibit a strong customer service focus. Your ability to respond with a calm, analytical purpose will go a long way toward gaining the respect of the user community.

- You are a professional. You exhibit a professional demeanor and attitude, which includes meeting the professional dress code of your organization.

Takes on Multiple Tasks

The DST is a "multitasker," possessing the ability to undertake numerous varied tasks simultaneously. On a daily basis, the DST responds to varied requests. The ability to prioritize the following varied tasks—which are only a sample of the tasks that you might encounter in the workplace—is a key to meeting these challenges:

- Respond to computer-generated problem tickets

- Resolve user desktop problems

- Establish and maintain hardware/software inventory logs

- Relocate desktops including moves/adds/changes

- Roll-out of new and reconfigured applications

- Maintain hardware/software on the desktops

- Coordinate off-site repairs

Knows Networking Environment

Your knowledge of the Microsoft networking environment permits you to interrelate the desktop with the networking environment. For example, you can visualize the relationship between the desktop computer and the other computers on the network. You use this visual image to troubleshoot the desktop computers that connect to the network.

You are aware that networks come in many sizes. Several desktops, a printer, and perhaps a file server could be connected to form a workgroup. As additional desktops, printers, and file servers are added, the network continues to grow in size. You will use your knowledge and skills to troubleshoot problems associated with various-sized networks.

Possesses Software Experience

Your software experience includes, in addition to the Microsoft Windows operating system, a wide range of Microsoft products, such as Internet Explorer and Outlook Express. Also, you must have knowledge of the Microsoft Office products: Excel, Word, Outlook, and PowerPoint. In many organizations, you will be required to learn additional software applications.

While Microsoft Office 2003, Internet Explorer, Outlook, and Outlook Express are the focus of the exams for the MCDST, you may be required to support many other applications. Some of the applications may have been developed in-house. Your users may select products from a number of commercial firms such as those listed in Table 1-1.

Table 1-1   Representative commercial software products

Category	Vendor	Application
Accounting	Best Software	Peachtree Accounting
	Intuit	QuickBooks
Antivirus	Symantec	Norton Antivirus
Database	Business Objects	Crystal Reports
	Filemaker	Filemaker Pro
Graphics	Adobe	Photoshop
Office Suite	Corel	WordPerfect Office
	Sun Microsystems	Star Office
Project Management	Microsoft	Project
Publishing	Adobe	Acrobat
	Scansoft	Omnipage
Security	Broderbund	Zone Alarm
	Symantec	Norton Personal Firewall
Utilities	Symantec	Norton System Works

Works Within a Team

You will work within a team of other technicians. In many organizations, the team size may be from two to five persons. Depending on the structure of the team, you may start as the "junior" member. Each team is normally assigned a "senior" member that possesses a deeper knowledge of the required technical skills. In addition to the user community, you and your teammates will interact with other teams in the IT community. Other teams in IT will be discussed in the "Relationships in the IT Department" section of this chapter.

Activity 1-1: Researching the Job Role of the DST

Time Required: 30 minutes

Objective: Describe the job role of the desktop support technician.

Description: In this project, you will research the career opportunities for the DST in order to visualize the responsibilities of your future job. To do so, access the following Web site, which provides DST job information.

1. Log on to your computer using the user name **user01** and password **Password1**. For this and all Activities, the students should substitute their assigned usernames (user02, user03, etc.).

2. Open your Web browser.

3. In the Address line, type **www.monster.com** (or the Web site suggested by your instructor) and press **Enter**.

To have Internet Explorer provide the prefix www. and suffix .com, type the site name (for example, monster) and press the Ctrl+Enter keys.

4. Click the **Search Jobs** button. If necessary, click the **Not today, thanks** option button, and click the **Next** button. Type **desktop support**, and press **Enter**.

5. Scroll to locate an interesting entry and click the entry.

You will be asked to record information, observations, and notes as you complete the Activities in this book. For your personal project log, select a hard-backed, lined notepad. Recording your findings will enable you to enhance your retention of the many facts that you will acquire as you prepare for both the MCDST exam and your future job.

6. Read the information on this job. Add this information to your project log and click the **Back** button.

7. Repeat Steps 5 and 6 for additional entries.

8. In your project log, write a brief summary describing the job role of the desktop support technician.

9. Close your Web browser.

RELATIONSHIPS WITHIN THE IT DEPARTMENT

The DST coordinates activities with other members of the Information Technology (IT) organization. Figure 1-1 illustrates the organization of a representative IT Department. Depending on the size of the organization, the titles may change. In smaller organizations, responsibilities may be merged. However, the reporting relationships are still representative.

The following sections discuss each organizational group.

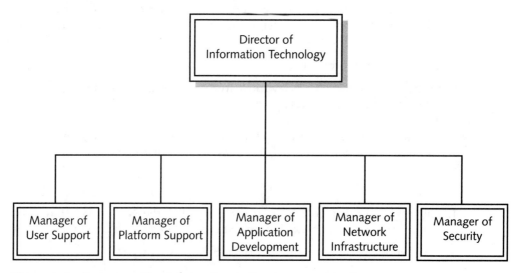

Figure 1-1   Representative information technology organization

Director of Information Technology

The Director of Information Technology is responsible for the IT Department. He or she provides direction to the managers that report to him. Managers reporting to the director manage groups of employees in organizational areas shown in the second row of Figure 1-1.

Manager of User Support

The Manager of User Support provides the user community with day-to-day user support. This manager is responsible for the management of teams of employees that provide the interface between the user community and the IT organization. The **Help Desk** (a place where a user can call to get assistance with a problem) provides a central contact point for the resolution of problems. When problems cannot be resolved by any member of the Help Desk, they are assigned to other personnel within IT. As a member of the Desktop Support team, you will be resolving problems assigned by the Help Desk.

Manager of Platform Support

The Manager of Platform Support provides primary support for the applications developed by the Application Development team. As you know, **servers** are computers deployed using Microsoft Windows Server 2003. The manager's analysts maintain the **database servers** (computers that maintain a collection of information organized for storage and retrieval) and **application servers** (computers that run programs to process the data housed on database servers) that provide mission critical applications to support the business objectives of the organization. In addition, these servers may use various forms of **UNIX** (an operating system that originated at Bell Labs in 1969). On database servers, you will find **database management systems** that provide for the storage and maintenance of the data required for the applications developed by the Application Development team. You may need to contact the Platform Support team when resolving problems of user access to the data and applications supported by the Platform Support team.

Manager of Application Development

The teams reporting to the Manager of Application Development develop and customize the applications used to support the **business processes** (the steps an organization takes to fulfill its objectives) of the organization. The teams develop computer programs in computer programming languages. Should the organization decide to purchase software packages, customization may be required to meet the business processes of the organization. Current trends include the development of Web-based applications for Internet servers. When resolving user problems related to applications developed by the team, you may need to contact the Application Development team. For example, your user needs assistance completing tasks related to the entry of data into a Web form.

Manager of Network Infrastructure

The Manager of Network Infrastructure supports the network infrastructure that provides connectivity for the organization. This network infrastructure includes **LANs** (Local Area Networks) and **WANs** (Wide Area Networks). The Network Infrastructure team members should also be familiar with **routers**, which are devices that forward packets to the next network, and **switches**, which are devices that channel data between computers. The manager's team configures routers and switches to move packets throughout the network. Physical cabling to connect the computers and network devices are an additional responsibility of the team. The team installs and configures a range of services for network servers including:

- **Domain Controller (DC):** Manages access to network resources
- **File and print services:** Stores data files and provides print support
- **Domain Name System (DNS):** Resolves computer names into Internet addresses

As a desktop support technician, you may need to contact the Network Infrastructure team to resolve a desktop problem related to the network. For example, your user may need assistance connecting to a printer located on the network or the user is unable to store a file on a network file server.

Manager of Security

The Manager of Security manages a small, but vital team. This group is charged with the responsibility to protect the assets of the organization. This security begins with **physical security** (protection for computer rooms and equipment) for the computers in use within the organization. An equally important responsibility is providing the security for the data of the organization, which includes the file and print servers. The Security team protects the organization's internal network from the threats on the Internet with a firewall; the Manager of Security creates and updates the **security policy** that specifies the procedures required to secure the organization's assets.

You may need to contact the Network Infrastructure team to resolve a desktop problem related to the network. For example, your user needs assistance connecting to a printer located on the network or the user is unable to store a file on a network file server.

ACTIVITY

Activity 1-2: Researching the Relationships Within Information Technology

Time Required: 30 minutes

Objective: Describe the relationship of the desktop support technician to other Information Technology areas.

Description: In this project, you will research information about the various work areas within the IT department so that you can visualize the potential work relationships in your new job. You will use a search engine to search for Web sites that provide information on the infrastructure for their Information Technology organization.

1. If necessary, log on to your computer using the user name **user01** and password **Password1**.

2. Open your Web browser.

3. In the Address line, type **www.google.com** (or the search engine suggested by your instructor) and press **Enter**.

4. Type **information technology infrastructure** (or the search text suggested by your instructor) in the Search text box and press **Enter**.

5. Scroll to locate an entry that appears interesting and click the entry.

6. Read the information on this entry. Add this information to your project log and click the **Back** button.

7. Repeat Steps 5 and 6 for additional entries.

8. In your project log, write a brief summary that describes the relationship of the desktop support technician to other Information Technology areas.

9. Close your Web browser.

RESOLVE USER PROBLEMS

One of the major tasks for the IT Department is to participate in the resolution of user problems. Problem tracking provides a vehicle to record timely information about the problem and its resolution. The following sections of this chapter describe the three scenarios depicted in Figure 1-2. Each scenario depicts the resolution of a problem by one of the three levels.

Level 1: Problem Resolved by the Help Desk

Level 1 support is the initial contact point for the resolution of user problems. Level 1 support is provided by the Help Desk.

Let's walk through a simple example of the steps for resolving a customer's problems:

1. The user calls the Help Desk to report a problem: The user cannot log on to his computer.

2. The Help Desk person resets the user's password.

3. The problem is solved. Life is good once again.

Industry analysts estimate that 65–80% of problem requests are resolved by the Help Desk at Level 1.

IN THE WORKPLACE

Level 2: Problem Resolved by the DST

Level 2 support includes addressing problems referred by the Help Desk. Where the problem cannot be resolved at Level 1, the Help Desk personnel will escalate (raise the problem status to higher level) or assign the problem to Level 2 support in the DST **queue** (a line of items waiting to be handled). In some organizations, you will be assigned the problem by your supervisor or the Help Desk personnel. In the remaining organizations, the DST will pick up the next assignment in the queue.

Let's walk through the steps for which the DST will be asked to resolve a problem while working at Level 2. The steps, as always, start with Level 1:

1. The user calls the Help Desk and reports that he has noticed that he does not have virus protection software installed.

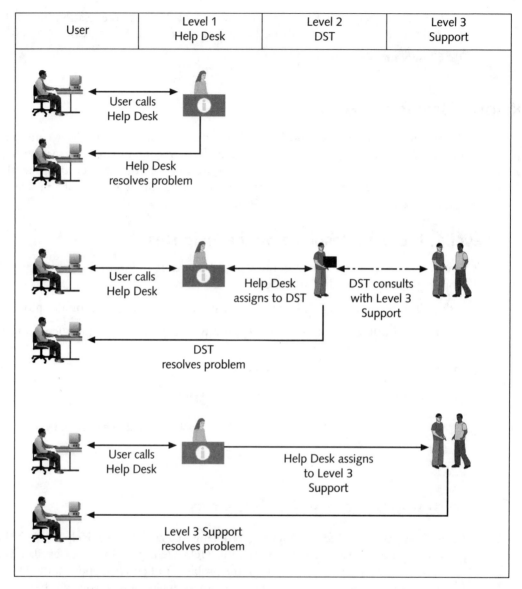

Figure 1-2   Work flow for problem resolution

2. The Help Desk records the user's request along with other pertinent information for the DST and provides this information to the DST.

3. The DST contacts the user. The DST addresses the problem. Occasionally, the DST may need to contact Level 3 support for assistance with the problem.

4. The DST reports the resolution of the problem to the Help Desk.

Level 3: Problem Resolved by Level 3 Support

Level 3 support also includes addressing problems referred by the Help Desk. If the problem involves multiple users, the Help Desk personnel may assign the problem to a Level 3 support team. Level 3 support consists of the various teams within the IT Department, such as the network infrastructure team. An example of a problem assigned to Level 3 support would be a network outage resulting from a failed network switch.

Let's walk through the steps for which the Level 3 support will be asked to resolve a problem. The steps, as always, start with Level 1:

1. Multiple users call the Help Desk and report that they are unable to access the resources on the network.

2. The Help Desk records the users' requests along with other pertinent information and provides this information to the particular Level 3 support team.

3. A member of the Network Infrastructure team investigates and resolves the problem.

4. The team member reports the resolution of the problem to the Help Desk.

Using Problem Tracking

As a DST, you will be required to use problem tracking as you resolve assigned problems. Your organization may use either a manual or an automated system. A manual system might use forms to record information. An automated system might use an in-house developed application or a commercial system.

Problem tracking maintains a record of the resolution of user problems. Multiple entries comprise the record for each problem. Each entry represents one action—a user call, a DST's action, and so on. The following sections present the use of problem-tracking software to support recording the information about a user problem.

Step 1: Create Problem Ticket

When the user calls the Help Desk, a problem ticket is created. The **problem ticket** contains the information provided by the user, which describes the problem. The Help Desk will triage the severity of the problem and assign the ticket to the proper level.

Step 2: Open Problem Ticket

When you open the problem ticket, the timer starts. Depending on the severity of the problem, you are given a specific number of hours to contact the user and resolve the problem. You develop a strategy to resolve the user's problem. Next, you implement the required actions to resolve the problem. At each step of the process, you record your actions using the problem tracking software.

Step 3: Research Known Solutions

Use the **problem tracking software** as a research vehicle. A helpful part of problem tracking software is the **knowledge base**, which optimizes collection, organization, and retrieval of information. You can avoid "reinventing the wheel" by viewing the knowledge base for solutions to the same or similar problems. You can determine if the user has experienced this problem previously. You will want to use the knowledge base to provide a quick response to recurring problems.

Although the problem tracking software provides information on the problems unique to the organization, let's not overlook the value of a search engine such as Google. Another good place to check for problem resolution information is the knowledge base provided on the Microsoft Web site.

Step 4: Close the Problem Ticket

When the problem is resolved, finalize the explanation in the problem resolution stage. Depending on the problem tracking software, your diagnosis, progress, and final resolution is available to your supervisor and his manager. You will need to enter your resolutions promptly and close your problem tickets. The job is not done until the paperwork is completed!

Activity 1-3: Describing the Use of Problem Tracking Software

Time Required: 30 minutes

Objective: Describe the steps in the problem resolution workflow and the use of problem tracking software.

Description: In this activity, you will provide a description of the use of problem tracking software. Recall that the DST is expected to use the problem tracking software to record the resolution for all user problems.

1. If necessary, log on to your computer using the user name **user01** and password **Password1**.

2. Open your Web browser.

3. In the Address line, type **www.google.com** (or the search engine suggested by your instructor) and press **Enter**.

4. Type **problem tracking software** (or the search text suggested by your instructor) in the Search text box and press **Enter**.

5. Scroll to locate an entry that appears interesting and click the entry.

6. Read the information on this software. Add this information to your project log and click the Back button.

7. Repeat Step 5 and Step 6 for additional entries.

8. In your project log, write a brief summary that describes the use of problem tracking software to record the problem ticket creation and problem resolution.

9. Close your Web browser.

OPERATING SYSTEM AND COMPUTER ENVIRONMENT

The actions that you take to resolve a problem are greatly influenced by the hardware platform, operating system, and applications in use. Microsoft provides Help and Support tools because they realize that information about the computer environment is required when troubleshooting and resolving problems. You should take advantage of these tools to reduce the time required to resolve problems. The following sections cover the information and sources of information needed to resolve problems.

My Computer Information

The My Computer Information tool provides summary information for the computer. This is a good tool to confirm the system configuration. The options displayed in Figure 1-3 are available. To access this tool, click **Help and Support** from **Start**, locate the **Pick a Task** section, click **Tools**, and click **My Computer Information** link.

To change the view for My Computer Information, click the **Change View** button.

TIP

General System Information

With the View general system information about this computer option, you can determine a wide variety of useful information. To access this option, click the **View general system information about this computer** option in Figure 1-3. Your screen should resemble Figure 1-4. You will use this information to gain insight into the configuration of a desktop computer.

System Status

How do you determine the health of a computer? You select the **View the status of my system hardware and software** option from Figure 1-3. Your screen would then resemble Figure 1-5. This screen provides information about problem areas to investigate. You should always check the health of each computer that you encounter when resolving problems.

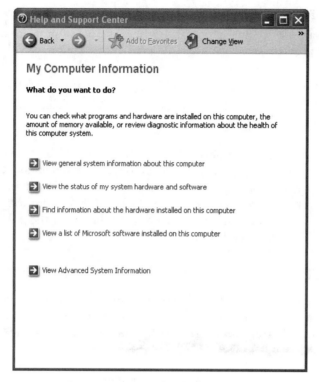

Figure 1-3   Display of My Computer Information

On this status screen are a number of entries that are important in the resolution of problems:

- **Obsolete Application and Device Drivers:** This should be empty
- **System software:** Operating system installed, date of install, and Help links
- **Hardware:** Status for various components, indication of whether an update is required, and Help links

Installed Hardware

If you need information about the hardware installed, select the **Find information about the hardware installed on this computer** link from Figure 1-3. Your screen should resemble Figure 1-6. This screen provides information about the installed hardware. This is useful when you need the manufacturer and model for an installed device. You will use this information to resolve problems involving interactions between devices and system software. Also, you will need this information to locate updated software for a device.

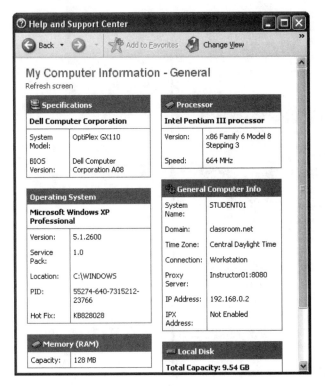

Figure 1-4   Display of My Computer Information - General

Microsoft Installed Software

If you need to know which Microsoft applications are installed, select the **View a list of Microsoft software installed on this computer** option from Figure 1-3. Your screen will resemble Figure 1-7. You might need to gather the information from this screen to resolve a problem related to Microsoft application software or a program that automatically starts.

This display provides useful information in two areas:

- **Microsoft Registered Software:** Used to determine if software licensing requirements have been met
- **Startup Program Group:** Used to determine which programs are being started at system startup.

Activity 1-4: Viewing System Information

Time Required: 15 minutes

Objective: Explain the importance of the operating system version and computer configuration for troubleshooting.

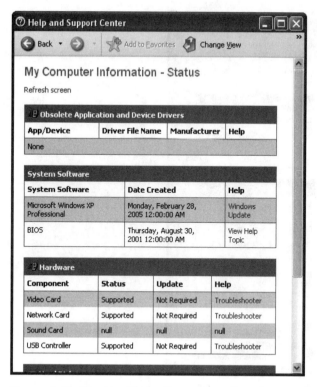

Figure 1-5 Display of My Computer Information - Status

Description: In this activity, you will view the system information for your desktop computer. You will practice locating and viewing this information because you will need to obtain similar information to resolve problems and to create inventory records when you get on the job.

1. If necessary, log on to your computer using the user name **user01** and password **Password1**.

2. Click **Start**, click **Help and Support**, locate the **Pick a task** section, and click **Use Tools to view your computer information and diagnose problems**.

3. Click **My Computer Information** and click **View general system information about this computer**.

4. Wait for the information to be collected.

5. In your project log, record the requested information in Table 1-2.

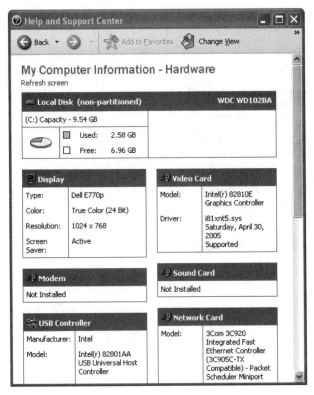

Figure 1-6   Display of My Computer Information - Hardware

Table 1-2   Requested information

Category	Item	Information
Specifications	Computer Vendor	
	System Model	
Processor	Description	
	Speed	
Operating System	Description	
	Version	
	Service Pack	
	Location	
	Hot Fix	
General Computer Info	System Name	
	Domain	
	IP Address	
Memory (RAM)	Memory Capacity	
Local Disk	Total Disk Capacity	
	Free Space	

Figure 1-7   Display of My Computer Information - Software

6. Close the Help and Support Center window.

7. Log off your computer.

ACTIVITY

Activity 1-5: Viewing Your Computer's Health

Time Required: 15 minutes

Objective: Explain the importance of the operating system version and computer configuration on troubleshooting.

Description: In this activity, you will the view the system information for your desktop computer. You are practicing locating and viewing this information because you will need to obtain similar information to resolve problems and to create inventory records when you get on the job.

1. Log on to your computer using the user name **admin01** and password **Password1**.

2. You will have two user accounts (userxx and adminxx). The two accounts have differing security privileges—the userxx (domain user privilege) and adminxx (domain administration privileges). For this Hands-on Activity, the adminxx account provides the necessary privileges.

3. Click **Start**, click **Help and Support**, locate the **Pick a Task** section, and click **Use Tools to view your computer information and diagnose problems.**

4. If you see the message, This feature is available to local administrators only, you have logged in as a user instead of as an administrator. Return to Step 1 and ensure that you sign in as admin01 and not as user01.

5. Click **My Computer Information** and click **View the status of my system hardware and software**.

6. Wait for the information to be collected.

7. In your project log, record the information indicated in Table 1-3. Note that when you copy this table into your project log, you might want to give yourself extra space for the cells in the Information column.

Table 1-3   Requested information

Category	Item	Information
Obsolete Application and Device Drivers	Names (if any)	
System Software	Date Created (date system software installed)	
Hardware	Names of Components	
	Names of Unsupported Hardware Components (if any)	
Hard Disk	Percentage of Hard Disk Usage	
Random Access Memory (RAM)	Memory (RAM) Detected	
	Minimum Requirement	

8. In your project log, place a note beside any problem indicated by the status check for your system and contact your instructor.

9. Locate the entry for the Video Card Hardware Component and click the **Troubleshooter** link.

10. Click the **Yes, I am having a problem using this device and want to resolve the conflict** option button and click **Next**.

11. View the offered suggestions.

12. Click **To determine whether your device has been installed more than once** link.

13. Click **Device Manager**.

14. To expand an item, click the + (plus symbol).

15. Expand **Display adapters** and verify that only one video controller is installed. If you have more than one video controller, contact your instructor.

16. Close the Device Manager window.

17. Close the Help and Support Center window.

18. Log off your computer.

ACTIVITY

Activity 1-6: Viewing Installed Software

Time Required: 15 minutes

Objective: Explain the importance of the operating system version and computer configuration on troubleshooting.

Description: In this activity, you will view a list of the software installed on your desktop computer. You will practice locating and viewing this information because you will need to obtain similar information to resolve problems and to create inventory records when you get on the job. You will discover that the List of Programs in the Startup Group can provide valuable insight into system startup behavior.

1. Log on to your computer using the user name **user01** and password **Password1**.

2. Click **Start**, click **Help and Support**, and click **Use Tools to view your computer information and diagnose problems**.

3. Click **My Computer Information** and click **View a list of Microsoft software installed on this computer**.

4. Wait for the information to be collected.

5. In your project log, record the information indicated in Table 1-4.

Table 1-4   Requested information

Category	Item	Information
Software	Microsoft Registered Software	
Startup Program Group	Software Installed	

6. Close the Help and Support Center window.

7. Log off your computer.

NETWORK MODELS

Using Windows, there are numerous ways to connect computers or to create a network. A network can be created with a pair of computers. A workgroup can be created for up to ten computers. Likewise, a large network or domain might have thousands of computers. You should have a strong working knowledge of operating desktop systems in a workgroup or Active Directory domain environment and how end users are impacted by each environment. For example, you must know the network environment for the desktop to correctly use the resources of the network.

Peer-to-Peer Model

For small offices, the most common model is **peer-to-peer networking** (a network in which computers directly communicate with each other). See Figure 1-8 for a network diagram of a peer-to-peer network.

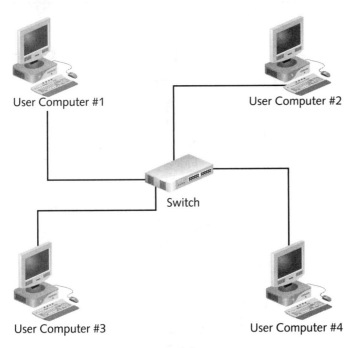

Figure 1-8   Peer-to-peer model

A peer-to-peer network, also called a **workgroup**, is commonly used for small office networks. They do not require a server to manage network resources. In general, a peer-to-peer network is most appropriate where there are less than ten computers located in the same office. The computers in a workgroup are considered peers because they are all equal. That is, these computers share resources among each other without requiring a file server, which is a server that consolidates data storage with centralized security. Instead of the security on the server controlling access, each user determines which data on his computer will be shared on the network. Sharing common resources allows users to print from a single printer and access information in shared folders.

Domain Model

Larger businesses or those with more complex networking needs rely on the **domain model**. In a domain model, computer tasks are split between a personal computer, which acts as the client, and a server, which provides access to network resources. The client contacts the server for resources, such as files and printers. The server stores files for users in a central location and provides access to other network resources, such as printers, CD-ROM drives, and software. In addition to sharing files, the server provides network services and security features. Figure 1-9 presents a representative domain model.

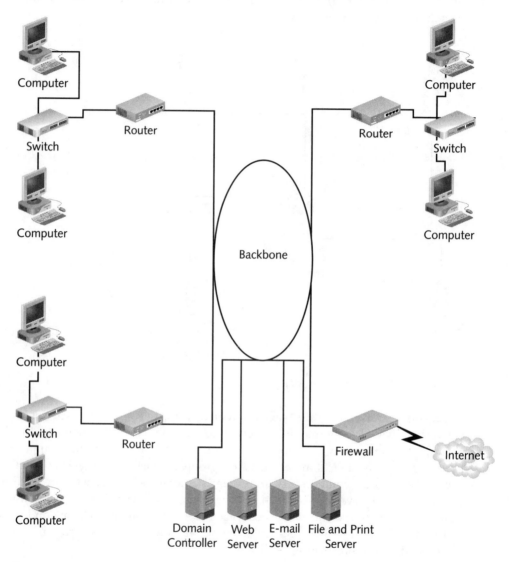

Figure 1-9   Domain model

The domain model has become the standard model for networking, primarily because it permits reliable management of network resources and a common security database. A network based on this model can support thousands of users, and servers are managed by a central group of administrators who oversee the network operation and ensure that security is maintained.

1

Setting up a domain model requires more personnel than a peer-to-peer network. The trained staff of network administrators must ensure that all of the necessary hardware, protocols, settings, and services are configured properly.

In a network based on the domain model, one or more computers can be used solely as network servers. The number of servers depends on the number of users, volume of traffic, number of peripherals, and so on. For example, you might use specialized servers—a print server, a communications server, and a database server—for a number of tasks.

Use of the domain model requires one or more centralized servers, which are domain controllers, to control the network resources, user accounts, and security settings for the client computers and other servers on the network. Domain controllers employ a **directory service**, which is a hierarchical structure that stores information about objects on the network, for the centralized control of security. **Active Directory**, Microsoft's directory service, provides the methods for storing directory data and making this data available to network users and administrators. For example, Active Directory stores information about user accounts, such as names, passwords, phone numbers, and so on, and enables other authorized users on the same network to access this information.

ACTIVITY

Activity 1-7: Viewing the Networking Model

Time Required: 15 minutes

Objective: Explain the importance of the operating system version and computer configuration for troubleshooting.

Description: In this activity, you will determine the network model used by the network. You will need the domain name when troubleshooting such items as user logins. The Full computer name is useful to troubleshoot name resolution problems.

1. Log on to your computer using the user name **admin01** and password **Password1**.

2. Click **Start**, right-click **My Computer** on the Start menu, and click **Properties**.

3. Click the **Computer Name** tab.

4. Your screen should resemble Figure 1-10. Locate and record in your project log the Full computer name and Domain.

5. Click **Cancel**.

COMPUTER MANAGEMENT

Computer Management contains three categories as shown in Figure 1-11. You access Computer Management from the Administrative Tools. You will use these tools to determine the source of problems with a desktop. The DST must master the tools of the trade. From Computer Management you can truly manage your computers.

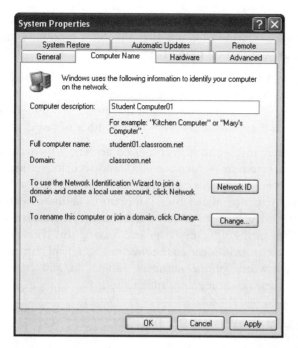

Figure 1-10 Location of computer name and domain name

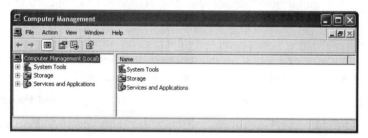

Figure 1-11 Display of Computer Management console

From this display, you will see three categories to manage your computer. The following sections discuss each category.

System Tools

The first item in the Computer Management console tree is System Tools, as shown in Figure 1-12. You can use these items to manage system events and performance on your computer.

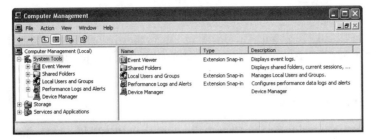

Figure 1-12   Display of Computer Management, System Tools

Event Viewer

Using the event logs in Event Viewer, you can gather information about hardware, software, and system problems. You can also monitor Windows XP security events. A computer running any version of Windows XP records events in three types of logs:

- The application log contains events logged by applications or programs. For example, a virus checking program might record a message in the application log.

- The security log might be used to audit events related to resource use, such as creating, opening, or deleting files or other objects. An administrator can specify which events are recorded in the security log.

- The system log contains events logged by Windows XP system components. For example, the failure of a device driver to load during startup is recorded in the system log. The event types logged by system components are predetermined by Windows XP.

These three logs are illustrated in Figure 1-13.

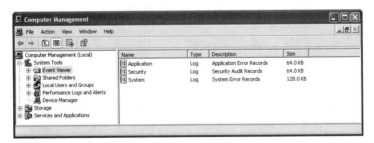

Figure 1-13   Display of Computer Management, Event Viewer

Shared Folders

This option gathers information about shared folders on a computer, users connected to a computer, and files currently opened by other users. Use Shared Folders to create, view, and set permissions for shared files and folders. A computer administrator account is required to perform these tasks.

Local Users and Groups

Using the entities in Local Users and Groups, you can gather information about local user accounts and user groups. A computer administrator account is required to perform these tasks.

Performance Logs and Alerts

This option permits the configuration of logs to record performance data. System alerts notify an administrator when a specified performance counter's value is above or below a defined threshold. A computer administrator account is required to perform these tasks.

Device Manager

Another system tool that you will frequently use is the Device Manager, which provides a graphical view of the devices. Figure 1-14 shows the hardware installed on a computer. You can use the Device Manager to update the drivers (or software) for hardware devices and modify hardware settings. The Device Manager links to aids that you can use to troubleshoot hardware problems.

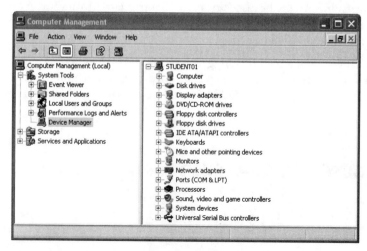

Figure 1-14   Display of Computer Management, Device Manager

From the display of the Computer Management Device Manager, you will find a list of the installed devices divided into a number of categories.

Storage

Storage is the second item in the Computer Management console tree. It displays storage devices installed on the computer. You can use the default tools, Removable Storage, Disk Defragmenter, and Disk Management, to manage the properties of storage devices. See Figure 1-15 for the storage options.

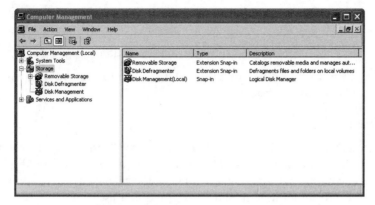

Figure 1-15   Display of Computer Management, Storage

Removable Storage

Removable Storage tracks removable storage media, such as CD-R discs. A person using the computer administrator account is required to perform these tasks.

Disk Defragmenter

The Disk Defragmenter, as shown in Figure 1-16, analyzes local volumes and consolidates fragmented files and folders so that each occupies a single, contiguous space on the volume. The process of consolidating fragmented files and folders is called defragmentation or defragging. After defragging, your system can access files and folders and save new ones more efficiently.

Figure 1-16   Display of Computer Management, Disk Defragmenter

From the display of the Computer Management Disk Defragmenter, you will see the following

- Statistics for each partition, or volume, on the computer
- Graphical analysis indicating the areas on the partition, or volume, that could benefit from defragmentation

Disk Management

The Disk Management is a system utility for managing hard disks and the volumes, or partitions, that they contain. With Disk Management, you can initialize disks, create volumes, and format volumes with file systems. The Disk Management window (Figure 1-17), displays disks and volumes in a graphical view and in a list view.

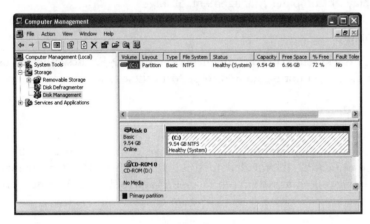

Figure 1-17   Display of Computer Management—Disk Management

From the display of the Computer Management—Disk Management, you will see:

- Statistics for each drive, including the hard drive and CD-ROM, on the computer
- Graphical representation of each partition or volume

Services and Applications

Services and Applications is the third item in the Computer Management console tree. It contains several tools to help manage services and applications on the target computer, as shown in Figure 1-18.

The following sections discuss each service and application.

Services

The Services option manages the services on your computer, such as scheduling recovery actions. A computer administrator account is required to perform these tasks.

1

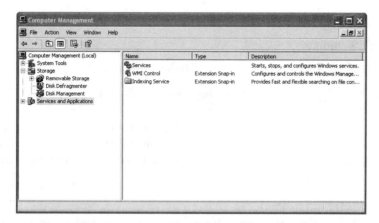

Figure 1-18 Display of Computer Management, Services and Applications

WMI Control

The Windows Management Instrumentation (WMI) control permits viewing and changing system properties on a remote or local computer. A computer administrator account is required to perform these tasks.

Indexing Service

For example, you can use Indexing for quick and easy access to system information through the Windows XP Search function. The Directories feature allows you to view items that are being indexed in the Directories folder (see Figure 1-19).

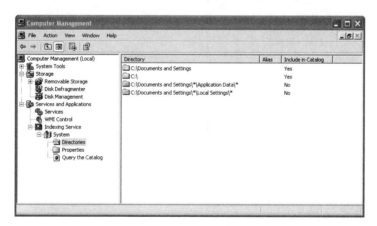

Figure 1-19 Display of Computer Management Services and Applications Indexing Service

Activity 1-8: Using Event Viewer

Time Required: 15 minutes

Objective: Use Computer Management to troubleshoot problems.

Description: In this activity, you will view the entries in the system logs with the Event Viewer. You will routinely use the Event Viewer to troubleshoot previous instances of system malfunction. You will want to start with the system log, which contains a record of system and service activities, when you start your troubleshooting. If you are resolving a problem with an application, such as Microsoft Office, you will want to start with the application log.

1. If necessary, log on to your computer using the user name **admin01** and password **Password1**.

2. Click **Start**, and click **Control Panel**. If necessary, click the **Switch to Classic View** hyperlink. Double-click **Administrative Tools** and double-click **Event Viewer**.

3. Click **System** in the console tree (located in the left pane).

4. Click **View** on the dialog menu, click **Filter**, clear the **Information** check box, uncheck the **Warning** check box (see Figure 1-20 for the correct settings), and click the **OK** button to display only the error messages in the system log.

Figure 1- 20   Correct filter settings

5. This should reveal a list of errors. If you do not see a list of errors, contact your instructor.

6. Double-click an error (W32Time would be a good choice).

7. In your project log, record the Date, Time, Source, Event ID, User (if any), Computer, and Description.

8. Close the Event Properties dialog box.

9. Click **Application** in the console tree.

10. Click **View** on the dialog menu, click **Filter**, uncheck the **Information** check box, and click the **OK** button to display only the warning and error messages in the system log.

11. This should reveal a list of warnings and possibly some errors. If you do not see a list of warnings and error messages, contact your instructor.

12. Double-click a warning or an error (WinMgmt would be a good choice).

13. In your project log, record the Date, Time, Source, Event ID, User (if any), Computer, and Description.

14. Write a brief description on how to use the Event Viewer in your project log.

15. Close the Event Properties dialog box, close the Event Viewer window, and close the Administrative Tools window.

Activity 1-9: Using Device Manager

Time Required: 15 minutes

Objective: Use Computer Management to troubleshoot problems.

Description: In this activity, you will view the hardware entries with the Device Manager. You will routinely use the Device Manager to troubleshoot hardware problems. With the Device Manager, you can determine and resolve hardware resource conflicts, such as IRQs (the Interrupt Request assignments made in hardware).

1. If necessary, log on to your computer using the user name **admin01** and password **Password1**.

To see the contents of the Control Panel in object (or classic view), click **Switch to Classic View** from the Control Panel window.

2. Click **Start**, click **Control Panel**, and double-click **Administrative Tools**.

3. Double-click **Computer Management**, and click **Device Manager** in the console tree (located in the left pane).

4. Expand the **Display adapters** in the right pane, right-click on the available display adapter, and click **Properties**.

5. View the **Device status** and record this status information in your project log. Is your video adapter working properly?

6. To practice using the Troubleshooter, click **Troubleshoot**, click the **My display flickers or is garbled** option, and click the **Next** button.

7. Click the **I don't know** option, and click the **Next** button.

8. Expand the **To change your display settings** view and continue on the screen with the suggested troubleshooting steps to change the color setting.

9. Close the Help and Support Center window and the video card's Properties window.

10. In Computer Management, click **View** on the menu bar, and click **Resources by type** to view hardware resources.

11. Expand **Interrupt request (IRQ)** in the right pane to view the IRQs.

12. Write a brief description on how to use the Device Manager in your project log.

13. Close the Computer Management window and close the Administrative Tools window.

ACTIVITY

Activity 1-10: Using Disk Tools

Time Required: 45 minutes

Objective: Use Computer Management to troubleshoot problems.

Description: In this activity, you will view the disk allocation entries with the Disk Management feature. You will routinely use Disk Management to troubleshoot disk allocation problems. With the Disk Defragmenter, you can improve the performance of your disk drives.

1. If necessary, log on to your computer using the user name **admin01** and password **Password1**.

2. Click **Start**, click **Control Panel**, and double-click **Administrative Tools**.

3. Double-click **Computer Management**, and click **Disk Management** in the console tree (located in the left pane) to view the disk allocations.

4. View the detail information to determine how much free space you have on your hard drive and record this information in your project log.

5. Right-click on the graphical representation of your hard drive and click **Properties** to view the properties dialog.

6. After viewing the statistics, click the **Cancel** button.

7. Click the **Disk Defragmenter** in the console tree and click the **Analyze** button.

8. Wait for the analysis to complete.

9. If recommended, click the **Defragment** button; otherwise, click **Close** and proceed to Step 11.

10. Wait for the defrag to complete (this may be a good time to check on the vending machines!).

11. Write a brief description on how to use the Disk Defragmenter in your project log.

12. Close all open windows.

13. Log off your computer.

USING THE REMOTE ASSISTANT

As a DST, you are expected to be able to use the Remote Assistant to view a user's desktop and, where policy permits, to take control temporarily to resolve problems. Both you and the user should be running Microsoft Windows XP for this tool to work.

Methods of Delivering Invitations

Your user will solicit your help by initiating a Remote Assistance invitation in one of the following ways:

- **File invitation:** A file saved as a Microsoft Remote Control Incident starts the process.

- **E-mail invitation:** An attachment in the message is used to initiate the session.

- **MSN buddy list:** Invitation is delivered through MSN Messenger Service accounts.

The following section discusses the first method, which is the most popular.

File Invitation

You may be familiar with the terms that Microsoft uses when discussing Remote Assistant. An **expert** is a computer savvy colleague and a **novice** is a person who desires help from the expert. Let's walk through a session in which a novice is asking an expert to view the desktop on the novice's computer. The novice will place an invitation in a shared folder on the expert's hard drive.

Step 1: Invite a Friend

The novice invites a friend by launching Help and Support from the Start menu. Under Ask for assistance, select **Invite a friend to connect to your computer with Remote Assistance**. As indicated in Figure 1-21, the novice can invite a friend, the expert, to connect to his or her computer with Remote Assistance by selecting Invite someone to help you.

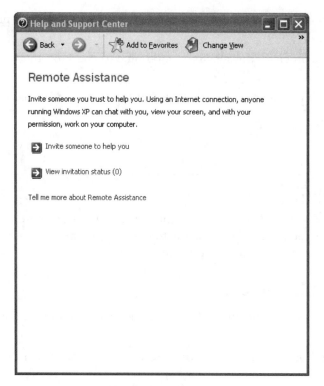

Figure 1-21   Inviting a friend

Step 2: Save the Invitation

The novice selects Save invitation as a file (Advanced). See the bottom of Figure 1–22 for the location of the option.

Step 3: Specify the User

The novice enters the name to appear on the invitation. (See Figure 1–23.) The default user name is acceptable, so continue to the next dialog box and type and confirm the password. It is recommended that you provide a password. The novice will need to communicate the password to the expert.

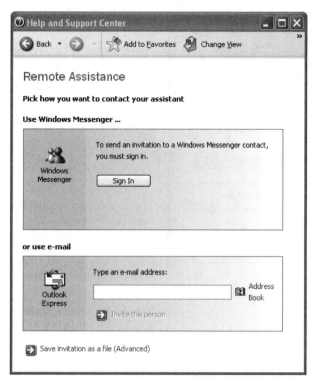

Figure 1-22   Save invitation as a file

Step 4: Connect to the Share

The novice will connect to the shared Invitations folder on the expert's computer. Figure 1-24 shows the expert's computer selected. Select **Save Invitation** to save the invitation request file on the expert's computer in the Invitations folder.

Step 5: Process the Invitation

The expert locates the invitation file in the Invitations folder and selects the file to initiate the connection to the novice's computer. A message appears on the novice's computer as indicated in Figure 1-25. The novice indicates that he is ready to permit the expert to connect by selecting Yes.

The expert will respond to the previous action of the novice. The expert is then asked to type the password that was furnished by the novice. After typing the password, the expert can view the novice's screen and chat with the novice. As a security precaution, the expert must request permission of the novice to take control of the novice's desktop.

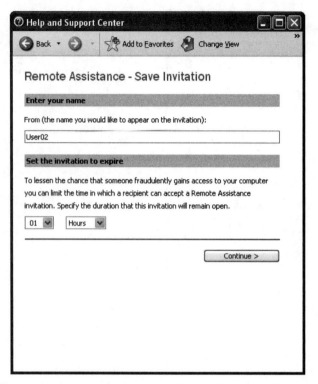

Figure 1-23   Specifying the user

Figure 1-24   Expert's computer selected

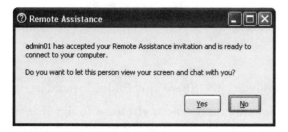

Figure 1-25 Remote Assistance invitation accepted

NOTE Where the computers are members of a domain, a security policy must be established to permit a second user to take over control of the first computer's keyboard and mouse.

ACTIVITY

Activity 1-11 Using the Remote Assistant

Time Required: 15 minutes

Objective: Use the Remote Assistant to resolve operating system/application problems.

Description: In this activity, you will use the Remote Assistant to connect to a second computer. You, the expert, will routinely use the Remote Assistant to connect to a user's computer (the novice) to configure the operating system and applications. Also, you will be able to show the novice the steps to perform tasks for which they have questions. As an example, you will set a value for the screensaver for the novice. Note that you will be working with a partner on this activity. The first computer, Student01, of the pair will be used by the expert and the second, Student02, by the novice. You and your partner will want to observe the activities on both computers.

NOTE For this Activity, the student should substitute Studentxx for Student01 (the expert's computer), and Adminxx for Admin01. Substitute Studentyy (the novice's computer) for Student02, and Useryy for User02.

1. Log on to the Student01 computer using the user name **admin01** and password **Password1**.

NOTE To remove an existing shared folder, right-click the folder, click **Delete**, and click the **Yes** button.

2. Click **Start**, click **My Documents**, click **Make a new folder**, type **Invitations**, and press **Enter**.

TIP

To rename a folder, click **New Folder** (or the folder name), wait, click a second time, and type the new folder name.

3. Click the **Invitations** folder and click the **Share this folder** hyperlink.

4. Click the **Share this folder** option button, type **Invitations** in the Share name text box (if necessary), click **Permissions**, click the **Full Control Allow** check box (see Figure 1-26 for the correct permissions), and click **OK**.

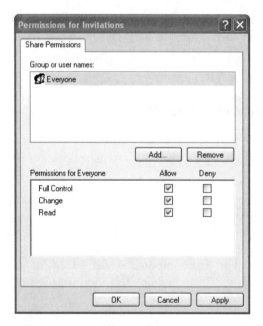

Figure 1-26   Setting full control

NOTE

When the folder is named "Invitations" by the expert and shared as "Invitations," the novice will automatically be positioned into the Invitations folder.

5. Click the **Security** tab, click **Add**, type **user02** in the Enter the object names to select text box (see Figure 1-27 for the user name), click **Check Names**, click **OK**, check the **Modify Allow** check box, and click the **OK** button.

NOTE

If you do not see the correct user name, ask your instructor for help.

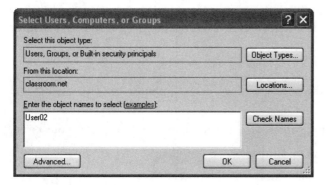

Figure 1-27   User name entered

6. Go to the Student02 computer.

7. Your partner should be logged on to the Student02 computer using the user name **User02** and password **Password1**.

8. Click **Start**, click **Help and Support**, and under the Ask for assistance section, click the **Invite a friend to your computer with Remote Assistance** hyperlink.

9. Click the **Invite someone to help you** link, click the **Save invitation as a file (Advanced)** hyperlink, and click the **Continue** button.

10. Type **Password1** in the Type password text box, press **Tab**, type **Password1** in the Confirm password text box, and click the **Save Invitation** button.

11. If needed, click the **My Network** icon, double-click **Entire Network**, double-click **Microsoft Windows Network**, double-click **Classroom**, double-click **Student Computer01 (Student01)**, and double-click **Invitations**.

12. Click the **Save** button. If needed, click the **Yes** button to replace the file.

13. Return to the Student01 computer.

14. Double-click the **Invitations** folder, double-click the **RAInvitation** file, type **Password1** in the Password text box, and click the **Yes** button to connect to the novice's screen.

15. Return to Student02 and click the **Yes** button to permit the connection.

16. Type a message in the Message Entry window and click the **Send** button.

17. Return to the Student01 computer and view the message.

18. Click **Take Control** on the menu bar.

19. Return to the Student02 computer and click the **Yes** button to permit the expert to control the desktop.

20. Return to Student01 and click the **OK** button for the expert to control the novice's desktop.

21. Right click on the novice's desktop, click **Properties**, click the **Settings** tab, view the **Display** settings, click the **Screen Saver** tab, type **30** in the Wait spin box, and click the **OK** button.

22. Return to Student02.

23. Type **Thank you** in the Message Entry, click the **Send** button and click the **Disconnect** button.

24. Write a brief description on how to use the Remote Assistant in your project log.

25. Close all open windows on Student01 and Student02.

26. Log off the Student01 and Student02 computers.

CERTIFICATIONS FOR THE DST

In this section, you will learn information that will help you navigate the employment field for DSTs.

Why Certifications?

One of the benefits for certification is recognition of your knowledge and proficiency with Microsoft products and technologies. You may want to consider certification as a potential inroad to a job as a DST. Having a professional certification gives you an edge when you're applying for a job. It's proof of your abilities and adds value to your resume. Many employers prefer to hire certified employees.

Microsoft Certified Desktop Support Technician

Microsoft describes the Microsoft Certified Desktop Support Technician (MCDST) as the possessor of the skills "to successfully support end users and troubleshoot desktop environments running the Microsoft Windows XP operating system." As you might expect, Microsoft expects the DST to have experience with the following Microsoft products in a corporate or home environment:

- Microsoft Windows XP Professional
- Microsoft Windows XP Home Edition
- Microsoft Internet Explorer
- Microsoft Outlook and Outlook Express
- Microsoft Office 2003 applications

Microsoft states that candidates should be able to resolve issues by telephone, by remote connection to an end user's system, or face-to-face at the end user's desktop. Finally, an

MCDST should have a strong working knowledge of operating desktop systems in a workgroup or Active Directory domain environment and the impact of each environment on the user.

Microsoft requires two examinations for the MCDST:

- Exam 70–271: Supporting Users and Troubleshooting a Microsoft Windows XP Operating System

- Exam 70-272: Supporting Users and Troubleshooting Desktop Applications on a Microsoft Windows XP Operating System

CompTIA Certifications

You may want to consider additional exams from **CompTIA**, the Computing Technology Industry Association. These examinations could be used to broaden the demonstrated skills of the DST. CompTIA states that vendor-neutral certifications are a great way to break into the information technology field because they provide a broad knowledge base and are not limited to only one product or company.

The CompTIA A+ exam consists of two exams—the A+ Core Hardware exam and the A+ OS Technologies exam. You become A+ certified by passing both exams. The hardware exam demonstrates your ability to install, configure, repair, upgrade, and troubleshoot personal computer hardware. The Operating System exam requires that you demonstrate basic knowledge of operating systems (Windows 95 through Windows XP).

Another exam worthy of consideration is the Network+ certification. A Network+ certification demonstrates your technical abilities in networking administration and support, and validates your knowledge of media and topologies, protocols and standards, network implementation, and network support.

ACTIVITY

Activity 1-12: Reviewing Certification Offerings

Time Required: 15 minutes

Objective: Describe certifications for the desktop support technician.

Description: In this project, you will research information about the various certifications for the desktop support technician. You will visit the Microsoft Web site work for information on the MCDST and CompTIA for the A+ and Network + certifications.

1. Log on to the Student01 computer using the user name **user01** and password **Password1**.

2. Open your Web browser.

3. In the Address line, type **www.microsoft.com** and press **Enter**.

4. Type **mcdst requirements** in the Search Microsoft.com for text box and click the **Go** button.

5. Locate and click the entry with the MCDST requirements.

6. Read the information about the MCDST. Add this information to your project log and click the **Back** button.

7. Repeat Steps 5 and 6 for additional entries.

8. In your project log, write a brief summary that describes the Microsoft certification for the desktop support technician.

9. In the Address line, type **www.comptia.com** and press **Enter**.

10. Click the **certification** button, click in the **I'm Interested in** drop-down menu, and click the **CompTIA A+** selection.

11. Locate and click the entry with the **A+ Objectives** under A+ Navigation.

12. Read the information about the A+ exam objectives. Add this information to your project log.

13. Repeat Steps 10 through 12 for the **Network+** requirements.

14. In your project log, write a brief summary that describes the CompTIA A+ and Network+ certifications.

15. Close your Web browser.

16. Log off your computer.

CHAPTER SUMMARY

◻ Note that as a DST, you are responsible for providing support and resolving problems for users of desktop computers. The successful DST combines social and technical skills.

◻ The DST coordinates activities with other teams in Information Technology to resolve user problems.

◻ The DST follows prescribed procedures for problem resolution and problem tracking.

◻ The DST uses the Help and Support tools to locate summary information.

◻ The DST uses Computer Management to troubleshoot problems.

◻ The DST uses the Remote Assistant to connect to a user's computer to resolve problems.

◻ Certification is often a job requirement for the DST. This text maps to the Microsoft Certified Desktop Support Technician certification. Additional certification alternatives, CompTIA A+ and N+, are suggested.

KEY TERMS

Active Directory — Microsoft's directory service, which is an integral part of the Windows Server 2003 architecture. Active Directory is a centralized and standardized system for network management of network resources and security.

application server — Computer that executes application programs in a network environment.

business process — Course of action taken by an organization to achieve desired results.

CompTIA — The Computing Technology Industry Association is the world's largest developer of vendor-neutral IT certification exams, including the A+ and Network+ exams.

database management system — Sometimes simply called a database manager, it is a program that permits one or more computer users to create and access data in a database.

database server — Computer that provides the environment to use a database management system.

desktop — Abbreviated form of desktop computer; it is a personal computer that fits on top of a desk.

desktop support technician — Person whose occupation provides hardware and software installation and repair support for personal computers in an office environment.

directory service — Service on a network that enables a user to locate resources on the network.

Domain Controller (DC) — A role that can be assigned to a server in a network of computers that use the Windows Server 2003 operating system. A domain controller manages the computers in the domain model.

domain model — A security model with centralized control to the access of shared resources.

Domain Name System (DNS) — A service that provides for the resolution of computer names to Internet addresses.

expert — With Remote Assistant, a person who responds to a request for help with a hardware or software problem.

File and print services — Computer that provides for the sharing of files and printing of documents.

Help Desk — The location a computer user can call for help with a computer hardware or software problem.

knowledge base — A centralized repository for information, it is a database of related information about a particular subject organized for easy retrieval.

LANs — A local area network is a group of computers and associated devices that share a common communications line.

Level 1 support — Support for customers or users provided by a Help Desk.

Level 2 support — Support for customers or users provided by a Desktop Support Technician.

Level 3 support — Includes addressing problems referred by the Help Desk.

Microsoft Certified Desktop Support Technician (MCDST) — Person who has passed the two Microsoft examinations for desktop support technicians.

novice — With Remote Assistant, a person who requests help with a hardware or software problem.

peer-to-peer networking — A security model in which each party has the same capabilities and either party can cmmunicate with the other to access shared resources.

physical security — Actions taken against theft or sabotage to protect the assets of the organization.

problem ticket — A form on a computer generated by problem tracking software. Used by the Desktop Support Technician to initiate the resolution of a problem.

problem tracking software — Program developed to trace the resolution of a user problem.

queue — Represents a series of problems waiting resolution by the Desktop Support Technician.

routers — Devices that determine the next network point to forward a packet in order to reach its destination.

security policy — Procedures implemented to control access to desktop computers, servers, and network resources.

server — Computer that runs the operating system software that provides access to shared resources.

switch — Device that passes incoming frames from any of multiple input ports to the specific output port that will take the data toward its intended device or computer.

UNIX — An operating system that originated at Bell Labs in 1969 as an interactive time-sharing system. Linux, a Unix derivative available in both "free software" and commercial versions, is increasing in popularity as an alternative to proprietary operating systems.

WANs — A geographically dispersed telecommunications network that is broader than the communications structure of a LAN.

workgroup — Synonym for a peer-to-peer network.

REVIEW QUESTIONS

1. Microsoft created a certification for desktop support technicians that is called the
   _____

   a. Microsoft Certified Developer Specialist Trainer

   b. Microsoft Certified Desktop Support Technician

   c. Microsoft Certificate for Desktop Support Technicians

   d. Microsoft Certificate for Developer Support Trainer

2. Which of the following is considered an advantage to having the MCDST? (Choose all that apply.)

    a. expected by employers

    b. looks impressive on a resume

    c. required by some employers

    d. none of the above

3. The desktop support technician is required to support which of the following? (Choose all that apply.)

    a. personal computers

    b. firewalls

    c. Microsoft Windows XP

    d. network servers

    e. Microsoft Office 2003

4. Which of the following is a capability of the DST? (Choose all that apply.)

    a. interacts effectively with various types of people

    b. resolves user desktop problems

    c. interrelates desktop computers to the networking environment

    d. works within a team of desktop support technicians

    e. correlates activities with other members of the Information Technology Department

5. The Platform Support team provides support for a wide range of servers, including _____ . (Choose all that apply.)

    a. Domain Controllers

    b. Domain Name System

    c. file and print servers

    d. database servers

    e. application servers

6. The _____ manager heads a team that creates and updates procedures that secure the organization's assets.

    a. platform support

    b. application development

    c. network infrastructure

    d. security

    e. user support

7. The Network Infrastructure team supports network devices, including (a)
   _____ , within the organization. (Choose all that apply.)

   a. Domain Controllers

   b. Domain Name System

   c. file and print servers

   d. routers

   e. switches

8. Which of the following statements regarding problem tracking software is true?
   (Choose all that apply.)

   a. maintains information about the resolution of user problems

   b. is initiated by the Help Desk when a user calls

   c. provides the time that the ticket has been opened

   d. contains the resolution of the problem

9. In many organizations, there are two levels of user support. Which of the following
   statements accurately describes these two levels? (Choose all that apply.)

   a. Level 1 support functions at the Help Desk level.

   b. Level 1 support functions at the desktop level.

   c. Level 2 support functions at the Help Desk level.

   d. Level 2 support functions at the desktop level.

10. The desktop support technician enters _____ into the problem track-
    ing system.

    a. knowledge base entries

    b. user's request issues

    c. request queue

    d. number of hours to contact the user

    e. actions taken to resolve the problem

11. The My Computer Information Tool - General screen can be used to provide infor-
    mation about which of the following items? (Choose all that apply.)

    a. hardware configuration

    b. operating system version

    c. applied operating system patches

    d. failed hardware devices

    e. hard disk statistics

    f. amount of installed RAM

12. The My Computer Information-Status screen can be used to collect information about which of the following items? (Choose all that apply.)

    a. hardware configuration

    b. operating system version

    c. applied operating system patches

    d. failed hardware devices

    e. hard disk statistics

    f. amount of installed RAM

13. The _____ screen can be used to obtain information about which programs are automatically started when the operating system starts.

    a. My Computer Information - General

    b. My Computer Information - Status

    c. My Computer Information - Started

    d. My Computer Information - Software

14. The workgroup networking model exhibits which of the following characteristics? (Choose all that apply.)

    a. deployed in small offices

    b. requires centralized security configuration by system administrators

    c. recommended for 10 or less computers

    d. requires Active Directory on Domain Controllers

15. The domain networking model exhibits which of the following characteristics? (Choose all that apply.)

    a. deployed in small offices

    b. requires centralized security configuration by system administrators

    c. recommended for 10 or less computers

    d. requires Active Directory on Domain Controllers

16. The Event Viewer permits which of the following logs to be viewed? (Choose all that apply.)

    a. configuration

    b. application

    c. audit

    d. security

    e. system

17. If you have a problem with a software application, you can use the
_____ to assist with the resolution of the problem.

    a. Device Manager

    b. software troubleshooter

    c. operating system troubleshooter

    d. system health

18. _____ is a system utility for managing hard disks.

    a. Disk Manager

    b. Disk Management

    c. Disk Allocator

    d. Disk Defragmenter

19. After running the Disk Defragmenter, your computer will be capable of
_____ . (Choose all that apply.)

    a. accessing files quicker

    b. restoring files

    c. storing new files more efficiently

    d. removing fragmented files

20. If you have a problem with a purchased program, you will want to view the
_____ log with the Event Viewer.

    a. configuration

    b. application

    c. system

    d. audit

    e. security

21. You can troubleshoot devices such as display adapters with
_____ .

    a. Display Manager

    b. Display Allocator

    c. Display Screen

    d. Device Manager

22. Which of the following can you accomplish using the Remote Assistant? (Choose all
that apply.)

    a. view a user's desktop

    b. reinstall the operating system

    c. chat with a user

    d. take control of the user's desktop

23. The novice can use a(n) _____ to request assistance from the expert using Remote Assistance. (Choose all that apply.)

   a. attachment in an e-mail message

   b. file saved as a Microsoft Remote Control Incident

   c. invitation sent through ICQ or AOL

   d. invitation is delivered through MSN Messenger

24. A Microsoft Certified Desktop Support Technician has to pass which of the following exams? (Choose all that apply.)

   a. Exam 70–271: Supporting Users and Troubleshooting on a Microsoft Windows XP Operating System

   b. Exam 70-272: Supporting Users and Troubleshooting Desktop Applications on a Microsoft Windows XP Operating System

   c. Exam 220-221: A+ Core Hardware

   d. Exam 220-222: A+ OS Technologies

   e. Exam N10-002: Network +

25. On the CompTIA Web site, A+ and Network+ certifications are described as _____ . (Choose all that apply.)

   a. vendor neutral

   b. industry standard for entry-level computer technicians

   c. possibly required by companies

   d. showing demonstrated skill in network administration and support

   e. highly recommended by corporations

CASE PROJECTS

CASE PROJECTS

Case 1-1: Understanding Other IT Areas

You are a desktop support technician at FlyHigh Airlines. Your network consists of a Windows 2003 Active Directory domain with 10 servers, including application and database servers and 120 computers running Windows XP Professional.

You are responding to a problem ticket created by the Help Desk. In that ticket, you read that Lisa uses the Flight Projection program to review the flight loadings. Today she cannot access the program. Which business areas in FlyHigh Airlines Information Technology might you need to contact to resolve her problem? What information might you request of each area?

You continue with the resolution of the problem. Describe how problem tracking software could be used in the resolution of the problem.

Case 1-2: Using Computer Management

You consult as a desktop support technician. Your customer's network consists of five computers configured as a workgroup.

Bob remarks that he saw a message on the screen when he started his computer. He does not remember the message. Also, he has downloaded a number of large video courses to his hard drive. He has added a printer to his computer and it does not print correctly.

How will you use Computer Management to rcsolves Bob's three problems?

Case 1-3: Using the Remote Assistant

You are a desktop support technician. Your network employs Windows 2003 Domain Controllers and has 12 Windows Server 2003 computers and 290 computers with Windows XP Professional installed. John asks you about the steps to configure his display. Describe the steps to use Remote Assistant to resolve John's problem.

2

OVERVIEW OF MICROSOFT USER APPLICATIONS

After reading this chapter and completing the exercises, you will be able to:

♦ Describe user applications provided with Windows XP Professional

♦ Work with common applications in Office 2003

♦ Describe Microsoft Office 2003 Editions and Licensing

The role of the DST requires that you be prepared to know the capabilities of both the user applications installed with Windows XP Professional and applications that are available in Microsoft Office 2003. Ultimately, you will need to be prepared to answer your users' questions on the capabilities of these applications.

The chapter starts with an overview of the user applications that are installed with Windows XP Professional. You will learn how these applications could be used by your users.

Next, the applications that make up Microsoft Office 2003 will be featured. Information will be presented on the major new features for these applications. Although the MCDST exam will not have direct questions regarding the use of Microsoft Office's many features, you still need to be aware of these new features.

Microsoft recognizes that the users may not need all seven major applications available in Microsoft Office 2003. Thus, it offers different combinations of components with five licensing programs. The chapter ends with a discussion of these programs.

USER APPLICATIONS PROVIDED WITH WINDOWS XP

Windows XP provides applications that your users may use to access the Internet. Other accessories could be used to type notes, prepare small documents, create graphic images, calculate results, and insert special characters in documents. The following sections discuss these and more. However, our first stop is Windows Explorer, which we like to think of as the file and folder manager for every good DST.

Using Windows Explorer

Windows Explorer is a utility in Windows XP that enables you to locate and open files and folders. Your users will expect you to answer their questions as they use Windows Explorer to manipulate files and folders. Figure 2-1 displays Windows Explorer when you start Windows Explorer from My Computer icon on the desktop.

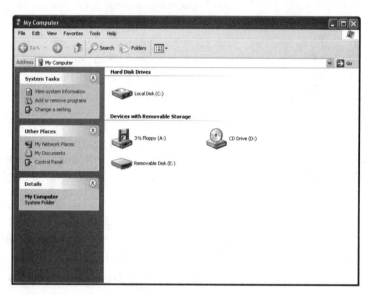

Figure 2-1   Windows Explorer

In the sections that follow, you will review the use of Windows Explorer.

My Documents

Documents you create or save are stored in your own My Documents folder, separate from the documents of others who also use the computer. As you use the Windows XP applications, you store your files in the My Documents folder. User accounts individualize Windows XP for each person sharing a computer. Your My Documents folder is tied to your user account. You will need administrator privileges to access the My Documents folder of other users.

2

Recycle Bin

You might know that the **Recycle Bin** provides you with a second chance when deleting files or folders. When you delete any of the files or folders from your hard disk, Windows XP places the file or folder in the Recycle Bin, as indicated in Figure 2-2. You can restore files and folders from the Recycle Bin to the original location. As the Recycle Bin fills up, older items are automatically removed to make room for the new items. Items in the Recycle Bin remain available until you decide to permanently delete them from your computer by emptying the Recycle Bin. If you're running low on hard disk space, you should empty the Recycle Bin. You will learn to manipulate the Recycle Bin in Activity 2-1.

Figure 2-2   Recycle Bin

Items deleted from a floppy disk or network drives are permanently deleted and are not sent to the Recycle Bin.

Search Companion

When you need to locate a file or folder, you use the Search Companion, as shown in Figure 2-3. You will learn to use the Search Companion in Activity 2-2.

You can use the Search Companion when:

- You are looking for common file types
- You remember all or part of the name
- You know when you last changed a file
- You know a word or phrase in the file

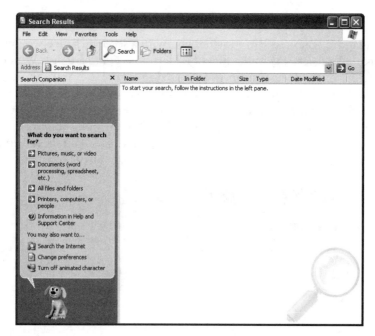

Figure 2-3 Search Results

 Tired of the animated dog? Right-click on the dog, and then you can choose a new character or turn the animated character off. Or better yet, ask the animated character to do a trick!

IN THE WORKPLACE

Consider the following search strategies that you can employ:

- If you know only part of the name, you can use wildcard characters to locate all files or folders that include that part in the name. You may know that a **wildcard character** is a keyboard character such as an asterisk (*) or a question mark (?). Use the asterisk as a substitute for zero or more characters and the question mark for a single character.

- If you are looking for a file that you know starts with "man" but you forget the rest of the file name, type the following: man*. (Do not type the terminal period.) This locates all files of any file type that begin with "man" including Manuscript.txt, Manuscript.doc, and Manual.doc.

- To narrow the search to a specific type of file, type: man*.doc. (Do not type the terminal period.) This locates all files that begin with "man" but have the file name extension .doc, such as Manuscript.doc and Manual.doc.

- You might use the question mark as a substitute for a single character in a filename. For example, to locate the file many.doc or man1.doc but not Manual.doc, type man?.doc. (Do not type the terminal period.)

File Menu

The File menu is tailored on-the-fly to meet the specifics of a selected file or folder. Figure 2-4 is a representative menu for a typical file. You may see something different for another file type.

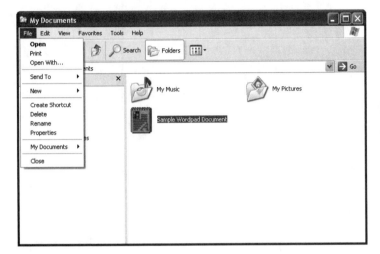

Figure 2-4   File menu for a file

When you select a folder and then click the File menu, you will see something different. For example, if you select the My Music folder and then click the File menu, you would see Explore to open the folder and Add to Playlist to add the sound files to a media player playlist, as shown in Figure 2-5.

When you highlight a document file in Windows Explorer and then select the File menu, you can choose from the following:

- Open: Open the file in the application that created the file (if the application is installed).

- Print: Open the file in the application that created the file and print the file.

- Open With: Select the application in which to open the file.

- Send To: Send the file to the target. The target might be a shortcut on the desktop, the Floppy Disk, or some other destination.

- New: Create a New Folder, a shortcut, or a new document.

- Create Shortcut: Create a shortcut to the selected item.

- Delete: Delete the selected item and send it to the Recycle Bin.

- Rename: Change the name of the selected item.

Figure 2-5 File menu for a folder

- Properties: Open the Properties dialog box for the selected item. This provides the properties, such as the size, date created, and so forth.

- My Documents: Permits access to the My Documents folder

- Close: Closes the Windows Explorer window.

NOTE You have two ways to open Windows Explorer: you can click the My Computer icon on the desktop, and you can click the Start menu and then click My Documents. When you open it the latter way, the My Documents folder appears by default.

Edit Menu

From the Edit menu, as shown in Figure 2-6, you perform operations related to a single file or group of selected files.

The Edit menu is tailored on-the-fly to meet the specifics of a selected file or folder. Operations that are not currently available are "grayed out."

When you highlight a document file or folder in the Windows Explorer Edit menu, you can choose from the following:

- Undo: Cancel the previous file operation.

- Cut: Removes the selected item(s) and copies them to the clipboard.

- Copy: Copies the selected item(s) to the clipboard.

- Paste: Places the items that were cut or copied.

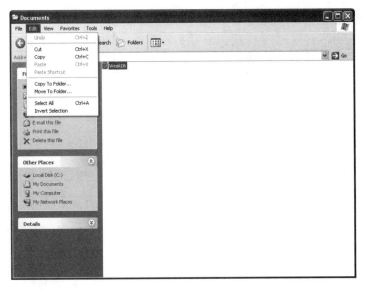

Figure 2-6   Windows Explorer - Edit menu

- Paste Shortcut: Places the shortcut that was cut or copied.

- Copy To Folder: Selects the folder into which the item is copied.

- Move To Folder: Selects the folder into which the item is moved.

- Select All: Selects all the items in the selected folder.

- Invert Selection: Changes the current selection such that everything previously unselected will now be selected and vice versa.

IN THE WORKPLACE

To select consecutive files or folders, click the first item, press and hold down the Shift key, and click the last item. To select nonconsecutive files or folders, press and hold down the Ctrl key, and click each item.

View Menu

From the View menu, you customize the display of items in the current window. Figure 2-7 displays the View menu in Windows Explorer.

From the View menu in Windows Explorer, you can choose from the following:

- Toolbars: Shows or hides toolbars.

- Status Bar: Adds or removes the Status bar information in the bottom of the window.

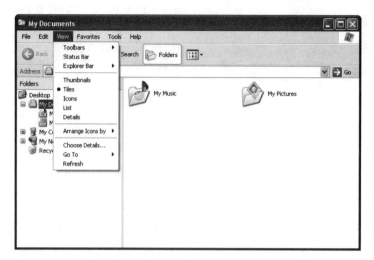

Figure 2-7 Windows Explorer - View menu

- Explorer Bar: Shows or hides the Explorer bar.

- Thumbnails: Displays items by using thumbnails.

- Tiles: Displays information for an item in the window using a tile.

- Icons: Displays items by using large icons.

- List: Displays items in a list.

- Details: Displays information about each item in the window.

- Arrange Icons by: Contains commands for arranging items in the window.

- Choose Details: Presents a dialog to include or remove details from the display.

- Go To: Navigates to another folder.

- Refresh: Refreshes the window contents.

Favorites Menu

From the Favorites menu, you can organize your Favorites List. Figure 2-8 displays the Favorites menu in Windows Explorer.

Tools Menu

The Tools menu offers tools that support the use of Windows Explorer. Figure 2-9 shows the Tools menu in Windows Explorer.

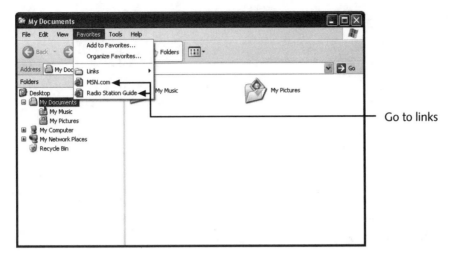

Figure 2-8   Windows Explorer - Favorites menu

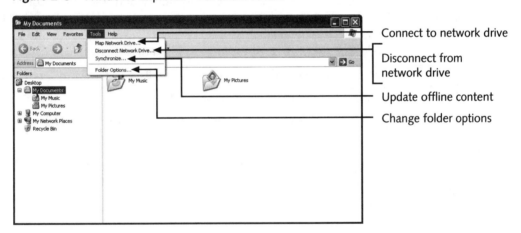

Figure 2-9   Windows Explorer - Tools menu

Help Menu

The Help menu offers information to assist you with the completion of a task. Figure 2-10 shows the Help menu in Windows Explorer.

Activity 2-1: Managing the Recycle Bin

Time Required: 10 minutes

Objective: Manage file and folder deletion or restoration using the Recycle Bin.

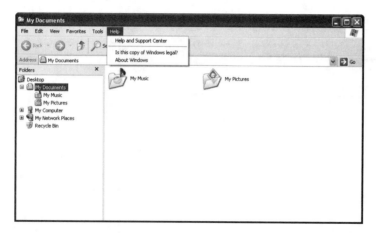

Figure 2-10   Windows Explorer - Help menu

Description: In this activity, you will delete a document and restore the document from the Recycle Bin. Next, you will practice emptying the Recycle Bin. You will find this activity useful in your career as a DST because, in order to answer users' questions about the use of the Recycle Bin, you will need to have explored these activities in detail.

1. Log on to your computer with the user name **user01** and password **Password1**.

2. Click **Start** and click the **My Documents** folder.

3. Right-click in the right pane, click **New**, click **Text Document**, type **Delete Me** over New Text Document, and press **Enter**.

4. Right-click the **Delete Me** text file, click **Delete**, and click the **Yes** button.

5. Double-click the **Recycle Bin** icon on the desktop.

6. Right-click the **Delete Me** text file, and click **Restore**.

7. Minimize the Recycle Bin window.

8. Verify that the Delete Me icon has returned to the My Documents folder.

9. Right-click the **Delete Me** text file, click **Delete**, and click the **Yes** button.

10. Maximize the Recycle Bin window.

11. Click the **Empty the Recycle Bin** link and click the **Yes** button.

12. Verify that the Delete Me icon has left the Recycle Bin folder.

13. In your project log, write a brief description of the steps to restore a file from the Recycle Bin and to empty the Recycle Bin.

14. Close any open windows.

ACTIVITY

Activity 2-2: Using the Search Companion

Time Required: 20 minutes

Objective: Use the Search Companion to locate files and folders.

Description: In this activity, you will use the Search Companion to find files that meet specified criteria. You will find this activity useful in your career as a DST because, in order to answer users' questions about using the Search Companion, you will need to have explored this feature in detail.

1. If necessary, log on to your computer with the user name **user01** and password **Password1**.

2. Click **Start** and click **Search**.

3. Under What do you want to search for?, click the **Pictures, music, or video** link.

4. Check the **Pictures and Photos** check box, type **blue** in the All or part of the file name text box, and click the **Search** button.

5. Wait for the search to complete.

6. Verify that you obtained one or more files with the word *blue* in the file name.

7. Click the **Search for all files of this type** link.

8. Wait for the search to complete.

9. Verify that you obtained one or more files of the same type as in Step 4.

10. Click the **Back** button twice.

11. Click the **All files and folders** link.

12. Type **B*.bmp** in the All or part of the file name text box and click the **Search** button.

13. Wait for the search to complete.

14. Verify that you obtained one or more files of the **.bmp** type that start with *b*.

15. Click the **Back** button.

16. Type ***.log** in the All or part of the file name text box, type **setup** in the A word or phrase in the file text box, click the **More advanced options** down arrow, check the **Search hidden files and folders** check box, and click the **Search** button.

17. Wait for the search to complete.

18. Verify that you obtained one or more files of the .log type.

19. In your project log, write a brief description of the various methods that you used to search for files.

20. Close any open windows.

Activity 2-3: Managing Files with Windows Explorer

Time Required: 20 minutes

Objective: Manage files and folders with Windows Explorer.

Description: In this activity, you will manage files and folders and explore Windows Explorer menus. You will find this activity useful in your career as a DST because, in order to answer users' questions about the management of files and folders, you will need to have explored this topic in detail.

1. If necessary, log on to your computer with the user name **user01** and password **Password1**.

2. Click **Start**, point to **All Programs**, point to **Accessories**, and click **Windows Explorer**.

3. Click the **File** menu and view the submenu options.

NOTE

If this activity has been completed previously and a Sample Folder#1 or Sample Folder#2 exists, right-click the folder icon, click Delete, and click the Yes button to delete the folder.

4. Point to **New**, click **Folder**, type **Sample Folder#1** over New Folder, and press **Enter**.

5. Click **File**, point **New**, click **Folder**, type **Sample Folder#2** over New Folder, and press **Enter**.

6. Double-click the **Sample Folder#1** icon.

7. Click **File**, point **New**, click **Text Document**, type **Sample Document#1** over New Text Document, and press **Enter**.

8. Click **File**, point **New**, click **Text Document**, type **Sample Document#2** over New Text Document, and press **Enter**.

9. Click the **Sample Document#1** icon, click the **File** menu, click **Rename**, type **Sample Rename** over Sample Document#1, and press **Enter**.

10. Click the **Edit** menu and view the submenu options.

11. Click **Undo Rename** and verify that the file was renamed Sample Document#1.

12. Click **Sample Document#1**, press the **Delete** key, and click the **Yes** button.

13. Click the **Edit** menu, click **Undo Delete**, and verify that the Sample Document#1 icon returned.

14. Click **Sample Document#1**, click the **Edit** menu, click **Move To Folder**, expand **My Documents**, click **Sample Folder#2**, and click the **Move** button.

15. Click **Sample Folder#2** and verify that the Sample Document#1 icon exists.

16. Click **My Pictures**, click the **View** menu, and click **Filmstrip**.

17. Click the **View** menu and click **Tiles**.

18. Repeat Step 17 with **Icons**, **List**, **Details** and **Thumbnails**.

19. Click the **View** menu, point to **Arrange Icons by**, and click **Size**.

20. Repeat Step 19 with **Type**, **Modified**, **Picture Taken On**, **Dimensions**, and **Name**.

21. Click the **View** menu, point to **Go To**, and click **My Documents**.

22. Click the **Favorites** menu and view the submenu options.

23. Point to the **Tools** menu and view the submenu options.

24. Point to the **Help** menu and view the submenu options.

25. In your project log, write a brief summary that describes the menu structure of Windows Explorer. Also, describe the file operations that you completed in this activity.

26. Close any open windows.

IN THE WORKPLACE

I'm really a "right mouser." I use the right mouse button frequently. After clicking the right mouse button over a file or folder, I can quickly click the following:

- Explore: Open a folder
- Open: Open a file with the associated application
- Open With: Select an application to open the file
- Search: Launch the search task
- Send To: Send a file to floppy disk, e-mail recipient, or a registered application
- Cut: Same as Edit and Cut
- Copy: Same as Edit and Copy
- Create Shortcut: Create a shortcut for a file or folder
- Delete: Delete a file or folder
- Rename: Rename a file or folder
- Properties: View information about a file or folder

Accessing the Internet

You know that the Internet is the largest computer network in the world, linking millions of computers. You may use a Web browser to locate information on a wide range of topics. And you may use e-mail to correspond with friends and family members. Your users will expect you to provide answers to their questions on the use of Internet Explorer and Outlook Express. These two Windows XP applications as well as two Internet security features will be overviewed in this chapter.

For additional information on Internet Explorer and Outlook Express configuration and troubleshooting, refer to Chapter 5.

NOTE

Internet Explorer

With Internet Explorer (shown in Figure 2-11) and an Internet connection, you can search for information on the World Wide Web. You can type the address of the Web page you want to visit into the Address bar or you can select addresses from your list of Favorites. If you want to find information quickly, you can type go, find, or ? followed by the text you want to search for in the Address bar of Internet Explorer.

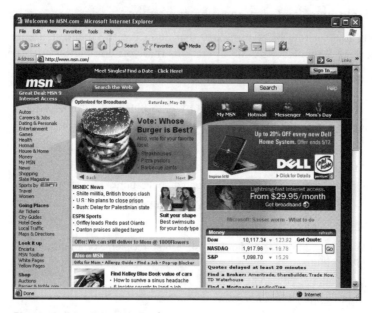

Figure 2-11   Internet Explorer

Outlook Express

With an Internet connection and Outlook Express, you can exchange e-mail messages with friends and colleagues on the Internet and join any number of newsgroups (Figure 2-12).

A **newsgroup** is a collection of messages posted by individuals to a **news server** (a computer with software supporting newsgroups). You can find newsgroups on practically any subject and can interact with subject matter experts. For example, you can submit questions to the MCDST newsgroup and provide answers to the questions of others.

Although some newsgroups are moderated, most are not. **Moderated newsgroups** are managed by someone who reviews the submissions prior to posting and might answer questions. Anyone can post messages to a newsgroup. Newsgroups do not require any kind of membership or fees.

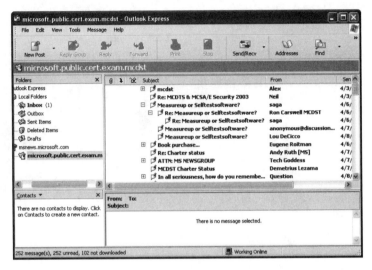

Figure 2-12   Newsgroup in Outlook Express

Internet Connection Sharing (ICS)

With **Internet Connection Sharing (ICS)**, you can connect computers on your small network to the Internet using just one connection. For an example see Figure 2-13, where you have one computer (labeled ICS Computer) that connects to the Internet using a DSL connection. When ICS is enabled on this computer, called the ICS host, other computers on the network connect to the Internet through this connection. You can use programs such as Internet Explorer and Outlook Express as if they were directly connected to the Internet.

Internet Connection Firewall (ICF)

A **firewall** is a security system that acts as a protective boundary between your network and the outside world. **Internet Connection Firewall (ICF)** is firewall software that you use to set restrictions on what information is communicated between your home or small office network and the Internet. Figure 2-14 shows the ICF software coexisting with ICS on the ICS/ICF computer.

ICF is considered a "stateful packet inspection" firewall. ICF uses **stateful packet inspection** (or dynamic packet filtering), which tracks the packets through the firewall and makes sure they are valid. A stateful inspection firewall monitors the state of the connection and compiles the information in a state table. Because of this, filtering decisions are based on the context that has been established by prior packets that have passed through the firewall.

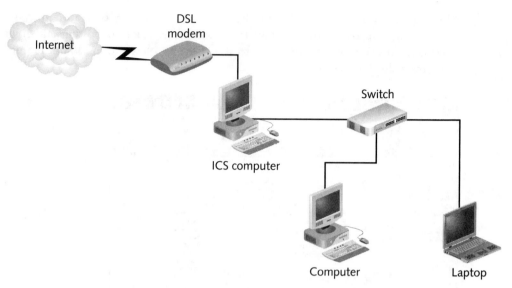

Figure 2-13   ICS in action

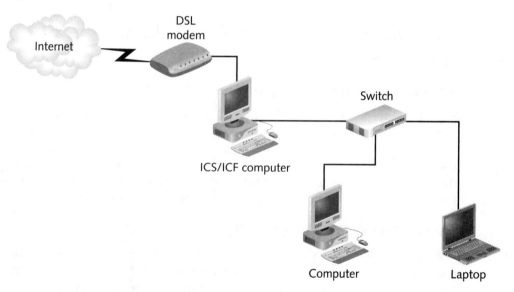

Figure 2-14   ICS with the addition of ICF

To prevent unsolicited traffic from the public side of the connection (the Internet/DSL side in Figure 2-14) from entering the private side, ICF keeps a table of all communications that have passed through the ICF computer. When used in conjunction with ICS, ICF tracks all traffic originated from the ICF/ICS computer and all traffic originated from private network computers. All inbound traffic from the Internet is compared against the entries in the table. Inbound Internet traffic is allowed to reach the computers in your network only when there is a matching entry in the table that shows that the communication exchange began from within your private network.

Working with Text and Word Processing

Notepad is a basic text editor that you can use for simple text files, such as configuration files or Web pages. To create or edit documents that require formatting, you might use WordPad. Both are discussed in the following sections.

Notepad

Notepad is a basic text editor that you can use to create and edit simple documents. The most common use for Notepad is to view and edit text (.txt) files. However, you can use Notepad to view the contents of other files containing text. Because there are only two formatting options (font and word wrap), you can safely use Notepad with HTML documents for Web pages. Figure 2-15 shows the rather stark window for Notepad.

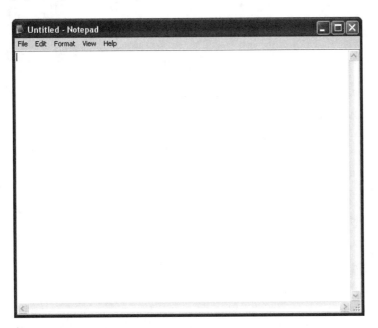

Figure 2-15   Notepad window

 I've routinely used Notepad to type notes when troubleshooting and resolving users' problems. To place a date and time stamp in the log, click Time/Date under the Edit menu or press the F5 key.

IN THE WORKPLACE

WordPad

With WordPad, you can create and edit a wide range of documents from simple text documents to documents with complex formatting and graphics, as shown in Figure 2-16.

In WordPad, you can perform the following functions needed for basic word processing:

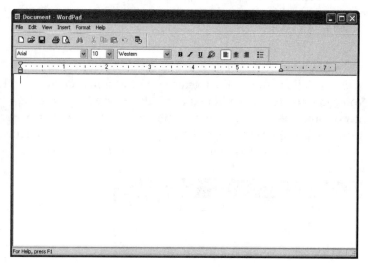

Figure 2-16   WordPad window

- Create a bulleted list
- Change font, style, size, and color
- Indent a paragraph
- Change the paragraph alignment
- Set or remove tabs
- Change paper size, source, and orientation
- Link or imbed an object

You may have noticed that no spell checking capability appears in the previous list. This is one big drawback to using WordPad for word processing. However, because WordPad is installed by default on all installations of Windows XP, WordPad is still an excellent choice for a basic document viewer. You can create documents that you know can be viewed by all of your users.

Activity 2-4: Discovering WordPad

Time Required: 15 minutes

Objective: Create documents requiring formatting with WordPad.

Description: In this activity, you will discover the organization of the menus for WordPad. In addition, you will prepare a simple formatted document. You will find this activity useful in your career as a DST because, in order to answer users' questions about WordPad, you will need to have explored this program in detail.

1. If necessary, log on to your computer with the user name **user01** and password **Password1**.

2. Click **Start**, point to **All Programs**, point to **Accessories**, and click **WordPad**.

3. Click the **File** menu to view the submenu options, point to **Edit** to view the submenu options, and then point to the **Format** menu to view the submenu options.

4. Click in the document window, type a line of text of your choosing at the cursor, and press **Enter**.

5. Click the **Bullets** icon, type a short line of text, and press **Enter**.

6. Type a short line of text and press **Enter**.

7. Click the **Bullets** icon and press **Enter**.

8. Click the **Insert** menu, click **Object**, click the **Create from File** option button, click the **Browse** button, double-click the **My Pictures** folder, double-click the **Sample Pictures** folder, click **Sunset**, click the **Open** button, and click the **OK** button.

9. Observe that the Sunset.jpg file appears as an object.

10. In your project log, write a brief summary that describes the menu structure of WordPad. Include a description of the available features.

11. Close any open windows. If needed, click the **No** button when asked to save the changes.

Working with Graphics

Paint is a drawing tool (see Figure 2-17) that you can use to create simple or elaborate drawings. You can use either black-and-white or color. Paint saves drawings in common bitmap formats (for example, .tif, .jpg, .gif, and .bmp). You can paste these drawings into common Microsoft Office documents.

IN THE WORKPLACE

As a network administrator, I've routinely used Paint to add the name of a computer to the desktop background. For example, open the Bliss.bmp, which is located in the C:\WINDOWS\Web\Wallpaper folder, and add the name of the computer to the upper-right corner of the graphic. Be sure to save the graphic with a new name.

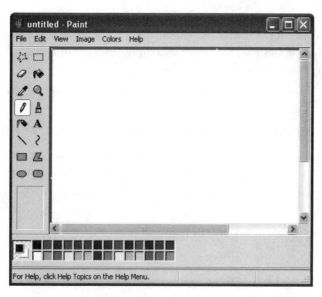

Figure 2-17 Paint window

Activity 2-5: Discovering Paint

Time Required: 15 minutes

Objective: Explore the features of the Paint program.

Description: In this activity, explore the menu structure and use the Help Topics of Paint. You will find this activity useful in your career as a DST because, in order to answer users' questions about using Paint, you will need to have explored the features of Paint in detail.

1. If necessary, log on to your computer with the user name **user01** and password **Password1**.

2. Click **Start**, point to **All Programs**, point to **Accessories**, and click **Paint**.

3. Click the **File** menu and view the submenu options. Do the same for **Edit**, **View**, **Image**, and **Colors**.

4. Click the **Help** menu, click **Help Topics**, click the **Paint** icon, and click **Common tasks**.

5. For each item listed in Common Tasks, expand the item, click the **Step-by-step procedure**, and follow the instructions. To return to the Common Tasks list, click the **Back** button.

6. If time permits, explore the remaining items in the Help Topics list.

7. In your project log, write a brief summary that describes the interaction between the Help and the creation of a drawing.

8. Close any open windows. If needed, click the **No** button when asked to save the changes.

Using the Additional Accessories

There are two handy programs that you might assist your users with. The first, Calculator, might be used as an on-screen version of a handheld calculator. If your users need a special character for a document, they will want to try the Character map, which is the second program.

These programs are presented in the next two sections.

Calculator

You can use the Calculator in Standard view to do simple calculations, or in Scientific view to do advanced scientific and statistical calculations. In Standard view, you can use the Calculator to perform any of the standard operations for which you would normally use a handheld calculator. Figure 2-18 shows the functions available in the Scientific view.

Figure 2-18   Calculator window

Character Map

You can use the Character Map to insert special characters into your documents. When creating your documents, you may need to use a special character in your text, such as a copyright (©) or a registered (®) symbol. See Figure 2-19 for a sample of the available characters.

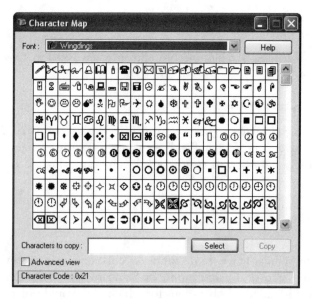

Figure 2-19   Character Map

ACTIVITY

Activity 2-6: Discovering the Calculator and Character Map

Time Required: 15 minutes

Objective: Describe user applications provided with Windows XP Professional.

Description: In this activity, you will use the Scientific view of the Calculator. Next, you will use the Character Map to place a character in the clipboard and copy the character to a WordPad document. You will find this activity useful in your career as a DST because, in order to answer users' questions about these two applications, you will need to have explored these applications in detail.

1. If necessary, log on to your computer with the user name **user01** and password **Password1**.

2. Click **Start**, point to **All Programs**, point to **Accessories**, and click **Calculator**.

3. Click the **Edit** menu and view the submenu options.

4. Point to the **View** menu and click **Scientific**.

5. With the calculator buttons, enter **255**.

6. Click the **Hex** option button and observe the change in radix (which is the base of a number system).

7. Repeat Step 6 for **Oct**, **Bin**, and **Dec**.

8. If time permits and you are familiar with scientific calculators, perform additional operations.

9. Close any open windows.

10. In your project log, write a brief summary that describes how you can use the Calculator to convert numbers between number systems.

11. Click **Start**, point to **All Programs**, point to **Accessories**, and click **WordPad**.

12. Click **Start**, point to **All Programs**, point to **Accessories**, point to **System Tools**, and click **Character Map**.

13. Move the Character Map window so that you can see the WordPad window.

14. Click the **Font** drop-down menu, and then scroll and click the **Wingdings** font.

15. Click the symbol that resembles an envelope, view the enlarged symbol, click the **Select** button, and click the **Copy** button.

16. Click the WordPad window title bar.

17. Click the **Edit** menu and click **Paste**.

18. In your project log, write a brief summary that describes how you can place a font character in a WordPad document.

19. Close any open windows. If needed, click the **No** button when asked to save the changes.

WORKING WITH THE APPLICATIONS OF OFFICE 2003

Microsoft Office is the dominant set of office applications. It's the de facto standard for nearly all tasks that your users might do on the desktop. In a break from the suite terminology, Microsoft calls its collection of applications and services the Office "System." In this part of the chapter, you will review the new common features of Microsoft Office and then follow up by exploring the three applications common to all editions of Microsoft Office.

NOTE

For information on Microsoft Office configuration and troubleshooting, refer to Chapter 8.

Using the New Features in Office 2003

Many of the new features in Office 2003 transcend the entire set of office applications. Microsoft touts that the Microsoft Office 2003 editions include new and enhanced functionality and productivity tools to connect people, information, and business processes, making it easier for people to take more effective action and get better results.

Although the MCDST exam will not have direct questions regarding the use of Office's many new features, you will need to be ready to answer your users' questions about these new features. In particular, you need to be aware of the impact that the new features might have on the way your users work with the Office applications. In the sections that follow, you will review the new features for Office 2003.

Help Integration with Office on Microsoft.com

The Help system extends past the individual desktop computer. If you are connected to the Internet when you choose a Help topic or type a phrase in the search box, the Help system displays both the local Help information and the Help information from Microsoft.com. For a representative Help screen, see Figure 2-20.

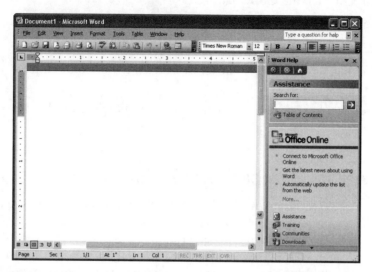

Figure 2-20   Help task pane

The screen in Figure 2-20 gives you the most current information about the topic for which you need help, as well as links to a number of new features, including the following:

- **Assistance Center Web page**: Provides articles that offer answers to common problems.

- **Office Online Training link**: Offers you online classes, Web-based interactive training, and self-paced exercises.

- **Templates link**: Takes you to a Template Gallery with dozens of professionally designed templates arranged by topic.

- **Clip Art and Media link**: Allows you to locate and download thousands of clip art files for use in your documents and presentations.

Topic Research

The Research task pane, which is accessed by clicking the Tools menu and then clicking Research, enables you and your users to search online references to locate information. Figure 2-21 shows a representative Research task pane.

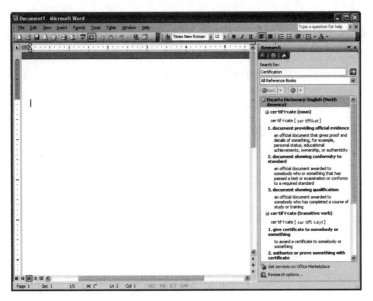

Figure 2-21 Research task pane

Through the Research task pane, Microsoft provides a number of free Internet services, such as Encarta Dictionary (which was shown in Figure 2-21), Thesaurus, Encarta Encyclopedia, MSN Search, MSN Money Stock Quotes, and Gale Company Profiles. For a usage fee, you can add third-party resources, such as Factiva iWorks, LexisNexis, and Safari HelpDesk Online.

Enhanced Collaboration

Microsoft Windows SharePoint Services and Microsoft Office SharePoint Portal Server 2003 are designed to help your organization share information. When used with Microsoft Office 2003, you can use a central repository for documents, as well as, an interactive work environment for collaboration, as follows:

- **Windows SharePoint Services**: Small or ad hoc workgroups that need an informal means to collaborate
- **Office SharePoint Portal Server**: Larger workgroups with structured processes that need greater management control over information flow

Both of the services in the preceding list permit the following:

- **Integrated file open and share**: Open files from and save files directly to SharePoint sites
- **Document check-out and check-in**: Checking a file out locks the file while it is being edited

Information Rights Management (IRM)

IRM is a feature designed to enhance collaboration methods while restricting access to the content of Office documents. IRM adds additional permissions to the file that allows you to specify who can access and use documents or e-mail messages. It helps prevent sensitive information from being printed, forwarded, or copied by unauthorized individuals.

If your organization elects to use IRM, you might get questions such as the following from your end users:

- How can I protect my organization's intellectual property?
- How can I prevent e-mail messages from being copied, forwarded, or printed?
- How can I use IRM with Internet Explorer?

Although the MCDST exam will not have direct questions regarding the use of IRM, you may need to be aware of IRM to answer your users' questions. As this is a new and developing technology, your best bet is to search the Microsoft Web site, *www.microsoft.com*, for irm.

Working with Documents

Microsoft Word is the word processing application in Microsoft Office 2003. Without a doubt, Microsoft Office Word 2003 is the world's leading word processing application. You—and your users—use it as a typing tool for creating correspondence: simple letters and memos. Some of your users may use it to create more sophisticated documents, such as large booklets, procedure manuals, and complex technical and legal documents.

Although the MCDST exam will not have direct questions regarding the use of Word's many features, you will need to be ready to answer your users' questions about using Word. In particular, you need to be aware of the new features. In the sections that follow, you will review two new features in Microsoft Word for Office 2003.

Reading Layout Mode

With Reading Layout mode, you can read through a document and navigate through the document without resorting to a printed copy. You can switch to the Reading Layout mode by clicking the Read tool on the Standard toolbar. If the text is too small to read comfortably, click the Increase Text Size tool, as shown in Figure 2-22. When you are through reading the document, click the Close tool.

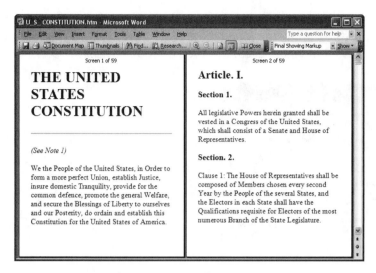

Figure 2-22   Reading Layout mode

Style Locking

You can limit what other users can change in your documents. You can block their attempts to boldface, underline, or reformat parts of a collaborative document. To enable style locking, check the Limit formatting to a selection of styles check box from the Protect Document task pane. To access the Protect Document task pane, click Protect Document from the Tools menu.

Activity 2-7: Installing Office

Time Required: 20 minutes

Objective: Install Office 2003.

Description: In this activity, you will install Microsoft Office 2003. You will find this activity useful in your career as a DST because you might be required to install Microsoft Office 2003 on your users' desktop computers.

In this chapter, you will perform a typical installation of Microsoft Office 2003 and remove the installation in Activity 2-12. In Chapter 6, you will learn more about the installation of Microsoft Office 2003.

NOTE

1. If necessary, log on to your computer with the user name **user01** and password **Password1**.

2. Insert the Microsoft Office 2003 CD in the appropriate drive.

3. If needed, click **Start**, click **My Computer**, right-click the **CD-ROM icon**, and click **AutoPlay**.

4. Click the **Run the program as the following user** option button, type **classroom\admin01** in the User name text box, type **Password1** in the Password text box, as indicated in Figure 2-23, and click the **OK** button.

Figure 2-23 Logon information

5. Wait for install preparation to complete.

6. Type the Product key, provided by your instructor, in the **Product Key** text boxes and click the **Next** button.

7. Type **Student01** in the User name text box, **S1** in the Initials text box, **Classroom** in the Organization text box, and click the **Next** button.

8. Read the End-User License Agreement, check the **I accept the terms in the License Agreement** check box, and click the **Next** button.

9. Verify that the **Typical Install** option button is selected and click the **Next** button.

10. Click the **Install** button to start the installation.

11. Wait for the installation to complete and click the **Finish** button.

12. In your project log, write a brief summary of the steps to install Microsoft Office 2003.

13. Close any open windows.

Activity 2-8: Discovering Word

Time Required: 30 minutes

Objective: Describe features in Word for Office 2003.

Description: In this activity, you will review the menus for Word. Also, you will create a memo with the assistance of the Help system. You will find this activity useful in your career as a DST because, in order to answer users' questions about Word, you will need to have explored these features in detail.

1. If necessary, log on to your computer with the user name **user01** and password **Password1**.

2. Click **Start**, point to **All Programs**, point to **Microsoft Office**, and click **Microsoft Office Word 2003**.

3. If the activation dialog box appears, click the **Cancel** button.

4. If necessary, type **First User** in the Name text box, type **FU** in the Initials text box, and click the **OK** button.

5. Click the **File** menu and view the submenu options.

6. Point to **Edit** and view the submenu options.

7. Repeat Step 6 for the remaining menu options.

8. Position the cursor over the first icon in the Standard toolbar. You should see New Blank Document.

9. Position the cursor over each of the remaining Standard toolbar icons.

10. Click the **Toolbar Options** button **(>>)** You should see icons appear that you can add to the Standard toolbar.

11. Click the **Toolbar Options** button **(>>)** to close the window.

12. Position the cursor over the first icon in the Formatting toolbar. You should see Styles and Formatting. Click the **Styles and Formatting** icon.

13. Click the **Styles and Formatting** icon to remove the task pane.

14. Click the **Font** drop-down menu. You should see a list of fonts.

15. Position the cursor over each of the remaining Formatting toolbar icons.

16. Click the **Toolbar Options** button **(>>)**. You should see icons that you can add to the Formatting toolbar.

17. Click the **Toolbar Options** button **(>>)** to close the window.

18. Click the **View** menu and point to **Toolbars**. You should see a list of toolbars that you can add.

19. Point to **Help** and click **Show the Office Assistant**.

20. If needed, click the **Yes** button to install the Office Assistant.

21. Wait for the Office Assistant to install.

22. Click the **Office Assistant** icon. (The default icon is Clippy.)

23. Type **write a memo** in the What would you like to do? text box and click the **Search** button.

24. Wait for a list of options to be displayed.

25. Click **Create a memo** and follow the steps presented in the Create a memo task pane.

26. Click the **Close** button and close the task pane.

27. Click **Help** and click **Hide the Office Assistant**.

28. Click **Help** and click **Microsoft Office Word Help**.

29. Click the **Assistance** link and select a topic of your choice.

30. Return to the Word Help task pane and click the **Training** link.

31. If time permits and you see a course in which you are interested, take a training course.

32. In your project log, write a brief summary that describes the menu structure of Microsoft Word. Include information about the toolbars. Also, include information about the various Help components that are available.

33. Close any open windows. If needed, click the **No** button when asked to save the changes.

Working with Worksheets

You know that Microsoft Excel is the worksheet or spreadsheet application in Microsoft Office 2003. When you build a worksheet, you enter text, numbers, and formulas into worksheet cells. If your users are accountants, they may have mastered building worksheets. Yet, worksheets can be developed by persons in other disciplines. For example, engineers use spreadsheets for engineering calculations and managers use worksheets for budgets.

Although the MCDST exam will not have direct questions regarding the use of Excel's many features, you will need to be ready to answer your users' questions about building worksheets in Excel. One feature that you need to know about is smart tags. Excel recognizes certain types of data and labels them with smart tags. The type of actions you can take depends on the data that Excel recognizes and labels with a smart tag.

The purple triangles in the corners of cells on your worksheet indicate the smart tags. After typing a U.S. stock symbol in a cell on a worksheet in Excel—for example DELL—you can use the smart tag options to gain instant access to published Web information about a company without having to open a separate Internet Explorer window. Of course, this access is dependent on your having an Internet connection already established.

Activity 2-9: Discovering Excel

Time Required: 20 minutes

Objective: Describe features in Excel for Office 2003.

2

Description: In this activity, you will review the menus for Excel. Also, you will create a worksheet with the assistance of the Help menu. You will find this activity useful in your career as a DST because, in order to answer users' questions about Excel, you will need to have explored the program in detail.

1. If necessary, log on to your computer with the user name **user01** and password **Password1**.

2. Click **Start**, point to **All Programs**, point to **Microsoft Office**, and click **Microsoft Office Excel 2003**.

3. If the activation dialog box appears, click the **Cancel** button.

4. Click the **File** menu and view the submenu options.

5. Point to **Edit** and view the submenu options.

6. Repeat Step 5 for the remaining menu options.

7. Position the cursor over the first icon in the Standard toolbar. You should see the text "New."

8. Position the cursor over each of the remaining Standard toolbar icons.

9. Click the Toolbar Options button **(>>)**. You should see icons that you can add to the Standard toolbar.

10. Click the Toolbar Options button **(>>)** to close the window.

11. Position the cursor over the first icon in the Formatting toolbar. You should see the text "Bold."

12. Click the **Toolbar Options** button **(>>)**. You should see icons that you can add to the Formatting toolbar.

13. Click the **Toolbar Options** button **(>>)** to close the window.

14. Click **Help** and click **Microsoft Excel Help**.

15. Type **loan** in the Search for text box, and click the green arrow.

16. Click the loan option of your choice and follow the steps in the wizard.

17. In your project log, write a brief summary that describes the menu structure of Microsoft Excel. Include information about the toolbars. Also, include information about the Help components that are available.

18. Close any open windows. If needed, click the **No** button when asked to save the changes.

Working with Presentations

For your last class, your instructor may have used a PowerPoint presentation. Using PowerPoint, you can create charts, graphs, slides, handouts, and overheads. PowerPoint is heavily used by professionals who need to make business presentations. These slide shows might be projected on a screen using a projection device. You can choose from dozens of professionally designed templates that speed the development of the presentation by allowing you to focus on the message.

Although the MCDST exam will not have direct questions regarding the use of Power-Point's many features, you will need to be ready to answer your users' questions about using PowerPoint. In particular, you need to be aware of the new features. In the sections that follow, you will review three new features in Microsoft PowerPoint for Office 2003.

Package Presentations

This feature allows you to prepare your presentation and burn it to a CD. Because the feature includes a PowerPoint viewer, your user does not need PowerPoint to view the presentation. You start the process by selecting Package for CD from the File menu. You name the CD and indicate which presentations to add. When you are ready, click the Copy to CD button.

Slide Show Annotations

You can make "handwritten" notes anywhere on a slide during a presentation. To do so, change the pointer to a pen or highlighter on the Slide Show toolbar and mark the slide with a tablet pen (the pen that comes with a tablet PC) or mouse.

Navigation Tools

The Slide Show toolbar displays only navigation-related options. You can move easily to another slide by selecting the Go to Slide submenu. You can pause the presentation and display a black or white slide while you discuss the topic. If you need to add a note, or perhaps an action item, you can display and edit the speaker notes. Another option allows you to switch to another running program. For example, your user could start Excel and open the budget worksheet and switch from the presentation when a manager asks to see the budget.

Activity 2-10: Discovering PowerPoint

Time Required: 20 minutes

Objective: Describe common features in PowerPoint for Office 2003.

Description: In this activity, you will review the menus for PowerPoint. Also, you will create a slide presentation with the assistance of the Help menu. You will find this activity useful in your career as a DST because, in order to answer users' questions about presentations, you will need to have explored this program in detail.

2

1. If necessary, log on to your computer with the user name **user01** and password **Password1**.

2. Click **Start**, point to **All Programs**, point to **Microsoft Office**, and click **Microsoft Office PowerPoint 2003**.

3. If the activation dialog box appears, click the **Cancel** button.

4. Click the **File** menu and view the submenu options.

5. Point to **Edit** and view the submenu options.

6. Repeat Step 5 for the remaining menu options.

7. Position the cursor over the first icon in the Standard toolbar. You should see "New" pop up.

8. Position the cursor over each of the remaining Standard toolbar icons.

9. Click the **Toolbar Options** button (**>>**). You should see icons that you can add to the Standard toolbar.

10. Click the **Toolbar Options** button (**>>**) to close the window.

11. Click **Help** and click **Microsoft Office PowerPoint Help**.

12. Type **project** in the Search for text box and click the green arrow.

13. Click the project option of your choice and follow the steps in the wizard.

14. In your project log, write a brief summary that describes the menu structure of Microsoft PowerPoint. Include information about the toolbars. Also, include information about the Help components that are available.

15. Close any open windows. If needed, click the **No** button when asked to save the changes.

Working with E-mail

You may know that with Microsoft Office Outlook you can track personal contacts and manage your e-mail. Microsoft Office Outlook provides an electronic version of a day-planner with features to schedule appointments, store contact information, and maintain to-do lists. It also sends and receives all your e-mail with features to compose messages and reply to messages. For additional information on Microsoft Outlook configuration and troubleshooting, refer to Chapter 9.

Although the MCDST exam will not have direct questions regarding the use of Outlook's many features, you will need to be ready to answer your users' questions about using Outlook. In particular, you need to be aware of the new features. In the sections that follow, you will review three new features in Microsoft Outlook for Office 2003.

New Interface

Microsoft Outlook 2003 sports a new user interface which is the first major change since Outlook 97. See Figure 2-24 for this new interface. The icon bar that appeared on the left, and took up space, has been replaced by a more functional Navigation Pane. By default, the four most used Outlook bars for views (Mail, Calendar, Contacts, and Tasks) occupy the lower third of the Navigation Pane.

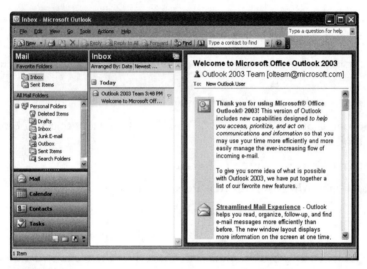

Figure 2-24   New Microsoft Outlook 2003 interface

Mail Improvements

By default, the Mail view is displayed when you start Outlook. The Preview Pane (see Figure 2-24) is larger, permitting you to read most of an average-length e-mail message. The e-mail folders are organized above the Navigation Pane where you can easily access them.

Junk E-mail Filter

The best new feature is the ability to filter **spam** (the electronic equivalent of junk mail). The filter examines the content and structure of the e-mail message to determine if it is junk e-mail. If it's junk, it's placed in the Junk E-mail folder. You can review the Junk E-mail folder and delete individual e-mails later. Why would you want to review junk e-mail? Because e-mail that you may need could be misclassified as junk!

Spam is more than annoying. Before spam filtering, I could count on 20 to 30 messages of the get rich quick or prescription drugs type each day. I would lose time sorting through these e-mails for the e-mail messages that I really wanted. My organization employs a spam filter that does not appear to be efficient as the one described in Outlook.

I've read that the filter in Microsoft Outlook 2003 can filter up to 95% of the spam because Microsoft has already looked at millions of spam and non-spam e-mails and created a filtering mechanism based on some 100,000 variables. This filter is installed as part of Outlook and is used to score each incoming message for its spam potential. Cross a certain threshold and the message goes to the spam folder. One of the editors that I worked with on this book found this filter to be very, very helpful.

Working with Compound Documents

A compound document is used to organize a number of user interfaces (for example, Word and Excel) to form a single integrated environment. A compound document is also an application environment containing program objects that can be interlinked and interacted with by a user. Compound documents are developed from information parts that originate from different applications and are assembled on–the–fly.

Object Linking and Embedding (OLE) is Microsoft's framework for a compound document technology. With OLE, each document object is an independent program entity that you can interact with and also use to communicate with other objects within the document. With OLE, you can do many tasks, including the following sample scenario:

1. Start with a Word document.

2. If you need a sales projection, drop in a table from Excel.

3. You notice that you could use a graph, so you drop in a graph also from Excel.

4. You then include the new corporate logo that you created in Paint.

5. Continuing with the example, you notice that the sales projections are not aggressive enough. By double-clicking on the object from Excel, your screen is transformed to that of Excel. You make the needed changes. Because the graph was linked to the sales projections, the line on the graph changes to reflect your new sales projection.

Although the MCDST exam will not have direct questions regarding the use of compound objects, you will need to be ready to answer your users' questions about using this productivity enhancement. In particular, you need to know the steps to build compound documents.

ACTIVITY

Activity 2-11: Working with Compound Documents

Time Required: 20 minutes

Objective: Describe compound documents in Office 2003.

Description: In this activity, you will create a compound document with a worksheet and a chart. You will find this activity useful in your career as a DST because, in order to answer users' questions about compound documents, you will need to have explored this option in detail.

1. If necessary, log on to your computer with the user name **user01** and password **Password1**.

2. Click **Start**, point to **All Programs**, point to **Microsoft Office**, and click **Microsoft Office Excel 2003**.

3. If the activation dialog box appears, click the **Cancel** button.

4. Starting in cell A1, enter the information in Table 2-1.

Table 2-1   Sales projections to enter into Excel

Units	Year
100,000	2004
125,000	2005
145,000	2006
100,000	2007
165,000	2008
195,000	2009
200,000	2010

5. Click the **Sheet2** tab.

6. Click **Insert** and click **Chart**.

7. Click the **Next** button and click the **Series** tab.

8. Click the **Add** button, type **Sales** in the Name text box, click the **Values** icon, click the **Sheet1** tab, click cell **A2** and drag your mouse down to cell **A8**, and close the **Chart Source Data – Values** window.

9. Click the **Category (X) axis labels** icon, click the **Sheet1** tab, click cell **B2** and drag your mouse down to cell **B8**, close the **Source Data – Category (X) axis labels** window, and click the **Finish** button. Your completed chart should resemble Figure 2-25.

10. Click **File**, click **Save As**, type **Sales Projections** in the File name text box, and click the **Save** button. If needed, click the **Yes** button to replace the file.

11. Click **Start**, point to **All Programs**, point to **Microsoft Office**, and click **Microsoft Office Word 2003**.

12. If the activation dialog box appears, click the **Cancel** button.

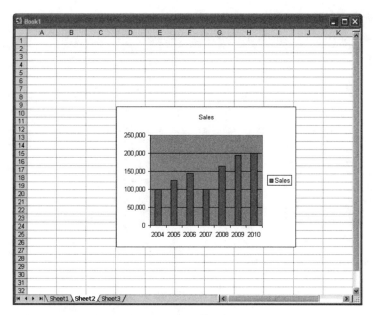

Figure 2-25   Completed Microsoft Excel chart

13. Type **We can expect steady sales through the year 2010. Sales projection numbers appear in the table below**. Press Enter **twice**.

14. Click the **Microsoft Excel – Sales Projections** button located on the Windows Taskbar located at the bottom of the screen.

15. Click the **Sheet1** tab, click cell **A1** and drag diagonally to cell **B8**, right-click the highlighted cells, and click **Copy**.

16. Click the **Document1 – Microsoft Word** button located on the Windows taskbar.

17. Click **Edit**, click **Paste Special**, click the **Paste link** option button, click **Microsoft Office Excel Worksheet Object** in the **As** list, and click the **OK** button.

18. Press **Enter** twice.

19. Type **And here is a chart that shows the sales projections**, and press Enter **twice**.

20. Click the **Microsoft Excel – Sales Projections** button located on the taskbar.

21. Click the **Sheet2** tab, click the white background of the chart, click the **Edit** menu, and click **Copy**.

22. Click the **Document1 – Microsoft Word** button located on the Windows taskbar.

23. Click **Edit**, click **Paste Special**, click the **Paste link** option button, and click the **OK** button. Your completed compound document should resemble Figure 2-26.

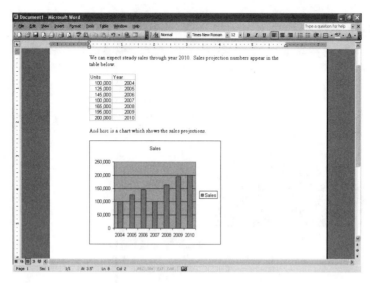

Figure 2-26 Completed Microsoft Word compound document

24. Oops! You notice that the unit projection for the year 2007 is incorrect. Double-click the spreadsheet located in the Microsoft Word document.

25. When the screen changes to Microsoft Excel, type **155,000** in cell **A5** and press **Enter**.

26. Click the **Document1 – Microsoft Word** button located on the Windows taskbar.

27. Notice that the edited value appears in the Microsoft Word document and that the chart reflects the change.

28. In your project log, write a brief summary that describes the steps to create compound documents.

29. Close any open windows. If needed, click the **No** button when asked to save the changes.

30. Log off the computer.

Activity 2-12: Uninstalling Office

Time Required: 20 minutes

Objective: Uninstall Office 2003.

Description: In this activity, you will uninstall Office 2003. You will find this activity useful in your career as a DST because you might be required to uninstall Microsoft Office 2003 on your users' desktop computers.

NOTE In this activity, you will uninstall the installation of Microsoft Office 2003 that you installed in Activity 2-7. In Chapter 6, you will learn more about the installation of Microsoft Office 2003.

1. If necessary, log on to your computer with the user name **admin01** and password **Password1**.

2. Click **Start**, point to **Control Panel**, and click the **Add or Remove Programs** icon.

3. Click **Microsoft Office Professional Edition 2003**, click the **Remove** button, and click the **Yes** button.

4. Wait for Microsoft Office Professional Edition 2003 to be removed.

5. In your project log, write a brief summary that describes the steps to uninstall Microsoft Office Professional Edition 2003.

6. Log off the computer.

MICROSOFT OFFICE 2003 EDITIONS AND LICENSING

Microsoft states that they have a Microsoft edition that's right for you. Whether you are a business large or small, student, academic entity, or volume-license business customer, you will find the right components in the respective Office 2003 editions. In the two sections that follow, you will view tables that indicate the components in the various editions and read a summary of the licensing options.

As a DST, you need to be aware of the various Microsoft Office 2003 editions to answer your users' questions about the components in each edition.

Microsoft Office 2003 Editions

In this section, you will encounter tables that provide the components for the various editions and licensing options.

In Table 2-2, you will find the Office 2003 editions that are available in the retail market. You can purchase them in your local electronics outlet and online from an Internet Web merchant.

Table 2-2   Microsoft Office 2003 retail editions

Retail Edition	Access	Excel	Outlook	Business Contact Manager	PowerPoint	Publisher	Word
Office Professional	Yes	Yes	Yes	Yes	Yes	Yes	Yes
Office Small Business	No	Yes	Yes	Yes	Yes	Yes	Yes
Office Standard	No	Yes	Yes	No	Yes	No	Yes
Office Student and Teacher	No	Yes	Yes	No	Yes	No	Yes

Table 2-3 lists the Office 2003 editions that are available as preinstalled editions. You would purchase these bundled with a computer from a major computer dealer.

Table 2-3   Microsoft Office 2003 preinstalled editions

Preinstalled Edition	Access	Excel	Outlook	Business Contact Manager	PowerPoint	Publisher	Word
Office Professional	Yes	Yes	Yes	Yes	Yes	Yes	Yes
Office Small Business	No	Yes	Yes	Yes	Yes	Yes	Yes
Office Basic Edition	No	Yes	Yes	No	No	No	Yes

If you work for a large organization, your organization will most likely negotiate a volume license with Microsoft or a major software distributor. Table 2-4 shows the Office 2003 editions that are available as volume-license editions.

Table 2-4   Microsoft Office 2003 volume license editions

Volume License Edition	Access	Excel	Outlook	Business Contact Manager	PowerPoint	Publisher	Word
Office Professional	Yes	Yes	Yes	Yes	Yes	Yes	Yes
Office Small Business	No	Yes	Yes	Yes	Yes	Yes	Yes
Office Standard Edition	No	Yes	Yes	No	Yes	No	Yes

If you work for a large educational organization, your school will most likely negotiate a volume license with Microsoft or a major software distributor. Table 2-5 lists the Office 2003 editions that are available to educational institutions through Microsoft academic licensing programs.

Table 2-5   Microsoft Office 2003 academic license editions

Academic License Edition	Access	Excel	Outlook	Business Contact Manager	PowerPoint	Publisher	Word
Office Professional	Yes	Yes	Yes	Yes	Yes	Yes	Yes
Office Standard Edition	No	Yes	Yes	No	Yes	No	Yes

If you attend or work for an educational organization, your school will most likely qualify to purchase a Qualifying Academic Edition. Table 2-6 lists the Office 2003 editions that are available to qualifying individuals.

IN THE WORKPLACE

The following individuals qualify for the academic edition:

- A student attending a public or private school or college. If you or a relative in your household attend a public or private school, purchase the Academic Edition. You will need proof that you or the household relative attends the school. A tuition receipt or grade report suffices.

- An employee of a public or private school or college. Again, you will need proof. A pay stub should suffice. At the time that this was written, the price was $149 for the Student and Teacher Edition.

Table 2-6   Microsoft Office 2003 qualifying academic editions

Qualifying Academic Edition	Access	Excel	Outlook	Business Contact Manager	PowerPoint	Publisher	Word
Office Professional	Yes	Yes	Yes	Yes	Yes	Yes	Yes
Office Standard	No	Yes	Yes	No	Yes	No	Yes
Office Student and Teacher	No	Yes	Yes	No	Yes	No	Yes

Licensing Options

In this section, you will find a recap of the various licensing options:

- **Retail editions**: Available online and in stores. You should purchase a retail edition only if you do not qualify for another licensing option.

- **Preinstalled editions**: Bundled with the purchase of a computer system. You might save considerable money by purchasing a computer with Microsoft Office 2003 preinstalled.

- **Volume-license editions**: Negotiated from Microsoft or a software distributor. Your organization can receive discounts by purchasing large quantities of Microsoft Office 2003 Editions.

- **Academic license editions**: Negotiated from Microsoft or a software distributor. Your educational organization can receive discounts by purchasing large quantities of Microsoft Office 2003 Editions.

- **Qualifying academic editions**: Tailored to students. If you qualify or your household members qualify, you can receive substantial discounts.

CHAPTER SUMMARY

- Windows XP Professional provides a number of user applications that your users can use to perform common tasks. With Windows Explorer, you manage files and folders. To learn the general structure of Windows menus, you examined the menus in Windows Explorer. Internet Explorer and Outlook Express permit access to Web sites, e-mail, and newsgroups.

- For text and light word processing, you reviewed Notepad and WordPad. To prepare graphics, your users might use Paint. For an on-screen calculator, your users might use Calculator. To insert characters, your users could use Character Map. You learned how these applications could be used by your users.

- Microsoft Office is the de facto standard for nearly all tasks that your users might perform on the desktop. In order to assist your users, you learned how to build a compound document. You reviewed the new features that were introduced in Microsoft Office 2003. You explored each of the following common applications:

  - Documents: Microsoft Word

  - Worksheets: Microsoft Excel

  - Presentations: Microsoft PowerPoint

  - E-mail: Microsoft Outlook

❏ Microsoft has licensing options for businesses large or small, student, academic entity, and volume-license business customers. Microsoft combines various components in the respective Office 2003 editions. You need to be aware of the various Microsoft Office 2003 editions to answer your users' questions about the components in each edition.

2

KEY TERMS

firewall — A security system that protects an organization's network from external threats.

Internet Connection Firewall (ICF) — Microsoft's implementation of a firewall in Windows XP.

Internet Connection Sharing (ICS) — Microsoft's implementation of a router connection between a private network and the Internet.

moderated newsgroups — Newsgroups that are managed by someone who reviews the submissions prior to posting and might answer questions.

newsgroup — A forum on the Internet for threaded discussions on a specified subject.

news server — A computer that exchanges Internet newsgroups with news reader clients and other servers.

Recycle Bin — A folder in Windows that holds files that are deleted and permits the files to be restored.

spam — An unsolicited e-mail message sent to many recipients at one time.

stateful packet inspection — A firewall architecture that works at the Network layer. Also referred to as dynamic packet filtering.

wildcard character — A keyboard character that represents one or more characters.

REVIEW QUESTIONS

1. The My Documents folder has which of the following characteristics? (Choose all that apply.)

   a. stores documents created by applications

   b. stores files created by operating system programs

   c. tied to an individual user account

   d. isolates individual documents from other documents

2. The Recycle Bin _____ . (Choose all that apply.)

   a. provides a second chance when deleting files or folders

   b. rejects newer files when full

   c. removes older files when adding newer files

   d. restores files from network drives

3. With the Search Companion, you can find files or folders by
   _____ . (Choose all that apply.)
   a. common file type
   b. all or part of the name
   c. date of the last change
   d. word or phrase in the file

4. The search characters fun*.doc will locate which file? (Choose all that apply.)
   a. Funnyface.doc
   b. Funnyface.txt
   c. Funandgames.doc
   d. Funandgames.txt
   e. Fun.doc

5. From the File menu in Windows Explorer, you can _____ . (Choose all
   that apply.)
   a. create an application file
   b. remove a file
   c. view the properties of a file
   d. copy the contents of a file
   e. access the My Documents folder by name

6. From the Edit menu in Windows Explorer, you can _____ . (Choose all
   that apply.)
   a. copy the contents of a file
   b. move a file to a folder
   c. open a file
   d. undo the previous file operation

7. From the View menu in Windows Explorer, you can _____ . (Choose
   all that apply.)
   a. show a toolbar
   b. add the Status bar
   c. hide the Explorer bar
   d. display the items by using images
   e. display the items by using thumbnails

2

8. With Windows Explorer, how can you access information on the Internet? (Choose all that apply.)

   a. type the search command in the Address bar

   b. type the address of the Web page in the Address bar

   c. select the address from your list of Favorites

   d. type find with the text to search for in the Address bar

9. Which of the following sentences about Internet Connection Sharing is true? (Choose all that apply.)

   a. It provides a protective boundary between your network and the Internet.

   b. It uses one connection to the Internet for a number of computers.

   c. It monitors all aspects of communications that cross its path.

   d. It sets restrictions on what information enters the private network.

10. Which of the following sentences about Internet Connection Firewall is true? (Choose all that apply.)

   a. It provides a protective boundary between your network and the Internet.

   b. It uses one connection to the Internet for a number of computers.

   c. It monitors all aspects of communications that cross its path.

   d. It sets restrictions on what information enters the private network.

11. You can use WordPad to _____ . (Choose all that apply.)

   a. spellcheck documents

   b. create a bulleted list

   c. link or imbed a graphic

   d. indent a paragraph

   e. change font, style, or size

12. You can use the Calculator accessory to _____ . (Choose all that apply.)

   a. enter numbers in decimal, binary, and octal

   b. calculate the square a number

   c. use trigonometric functions

   d. use as an on-screen four-function calculator

13. From the integrated Help in Microsoft Office, you can link to _____ . (Choose all that apply.)

   a. Office online training

   b. the Template Gallery

   c. the Clip Art feature

   d. the Assistance Center

14. When you use Topic Research, you can access which of the following free services? (Choose all that apply.)

    a. Encarta dictionary and Encarta encyclopedia

    b. MSN Search

    c. Factiva iWorks

    d. LexisNexis

    e. Safari HelpDesk

15. With SharePoint Services or SharePoint Portal Server 2003, you can
    _____ . (Choose all that apply.)

    a. collaborate between small workgroups

    b. open files and save directly to SharePoint sites

    c. check documents in and out

    d. have a central repository for documents

16. To enhance the reading of Microsoft Word documents, you use the
    _____ view.

    a. Normal

    b. Web layout

    c. Print layout

    d. Reading layout

17. When using smart tags, Microsoft Excel _____ . (Choose all that apply.)

    a. recognizes certain types of data and labels

    b. indicates that smart tags are available by highlighting the cell in purple

    c. creates an address to paste in the Address bar of Internet Explorer

    d. provides instant access to published Web information

18. To burn a set of slides to a CD in PowerPoint, access the _____
    submenu.

    a. Package presentation

    b. Burn CD

    c. Package for CD

    d. Package slides

19. When using Microsoft Outlook, you have access to _____ . (Choose all
    that apply.)

    a. calendars for appointments

    b. message generators

2

c. contact information

d. to-do lists

e. junk mail filters

20. Compound documents _____ . (Choose all that apply.)

    a. are assembled on-the-fly

    b. link objects from other applications

    c. open programs from an object

    d. require specialized add-in software

CASE PROJECTS

Case 2-1: Describing the Windows XP User Applications

You are a desktop support technician. Your network consists of a Windows 2003 Active Directory domain with 10 servers, including application and database servers and 500 computers running Windows XP Professional.

You are preparing a short hand-out for your users on the Windows XP user applications. Which applications will you include on your handout? Provide a description of each application. Include one specific task that a user could perform for each application that would motivate a user to try the user application.

Case 2-2: Describing the Common Applications in Microsoft Office 2003

You are a desktop support technician. Your network consists of a Windows 2003 Active Directory domain with 10 servers, including application and database servers and 800 computers running Windows XP Professional. Your organization is in the process of adopting and installing Microsoft Office 2003.

You recognize that your users will have questions about the new edition of Microsoft Office. You are preparing notes on the common applications in Microsoft Office 2003. Which applications will you include on your notes? Provide a description of each application. Include descriptions of the new features.

Case 2-3: Describing the Microsoft Office 2003 Editions and Licensing

You are a desktop support technician. Your network consists of a Windows 2003 Active Directory domain with eight servers, including application and database servers and 600 computers running Windows XP Professional. Your organization is in the process of adopting and installing Microsoft Office 2003.

You are responding to an e-mail message that you received from a friend in your organization. Rachel has asked your recommendations on the following points:

1. We will need Word, Excel, PowerPoint, and Outlook for the accountants. Which edition should we request?

2. The analysts need the same applications as the accountants with the addition of Access. Which edition should we request?

3. Could we save money by buying Office with the new computers?

4. What is the difference between retail licensing, preinstalled, and volume licensing? Where do we use each?

Because Rachel is a trusted friend, you will want to respond quickly and accurately to her e-mail. Create a draft of your e-mail response.

3

RESOLVE ISSUES RELATED TO OPERATING SYSTEM CUSTOMIZATION

After reading this chapter and completing the exercises, you will be able to:

- ◆ Customize the Start menu and taskbar
- ◆ Customize regional and language settings
- ◆ Customize accessibility settings
- ◆ Customize display fonts
- ◆ Customize folder settings

As you are aware, the role of the DST requires that you be prepared to resolve issues related to operating system customization. The operating system is the backbone that supports applications such as Microsoft Office. You will need to be prepared to answer your user's questions on customization of the operating system.

This chapter starts with the skills to customize the Start menu and taskbar. In Windows XP, Microsoft provides a new, simple organization for the menu used to start programs. You will learn customization features for both the Start menu and the taskbar.

Next, you will learn the steps to implement multiple language computers deploying Windows XP. These language customizations permit the preparation of documents in multiple languages. Regional settings permit the formatting of currencies, dates, and times for various languages.

Microsoft recognizes the needs of users that have difficulty using the computer because of accessibility issues. You will learn how to assist persons with special needs to use the accessibility features provided by Windows XP. For example, these features permit customization of the mouse, keyboard, and display.

You can change the visual elements of your computer by changing fonts and by customizing folder content. These two topics round out the chapter's discussion.

Customizing the Start Menu and Taskbar

The most useful items on your computer are accessed by clicking Start on the lower-left corner of the screen. Items that you can access include All Programs, My Documents, and My Computer. Customization permits control over the display of the items on the Start menu.

The **taskbar** is used to rapidly switch between running programs. The taskbar contains a button for each open window. The button for the active window is visually highlighted. Simply click on a taskbar button to switch to another window.

Elements surrounding the Start menu and the taskbar are discussed in the following sections.

Start Menu Views

There are two views for the Start menu in Windows XP. The Simple Start menu is the default Start menu and will be discussed first. The **Simple Start menu**, as shown in Figure 3-1, is the Start menu that is available when you start Windows XP for the first time. Note that your pinned items and most frequently used programs lists will vary.

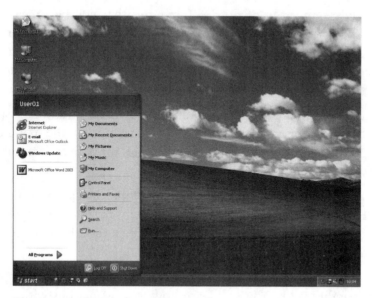

Figure 3-1   Simple Start menu

The second view is the Classic view, as shown in Figure 3-2. If you or your users used a version of Windows prior to Windows XP, you may prefer the **Classic Start menu**. In Activity 3-1, you will learn to switch between the Start menu views.

Figure 3-2   Classic Start menu

ACTIVITY

Activity 3-1: Switching Between Start Menus

Time Required: 15 minutes

Objective: Customize the Start menu and taskbar.

Description: In this activity, you will switch between the Simple and Classic Start menus. You will find this activity useful in your career as a DST because you will need to have explored these menus in detail to answer user questions about the contents of the two menus.

1. Log on to your computer with the user name **user01** and password **Password1**.

2. Right-click **Start**, click **Properties**, click the **Classic Start menu** option button, and then click the **OK** button to change to the Classic Start menu.

3. Click **Start**, and then click **Programs** and view the available programs.

4. Click **Documents** and view the list of previously opened documents.

5. Click **Run** to view the Run dialog box, and then click the **Cancel** button.

6. View any other items of interest.

7. Right-click **Start**, click **Properties**, click the **Start menu** option button, and then click the **OK** button to change to the Simple Start menu.

8. Click **Start**, and then point to **All Programs** to view the available programs.

9. Click **Start**, and then click **My Documents** to view the list documents in the My Documents folder.

10. Click **Start**, and then point to **My Recent Documents** to view the list of previously opened documents.

11. Click **Run**, view the Run dialog box, and then click the **Cancel** button.

12. View any other items of interest.

13. Close any open windows.

14. In your project log, write a brief summary that describes the steps to switch between the Simple Start menu and the Classic Start menu. Also, describe the visual differences between the two menu views.

Customizing the Simple Start Menu

The new Start menu in Windows XP provides more customization options than before. For instance, it shows you who is logged on. It also automatically adds the most frequently used programs to the top-level menu. You can add **shortcuts** to the Simple Start menu for any programs that you want to access quickly. Frequently used items, such as the My Pictures and My Documents folders, are now readily accessible from the Start menu.

The list of programs on the Start menu is divided into two parts:

■ **Pinned items list:** These are the programs that are displayed above the separator line, as shown in Figure 3-3. The programs remain there and are always available for you to click to start. (You will add to the Pinned items list in Activity 3-2).

■ **Most frequently used programs list:** These are the programs displayed below the separator line, as shown in Figure 3-3. By default, this list contains six programs. As new programs are run with more frequency than the previously listed programs, the new programs replace the old in the list.

If your users prefer the Start menu in Simple view, you will need to be able to answer questions about the customization of the Simple Start menu. You can customize the Simple Start menu by opening the Customize Start Menu dialog box by selecting Taskbar and Start Menu from the Control Panel, selecting the Start Menu tab, and then clicking the Customize button.

Location of separator

Figure 3-3   Simple Start menu showing the pinned items list

From the General tab of Customize Start Menu dialog box (see Figure 3-4), you can customize four global items. See Table 3-1 for an explanation of these items.

Table 3-1   Start menu global settings

Simple Start menu General item	Options
Select an icon size of icons for programs	Large or small
Number of programs on Start menu	From zero to 30 programs
Show Internet browser	Only Internet Explorer
Show E-mail client	Pick from Hotmail, Microsoft Office Outlook, Outlook Express

From the Advanced tab of the Customize Start Menu dialog box, as shown in Figure 3-5, you can customize specific menu settings. These settings are discussed in Table 3-2. (You will work with these settings in Activity 3-3.)

Table 3-2   Simple Start menu settings

Simple Start menu item	Purpose
Open menus when I pause on them with my mouse	Point to a menu to open the menu
Highlight newly installed programs	Spot the newly installed programs
List my most recently opened documents	Display up to 15 of the documents or files that were opened recently

Figure 3-4   General tab of the Customize Start Menu dialog box

Figure 3-5   Advanced tab of the Customize Start Menu dialog box

In the middle of the Advanced tab is the Start menu items list box. Table 3–3 discusses the menu items in this list box. (You will customize some of these items in Activity 3–5.)

Table 3-3   Entries in the Start menu items list box

Advanced Start menu item	Purpose
Control Panel	Display as link, Display as a menu, Don't display this item
Enable dragging and dropping	Permits shortcuts to be added by dragging and dropping the shortcut to the Start menu or a submenu
Favorites menu	Adds the Favorites menu. Enable this option when your users use Internet favorites frequently.
Help and Support	Adds a link to Help and Support
My Computer	Display as link, Display as a menu, Don't display this item
My Documents	Display as link, Display as a menu, Don't display this item
My Music	Display as link, Display as a menu, Don't display this item
My Network Places	Adds the shortcut to My Network Places
My Pictures	Display as link, Display as a menu, Don't display this item
Network Connections	Display as Connect to menu, Don't display this item, Link to Network Connections Folder
Printers and Faxes	Adds the shortcut to the Printers folder
Run command	Adds the shortcut to the Run command
Scroll Programs	Scroll through the list when the list of programs exceeds the number of programs that can be displayed on the Start menu
Search	Adds the shortcut to the folder and file search routine
System Administrative Tools	Display on the All Programs menu, Display on the All Programs menu and the Start Menu, Don't display this item

Because the Simple Start menu is highly customizable, you must become familiar with the Start menu to resolve your user's problems. The first customization with which you must become familiar is to add a program shortcut to the Simple Start menu.

As previously noted, the new Simple Start menu offers a number of new features. However, these new features can be bewildering for users who have used a previous version of Windows. This is a good opportunity for one-on-one training with your users on the new features.

Activity 3-2: Adding a Shortcut to the Simple Start Menu

Time Required: 15 minutes

Objective: Customize the Start menu and taskbar.

Description: In this activity, you will add a program shortcut on the Simple Start menu. You will find this activity useful in your career as a DST because, in order to answer user questions, such as how to add a program shortcut to the Start menu, you will need to be comfortable with adding a program shortcut to the Simple Start menu.

1. If necessary, log on to your computer with the user name **user01** and password **Password1**.

2. Right-click **Start**, click **Properties**, click the **Start menu** option button, and then click the **OK** button to change to the Simple Start menu.

3. Right-click **Start**, click **Properties**, click the **Customize** button, and then click the **Advanced** tab to display the Advanced Start Menu options.

4. If needed, check the **Enable dragging and dropping** check box to permit shortcuts to be dropped on the Start menu.

5. Click the two **OK** buttons.

6. Right-click the desktop in an empty place, point to **New**, and then click **Shortcut** to start the Create Shortcut wizard.

7. Click the **Browse** button, expand **My Computer**, expand **Local Disk (C:)**, expand **WINDOWS**, expand **system32**, and then scroll, locate, and click **sol** to select the Solitaire program.

8. Click the **OK** button, click the **Next** button, and then click the **Finish** button to add the Solitaire program to the desktop.

9. Right-click the **sol** icon on the desktop, and then click **Pin to Start menu**.

10. Click **Start**, locate your **sol** menu shortcut on the pinned items list, then click the **sol** shortcut to test your addition to the Start menu.

11. Click **Start**, right-click the **sol** icon, and then click **Unpin from Start menu** to remove your addition from the pinned items list.

12. In your project log, write a brief summary that presents the steps to pin and unpin an icon to the Simple Start menu.

13. Close any open windows.

ACTIVITY

Activity 3-3: Customizing the Simple Start Menu

Time Required: 15 minutes

Objective: Customize the Start menu and taskbar.

Description: In this activity, you will customize the Simple Start menu. You will find this activity useful in your career as a DST because, in order to answer user questions, such as how to control the way the Control Panel **applets** (small single function utility programs) are displayed on the Start menu, you will need to become comfortable with these types of customizations.

1. If necessary, log on to your computer with the user name **user01** and password **Password1**.

2. Right-click **Start**, click **Properties**, click the **Customize** button, and then click the **Advanced** tab to display the Advanced Start Menu options.

3. Clear the **Open submenus when I pause on them with my mouse** check box.

4. Click the two **OK** buttons.

5. Click **Start**, click **All Programs**, point to **Accessories**, and then click **Calculator**. Close the Calculator window.

6. Repeat Step 2, and then check the **Open submenus when I pause on them with my mouse** check box. Click two **OK** buttons.

7. Click **Start**, point to **All Programs**, point to **Accessories**, and then click **Calculator**. Close the Calculator window. Notice that the All Programs window opened without clicking!

8. Click **Start**, and then click **Control Panel** to open the Control Panel folder.

9. Repeat Step 2, and then click the **Control Panel – Display as a menu** option button. Click the two **OK** buttons.

10. Click **Start**, and then point to **Control Panel** to open the Control Panel menu.

11. Close any open windows.

12. In your project log, provide a list of the customizations that your users might use.

Customizing the Classic Start Menu

If your users prefer the Start menu in Classic view, you will need to be able to answer questions about the customization of the Classic Start menu. For example, you will need to explain how to add program shortcuts to the Classic Start menu. (You will add program shortcuts in Activity 3-4.) You also will be asked to teach users how to control the shortcuts that appear on the Start menu and the arrangement of those items.

You can help your users add a number of frequently used menus, such as the Control Panel, Network Connections, Printers and Faxes, and Internet Favorites. Figure 3-6 shows the check boxes to add icons to the Classic Start menu. Table 3-4 lists the Classic Start menu items and their descriptions. (In Activity 3-5, you will configure the Classic Start menu.)

Table 3-4   Classic Start menu items

Classic Start Menu Item	Purpose
Display Administrative Tools	Adds the Administrative Tools menu
Display Favorites	Adds the Favorites menu. Enable this option when your users use Internet favorites frequently
Display Log Off	Adds the Logoff command to the menu
Display Run	Permits the use of the Run command
Enable dragging and dropping	Permits shortcuts to be added by dragging and dropping the shortcut to the Start menu
Expand Control Panel	When enabled, the Control Panel options appear as a submenu. Otherwise, the Control Panel window opens.
Expand My Documents	Same as Control Panel, but applies to the My Documents folder

Table 3-4 Classic Start menu items (continued)

Classic Start Menu Item	Purpose
Expand My Pictures	Same as Control Panel, but applies to the My Pictures folder
Expand Network Connections	Same as Control Panel, but applies to the Network Connections folder.
Expand Printers	Same as Control Panel, but applies to the Printers folder
Scroll Programs	Controls whether program menu displays all options or permits horizontal scrolling
Show Small Icons in Start menu	Reduces the size of the icons on the Start menu
Use Personalized Menus	Tracks the menu options as you work, displaying only a partial list

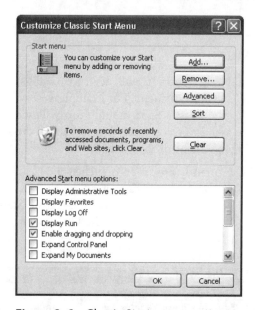

Figure 3-6 Classic Start menu options

 The Scroll Programs and Personalized Menus options can become annoying because items disappear from the Start menu. I recommend that these items not be selected. Your users will be happier and you will receive fewer questions about the disappearing menu items that require your users to remember to click on the arrows to view the items.

In order to troubleshoot your users' Start menus, you will need to become familiar with the new features. In addition, you will need to know the locations of the various option buttons and check boxes to configure the Start menu.

ACTIVITY

Activity 3-4: Adding a Shortcut to the Classic Start Menu

Time Required: 15 minutes

Objective: Customize the Start menu and taskbar.

Description: In this activity, you will add a program shortcut for the Solitaire program to the Classic Start menu. You will find this activity useful in your career as a DST because, in order to answer user questions about the customization of the Classic Start menu, you will need to know how to add a shortcut to this menu.

1. If necessary, log on to your computer with the user name **user01** and password **Password1**.

2. If needed, right-click **Start**, click **Properties**, click the **Classic Start Menu** option button, and then click the **OK** button to change to the Classic Start menu.

3. Click and hold on the **sol** icon on the Desktop, drag the **sol** icon on top of the **Start**. Wait until the Start menu is displayed. Drag the **sol** icon to the **Programs** item on the **Start** menu, then release the mouse button in the **Programs** submenu.

4. Click **Start**, click **Programs**, and then click **sol** to check access to Solitaire.

5. Right-click **Start**, click **Properties**, click the **Customize** button, click the **Sort** button to rearrange the entries on the Start menu, then click the two **OK** buttons.

6. Click **Start**, click **Programs**, and then view the sorted Start menu entries.

7. Close any open windows.

8. In your project log, write a brief description of the steps to add a shortcut to the Classic Start menu.

ACTIVITY

Activity 3-5: Customizing the Classic Start Menu

Time Required: 15 minutes

Objective: Customize the Start menu and taskbar.

Description: In this activity, you will customize the Classic Start menu. You will find this activity useful in your career as a DST because, in order to answer user questions, such as how to display the Internet favorites, you will need to know how to customize this menu.

1. If necessary, log on to your computer with the user name **user01** and password **Password1**.

2. If needed, right-click **Start**, click **Properties**, click the **Classic Start menu** option button, and then click the **OK** button to change to the Classic Start menu.

3. Right-click **Start**, click **Properties**, and then click the **Customize** button to display the customize Classic Start Menu options.

4. Check the **Display Favorites** check box.

5. If needed, check the **Enable dragging and dropping** check box to permit short-cuts to be dropped on the Start menu. See Figure 3-7 for these selections.

6. Uncheck the **Use Personalized Menus** check box to permit all of the Start menu items to be displayed.

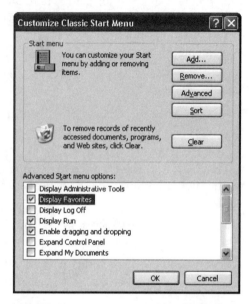

Figure 3-7   Custom options selected

7. Click the two **OK** buttons.

8. Click **Start**, and then point to **Favorites** to see the Internet shortcuts.

9. Close any open windows.

10. In your project log, provide a list of the customizations that your users might use.

Customizing the Taskbar

The **taskbar** (the box across the bottom of the screen) is a key element in the use of the Windows XP interface. From left to right, locate these items in Figure 3-8:

- Start button: Starts a program or locates a document

- Quick Launch toolbar: Adds shortcuts to frequently used items

- Application buttons: Provides a button for each open application

- Notification area: Displays a digital clock and a few other icons

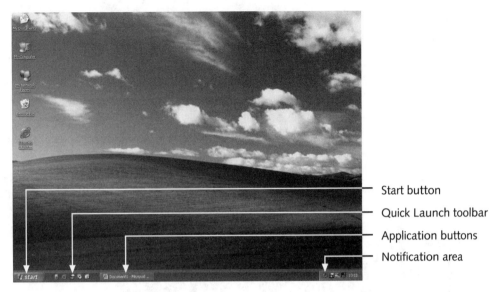

Figure 3-8 Taskbar items displayed

Moving and Resizing the Taskbar

Your users can increase the size and location of the taskbar on the screen. If you need to increase the size of the taskbar, position the mouse pointer over the taskbar's outer edge and drag the pointer to increase the size. To move the taskbar, click an empty area in the taskbar and drag it to the desired location. You will position, resize, and hide the taskbar in Activity 3-6.

Adding Toolbars to the Taskbar

You can add the toolbars listed in Table 3-5 to the taskbar. You will see how to do this in Activity 3-7.

Table 3-5 Toolbars that can be added to the taskbar

Toolbar	Content added
Address	A Web page address
Links	An Internet Explorer Link
Language bar	Text services
Desktop	Copies of all Desktop icons
Quick Launch	Shortcut to start an indicated application
New Toolbar	Contents of a set of icons from a folder

Grouping Programs on the Taskbar

The taskbar can become crowded with buttons when you are working with multiple programs at the same time. Windows provides a grouping feature (shown in Figure 3-9) to help you manage a large number of open documents and program items:

- Taskbar buttons for documents opened by the same program are always displayed in the same area of the taskbar so you can find your documents easily.

- Windows combines all the documents into one taskbar button that is labeled with the name of the program.

- A triangle on the right side of the button indicates that many documents are open in this program. The single button provides access to all the open documents.

Figure 3-9 Five documents grouped

Activity 3-6: Positioning, Resizing, and Hiding the Taskbar

Time Required: 15 minutes

Objective: Customize the Start menu and taskbar.

Description: In this activity, you will position the taskbar to another location on the desktop. You will find this activity useful in your career as a DST because, in order to answer user questions, such as how to resize the taskbar, you will need to know how to manipulate the taskbar.

1. If necessary, log on to your computer with the user name **user01** and password **Password1**.

3

2. Right-click an empty area of the taskbar, then uncheck the **Lock the Taskbar** menu entry.

3. Position the mouse pointer over an empty area of the taskbar, and then click and drag the taskbar to another location (top, left, or right edge).

4. Move the taskbar back to the screen bottom.

5. Grab the edge of the taskbar with the mouse and stretch it taller. Then shrink it back to its original size.

6. Right-click an empty area of the taskbar, click **Properties**, check the **Auto-hide the taskbar** check box, check the **Keep the taskbar on top of other windows** check box, check the **Group similar taskbar buttons** check box, and then check the **Show Quick Launch** check box, as indicated in Figure 3-10.

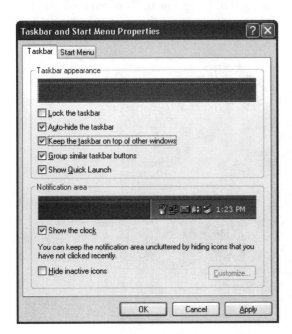

Figure 3-10   Taskbar properties selected

7. Click the **OK** button. Notice that the taskbar disappears. To bring the taskbar back, move the mouse pointer to the bottom of the screen.

8. Right-click an empty area of the taskbar, click **Properties**, uncheck the **Auto-hide the taskbar** check box, and then click the **OK** button.

9. Close all open windows.

10. In your project log, provide a brief description of the steps to position, resize, and hide the taskbar.

ACTIVITY

Activity 3-7: Customizing the Taskbar Toolbars

Time Required: 15 minutes

Objective: Customize the Start menu and taskbar.

Description: In this activity, you will customize the toolbars located on the taskbar, such as Internet links. You may already be aware that the Quick Launch toolbar exists to provide an area on the taskbar to hold the shortcuts to make frequently used programs available without having to use the Start menu. You will find this activity useful in your career as a DST because users will expect you to be able to help them customize the taskbar toolbars.

1. If necessary, log on to your computer with the user name **user01** and password **Password1**.

2. Right-click an empty portion of the taskbar, point to **Toolbars**, as shown in Figure 3-11, click **Links**, right-click an empty portion of the taskbar, point to **Toolbars**, and then click **Desktop**.

Figure 3-11   Toolbars submenu displayed

3. Click the **double chevron (>>)** next to **Links** on the taskbar to view the contents of the Internet links toolbar.

4. Click the **double chevron (>>)** next to **Desktop** on the taskbar to view the contents of the Desktop toolbar.

5. Right-click an empty portion of the taskbar, point to **Toolbars**, and then click **Quick Launch**.

NOTE

To delete an existing sol icon from the taskbar, right-click the **sol** icon, click **Delete**, and then click the **Yes** button.

6. Drag the **sol** icon from the Desktop and drop it next to the **Start** icon.

7. Click the **sol** icon on the Quick Launch.

8. Close all open windows.

9. In your project log, write a brief description of the steps to customize the taskbar toolbars.

CUSTOMIZING REGIONAL AND LANGUAGE SETTINGS

You may know that your users prepare documents in numerous languages throughout the world. To assist your users with these languages, you must learn to configure the settings for these languages. In the sections that follow, Regional settings and Language settings are presented.

Regional Settings

With Regional and Language Options in Control Panel, you can change the format of displaying dates, times, currency amounts, large numbers, and numbers with decimal fractions. You can also choose from a large number of input languages and text services, such as different keyboard layouts.

If your users work with others in different countries, you can change how programs format numbers, currency, times, and dates. You usually select the format that matches your location, such as English (United States) or English (United Kingdom). See Figure 3-12 for the formats that are used in England. You will practice using these options in Activity 3-8.

You—or your users—can change the clock to 24-hour format. You can customize how time is displayed by choosing 12-hour and 24-hour formats, the time separator, and A.M. and P.M. symbols. See Figure 3-13 for an example of the various time formats.

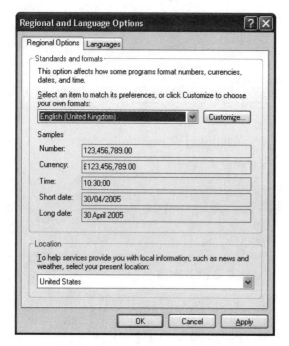

Figure 3-12   Formatting for the United Kingdom

Figure 3-13   Time formats displayed

Language Settings

You—or your users—might also need to switch to another input language. Each language has a default keyboard layout, but many languages have alternate versions. Even if your users do most of their work in one language, they might want to try other layouts. In English, for example, typing letters with accents might be simpler with the U.S.-International layout. If you compose documents using multiple languages, you can easily switch from one input language to another by using buttons on the taskbar. See Figure 3-14 for an example of the selection of a second language. If you want to enter or display text in that language, you have to add the language. In Activity 3-9, you will add a second language to the language bar.

Figure 3-14   Second language added

By default, Windows XP installs the files for most input languages supported by Windows. However, if you want to enter or display text in the East Asian languages or the complex script and right-to-left languages, you must install the proper language files located on the Windows CD-ROM.

You can add another keyboard layout or **Input Method Editor** (which permits users to enter languages such as Japanese). Keyboard layouts and Input Method Editors (IMEs) vary to accommodate the special characters and symbols used in different languages. Figure 3-15 shows a second keyboard layout added.

Figure 3-15   Second keyboard added

What is an IME, you ask? For years, Windows has used IMEs to permit users to enter the thousands of characters needed to write Chinese, Japanese, and Korean. An IME is a program that allows computer users to enter complex characters and symbols, such as Japanese characters, using a standard keyboard. Windows XP ships with standard IMEs that are based on the most popular input methods used in each target market.

ACTIVITY

Activity 3-8: Customizing Regional Settings

Time Required: 15 minutes

Objective: Customize Regional and Language Settings.

Description: In this activity, you will customize the regional settings to permit the use of settings for special currencies or localized date and time formats. You will find this activity useful in your career as a DST because end users will expect you to help them customize regional settings.

1. If necessary, log on to your computer with the user name **user01** and password **Password1**.

2. Right-click **Start**, click **Properties**, click the **Start menu** option button, and then click the **OK** button to change to the Simple Start menu.

3. Click **Start**, point to **Control Panel**, and then click **Regional and Language Options**.

4. Click the **Customize** button to display the Customize Regional Options properties box and view the Numbers customization options.

5. Click the **Currency** tab and view the Currency customization options.

6. Click the **Time** tab to view the Time customization options.

7. Click the **Time format** drop-down arrow, click the **H:mm:ss** to change the time format. Click the **Apply** button.

8. Click the **Date** tab, and then click the **Long date format** drop-down arrow (as shown in Figure 3-16). Click the **MMMM dd, yyyy** option to change the date format. Click the **OK** button.

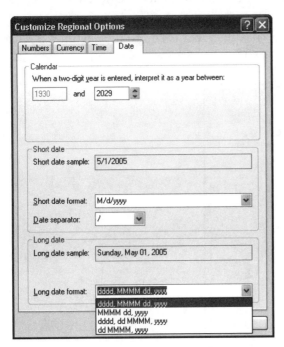

Figure 3-16   Date formats displayed

9. Click the **OK** button.

10. Close all open windows.

11. In your project log, write a brief description of the options that can be customized for the Regional settings.

Activity 3-9: Customizing Language Settings

Time Required: 15 minutes

Objective: Customize Regional and Language settings.

Description: In this activity, you will customize the language settings for Canadian French users. You will find this activity useful in your career as a DST because as companies become more internationalized, queries about languages and keyboards will become more common.

1. If necessary, log on to your computer with the user name **user01** and password **Password1**.

2. Click **Start**, point to **Control Panel**, and then click **Regional and Language Options**.

3. Click the **Languages** tab and click the **Details** button to view the language customization options. See Figure 3-17.

Figure 3-17   Settings tab of the Text Services and Input Languages dialog box

To remove an existing Input language, click the language to be removed, and then click the **Remove** button.

4. Click the **Add** button, click the **Input language** drop-down arrow, click

French(Canada), as shown in Figure 3-18, and then click the **OK** button to add Canadian French support.

Figure 3-18   French (Canada) selected

5. Click the **Default input language** drop-down list arrow, click **French (Canada) – Canadian Multilingual Standard** (as shown in Figure 3-19), and then click the **Apply** button to practice setting a default input language.

6. View the changes to the Text Services and Input Languages property box. Note that French (Canada) is the default input language and has been changed to bold text in the Installed services section, as shown in Figure 3-20.

7. Click the **Default input language** drop-down arrow, click **English (United States) – US,** and then click the **Apply** button to return to US English.

8. Click the **Language Bar** button, and check the **Show additional Language bar icons on the taskbar** check box to place the icons to switch between the two languages on the taskbar.

9. Click the three **OK** buttons.

10. Note the Language bar at the top of the screen.

11. Click the **Minimize** button on the right side of the language bar to place it on the taskbar.

12. Close all open windows.

13. In your project log, write a brief description of the language options that can be customized for the language settings.

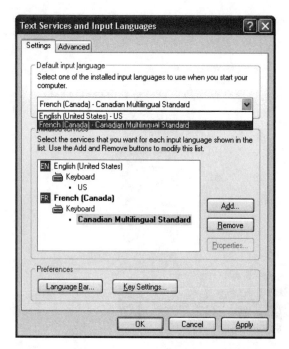

Figure 3-19   French (Canada) input selected

Figure 3-20   French (Canada) as the installed service

CUSTOMIZING ACCESSIBILITY SETTINGS

If your users have difficulty seeing things on screen, hearing sounds from the computer, or using the keyboard or mouse, you should consider using the Accessibility settings. You can quickly set accessibility-related options by using the Accessibility wizard. For your users with special needs, you can configure the options discussed in Table 3-6. You will practice setting representative options in Activity 3-10.

Table 3-6 Accessibility options

Accessibility option	Task
StickyKeys	Enables simultaneous keystrokes while pressing one key at a time
FilterKeys	Adjusts the response of your keyboard
ToggleKeys	Emits sounds when locking keys such as Caps Lock, Scroll Lock, and Num Lock are pressed
SoundSentry	Provides visual warnings for system sounds
ShowSounds	Instructs programs to display captions for program speech and sounds
High Contrast	Improves screen contrast with alternative colors and font sizes
MouseKeys	Enables the keyboard to perform mouse functions
SerialKeys	Allows the use of alternative input devices instead of a keyboard and mouse
Magnifier	Displays an enlarged version of the selected portion of the screen
Narrator	Reads the content of the screen aloud
On-Screen Keyboard	Types data by pointing and clicking with a pointing device

StickyKeys Option

StickyKeys is designed for people who have difficulty holding down two or more keys at a time. When a shortcut requires a key combination such as Ctrl+P, you can press one key at a time instead of pressing them simultaneously. This option, among others, is shown in Figure 3-21.

FilterKeys Option

FilterKeys adjusts the keyboard response so that inadvertently repeated keystrokes are ignored. Using FilterKeys, you can also slow the rate at which a key repeats when you hold it down.

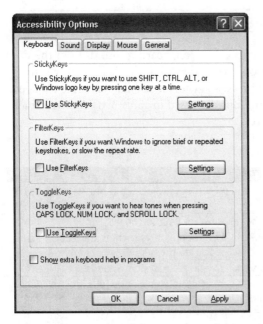

Figure 3-21   Accessibility Options displayed

ToggleKeys Option

ToggleKeys is for persons who have a vision impairment. When ToggleKeys is turned on, your computer will provide sound cues when the locking keys (Caps Lock, Num Lock, or Scroll Lock) are pressed. A high-pitched sound plays when the keys are switched on and a low-pitched sound plays when they are switched off.

IN THE WORKPLACE

As I type, I frequently find myself hitting the Caps Lock rather than the Shift Key. This results in sOMETHING LIKE THIS rather than Something like this. The emitted sound for the ToggleKeys option reminds me that I pressed the wrong key.

SoundSentry Option

SoundSentry is designed for people who have difficulty hearing system sounds generated by the computer. You can change the settings to generate visual warnings, such as a blinking title bar or a screen flash, whenever the computer you are using generates a sound.

ShowSounds Option

ShowSounds instructs programs that usually convey information only by sound to also provide all information visually, such as by displaying text captions or informative icons.

High Contrast Option

High Contrast is for people who have a vision impairment. High–contrast color schemes can increase legibility for some users by heightening screen contrast with alternative color combinations. Some of the schemes also change font sizes for greater legibility.

MouseKeys Option

MouseKeys is designed for people who have difficulty using a mouse. You can use the numeric keypad to control the movement of the mouse pointer.

SerialKeys Option

SerialKeys is designed for people who have difficulty using the computer's standard keyboard or mouse. SerialKeys provides support so that alternative input devices, such as puff and sip devices (enables a person to operate a switch-activated device without using his or her hands), can be attached.

Magnifier Option

Magnifier is a program designed for people with limited but viable vision. Magnifier displays an enlarged version of the selected portion of the screen. Magnifier is intended to provide a minimum level of functionality for users with slight visual impairments.

Narrator Option

Narrator is a program designed for those of more limited vision. It reads the contents of the screen aloud.

On-Screen Keyboard Option

The **On–Screen Keyboard** utility displays a **virtual keyboard** (software written to mimic the performance of a keyboard on the screen) and allows users with mobility impairments to type data by pointing and clicking with a pointing device.

You will configure the Magnifier and the On–Screen Keyboard in Activity 3-11.

IN THE WORKPLACE

At a course that I was attending, the keyboard on the instructor's laptop failed. With his mouse, the instructor started the on-screen keyboard, "typed" the commands, and completed his presentation. And we did not see him sweat!

Activity 3-10: Customizing Accessibility Settings

Time Required: 15 minutes

Objective: Customize the Accessibility settings.

Description: In this activity, you will customize several of the available accessibility options. You will find this activity useful in your career as a DST because the workplace is becoming more diverse and your skills must be ready to meet that diversity.

1. If necessary, log on to your computer with the user name **user01** and password **Password1**.

2. Click **Start**, point to **Control Panel**, and then click **Accessibility Options** to display the Keyboard options.

3. Check the **Use ToggleKeys** check box, click the **Settings** button in the ToggleKeys section, and read the explanation for the shortcut. Click the **OK** button, and then click the **Apply** button.

4. Tap the Caps Lock key several times and listen for the sound from the internal speaker.

5. Click the **Sound** tab, check the **Use SoundSentry** check box, check the **Use ShowSounds** check box, as shown in Figure 3-22, and then click **Apply**.

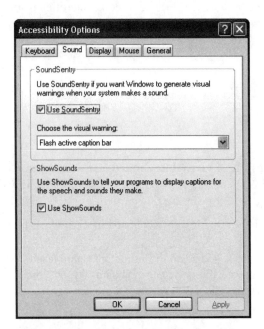

Figure 3-22   Sound options displayed

6. Click the **Display** tab, check the **Use High Contrast** check box, and then click the **Apply** button to change to the high-contrast theme.

7. Clear the **Use High Contrast** check box, and then click the **Apply** button to revert back to the previous theme.

8. Click the Mouse tab, check the **Use MouseKeys** check box, and then click the **Apply** button.

9. Press the **Num Lock** key and then use the arrow keys on the number pad to move the mouse pointer.

10. Uncheck the **Use MouseKeys** checkbox.

11. Click the **OK** button.

12. In your project log, write a list of the Accessibility options with a brief explanation of each.

ACTIVITY

Activity 3-11: Using Magnifier and the On-Screen Keyboard

Time Required: 20 minutes

Objective: Customize the Accessibility settings.

Description: In this activity, you will sample two accessibility programs: the magnifier and the on-screen keyboard. You will find this activity useful in your career as a DST because users are becoming more adept at requesting and using features that make them more productive.

1. If necessary, log on to your computer with the user name **user01** and password **Password1**.

2. Click **Start**, point to **All Programs**, point to **Accessories**, point to **Accessibility**, and then click **Magnifier**.

3. Read the marketing information, and then click the **OK** button.

4. Minimize the Magnifier Settings window to the taskbar.

5. Move your mouse pointer and observe that the pointer is tracked in magnifier window at the top of the screen.

6. Restore the Magnifier Settings window, and then close the Magnifier Settings window to stop the Magnifier.

7. Click **Start**, point to **All Programs**, point to **Accessories**, point to **Accessibility**, and then click **On-Screen Keyboard**.

8. Read the marketing information, and then click the **OK** button.

9. Click **Start**, point to **All Programs**, point to **Accessories**, and then click **Notepad**.

10. If needed, resize Notepad so that the Screen Keyboard and Notepad are both visible.

11. Type by clicking different letters on the On-Screen Keyboard. See Figure 3-23 for sample output. Note that you can "type" two keys (for example, Ctrl+V) by clicking the on-screen Ctrl key and then clicking on the screen character key.

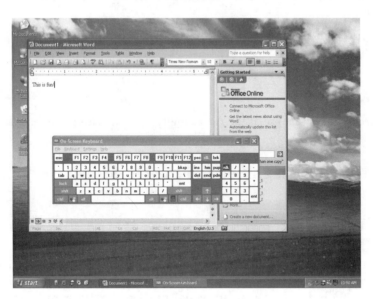

Figure 3-23   Example On-Screen keyboard input

12. Close the On-Screen Keyboard keyboard.

13. Close the Notepad window, and then click the **No** button.

14. In your project log, write a brief description of how your users might use the Magnifier, Narrator, and On-Screen Keyboard.

CUSTOMIZING THE DISPLAY FONTS

If your users have difficulty seeing text on the screen, you should consider customizing the Display fonts. You can quickly access the Display settings by right-clicking on the Desktop and choosing Properties. In the next two sections, you will learn to customize the display fonts. For a task related to customizing the display fonts, you will learn to set the display resolution (total number of pixels displayed horizontally and vertically).

Increasing the Size of Windows Text Fonts

If your users remark that the text on their screens is too small for easy reading, you can show them how to increase the size of the fonts used in Windows menus, headings, and icon labels. From the Display Properties dialog box, click the **Appearance** tab. See Figure 3-24 for the display of the Appearance tab.

Figure 3-24 Display Properties – Appearance Tab

Selecting ClearType Fonts

If you—or your users—have a laptop or a flat panel monitor, you may notice that your text outlines can get a little fuzzy at times. **ClearType** (Microsoft technology that improves the readability of text) improves readability on **Liquid Crystal Display (LCD)** displays with a digital interface, such as those in laptops and high-quality flat panel displays. To "turn-on" ClearType from the Appearance tab, click **Effects**. In the Effects dialog box, select the **Use the following method to smooth edges of screen fonts** check box, and then click **ClearType**.

IN THE WORKPLACE

For your users who are using LCD panels (such as those found on portable computer and other flat screen monitors), you should consider the ClearType font technology. However, ClearType fonts may appear slightly blurry on desktop computer CRT monitors; thus, you should select the Standard setting for the CRT on a desktop computer. This option is available under the **Use the following method to smooth edges of screen fonts** check box.

Changing Your Screen Resolution

To change the amount of information displayed on the screen, your users will change the screen resolution. When you customize the screen resolution, you change the apparent size of the screen fonts. To answer your users' questions, you must know how to make these changes. The screen resolution affects the amount of information displayed. Consider the following:

- To view more information at one time, increase your screen resolution. Everything will appear smaller on your screen, including text.

- To increase the size of items on your screen, decrease your screen resolution. Although you will be able to view less information at one time, the text and other information will be larger.

ACTIVITY

Activity 3-12: Customizing Display Fonts

Time Required: 15 minutes

Objective: Customize the Display fonts.

Description: In this activity, you will manipulate the on-screen fonts. You will also change the screen resolution. You will find this activity useful in your career as a DST because users are exploring font and display issues more and will often need your help.

1. If necessary, log on to your computer with the user name **user01** and password **Password1**.

2. Right-click an open place on the Desktop, click **Properties**, click the **Appearance** tab, click the **Font size** drop-down list arrow, click **Large Fonts**, and then click the **Apply** button.

3. Click the **Font size** drop-down list arrow, click **Normal**, and then click the **OK** button.

4. Right-click an open area on the Desktop, click **Properties**, click the **Appearance** tab, click the **Effects** button, click **Use the following method to smooth edges of screen fonts** drop-down list arrow, click **ClearType**, and then click **OK** twice.

5. Right-click an open area on the Desktop, click **Properties**, click the **Appearance** tab, click the **Effects** button, click **Use the following method to smooth edges of screen fonts** drop-down list arrow, click **Standard**, and then click **OK** twice.

6. Right-click an open area on the desktop, click **Properties**, click the **Settings** tab, drag the **Screen resolution** slider to change the resolution, and then click the **Apply** button. Wait for the screen resolution to change. If needed, click the **Yes** button to accept the change. Click the **OK** button.

7. Close all the windows.

8. In your project log, write a brief description of the steps to customize the display fonts and screen resolution.

CUSTOMIZING FOLDER SETTINGS

Your users can use Folder Options to change the appearance of folder content. For example, they can open each folder in a new window, display the full path to a folder, or hide the file name extensions. Opening items with either a single or a double click is one item that you will need to remember to discuss with your users. If your users open files from folders, you will need to know about changing the program that opens a file type.

You can perform the following tasks to customize folders:

- **Show common tasks in folders:** Display links to common tasks in the left pane of your folder windows. The links provide quick access to file and folder management activities and other places on your computer. By default, My Computer and My Network Places are displayed.

- **Open each folder in same or own window:** Specifies to open a folder in the same window or a new window.

- **Change the number of mouse clicks required to open items:** Use one or two clicks to open files and folders, and specify when you want the items to be underlined.

- **Display simple folder view in Explorer's Folders List:** Automatically display the folder contents and all subfolders within that folder. All other folders are automatically closed when a folder is selected.

- **Display full path in the address bar:** Complete path to the folder is displayed in the address bar.

- **Display full path in the title bar:** Complete path to the folder is displayed in the title bar.

- **Show hidden files and folders:** Choose to display these hidden files and folders that have the hidden file attribute.

- **Hide file name extensions:** By default, the file extensions for common file types are hidden.

- **Hide operating system files:** By default, the protected operating system files are not displayed.

IN THE WORKPLACE

To click or not to click, that is the question. Changing the number of mouse clicks required to open items—using one or two clicks to open files and folders—is a problem for which you may expect questions from your users. You will want to remember:

- If your user wants to point to a folder and click the file, choose the "Single-click to open an item (point to select)" option.

- If your user wants to click a folder and double-click the file, choose the "Double-click to open an item (single-click to select)" option.

ACTIVITY

Activity 3-13: Customizing Folders

Time Required: 15 minutes

Objective: Customize the Folder settings.

Description: In this activity, you will customize representative folder options. One useful option is to enable single-clicking and pointing to access folder objects. You will add two additional options: Display the full path in the title bar and Show hidden files and folders. You will find this activity useful in your career as a DST because end users will frequently want to customize elements and might need your expertise to do so.

1. If necessary, log on to your computer with the user name **user01** and password **Password1**.

2. Click **Start**, click **My Documents**, click **Tools**, and then click **Folder Options**.

3. Click the **Single-click to open an item (point to select)** option button, as shown in Figure 3-25.

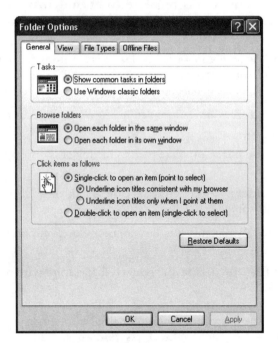

Figure 3-25 Folder Options dialog box

4. Click the **View tab** to display the view options.

5. Click the **Restore Defaults** button.

6. Check the **Display the full path in the title bar** check box.

7. Click the **Show hidden files and folders** option button, as shown in Figure 3-26.

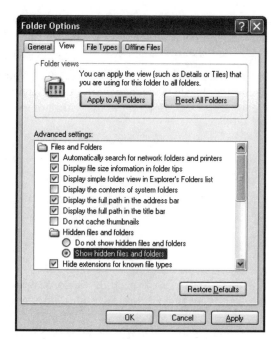

Figure 3-26   View tab of the Folder Options dialog box

8. Click **OK**.

9. Close all open windows.

10. In your project log, write a list of the Folder options with a brief explanation of each.

11. Log off the computer.

Chapter Summary

- ❏ Windows XP provides useful tools to access items on your computer. You will be prepared to answer questions on the two Start menus: Classic Start menu and Simple Start menu. In addition, your users will use the taskbar to rapidly switch between running programs and to launch programs.

- ❏ Windows XP supports numerous languages, which provide users with the ability to switch from one input language to another. You are prepared to answer questions on these language settings. With regional settings, you can choose the formats for such items as dates and times.

- ❏ If your users have physical limitations, you should consider the Accessibility options. Windows XP provides aids for users that have difficulty seeing things on screen, hearing sounds from the computer, or using the keyboard or mouse.

❏ Fonts are used to display text on the screen and in print. You are prepared to answer user questions regarding the use of ClearType, increasing/decreasing the size of on-screen fonts, and viewing and changing the screen resolution.

❏ Windows XP provides options to change the appearance of folder content. You will be able to answer user questions on: opening each folder in a new window, displaying the full path to a folder, hiding the file name extensions, or opening items with either a single or a double click.

Key Terms

applets — Small single-function programs on the Control Panel menu that perform operating system configuration.

Classic Start menu — Program menu used by Windows operating systems prior to Windows XP.

ClearType — Microsoft font technology that improves the text of LCD displays.

FilterKeys — Accessibility Control Panel option that permits persons with physical disabilities to use a keyboard. Ignores brief and repeated keystrokes resulting from slow finger movements.

High Contrast — Accessibility option in which a large degree of difference between light and dark extremes on a monitor is utilized.

Input Method Editor — Program that permits the thousands of characters written to be entered with a standard keyboard.

Liquid Crystal Display (LCD) — Type of display used in a laptop computer.

Magnifier — Microsoft accessibility program that enlarges the area of the screen where the mouse pointer currently resides.

Most frequently used programs list — List of programs on the Simple Start menu that appear below the separator line. Windows adds programs to this list.

MouseKeys — Accessibility Control Panel option that permits persons with physical limitations to move the mouse pointer with the arrow keys on the numeric keyboard.

Narrator — Microsoft accessibility program that reads what is displayed on screen: the contents of the active window, menu options, or the typed text.

On-Screen Keyboard — Microsoft accessibility program that displays a virtual keyboard on the screen and allows users with mobility impairments to type data using a pointing device.

Pinned items list — List of programs on the Simple Start menu that appear above the separator line. You can add programs to the pinned programs list.

SerialKeys — Accessibility Control Panel option that is used with a communications aid device, which allows keyboard and mouse controls to be accepted through the serial port.

shortcuts — An icon on the desktop or Start menu that permits access to a program, folder, or file.

ShowSounds — Accessibility Control Panel option that instructs application programs to provide a visual indication that the program is generating a sound. Used to alert users with hearing impairments.

Simple Start menu — Program menu used by Windows XP that is simple to use.

SoundSentry — Accessibility Control Panel option that instructs Windows to provide a visual clue such as a blinking bar when a system beeps. Used to alert users with hearing impairments.

StickyKeys — Accessibility Control Panel option that causes modifier keys, such as the Shift key, to stay on after they are pressed, eliminating the need to press multiple keys together.

taskbar — Graphical toolbar used by Windows to permit selections with the mouse.

ToggleKeys — Accessibility Control Panel option that instructs Windows to produce a high- or low-pitched sound when one of the toggle keys (Caps Lock, Num Lock, or Scroll Lock) are turned on or off.

virtual keyboard — Software written to mimic the performance of a keyboard.

REVIEW QUESTIONS

1. Which of the following is an option in the Classic Start menu? (Choose all that apply.)
   - a. Display Favorites
   - b. Display Programs
   - c. Display Menus
   - d. Enable Dragging and Dropping

2. Which of the following is an option in the Simple Start menu? (Choose all that apply.)
   - a. Size of icons
   - b. Control Panel
   - c. My Computer
   - d. Network Neighborhood

3. Which of the following can be added to the Classic Start menu? (Choose all that apply.)
   - a. Administrative Tools
   - b. Favorites
   - c. Run
   - d. Printers
   - e. Panels

4. Which statement is true regarding the pinned items list in the Simple Start menu? (Choose all that apply.)

    a. You added those pinned items.

    b. Programs are displayed above the separator line.

    c. Pinned items are added as programs are run.

    d. Programs are displayed below the separator line.

5. For the Simple Start menu, how many program shortcuts can be on the Most frequently used programs list? (Choose all that apply.)

    a. none

    b. default of 6

    c. maximum of 30

    d. maximum of 100

6. If you select "Open submenus when I pause on them with my mouse" in the Simple Start menu, what is then true? (Choose all that apply.)

    a. You must click to open menus.

    b. You must click to run a program.

    c. You must point to open menus.

    d. You must double-click to run a program.

7. Which of the following is a Start menu item for the Control Panel of the Simple Start menu? (Choose all that apply.)

    a. Display as a link

    b. Display as a menu

    c. Display as a pointer

    d. Display as a program

    e. Don't display this item

8. Which of the following can exist on the taskbar? (Choose all that apply.)

    a. Start menu

    b. Quick Launch toolbar

    c. application buttons

    d. notification area

9. Which action can you take with the taskbar? (Choose all that apply.)

    a. remove

    b. hide

    c. move

    d. resize

10. Which toolbar can be added to the taskbar? (Choose all that apply.)

    a. Address

    b. Sound

    c. Desktop

    d. Quick Launch

11. With the Regional options in Windows XP, you can change the format for
_____ . (Choose all that apply.)

    a. dates

    b. times

    c. currencies

    d. languages

    e. keyboards

12. What customization is available for the clock formats in Windows XP? (Choose all
that apply.)

    a. 12-hour format

    b. 24-hour format

    c. AM symbol

    d. PM symbol

    e. the separator symbol

13. If you need to use the East Asian languages with Windows XP, you must
_____ .

    a. do nothing as the East Asian languages are installed when Windows XP is installed

    b. purchase a third-party utility

    c. install the East Asian languages from the Windows XP CD-ROM

    d. download the East Asian languages from the Microsoft Web site

14. Microsoft provides IMEs for which language? (Choose all that apply.)

    a. English

    b. French

    c. Chinese

    d. Japanese

    e. Korean

15. To switch between input languages, you can click _____ . (Choose all that apply.)

    a. Control Panel Languages

    b. the language button on the Language Bar

    c. the language button on the taskbar

    d. the Quick Launch button

16. Microsoft provides Accessibility settings to assist persons who have difficulty _____ . (Choose all that apply.)

    a. seeing things on screen

    b. hearing sounds from the computer

    c. using the keyboard

    d. using the mouse

17. Which of the following is an Accessibility setting for the keyboard? (Choose all that apply.)

    a. StickyKeys

    b. FilterKeys

    c. ToggleKeys

    d. MouseKeys

18. Which of the following Accessibility options would assist persons with limited hearing? (Choose all that apply.)

    a. SoundSentry

    b. Narrator

    c. Speaker

    d. ShowSounds

19. Which of the following is a utility program that Microsoft provides for persons with accessibility issues? (Choose all that apply.)

    a. Narrator

    b. Speaker

    c. On-Screen Keyboard

    d. Magnifier

20. Microsoft developed ClearType especially for use with _____ .

    a. laser printers

    b. inkjet printers

    c. LCD panels

    d. monitors

21. Windows XP supports _____ fonts. (Choose all that apply.)

    a. rendered

    b. outline

    c. vector

    d. raster

3

22. Which option will permit you to point to select an item and single-click an item to open that item?

    a. Point to click

    b. Single-click to open an item (point to select)

    c. Single-click to open an item

    d. Single-click to point

23. When setting the options for browsing folders, select the _____ option under the Browse folders. (Choose all that apply.)

    a. Open each folder in the same window

    b. Open each folder in its own window

    c. Open each window in the same folder

    d. Open each window in its own folder

24. When setting the full path options, the location of the folders is ultimately displayed in the _____ . (Choose all that apply.)

    a. Address bar

    b. Browser bar

    c. taskbar

    d. Title bar

25. Which items in the View – Advanced check boxes can be marked as hidden? (Choose all that apply.)

    a. files

    b. folders

    c. system files

    d. Web files

CASE PROJECTS

CASE
PROJECTS

Case 3-1: Customizing the Start Menu and Taskbar

You are a desktop support technician. Your network consists of a Windows 2003 Active Directory domain with ten servers, including application and database servers and 500 computers running Windows XP Professional.

You are responding to a question posed by George. He has used Windows NT workstation and Windows 2000 Professional prior to the upgrade to Windows XP Professional. He wants your advice on choosing between the Simple Start menu and the Classic Start menu.

What advice will you be giving George? George will want to know about the features in the Simple Start menu. You will want to provide him with your experiences using this new Start menu. Point out what features he will lose by going to the Classic Start menu.

CASE
PROJECTS

Case 3-2: Customizing Regional and Language Settings

You are a desktop support technician for an international corporation with employees on five continents. Your network consists of ten Windows 2003 Active Directory domains with 5000 computers running Windows XP Professional.

You are responding to a question posed by a Japanese employee who desires to prepare documents in his native language.

How will you respond to the employee's business need? You should be prepared to communicate on all aspects of the Regional and Language settings.

CASE
PROJECTS

Case 3-3: Customizing Accessibility Settings

You are a desktop support technician for a nonprofit company that hires and trains people with hearing difficulties. Your network consists of ten computers running Windows XP Professional.

You are responding to a question posed by the director who desires to use the Accessibility options in Windows XP to aid his staff.

What recommendations will you make? You will need to communicate on all the aspects of the selected Accessibility options for people with hearing difficulties.

4

CONFIGURE USER-RELATED ISSUES

After reading this chapter and completing the exercises, you will be able to:

♦ Configure Access to Applications on Multiuser Computers

♦ Configure the Operating System to Support Applications

A s you are aware, the role of the DST requires that you be prepared to resolve issues related to user configurations. You should know how to configure the Windows XP operating system to support multiple users. User applications, such as Microsoft Office, may require additional configuration of the Windows XP operating system.

This chapter starts with the necessary skills to customize access to applications on computers with multiple users. For example, you will learn to create and configure multiple user accounts including the processing of the various types of logons. Next, you will learn the steps to configure Windows XP to support applications.

Configuring Access to Applications on Multiuser Computers

Just as there are two basic types of computers designed for small and larger businesses, there are two versions of Windows XP:

- Windows XP Home, which is designed for usage in the Small Office Home Office (SOHO) setting
- Windows XP Professional, which is designed for usage in the corporate business environment

On SOHO computers, you may log on from the Welcome screen. With fast user switching, users can rapidly switch between two or more running sets of applications. You will need to create user accounts for each user of the SOHO computers.

For larger networks, such as corporate networks, the configuration for multiusers differs from the SOHO network. For example, fast user switching cannot be used on corporate networks. User profiles, such as customization settings for the desktop, might be stored on servers that permit these customizations to be readily available as the user moves from computer to computer. User logons become an issue for corporate networks in which the user accounts may be validated from one or more sources.

These topics are discussed in the following sections.

Multiuser Desktop for SOHO Networks

If you support users on SOHO networks, you must know the details of user accounts and fast user switching. If you support corporate networks, you will need to know these details for two reasons:

- Your users have questions about their home networks and as the DST you are expected to know the answers.
- Your users want to understand the differences between home networks and corporate networks.

Using User Accounts

User accounts personalize Windows for each user who is sharing a computer. You—or your user—can choose his or her personal account name, picture, and password. This user account gives your user a personalized view of his or her files. With a user account, documents your users create or save are stored in his or her My Documents folder, separate from the documents of others who also use the computer. If your users use passwords for their user accounts, all of their files are kept secure and private so that other users cannot see them.

You manage user accounts from the User accounts window, as shown Figure 4-1. You access user accounts from the Start menu and then the Control Panel.

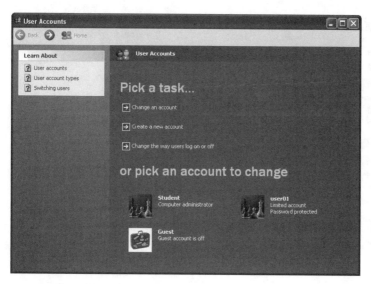

Figure 4-1   User Accounts window

Change an Account

By clicking the Change an account link, you will see the Pick an account to change window, as shown in Figure 4-2. From this window, you can pick the account that you wish to change.

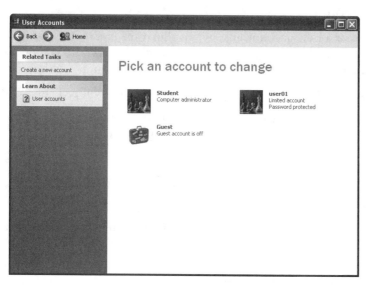

Figure 4-2   Pick an account to change screen

Figure 4-3 shows the actions that you can perform for a user account.

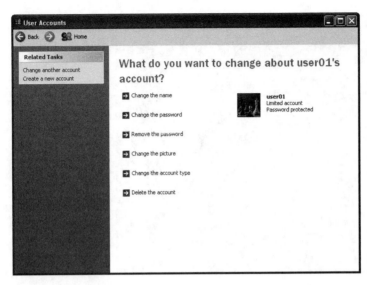

Figure 4-3   What do you want to change about user01's account? screen

    Pictures on the Welcome screen are clever! The pictures can aid in the identification of individual users. Take a picture of the individual with a digital camera. You'll find all sorts of opportunities for pictures—recent promotions, the last office party, league play, and so on.

Create a New Account

By clicking the Create a new account link, as was shown in Figure 4-1, you can start the New Account wizard. The initial window for the New Account wizard is shown in Figure 4-4. Within this window, you will type a name for the user account.

In the next, and last, window in the New Account wizard, you will pick an account type:

- **Computer administrator:** The person with this account type can create, change, and delete accounts; make system wide changes; install programs; and access all files.

- **Limited:** The person with this account type can change or remove his or her own password, change desktop settings, view files, and view files in the Shared Documents folder.

Also, older programs, designed before Windows 2000 and Windows XP, might not work properly with limited accounts. Microsoft recommends that you select programs designed to work with Microsoft XP. This means that you might be wise to upgrade your programs when you make the move to Windows XP.

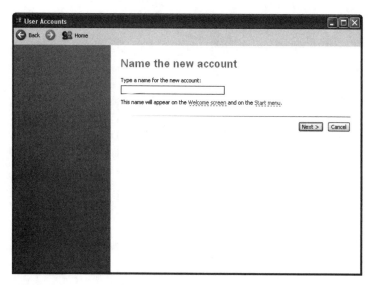

Figure 4-4   Name the new account screen

IN THE WORKPLACE

Users with Limited privileges cannot always install programs. To install some programs, you may have to change the User account type to Administrator.

Your users might find out about these restrictions when they try to install the latest and greatest unauthorized software on your system. Be prepared for some grumbling when they find out that they have been effectively blocked.

Fast User Switching

With Fast User Switching, you and your users can switch among user accounts without closing programs. This is beneficial in situations where users swap a single computer several times a day. From the window shown in Figure 4-1, click the Change the way users log on or off link to start the configuration for Fast User Switching. You then must choose both options in Figure 4-5 to enable Fast User Switching.

As the window cautions, when combining these two options you have added flexibility at the expense of security. These options should be used only in an environment where security is not a concern. In a secure environment, you may want to clear the Use the Welcome screen check box and use the classic logon prompt.

When Fast User Switching is enabled on a computer, the end user will see the following when he or she tries to log off:

- **Switch User:** Switch to any running user. Also, log on to other users that are currently not running.
- **Log Off:** Log off the user account.

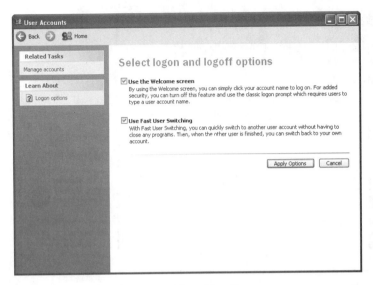

Figure 4-5   Select logon and logoff options screen

When the Switch User icon is clicked, you are presented with a window to select a user. In this window, as shown in Figure 4-6, you click on the user environment that you want to access. The two user accounts, user01 and user02, are logged on. You could switch to either by clicking the user icon and resuming the active applications. You could also log on to Student by clicking that icon and typing a password.

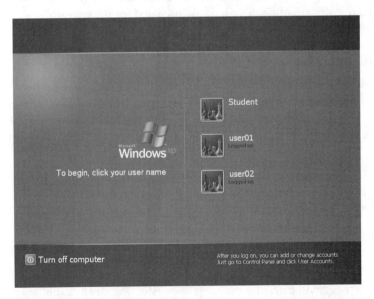

Figure 4-6   Select User window

Activity 4-1: Placing a Computer in a Workgroup

Time Required: 15 minutes

Objective: Change the membership of a computer from a domain to a workgroup.

Description: In this activity, you will remove a computer from the classroom domain and place it in the WORKGROUP workgroup. You will find this activity useful in your career as a DST because, in order to troubleshoot the differences between domains and workgroups, you will need to have explored these two types of networks in detail.

1. Log on to your computer with the user name **admin01** and password **Password1**.

2. Click **Start**, right-click **My Computer**, click **Properties**, and click the **Computer Name** tab, as shown in Figure 4-7.

Figure 4-7   Computer Name tab

3. Click the **Change** button. Under the Member of, click the **Workgroup** option button, type **WORKGROUP** in the Workgroup text box, and click the **OK** button.

4. Type **admin01** in the User name textbox, type **Password1** in the Password text box, and click the **OK** button.

5. Wait for the **Welcome to the WORKGROUP workgroup** message to be displayed. On three consecutive screens, click the **OK** button, and then click the **Yes** button.

6. Wait for the computer to restart.

7. In your project log, write a detailed summary that describes the steps to remove a computer from a domain and place it in a workgroup.

Activity 4-2: Creating User Accounts

Time Required: 15 minutes

Objective: Create local user accounts.

Description: In this activity, you will create local user accounts. You will find this activity useful in your career as a DST because, in order to answer questions regarding adding and modifying user accounts, you will need to have explored user accounts in detail.

1. If necessary, log on to your computer with the user name **student** and password **Password1**.

2. Click **Start**, point to **Control Panel**, and click **User Accounts**.

3. If this activity has been previously completed and it is necessary to remove the existing user accounts, click **user01**, click the **Delete the account** link, click the **Keep Files** button, and click the **Delete Account** button. Repeat for user02.

4. Click the **Create a new account** link, type **user01** in the Type a name for the new account text box, click the **Next** button, and click the **Create Account** button.

5. Click the **user01** account, click the **Create a password** link, type **Password1**, press the **Tab** key, type **Password1**, click the **Create Password** button, and click the **Back** button.

6. Repeat Steps 4 and 5 for the **user02** account.

7. In your project log, write a brief summary that describes the steps to create local user accounts.

8. Close all open windows.

Activity 4-3: Implementing Fast User Switching

Time Required: 20 minutes

Objective: Configure Fast User Switching.

Description: In this activity, you will implement Fast User Switching. You will find this activity useful in your career as a DST because, in order to answer questions regarding Fast User Switching , you will need to have explored Fast User Switching in detail.

1. If necessary, log on to your computer with the user name **student** and password **Password1**.

2. Click **Start**, click **Control Panel**, and click **User Accounts**.

3. Click the **Change the way users log on or off** link.

4. If the **Fast User Switching cannot be used because Offline Files is currently enabled** message is displayed, click the **OK** button. Uncheck the **Enable Offline Files** check box, click the **OK** button, and repeat Step 3.

5. Check the **Use the Welcome Screen** check box, check the **Use Fast User Switching** check box, and click the **Apply Options** button.

6. In your project log, write a brief summary that describes the steps to implement Fast User Switching.

7. Close any open windows.

8. Log off the computer, click the **Switch User** icon, click the **user01** icon, type **Password1**, and press **Enter**.

9. Wait for the personal settings to be applied.

10. Click **Start**, point to **All Programs**, point to **Accessories**, and click **Notepad**.

11. Repeat Steps 8 through 10 for **user02**.

12. Log off the computer, click the **Switch User** icon, and click the **user01** icon, type **Password1**, and press **Enter**.

13. If necessary, click **Start** and verify that user01 is at the top of the Start menu.

14. Repeat Steps 12 and 13 for **user02**. Notice how fast you can switch users using Fast User Switching once the personal settings have been applied.

15. Close any open windows.

16. Click **Start**, click the **Turn Off Computer** icon, and click **Turn Off**.

17. Read the **Other people are logged on** message and click the **No** button.

18. Log off the computer and click the **Log Off** icon.

19. Click the **user01** icon, type a password of **Password1**, close any open windows, log off the computer, and click the **Log Off** icon.

20. Repeat Step 19 for **student**.

21. In your project log, write a brief summary that describes the steps required to verify that Fast User Switching works.

Multiuser Desktop for Corporate Networks

In the land of networks, we define "desktop" as the settings that control how the desktop appears and the "multiuser" desktop as individualized desktop settings for each one of the multiusers. The multiuser desktop is ideal for computers that are shared by multiple users, such as multiple employees working different shifts. In such a situation, each user is provided a unique user name and password. This user account may be a local account or a domain account. In order to troubleshoot your user's logon problems, you must know the difference between local user accounts and domain user accounts. For example, if your user logs on to a local user account, he or she may not have access to the network files and printers that he or she could access by logging on using a domain user account.

To be an effective DST, you need to know what aspects of the desktop, such as desktop wallpaper and color scheme, can be changed for each individual user. You also need to know which parts of the desktop environment, such as hardware or network connection settings, you cannot permit to be changed. Knowing the **security policies** that have been applied by the Security team is crucial to resolving your users' customization problems.

How do I explain to my users the difference between the multiuser desktop and Fast User Switching? When the multiuser desktop is implemented, there is one user logged on at a time and the first user must log off to permit a second user to log on. With Fast User Switching, more than one user may be logged on at a time and each user can start and run a set of applications. In either case, they get their own personalized desktop settings.

Note that with the multiuser desktop configuration on one computer, individual users can:

- Modify Internet Explorer settings
- Modify the desktop settings, such as themes and screensavers
- Run installed applications
- Configure some Control Panel options, such as Display and Mouse

However, your users may not be able to:

- Use the Run command in the Start menu
- Add, remove, or configure hardware devices
- Change the settings of other users

"Why does my desktop look different at work?" The question might be worded differently, but users will want an explanation as to why they can do things at home that they cannot do at work. This is more of a business issue than a technical issue. In order to reduce the number of support calls, the business has the right to control or "lock down" the desktop. This is why the desktop looks different.

Problems with Logons

There are two types of logon processes that your users can encounter:

- **Interactive:** With this type of logon, the user logs on to a local computer at which he or she is seated
- **Network:** With this type of logon, the user logs on to a system that is running an operating system, such as Windows Server 2003, on a computer other than the one on which the user is logged.

The following sections discuss each in turn.

Interactive Logon

In the **interactive logon**, the user will be **authenticated** (that is, user logon information will be validated) against the **user accounts database** (which is a database of user logon accounts and related user information) on the local computer. This is an interactive logon in which your user will be accessing the resources on the local computer. Your user can create and update files on the computer's local hard drive. The local printer is available to print letters and reports.

Stated another way, an interactive logon process confirms the user's identity, by user name and password, to a local computer or domain account. The interactive logon process is overviewed in Figure 4-8.

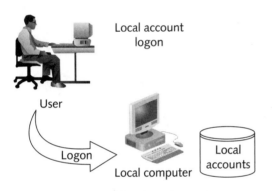

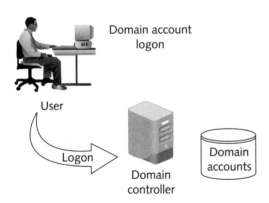

Figure 4-8   A Local user account compared to a domain account

The logon process differs depending on the location of the user account, as follows:

- **Local user account:** User logs on matching the user name and password in the local accounts database. Only the resources on the local computer can be accessed.

- **Domain account:** User logs on matching the user name and password in the Active Directory. An authorized user can access the resources in the domain on any server in the domain.

When your user performs an interactive logon, a number of components are invoked that are not visible to your user. The relationship of these components is depicted in Figure 4-9.

The logon process involves these components:

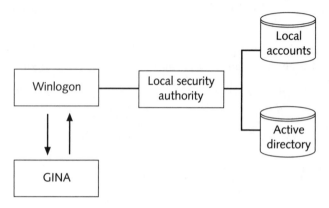

Figure 4-9 Components involved in an interactive logon

- **Winlogon:** Coordinates the security-related user interactions and then starts the Windows Explorer to display the desktop.

- **Graphical Identification and Authentication (GINA):** Obtains the user name and password and passes it back to Winlogon. This is the familiar logon dialog box.

- **Local Security Authority (LSA):** Obtains the username and password and determines if the authentication will be against the local accounts database or the Active Directory.

- **Security Account Manager (SAM):** Accesses the local accounts database to verify the user name and password. This accounts database would be on a local computer.

- **Active Directory:** Accesses the Active Directory to verify the user name and password. This accounts database would be on a domain controller.

Network Logon

In the **network logon**, your user will be authenticated against the user accounts database on a network server. Your user will be accessing the resources on the network server. Your user's files can be saved in the folders on the network server. Your user can print letters and worksheets using the printer attached on the network server. Local files and any attached printers on the user's computer can still be used.

When your user attempts to access resources across the network, a network logon (person logs onto a computer across the network) is required. In this case, the LSA on the user's computer will attempt to present his or her credentials to the LSA on the server, as illustrated by Figure 4-10. The credentials are the user name and password that he or she used for the interactive logon.

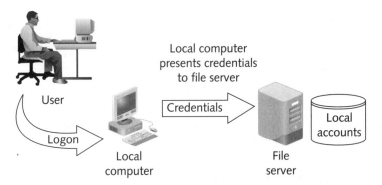

Figure 4-10 Client presents credentials to the server

The LSA on the server will take these credentials and determine if the credentials match an entry on the local accounts database or the Active Directory. The LSA on the server will use the Active Directory, if the server is a member of the Active Directory domain. Otherwise, the LSA will use the local accounts database on the file server. If the credentials are acceptable and your user is authorized to access the resource, the resource is made available to your user.

NOTE

You will learn more about using network resources in Chapter 10, "Configure and Troubleshoot Devices and Connectivity for Applications."

Because the network logon uses the existing credentials, a logon box, as discussed in the following section, is not required for the network logon.

Logon Dialog Boxes

The interactive logon dialog box is displayed for your user to enter the user name and password. This logon dialog box controls your users' access to the local computer. Your users' will see two varieties of dialog boxes: two-line and three-line.

In Figure 4-11, the user is logging on interactively against the local accounts database for a standalone or workgroup computer. This is called a two-line logon because there are only entries for the user name and password.

In Figure 4-12, the user is logging on interactively against the domain accounts database located on a Windows 2003 Server that is a domain controller. The domain controller uses

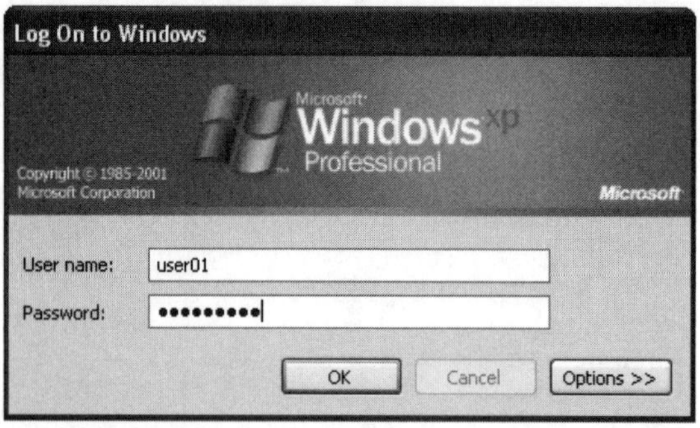

Figure 4-11 Two-line screen

Active Directory for the domain accounts database. In the three-line logon, there is a third line where the domain name is selected.

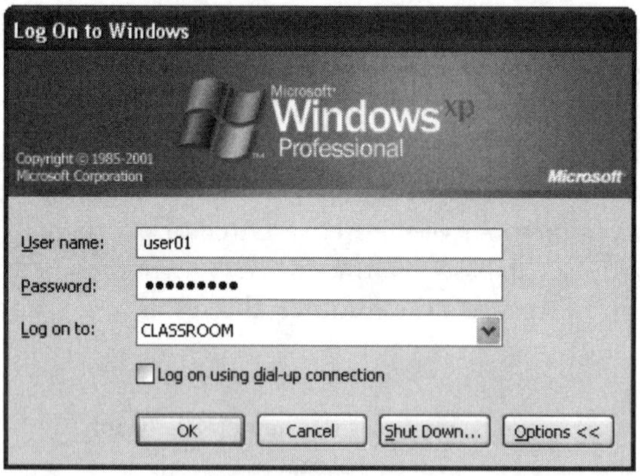

Figure 4-12 Three-line screen

Using Strong Passwords

The first defense against malicious intruders is a strong user password. Passwords can be the weakest link in a computer security scheme. When your users use weak passwords, the passwords can be broken within hours. Your users should use strong passwords. A strong password, which might take days or weeks to break, has these characteristics:

- Contains at least six characters
- Contains characters from each of these three groups:
  - Uppercase and lowercase letters (A, a, B, b, and so on)
  - Numerals (0 through 9)
  - Symbols (Special characters, not letters or numerals, such as !, @, #, and so on)

- Contains at least one symbol between the second through sixth positions
- Is significantly different from prior passwords
- Does not contain a name or user name
- Is not a common name or word

Windows XP Professional passwords can be up to 127 characters long. Instead of passwords, you may want to train your users to use pass phrases. Pass phrases are easier to remember than cryptic passwords. When passwords are cryptic, users write them down and post them in their cubicles. Recall, that when you need a user password, one of the first places to look is under the keyboard!

IN THE WORKPLACE

Here is an example of a pass phrase that, due to its length and use of capitalization and special characters, would be hard to break, yet it will be easy to remember:

`Micro$oftDesktopSupportTechsare#1`

ACTIVITY

Activity 4-4: Creating Strong Passwords

Time Required: 10 minutes

Objective: Verify and create passwords that meet the criteria for acceptable passwords.

Description: In this activity, you will review samples of passwords to determine if they meet the requirements of strong passwords. You will find this activity useful in your career as a DST because, in order to answer questions regarding strong passwords, you will need to have explored strong passwords in detail.

1. For each of the passwords in Table 4-1 verify if the password meets the requirements of a strong password. If the password does not meet the requirements for a strong password, explain the reasons why it does not meet the requirements.

Table 4-1 Specify if a password is a strong password

Password	Meets requirements	Reason(s) it fails to meet requirements
Office		
Office2003		
Office_2003		
_Office2003		
Office2003		
Office2003rules		
Office#2003#rules		
Iwilluseoffice#1		

2. For each of the sample passwords in Table 4-2, rewrite the password so that it meets the requirements of a strong password.

Table 4-2 Rewrite passwords as strong passwords

Sample Password	Corrected Password
office	
Mark	
password1	
windows	
Mark1	
short	
VeryLongPassword	
_Office2003	
Office	
########	

Activity 4-5: Placing a Computer in a Domain

Time Required: 15 minutes

Objective: Add a computer to the domain.

Description: In this activity, you will add a computer to the classroom domain from the WORKGROUP workgroup. You will find this activity useful in your career as a DST because, in order to troubleshoot the differences between domains and workgroups, you will need to have explored these two types of networks in detail.

1. If necessary, log on to your computer with the user name **student** and password **Password1**.

2. Click **Start**, right-click **My Computer**, click **Properties**, and click the **Computer Name** tab.

3. Click the **Change** button. Under the Member of, click the **Domain** option button, type **classroom** in the Domain text box, and click the **OK** button.

4. Type **admin01** in the user name text box, type **Password1** in the Password text box, and click the **OK** button.

5. Wait for the **Welcome to the classroom domain** message to be displayed, then click the three **OK** buttons and the **Yes** button.

6. Wait for the computer to restart.

7. In your project log, write a brief summary that describes the steps to add a computer to a domain. Include a description of the workgroup and domain names including capitalization of the two names WORKGROUP and classroom.

Activity 4-6: Practicing Local and Domain Logons

Time Required: 15 minutes

Objective: Practice logons using the local accounts database and the Active Directory.

Description: In this activity, you will log on to a computer with the local user account and then log on using the domain user account. You will find this activity useful in your career as a DST because, in order to troubleshoot logons to local and domain accounts, you will need to have explored these two types of logons in detail.

1. If necessary, log on to your computer with the user name **user01**, password **Password1**, and computer **Student01 (this computer)**.

2. Click **Start**, click **Run**, type **msinfo32** in the Open text box, and click the **OK** button.

3. Locate the item **User Name** and read the **STUDENT01\user01** value, which indicates that a local logon was used.

4. Close any open windows and log off the computer.

5. Log on to your computer with the user name **user01**, password **Password1**, and domain **CLASSROOM.**

6. Click **Start**, click **Run**, type **msinfo32** in the Open text box, and click the **OK** button.

7. Locate the item **User Name** and read the **CLASSROOM\user01** value, which indicates that a domain logon was used.

8. In your project log, write a brief summary that describes the steps to log on to a computer with a local user account and domain user account. Include a description of the third line in the logon dialog box. Also, include a description of one method to verify the type of logon.

9. Close any open windows and log off the computer.

Problems with User Profiles

Your users may have problems with user profiles. For example, the desktop settings may not migrate from machine to machine as your users work on multiple computers. This section presents the technical information about the three types of **user profiles** (records maintained for the user of a computer system that contains the user's personalization settings) for which you will need to resolve problems.

Local User Profiles

A local user profile is one that is stored on the hard drive of the local computer. To locate the local user profiles, open the System Properties dialog box by right-clicking My Computer and clicking Properties. Click the Advanced tab, and click Settings under User Profiles, as shown in Figure 4-13.

The dialog box provides the following information:

- **Name:** Location of the user account and user name.
- **Size:** Size of the user profile in kilobytes or megabytes.

Figure 4-13 Local User Profiles

- **Type:** Roaming or local.
- **Status:** Profile is local or roaming (on a server).
- **Modified:** Date that profile was last modified.

Roaming User Profiles

Your organization's network administrator can set the profile on the user account to permit roaming profiles. When the user logs off, the user profile is copied back to a file server. As the users migrate from machine to machine, the desktop settings follow each user.

Although you as a DST probably do not have the authority to make this change, you need to know how to verify that roaming profiles are being used on the desktop computer.

Figure 4-14 shows a roaming profile in use for a user. From the Change Type button, you can change the profile type back to a local profile. If you make this change, on the next logon for this user, the computer will use the locally cached copy of the roaming profile. You will practice identifying user profiles in Activity 4-7.

Mandatory User Profiles

There are situations in which the network administrators would like to configure user profiles but prohibit changes from being saved back to the file server. This would be useful for a computer that was accessed in an open area, such as a school library or kiosk.

The mandatory user profile meets this need—functions like a roaming profile but prohibits any changes to the profile to be saved on the file server.

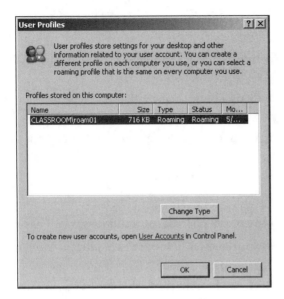

Figure 4-14   Roaming User Profiles

Repairing a Damaged Profile

When you log on to the computer, your user may receive this error message: The system has recovered from a serious error. The problem occurs because your user's profile is damaged. When this occurs, Windows may create a new profile for you to use, but the new profile does not reflect the My Documents folder that was used by the damaged profile. Windows creates a new profile in the C:\Documents and Settings*new user name* folder, where *new user name* is the name that Windows is now using for your profile. You will learn to repair the user profile with a System Restore in Activity 4-8.

I watched my wife lose time because of a damaged profile. Then, I noticed that she did a System Restore, recovered her profile, and grinned from ear-to-ear. And I thought that I was the only geek in the family.

IN THE WORKPLACE

ACTIVITY

Activity 4-7: Working with Profiles

Time Required: 15 minutes

Objective: Explore the use of roaming profiles.

Description: In this activity, you will log on to a computer with a domain user account that was configured to use a roaming profile. You will find this activity useful in your career as a DST because, in order to troubleshoot the profile types to local and domain accounts, you will need to have explored the local and roaming profiles in detail.

1. If necessary, log on to your computer with the user name **user01** and password **Password1**.

2. Click **Start**, right-click **My Computer**, click **Properties**, and click the **Advanced** tab.

3. Under User Profiles, click the **Settings** button. Verify that the Type and Status are Local.

4. Click the **Change Type** button. Verify that the Roaming Profile button is grayed out.

5. Click the **Cancel** button on three consecutive screens.

6. Log off your computer.

7. Log on to your computer with the user name **roam01** and password **Password1**.

8. Click **Start**, right-click **My Computer**, click **Properties**, and click the **Advanced** tab.

9. Under User Profiles, click the **Settings** button. Verify that the Type and Status are Roaming.

10. Click the **Change Type** button. Verify that the Roaming Profile button is not grayed out.

11. Click the **Local profile** option button and click the **OK** button. Verify that the Type is Local and the Status is Roaming.

12. Click the **Change Type** button, click the **Roaming profile** option button, and click the **OK** button. Verify that the Type and Status are Roaming.

13. Click the **OK** button on two consecutive screens.

14. In your project log, write a brief summary that describes the steps to verify the type and status of a user profile.

15. Close any open windows and log off the computer.

ACTIVITY

Activity 4-8: Working with Damaged Profiles

Time Required: Up to 45 minutes

Objective: Practice repairing a damaged local user profile.

Description: In this activity, you will practice repairing a damaged local user profile. You will use System Restore to return the profile to a state prior to when the profile was damaged. You will find this activity useful in your career as a DST because, in order to repair a damaged local user profile, you will need to have completed the steps to repair a damaged local profile.

1. If necessary, log on to your computer with the user name **admin01** and password **Password1**.

4

2. Click **Start**, point to **All Programs**, point to **Accessories**, and click **Windows Explorer**.

3. Expand **My Computer** and Expand **Local Disk (C:)**.

4. If necessary, right-click the **Backup** folder, click **Delete**, and click the **Yes** button.

5. Right-click in the right pane, point to **New**, click **Folder**, type **Backup** over New Folder, and press **Enter**.

6. Expand the **Documents and Settings** folder, expand **user01**, right-click **User01's Documents**, and click **Copy**.

7. Collapse the **Documents and Settings** folder, right-click the **Backup** folder, and click **Paste**.

8. Expand the **Documents and Settings** folder, expand **user01**, right-click **Favorites**, and click **Copy**.

9. Collapse the **Documents and Settings** folder, right-click the **Backup** folder, and click **Paste.**

10. Close the Windows Explorer window.

11. Click **Start**, point to **All Programs**, point to **Accessories**, point to **System Tools**, right-click **System Restore**, click **Run as**, click the **The following user** option button, type **student01\administrator** in the User name text box, type **Password1** in the Password text box, and click the **OK** button.

12. When the Welcome to System Restore dialog box is displayed, click the **Next** button.

13. Click a previous date in the calendar on the left, select a restore point on the right, and click the **Next** button.

14. View the text displayed and click the **Next** button.

15. Wait for the computer to restart and complete the System Restore.

16. Log on to your computer with the user name **admin01** and password **Password1**.

17. Verify that your computer was restored correctly and click the **OK** button.

18. In your project log, write a brief summary that describes the steps to repair a damaged local user profile. Provide an explanation for the tasks you completed in Steps 3 through 9.

19. Log off the computer.

IN THE WORKPLACE I feel a need to remind you that when you make changes to a person's computer, you should test your changes. This testing may permit you to avoid having to go back to the user to back out the change or finish the job. Remember: Embarrassed, red faces are unbecoming!

CONFIGURING THE OPERATING SYSTEM TO SUPPORT APPLICATIONS

To effectively run applications, you must configure the operating system to support these applications. As a DST, your users expect you to know these configuration options in case they come to you with questions like the following:

- Why can Bob run the new program and I cannot?
- Why don't I see the Administrative Tools?
- How can I change the order of the items on the All Programs menu?

As you go through this part of the chapter, you will learn more about the following:

- When Windows applications are installed, the program files are usually stored in subordinate folders to the C:\Program Files folder.
- The All Programs menu, which contains the program shortcuts, is located on the Start menu.
- From the Windows Explorer, you can click a document icon and the proper application will start to process the document. This occurs because the file type is a **registered file type** (associated with a particular application). You will learn to build associations between file extensions and file types and applications.

Location of Programs Files

In addition, when troubleshooting application programs, the problem-solving steps provided by the vendor may require that you locate the program files. The first place you should look is in the specific folder for the program in the C:\Program Files folder, unless the program developer made a decision to place the files in an alternate location.

 The Program Files can be located by opening Windows Explorer and navigating to the C:\Program Files folder. Because removing program files could break an application, you should caution your users to develop a hands-off policy for these files!

Location of Program Shortcuts on Start Menu

As you know, you can click the program shortcut on the Start menu to start a program. In order to answer your users' questions about the Start menu, you must learn how the Start menu is constructed. For instance, one user can access a program from the Start menu but another cannot locate the shortcut for the program on the Start menu.

Folders that Hold the Start Menu Shortcuts

Let's start with the fact that the Start menu is built from the information in two folders. If you were troubleshooting a problem for User01, you would look at these two folders:

- **C:\Documents and Settings\All Users\Start Menu\:** Start menu entries for all users of the computer.
- **C:\Documents and Settings\User01\Start Menu\:** Start menu entries for a specific user of the computer. The specific user in this case is User01 with a display name of First User.

The structure for these two folders is diagrammed in Figure 4-15.

4

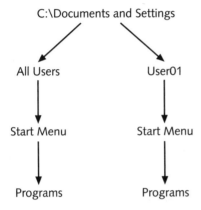

Figure 4-15   Diagram of folder structure

Figure 4-16 shows the All Users\Start Menu folder and files. You will see one folder, Programs, and two files, Windows Catalog and Windows Update.

Figure 4-16   Windows Explorer showing All Users\Start Menu folder

Figure 4-17 shows the folders and files for the All Users\Start Menu\Programs folder. Notice that there are four folders: Accessories, Administrative Tools, Games, and Startup.

Figure 4-17   Windows Explorer showing the All Users\Start Menu\Programs

Figure 4-18 shows the folders and files at the User01.CLASSROOM\Start Menu\Programs folder. Recall that User01 is a user account in the CLASSROOM domain. Notice that there are two folders: Accessories and Startup in Figure 4-18.

Figure 4-19 shows the All Programs menu for the First User. Notice the line that divides the menu. The shortcuts above the line are sourced from the All Users folder. The shortcuts below the line are sourced from either the All Users and User01 folders, with the ones sourced from the All Users folder coming first.

Notice that the Windows Catalog and Windows Update shortcuts appear above the line in Figure 4-19. Locate the Accessories, Games, and Startup folders that appear on the merged All Programs menu in Figure 4-19. You might wonder where the Administrative Tools folder is located on the All Programs menu. Well, in this case, User01 is a limited access user account and an option was set to restrict the display of this folder, even though the folder still exists behind the scenes. Last, notice that there are two shortcuts: MSN Explorer and Windows Messenger in Figure 4-17. These shortcuts also appear on the merged All Programs menu in Figure 4-19.

Take a look at Figure 4-17. Notice that the Accessories and Startup folders also appear in the Programs folder for All Users. Locate these two folders in Figure 4-19. You will see that the folders are not duplicated. Instead, the contents of the corresponding folders are merged into one instance of each folder. Last, notice that there are four program shortcuts: Internet

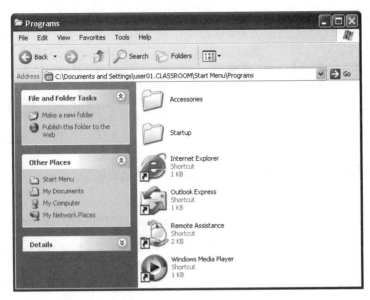

Figure 4-18 Windows Explorer showing the User01.CLASSROOM\Start Menu\Programs folder

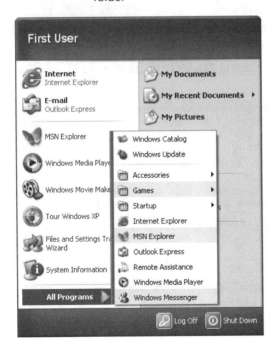

Figure 4-19 All Programs menu for User01

Explorer, Outlook Express, Remote Assistance, and Windows Media Player in Figure 4–18. Locate these four shortcuts on the All Programs menu for User01 in Figure 4–19.

As programs are added to your computer, they appear in an **ordinal sequence** on the Start menu. (Ordinal sequence is a number whose form indicates position in an ordered sequence of items.) You and your users may prefer that the program shortcuts be presented in alphabetical order. No problem! Click Start, point to All Programs, right-click on any shortcut, and click Sort by Name.

Activity 4-9: Exploring the All Programs Menu

Time Required: 25 minutes

Objective: Explore the folders that are merged to create the All Programs menu.

Description: In this activity, you will explore the two folders that are merged to create the All Programs menu. You will find this activity useful in your career as a DST because, in order to answer your users' questions about the All Programs menu, you will need to have explored this in detail.

1. If necessary, log on to your computer with the user name **user01** and password **Password1**.

2. Click **Start**, point to **All Programs**, point to **Accessories**, and click **Windows Explorer**.

3. Expand **My Computer**, expand **Local Disk (C:)**, and expand **Documents and Settings**.

4. Expand **All Users**, expand **Start Menu**, expand **Programs**, expand **Accessories**, and click **Accessories**.

5. Drag the lower-right corner of the Windows Explorer window so that the window is about 25% of the screen size, and then drag the window itself to the upper-right corner.

6. Click **Start**, point to **All Programs**, and point to **Accessories**.

7. Notice the folders that are common to both the Accessories menu and Accessories folder.

8. Click the **System Tools** folder in the Windows Explorer window.

9. Click **Start**, point to **All Programs**, point to **Accessories**, and point to **System Tools**.

10. Notice the shortcuts that are common to both the System Tools menu and System Tools folder.

11. Click the **Accessories** folder in the Windows Explorer window and scroll the right pane to display the program shortcuts.

12. Click **Start**, point to **All Programs**, point to **Accessories**, and click **Windows Explorer**.

13. Expand **My Computer**, expand **Local Disk (C:)**, and expand **Documents and Settings**.

14. Expand **user01.CLASSROOM**, expand **Start Menu**, expand **Programs**, and click **Programs**.

15. Click the **Accessories** folder in the Windows Explorer window and scroll the right pane to display the program shortcuts.

16. Resize the Windows Explorer window to about 25% of the screen size and drag it to the lower-right corner.

17. Click **Start**, point to **All Programs**, and point to **Accessories**.

18. Note the **Calculator** and **Paint** shortcuts in the All Users folder in the Windows Explorer located in the upper-right corner and note their inclusion in the Accessories menu as well.

19. Note the **Address Book** and **Command Prompt** shortcuts from the user01 folder in the Windows Explorer located in the lower-right corner and note their inclusion in the Accessories menu as well.

20. In your project log, write a brief summary that describes the methods Windows XP uses to construct an All Programs menu from the All Users folders and the user folder.

21. Close all open windows.

22. Log off your computer.

Activity 4-10: Modifying the All Programs Menu

Time Required: 15 minutes

Objective: Explore changes to the All Programs menu.

Description: In this activity, you will modify the All Users folder to include a program shortcut located in the User01 folder. This change will be reflected on the All Programs menu. You will find this activity useful in your career as a DST because, in order to assist your users with modifications to the All Programs menu, you will need to have explored this in detail.

1. Log on to your computer with the user name **admin01** and password **Password1**.

2. Click **Start**, point to **All Programs**, point to **Accessories**, and click **Windows Explorer**.

3. Expand **My Computer**, expand **Local Disk (C:)**, and expand **Documents and Settings**.

4. Expand **All Users**, expand **Start Menu**, and click **Start Menu**.

5. Resize the Windows Explorer window to about 25% of the screen size and drag it to the upper-right corner.

6. Click **Start**, point to **All Programs**, point to **Accessories**, and click **Windows Explorer**.

7. Expand **My Computer**, expand **Local Disk (C:)**, and expand **Documents and Settings**.

8. Expand **User01**, expand **Start Menu**, expand **Programs**, and click **Programs**.

9. Resize the Windows Explorer window to about 25% of the screen size and drag it to the lower-right corner.

10. Right-click **Windows Media Player** in the lower-right Windows Explorer window and click **Copy**.

11. Right-click in the upper-right Windows Explorer window, and click **Paste**.

12. Click **Start** and point to **All Programs**.

13. Notice that Windows Media Player has been copied above the line in the All Programs menu.

14. In your project log, write a brief summary that describes the steps to modify the folders that Windows XP uses to construct an All Programs menu.

15. Close all open windows and log off the computer.

Register File Types

As you know, you can open certain documents by double-clicking (or simply clicking, if your settings allow this) their icons from Windows Explorer. When you double-click the icon, the application associated with that document starts and the document opens within the application. It's in your interest as a DST to know how this all works because you will want to share this technique with your users.

Details View

When you create a document and save the document, the application adds a file extension to the file name you typed. You can see the file types in Windows Explorer by selecting Details from the View menu. Figure 4-20 shows the Details view for the My Samples folder.

The Type column entry is built according to these rules:

- If the file extension is registered and will be recognized by Windows XP, the corresponding file type is displayed. This rule applies to the HTML document in Figure 4-20.

- If the file has an extension, but is not registered, its type is the extension itself. This rule applies to the XPQ file in Figure 4-20.

- If the file has no extension, then its type is simply File. This rule applies to the first entry in Figure 4-20.

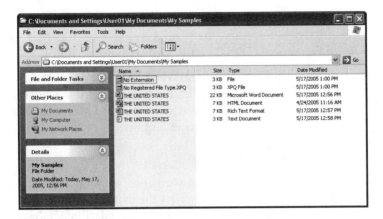

Figure 4-20   Windows Explorer in Details view

IN THE WORKPLACE   Because the file extension is hidden by default, your users may not be able to match like files to the application that created the file. By arranging the files by type, it may help your users determine which files were created by the same application.

You see four files in Figure 4-20 with the same file name: THE UNITED STATES. But how can that be? There are four different file extensions. The icon and corresponding file type is a clue to which program would open if the file name was clicked. Figure 4-21 shows an enlarged view of one part of Figure 4-20.

THE UNITED STATES	22 KB	Microsoft Word Document
THE UNITED STATES	7 KB	HTML Document
THE UNITED STATES	7 KB	Rich Text Format
THE UNITED STATES	3 KB	Text Document

Figure 4-21   Exploded section of Details view

Here is an explanation for each of the four THE UNITED STATES icons:

- The first was created using Microsoft Word, stored as a .DOC file, and will open in Microsoft Word. The icon indicates a Microsoft Word document.

- The second was created using Microsoft Word, stored as a .HTML file, and will open in Internet Explorer. The icon shows a Microsoft Word imposed over an Internet Explorer icon.

- The third was created using Microsoft Word, stored as a .RTF file, and will open in Microsoft Word. The icon indicates a Microsoft Word document.

- The fourth was created using Notepad, stored as a .TXT file, and will open in Notepad. The icon indicates text.

The first and third THE UNITED STATES files share the same icon and will open in Microsoft Word. However, they are stored using two different document formats—Microsoft Word Document (DOC) and Rich Text Format (RTF).

The icon of the second entry shows a Microsoft Word icon imposed over an Internet Explorer icon. The second THE UNITED STATES file was created using Microsoft Word but will open in the Internet Explorer because it was saved as an HTML document. HTML documents are registered, or associated, with Internet Explorer.

View Existing Registered File Types

In order to answer your users' questions about file associations, you should view the existing extensions and file types that your users can use. To view the existing file types, select Folder Options from the Tools menu in Windows Explorer. When the Files Types tab is selected, a list of registered file types is displayed. The information for Microsoft Word, among other applications, is shown in Figure 4-22. You can see more types by scrolling within the Registered file types list.

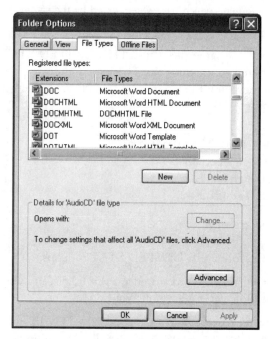

Figure 4-22   Registered file types for Microsoft Word

Microsoft Word can be used as the application for several file types, such as Word documents, HTML documents, and Word templates. Notice that the Extension ties to the File type. DOC ties to Microsoft Word document, DOCHTML ties to Microsoft Word HTML document, DOT ties to Microsoft Word template, and so on.

Create a New Registered File Type

You can create new file types by registering extensions that are currently unregistered. You might do this to create an association between a file type and a particular application. To register a file type, select Folder Options from the Tools menu in Windows Explorer. When the Files Types tab is selected, a list of registered file types is displayed, as shown in Figure 4-23.

4

Figure 4-23   Registered file types

From the dialog box shown in Figure 4-23, you can choose from the following:

- **New:** Creates a new association between a file extension and a file type. It also creates and registers a new file type with Windows.

- **Delete:** Removes the association between the selected extension and file type. Also deletes the extension from the list.

- **Change:** Changes the program that opens files of this type.

- **Advanced:** Modifies the settings of the selected file type.

Create New Extension

To create a new extension, you select the New button in Figure 4-23 to display the Create New Extension dialog box (see Figure 4-24). Type the extension in the File Extension text box that you want to register. For example, if you want to use the file extension REP for your weekly progress reports that you will be writing in WordPad, type REP in the File Extension text box.

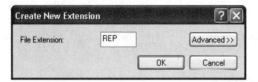

Figure 4-24   Create New Extension dialog box

At this point, you need to make a decision. Your choices are the following:

- **Use an existing file type:** Associate the extension with existing file type.
- **Create a new file type:** Associate the extension with the new file type. Define the actions for the new file type.

The best choice is to associate the new extension with an existing file type. The existing file type is already tied to an application. After typing the new extension, click the Advanced button to display the expanded Create New Extension dialog box. Open the Associated File Type drop-down and choose the desired file type (for example, Wordpad document) as shown in Figure 4-25. You have registered your new extension and associated it with the same application that you selected from the list.

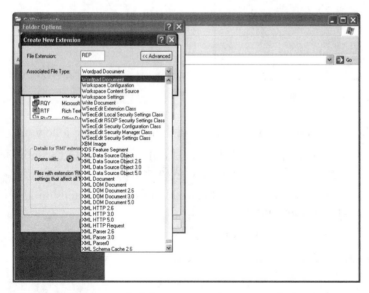

Figure 4-25   Expanded Create New Extension dialog box

NOTE

You will learn to create a new file extension in Activity 4-11.

If you decide to create a new file type, click the OK button after typing the desired extension. Your new file type will appear as in Figure 4-26.

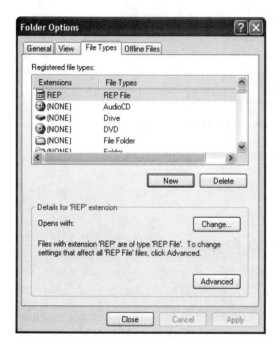

Figure 4-26   REP extension now appears on the File Types tab

Click the **Advanced** button and the Edit File Type dialog box is displayed. A completed Edit File Type dialog box is shown in Figure 4-27. You now have a number of tasks to complete:

- **Name the File Type:** Type a name for the file type in the text box.
- **Change Icon:** Select an icon for the file type. This icon will be displayed by Windows Explorer for the file type.
- **New:** Define the action. For example, open the file.
- **Edit:** Update or correct an existing action.
- **Set Default:** The default behavior when the file is accessed.

Figure 4-27   Completed Edit File Type dialog box

You will learn to create a new file type in Activity 4-11.

NOTE

ACTIVITY

Activity 4-11: Working with Registered File Types

Time Required: 20 minutes

Objective: Explore and create file types.

Description: In this activity, you will explore the association of a file extension with an existing file type. Then, you will create an association to a new file type. You will find this activity useful in your career as a DST because, in order to answer your users' questions about the file extensions Programs menu, you will need to have explored file extensions and file types in detail.

1. If necessary, log on to your computer with the user name **admin01** and password **Password1**.

2. Click **Start**, point to **All Programs**, point to **Accessories**, and click **Windows Explorer**.

3. Click **Tools**, click **Folder Options**, and click the **File Types** tab.

4. If necessary, scroll and locate TRK under Extensions, click **TRK**, click the **Delete** button, and click the **Yes** button.

5. Click the New button, type **TRK** in File Extension text box, click the **Advanced** button, click the **Associated File Type** drop-down menu, scroll and select **Text Document**, click the **OK** button, and click the **Close** button.

6. Click **Start**, point to **All Programs**, point to **Accessories**, and click **Notepad**.

4

7. Type a short message, click **File**, click **Save As**, type **"Test.TRK"** in the File name text box, and click **Save**. If necessary, click the **Yes** button.

8. Close the Notepad window and double-click **Test** in the Windows Explorer window.

9. Close the Notepad window.

10. Click **Tools**, click **Folder Options**, and click the **File Types** tab.

11. Scroll and click the **TRK** extension, click the **Delete** button, and click the **Yes** button.

12. Click the **New** button, type **TRK** in File Extension text box, and click the **OK** button.

13. Click **TRK** in the Registered file types list, click the **Advanced** button, type **Problem Tracking** in the text box, click the **Change Icon** button, click on an appropriate icon, and click the **OK** button.

14. Click the **New** button, type **Open** in the Action text box, click the **Browse** button, navigate to and click **C:\WINDOWS\Notepad**, click the **Open** button, and click the **OK** button.

15. Click the **New** button, type **Print** in the Action text box, click the **Browse** button, navigate to and click **C:\WINDOWS\Notepad**, click the **Open** button, and click the **OK** button.

16. Click **Print**, click the **Edit** button, type **/p** before the "%1", click the two **OK** buttons, and click the **Close** button.

17. Double-click **Test** in the Windows Explorer window.

18. Close the Notepad window.

19. If you have a printer, right-click **Test** and click **Print**.

20. In your project log, write a brief summary that describes the steps to create a file extension association with an icon and an application.

21. Close all open windows and log off the computer.

IN THE WORKPLACE

Because I spent a number of years as a programmer in a previous career, I've grown accustomed to using a programmer's text editor to type text. From time to time, I respond to questions on the MCDST newsgroup. I've discovered that questions are repeated. Because I can save time by not repeating the answers, I copy and paste the answers from a document that was designed to fit the line length of newsgroup responses. By registering the DST extension, I can have the file open in the text editor.

Disable Error Reporting

When an illegal operation or other error occurs in a program, such as Microsoft Word, the program stops working. You can elect to report system and program errors to Microsoft. This reporting system allows Microsoft to track and address operating system, Windows component, and program errors.

You can configure error reporting to send only specified information. For example, if you want to report only system errors, you can specify that reports be generated only for the operating system. The same is true for Windows components, such as Windows Explorer or Internet Explorer, and for programs, such as Microsoft Word, installed on your computer. Your organization may decide to disable this error reporting for your users' computers. You will learn more about this error reporting in Chapter 7, "Configuring and Troubleshooting Operating System Features."

To access the Error Reporting dialog box, as shown in Figure 4-28, right-click My Computer on the Start menu, click Properties, click the Advanced tab, and click the Error Reporting button.

Figure 4-28 Error Reporting dialog box

From the dialog box, you see these choices:

- **Disable error reporting:** Error reports will not be generated.
- **But notify me when critical errors occur:** Notify you if a critical error occurs, even if you have disabled error reporting.
- **Enable error reporting:** Error reports will be generated.
- **Windows operating system:** Report errors in the Windows XP operating system.
- **Programs:** Report errors in application programs.

- **Choose Programs:** Specify which programs to include or exclude from reporting.

Clicking the Choose Programs button opens the Choose Programs dialog box, as shown in Figure 4-29.

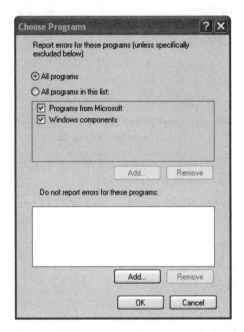

Figure 4-29   Choose Programs dialog box

From this dialog box, you see these choices:

- **All programs:** Report errors in all programs.
- **All programs in this list:** Include all programs from Microsoft, all Windows programs, or individual programs in error reporting.
- **Programs from Microsoft:** Check to include all programs from Microsoft.
- **Windows components:** Windows XP operating system programs.
- **Do not report errors for these programs:** Exclude individual programs from error reporting.
- **Add:** Add programs to include/exclude from the respective list.
- **Remove button:** Remove programs to include/exclude from the respective list.

You will practice configuring error reporting in Activity 4-12.

Do you like to be nagged by Microsoft? It's bad enough when an application fails. But then you are asked to report the problem to Microsoft. I prefer to disable the Error Reporting. I still get the message but I don't have to click on the Don't Send button.

Activity 4-12: Disabling Error Reporting

Time Required: 15 minutes

Objective: Disable Error Reporting to Microsoft.

Description: In this activity, you will practice disabling Error Reporting to Microsoft. You will find this activity useful in your career as a DST because, in order to disable Error Reporting to Microsoft, you will need to have explored the configuration of Error Reporting in detail.

1. If necessary, log on to your computer with the user name **admin01** and password **Password1**.

2. Click **Start**, right-click **My Computer**, click **Properties**, click the **Advanced** tab, and click the **Error Reporting** button.

3. Click the **Disable error reporting** option button and notice the changes to the bottom of the Error Reporting dialog box.

4. Click the **Enable error reporting** option button and notice that Error Reporting is activated.

5. Click the **Choose Programs** button.

6. Click the **Add** button located at the bottom of the screen, type **paint.exe** in the text box, and click the **OK** button.

7. Repeat Step 6 for **notepad.exe** and **wordpad.exe**.

8. Click the three **OK** buttons.

9. In your project log, write a brief summary that describes the steps to disable and enable Error Reporting. Include information on excluding programs from Error Reporting.

10. Close all windows and log off the computer.

CHAPTER SUMMARY

◻ Windows XP permits multiple users to use applications on the same computer. You explored some of the differences between Windows XP Home versus Windows XP Professional. With multiple user accounts on a home computer, you can implement Fast User Switching to rapidly switch between sets of running applications.

❏ Windows XP is used in both small networks, workgroups, larger networks, and domains. You learned about the various types of logons and the types of logon dialog boxes.

❏ You learned the rules for strong passwords: six or more characters, letters, numbers, and special characters, no common words.

❏ User profiles retain your user's customization from logon to logon. With roaming profiles, your users can retain these settings from computer to computer. You learned to repair damaged profiles with a System Restore.

❏ In order to support applications, you learned to configure the operating system. You learned where windows applications store program files. You observed how Windows XP constructs the Start menu.

❏ With registered file types, your users open an application by clicking the file with a registered file extension. You learned how to view the existing files types and to create new file types.

❏ By disabling Error Reporting, you can avoid sending personal information to Microsoft when a Windows program fails.

KEY TERMS

Active Directory — Microsoft's directory service, which is an integral part of the Windows Server 2003 architecture. Active Directory is a centralized and standardized system for network management of network resources and security.

authenticated — Process during which an operating system validates a user's logon information.

Graphical Identification and Authentication (GINA) — User interface that supports the logon to a computer requesting the user's identity and proof of identity.

interactive logon — Logon activity that occurs when the person logs on to the computer at which he or she is seated.

Local Security Authority (LSA) — Software component that provides the user's user name and password to the Security Account Manager or Active Directory to validate the user's identity.

network logon — Logon activity that occurs when the person logs onto the computer across the network.

ordinal sequence — A number whose form indicates position in an ordered sequence of items.

registered file type — A file type that is tracked by the system registry and recognized by the applications on the system.

Security Account Manager (SAM) — Software component that processes the user's user name and password against an accounts database to validate the user's identity.

security policies — Policies that define the rules to which a user must comply regarding changes a user may or may not make to the customization of a desktop computer.

user accounts database — Database consisting of user logon accounts and related user information and privileges.

user profiles — Record maintained for the user of a computer system that contains the user's personalization settings.

Winlogon — Process that manages user-related security interactions.

Review Questions

1. Microsoft markets which versions of Windows XP that could be deployed in a business? (Choose all that apply.)

   a. Home

   b. Corporate

   c. Enterprise

   d. Professional

2. The Fast User Switching Between Users feature is available in which versions of Windows XP? (Choose all that apply.)

   a. Home

   b. Corporate

   c. Enterprise

   d. Professional

3. Roaming user profiles are available with the _____ version of Windows XP.

   a. Home

   b. Corporate

   c. Enterprise

   d. Professional

4. Which items can be configured on a SOHO computer for a user account? (Choose all that apply.)

   a. account name

   b. computer name

   c. picture

   d. password

5. A user of a limited account can _____ . (Choose all that apply.)

   a. install all programs

   b. access the files of other users' My Documents folders.

   c. create accounts

d. view files in the Shared Documents folder

e. view files in your My Documents folder.

6. With _____ , you and your peers can switch to each other's programs without closing programs.

a. Quick Launch

b. Rapid Accounts

c. Fast User Switching

d. All Users

7. With the multiuser desktop configuration in a corporate network, you can _____ . (Choose all that apply.)

a. modify Internet Explorer

b. run installed applications

c. use the Run command from the Start menu

d. configure all Control Panel options

8. Which of the following is the type of profile that could be used in a corporate environment? (Choose all that apply.)

a. Mandatory

b. Optional

c. Local

d. Roaming

9. When a user on a network using roaming profiles logs off, what takes place?

a. Changes are not permitted to the profile.

b. The profile replaces the All User profile.

c. The user profile is copied back to the server.

d. The user profile is dropped from the computer.

10. _____ processes are logon processes that your users can use to access local resources. (Choose all that apply.)

a. Interactive

b. Seated

c. Network

d. Foreign

11. In the _____ logon, the user logs on matching the user name and password located in Active Directory.

a. Local user account

b. Interactive user account

c. Domain user account

d. Workgroup user account

12. In the _____ -line logon dialog box, the user selects the desired domain name.

    a. one

    b. two

    c. three

    d. four

13. To create a strong password, a user should create a password that _____ . (Choose all that apply.)

    a. contains no more than six characters

    b. contains upper- and lower-case letters

    c. contains a symbol after the first character

    d. is a common word

14. During installation, programs are typically placed in the _____ folder.

    a. Start

    b. All Programs

    c. Program Files

    d. Windows

15. For User01, which folder would be used to construct the All Programs menu? (Choose all that apply.)

    a. C:\Documents and Settings\All Users\Start Menu\

    b. C:\My Documents\All Users\Start Menu\

    c. C:\Documents and Settings\User01\Start Menu\

    d. C:\My Documents\User01\Start Menu\

16. For a registered file extension, which of the following is true? (Choose all that apply.)

    a. The icon for the application appears in Windows Explorer.

    b. The application starts with a blank document when the file name is clicked.

    c. The application starts when the file name is clicked.

    d. The file extension is appended when the file is saved.

17. When viewing the Type column in Windows Explorer, which of the following column entries would be available for a Microsoft DOC document?

    a. Microsoft Word Document

    b. HTML Document

   c. Microsoft Word Template

   d. Microsoft DOC Document

18. From the Registered File Types dialog box, you can _____ . (Choose all that apply.)

   a. create a new association

   b. delete an existing association

   c. change the program that opens the file

   d. modify the settings of a selected file type

19. From the Error Reporting dialog box, you can _____ . (Choose all that apply.)

   a. disable error reporting

   b. notify the user when critical errors occur

   c. enable error reporting

   d. access the Choose Programs dialog box

20. From the Choose Programs dialog box in Error Reporting, you can _____ . (Choose all that apply.)

   a. report errors on all Microsoft Windows XP programs

   b. include all programs from Microsoft

   c. include all programs from other vendors

   d. exclude programs from reporting

CASE PROJECTS

CASE PROJECTS

Case 4-1: Implementing Fast User Switching

Your firm provides desktop support for users of home computers. The typical software configuration that you install consists of Windows XP and Microsoft Office 2003.

You are responding to a question posed by a customer. Ray wants to know if there is a way to personalize the logon window for Ray, Linda, and the three children: Susan, Ray Jr., and Mike. What will you tell Ray? Describe, in detail, the steps that you will take to fulfill Ray's request.

CASE PROJECTS

Case 4-2: Implementing User Profiles

You are a desktop support technician. Your network consists of a Windows 2003 Active Directory domain with 10 servers, including application and database servers and 500 computers running Windows XP Professional.

Julie, the manager for the customer service department, has asked you to find a solution for a problem. She has 24 user computers and a total 60 employees on three shifts.

She wants the freedom to place any of the 60 employees on any of the 24 computers. When she tried this before, the employees complained that the "other reps" messed with the computers. The most common complaint was that the desktop settings were changed.

What will you recommend? How will you implement your solution? Will you need to work with any other teams to implement your solution? If so, what will the other teams need to do?

**CASE
PROJECTS**

Case 4-3: Implementing File Associations

You are a desktop support technician. Your network consists of a Windows 2003 Active Directory domain with 12 servers, including application and database servers and 680 computers running Windows XP Professional.

The programming team has implemented an application for the Engineering Department. The engineers were complaining that although the data files created by the engineering application were listed in Windows Explorer they could not be opened by the engineering application.

Do you have a solution for the engineers that will permit them to run the engineering application by clicking on the engineering data files in the Windows Explorer? How will you implement your recommendation? Because there are 20 computers in the Engineering Department, you will need the assistance of another DST to complete the tasks. Provide a detailed list of the steps for the other DST. (Hint: Do you have all of the information that you will need to implement your solution?)

5

CONFIGURE AND TROUBLESHOOT INTERNET EXPLORER AND OUTLOOK EXPRESS

After reading this chapter and completing the exercises, you will be able to:

♦ Repair Internet Explorer

♦ Configure Internet Explorer

♦ Work with the Internet Explorer Error Reporting Tool

♦ Interpret Internet Explorer Error Messages

♦ Work with and Repair Outlook Express

♦ Configure Outlook Express

♦ Interpret Outlook Express Error Messages

The first part of the chapter provides information about Internet Explorer. You will learn to repair Internet Explorer when files are damaged. Using the security features of Internet Explorer, your organization can create a secure environment that protects users' personal information on the Internet. You can configure Internet Explorer's privacy options to protect your users as they surf the Internet.

You will be prepared to troubleshoot some of the problems that you may encounter during and after installation of Internet Explorer. Typical problems are outdated or corrupted files, failed setup, download connection failures, and configuration errors.

After you have repaired, configured, and resolved error messages for Internet Explorer, you will perform similar tasks for Outlook Express. You setup Outlook Express to access various types of mail servers. You configure Outlook Express to access news servers. You must be prepared to troubleshoot some of the problems that you may encounter during and after installation of Outlook Express.

REPAIRING INTERNET EXPLORER

Internet Explorer version 6 is automatically preinstalled when you purchase a new computer with Windows XP Home or Windows XP Professional. When you upgrade to Windows XP Professional, Internet Explorer is upgraded to version 6. Therefore, if you are using Windows XP Home or Professional, you have Internet Explorer version 6 available for your Web browsing.

Microsoft states in the Knowledge Base article "How to Reinstall or Repair Internet Explorer and Outlook Express in Windows XP" that Internet Explorer is preinstalled in all versions of Windows XP. Furthermore, Microsoft states that it cannot be removed. At some point in your career, an end user will ask you about this—guaranteed.

To repair an existing copy of Internet Explorer version 6, you should run the System File Checker. This procedure replaces the system files that may be corrupt or missing. You may have to perform these steps if you or your user is having problems with Internet Explorer because of damaged files. You will need to be logged on as an administrator and have the Windows XP CD available.

Activity 5-1: Repairing Internet Explorer

Time Required: 30 minutes

Objective: Repair damaged Internet Explorer files.

Description: In this activity, you will repair Internet Explorer by replacing files that may be corrupt or missing. You will find this activity useful in your career as a DST because if you or your users are having problems with Internet Explorer because of damaged files, you will need to have explored this activity in detail.

1. Log on to your computer with the user name **admin01** and password **Password1**.

2. Insert the Windows XP CD and, if necessary, click the **Exit** link.

3. Click **Start**, click **Run**, type **sfc /scannow**, and click the **OK** button.

4. Wait for the file scan to complete.

5. In your project log, write a brief summary on this process to repair Internet Explorer.

6. Close any open windows.

7. Log off the computer.

When running the System File Checker, I've had it display a message that it could not locate a file on the CD. If this happens to you, take the CD out and clean the CD with a CD cleaning kit.

**IN THE
WORKPLACE**

Configuring Internet Explorer

5

Many users assume that the default installation of Internet Explorer will suffice for their uses and that no further configuration will be necessary. However, that's not the case. In fact, if you accept the default installation, you might run into problems such as the following:

- The default home page is MSN and your organization might desire to use a company home page

- Your users may not be able to access Web pages that they need to accomplish a business task

- Users may have to respond to numerous prompts to continue as they access Web pages

Obviously, these would be inconvenient to say the least. So, in this section, you will learn how to open the Internet Options dialog box, as shown in Figure 5-1, in order to configure the different options on the different tabs.

Access the Internet Explorer properties dialog box by selecting Internet Options from the Tools menu.

General Settings

You can customize Internet Explorer to fit the preferences of your organization. Your users expect your assistance with the configuration of these General settings. In Activity 5-2, you will configure the General settings in Internet Explorer.

You can customize these items:

- **Set your Home page**: Your **home page** is the page that appears every time you open Internet Explorer. Your users may need help setting this page from the default *www.msn.com* Web page.

- **Manage Temporary Internet files**: Your users can regain disk space by deleting these files that were stored on the computer as they surfed the Web.

- **Manage the History**: The **History** can grow rapidly as links for Web sites and pages visited in previous days and weeks are added to the History. This list is displayed from the Address bar as you type an address. When the list gets too long, it may be difficult to select a Web site from the History.

Figure 5-1   Internet Options dialog box

Activity 5-2: Setting the General Settings

Time Required: 15 minutes

Objective: Configure the General settings for Internet Explorer.

Description: In this activity, you will perform a number of routine tasks. You will set the home page to a recently visited site. Depending on usage, you should clean up the cookies, saved Internet files, and the History. You will find this activity useful in your career as a DST because, in order to answer user questions, such as how to clean up cookies or the History, you will need to be comfortable with configuring the General settings.

1. Log on to your computer with the user name **user01** and password **Password1**.

2. Click **Start**, and click **Internet** in the pinned area to start Internet Explorer.

3. Type *www.msn.com* in the Address bar and click the **Go** button.

4. Click **Tools** in the menu bar, and click **Internet Options**.

5. Click the **Use Current** button to set *www.msn.com* as the home page.

6. In your project log, write a brief description of the steps to set a home page for Internet Explorer.

7. Click the **Delete Cookies** button, then click the **OK** button.

8. Click the **Delete Files** button, check the **Delete all offline content** check box, then click the **OK** button.

9. Click the **Settings** button, grasp, and drag the slider to change the **Amount of disk space to use**, as indicated in Figure 5-2, to a value that represents about 1% of your hard disk capacity, and click the **OK** button.

Figure 5-2   Amount of disk space to use

10. In your project log, write a brief description of the steps to remove files after Internet Explorer has been used for a period of time.

11. Click the **Clear History** button, then click the **Yes** button.

12. Click the **OK** button and close any open windows.

Security Zones

Security zones offer an easy and flexible method for managing a secure Web environment. Your organization's Security Manager uses security zones to implement your organization's Internet security policy by grouping sets of sites together and assigning a security level to each zone.

The Security tab of the Internet Options dialog box is shown in Figure 5-3.

The following section will discuss the options that can be accessed from this tab.

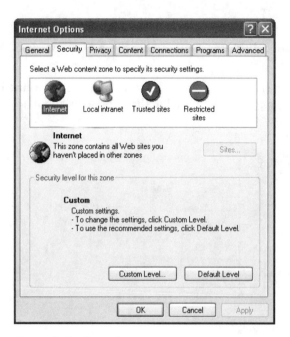

Figure 5-3 Security zones

The Zones

A zone is group of Web sites that can be separated in order to manage security. You see the zones at the top of Figure 5-3. When you first install Internet Explorer 6, it corrals all Web sites into a single zone, the Internet zone, and stands guard with a medium level of security. This helps you browse securely, but should prompt you before downloading potentially unsafe content.

Internet Explorer includes these Security zones:

- **Internet zone:** Internet Web sites that are not within the Trusted sites or Restricted sites or Local intranet zones. The Internet zone consists of all Web sites that are not included in the other security zones. By default, this zone is set to the Medium security level. If your organization is concerned about possible security problems when users browse the Web, change the security level to High. However, this change may cause some pages to malfunction or be displayed improperly. Consider specifying a Custom level that permits controlling each security decision for the zone.

- **Local intranet zone:** Web sites on an organization's intranet. You set up the Local intranet zone in conjunction with the firewall. All sites in this zone should be inside the firewall. Obtain detailed information about your internal network from the network administrators. By default, this zone consists of local domain names.

- **Trusted sites zone:** Internet sites that are trusted. These sites include the Web sites of business partners or reliable public entities. You can add trusted Web sites to the Trusted sites. By default, the Trusted zone is assigned the Low security level. The Web site will be allowed to perform a wider range of actions. This zone is intended for highly trusted Web sites, such as the sites of trusted business partners.

- **Restricted sites zone:** All sites that you do not trust. When you assign a Web site to the Restricted sites zone, it will be allowed to perform only minimal, very safe actions. By default, this zone is set to the High security level. Because a High security level is assigned to this zone, pages may not function or be displayed properly.

Figure 5-4 shows all these zones. Note that a firewall acts as a protective boundary between the internal networks and the outside world. **Proxy servers** act as intermediaries between computers and the Internet and filter access to Internet Web sites. As you may know, you define the location of the Security zones relative to the firewall. The local intranet zone resides behind the firewall. Typically, the other three zones reside outside of the firewall.

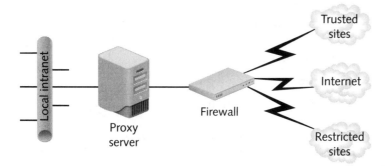

Figure 5-4 Security zones and a firewall

Security Settings Dialog Box

Clicking the Custom Level button on the Internet Properties dialog box opens the Security Settings dialog box, as shown in Figure 5-5.

At the top of the dialog box is the Settings list box. You can enable or disable the specific security options in this box depending on the security policies established by your organization.

The custom level options are grouped into the following categories:

- **ActiveX controls:** approves, downloads, runs scripts with **ActiveX controls** (software components to interact with one another in a networked environment)

- **Downloads:** file or font downloads can be downloaded

Figure 5-5   Security Settings dialog box

- **Scripting:** scripts are permitted
- **User authentication:** method to log on to a Web site
- **Miscellaneous:** wide range of actions are permitted or rejected

The Security team establishes the respective Security zone settings for each organization. You will want to contact them to find out the settings. If your users cannot access Web sites, you will need to be ready to answer their questions about Internet security.

Microsoft provides client-side software that watches for the downloading of supported software such as ActiveX controls and executable files. If a piece of software has been digitally signed, Internet Explorer can verify that the software originated from the developer and that no one has tampered with the software. A valid digital signature does not guarantee that the software is without problems. It means that the software has not been modified. Likewise, software without a signature does not prove the software is dangerous. However, it does alert the user to potential problems.

Now take a look at the Reset list box at the bottom of the tab. Table 5-1 gives a summary of the security levels available through this list box.

Table 5-1   Security levels

Level	Safeguards	Content	Appropriate zone
Low	Minimal safeguards and warning prompts	Most content is downloadable and runs	Trusted sites
Medium-Low	Minimal safeguards and warning prompts	Most content is downloadable and runs	Local intranet
Medium	Safe browsing and still functional	Prompts before downloading potentially unsafe content	Internet
High	Safest, yet least functional	Less secure features are disabled	Untrusted sites

5

Preserving the security of your computer when you browse the Web is a balancing act. The more open you are to downloads of software and other content, the greater your exposure to risk. For example, you want to avoid the risk of downloading software that could damage data on your hard drive. However, the more restrictive your settings, the less usable and useful the Web becomes.

Activity 5-3: Setting the Security Zones

Time Required: 20 minutes

Objective: Configure the Internet Explorer Security zones.

Description: In this project, you will review and set the default security settings for each of the four Security zones. For the Trusted sites zone, you will add the Microsoft Web site. You will find this activity useful in your career as a DST because, in order to answer user questions, such as setting the Security settings for a Security zone, you will need to be comfortable with configuring Security zones.

1. If necessary, log on to your computer with the user name **user01** and password **Password1**.

2. Click **Start**, then click **Internet** in the pinned area to start Internet Explorer.

3. Click **Tools** in the menu bar, click **Internet Options**, then click the **Security** tab to open the Security options.

4. If necessary, click the **Internet** icon in the **Select a Web content zone to specify its security settings** area.

When the Default Level button is grayed out, it must be activated for this lab. To activate the Default Level button, click the **Custom Level** button, click the **Reset** button, click the **Yes** button, and click the **OK** button.

5. Click the **Default Level** button to set the security level to Medium, as illustrated in Figure 5-6.

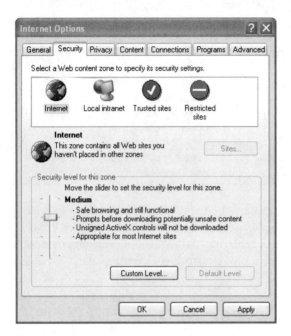

Figure 5-6   Internet zone security level set to Medium

6. Grasp the slider with the mouse pointer and pull it down to **Medium-low**, view the warning message, and click the **Yes** button.

7. Notice the security changes that have occurred when compared to Figure 5-6.

8. Click the **Default Level** button to set the Security level to Medium.

9. Click the **Local intranet** icon in the **Select a Web content zone to specify its security settings** area.

10. Click the **Default Level** button to set the Security level to **Medium-low**.

11. Click the **Trusted sites** icon in the **Select a Web content zone to specify its security settings** area.

If this activity has been completed previously, you can remove an existing approved site by clicking **www.microsoft.com** and clicking the **Remove** button.

NOTE

12. Click the **Sites** button, clear the **Require server verification (https:) for all sites in this zone** check box, type **www.microsoft.com** in the Add this Web site to the zone text box (see Figure 5-7), click the **Add** button, and click the **OK** button to add Microsoft as a trusted site.

Figure 5-7   Microsoft Web site added to Trusted zone

13. Click the **Default Level** button to set the Security level to **Low**.

14. Click the **Restricted sites** icon in the Select a Web content zone to specify its security settings area.

15. Click the **Default Level** button to set the Security level to **High**.

16. In your project log, write a detailed description of the four Security zones and how to set the Security level for each.

17. Click the **OK** button, and close any open windows.

Activity 5-4: Setting the Privacy Setting for the Internet Zone

Time Required: 15 minutes

Objective: Configure Internet Explorer privacy settings for the Internet zone.

Description: In this activity, you will set the privacy settings for the Internet zone. By configuring the privacy settings, you protect the privacy of your users as they surf the Web. You want the assurance that other people cannot intercept and read the information that you send and receive. You want to control how Web sites use the personal information that you provide. You will find this activity useful in your career as a DST because, in order to answer user questions, such as controlling file downloads, you will need to have explored configuring privacy settings in detail.

1. If necessary, log on to your computer with the user name **user01** and password **Password1**.

2. Click **Start**, then click **Internet** in the pinned area to start Internet Explorer.

3. Click **Tools** in the menu bar, click **Internet Options**, then click the **Privacy** tab to open the Privacy options.

4. Grasp the slider with the mouse pointer and pull it up to **Block All Cookies.** View the explanation as identified in Figure 5-8.

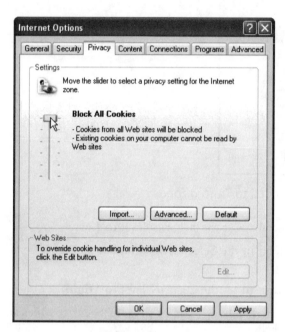

Figure 5-8   Cookie settings for Block All Cookies

5. Grasp the slider with the mouse pointer and pull it down to **High.** View the explanation.

6. Repeat Step 5 for **Medium High**, **Medium**, **Low**, and **Accept All Cookies**.

7. Click the **Default** button to set the Security level to **Medium**.

8. In your project log, write a detailed description of the six security levels for cookies with a summary of privacy settings for each of the six security levels.

If this activity has been completed previously, you can remove an existing approved site by clicking **www.2test.com** and clicking the **Remove** button.

NOTE

9. Click the **Edit** button, type **www.2test.com** in the Address of Web site text box (see Figure 5-9), click the **Allow** button, then click the **OK** button to permit cookies for the Prometric Web site *www.2test.com*.

Figure 5-9 Accept cookies from the Prometric Web site

10. In your project log, write a brief description of the steps to allow cookies from a Web site.

11. Click the **OK** button and close any open windows.

12. Log off your computer.

Privacy Tab

You configure privacy preferences on the Privacy tab located on the Internet Explorer properties dialog box, as shown in Figure 5-10. On the Privacy tab, you can perform the following activities:

- **Set your privacy level for the Internet zone:** By default, your privacy level for the Internet zone is set to Medium.

- **Import custom privacy settings:** You can import a custom privacy preferences file.

- **Customize your privacy settings for cookie handling:** You can specify privacy settings that override cookie handling for your selected privacy level.

- **Customize your privacy settings for individual Web sites:** You can define cookie management on a per-site basis.

Figure 5-10 Privacy tab

The following sections discuss each setting in turn.

Configuring Privacy Preferences

Using the privacy features, your organization creates a secure environment that protects users' personal information on the Internet. When you communicate over the Internet with a Web browser, you need the assurance that other people cannot intercept and read the information that you send and receive. Your users do not want others to use their passwords or share other private information. You and your users want to ensure that Web sites cannot access information on computers without your knowledge.

Web sites use cookies to maintain information and settings such as your personal surfing preferences. Two types of cookies are used by Web sites:

- **Persistent cookies are more permanent:** An expiration date in the cookie indicates when the browser can delete them.

- **Session cookies do not have an expiration date:** They are deleted when you close your browser.

Using P3P, a Web site can provide policy information for the cookies that it may attempt to store on your computer. You specify your privacy preferences to Internet Explorer. By comparing your preferences to the Web site's stated intentions, Internet Explorer determines if the Web should be permitted to store the cookie.

Move a slider on the Privacy tab to set the privacy level that you want:

- **Block All Cookies:** Prevents all Web sites from storing cookies. Web sites cannot read existing cookies. Per site privacy actions do not override these settings.

- **High:** Prevents Web sites from storing cookies that do not have a **compact privacy policy** (condensed computer readable P3P privacy statement). Web sites are unable to obtain **personally identifiable information** without your consent. Per site privacy actions do override these settings.

- **Medium-High:** Prevents Web sites from storing third-party cookies that do not have a compact privacy policy or use personally identifiable information without your consent. Also, prevents Web sites from storing first-party cookies that use personally identifiable information without your consent. Restricts access to first-party cookies that do not have a compact privacy policy so that they can be read only in a first-party context. Per site privacy actions do override these settings.

- **Medium (default):** Prevents Web sites from storing third-party cookies that do not have a compact privacy policy or use personally identifiable information without your consent. Permits first-party cookies that use personally identifiable information without your consent but deletes when you close the browser. Restricts access to first-party cookies that do not have a compact privacy policy so that they can be read only in a first-party context. Per site privacy actions do override these settings.

- **Low:** Permits Web sites to store cookies on your computer including third-party cookies that do not have a compact privacy policy or use personally identifiable information without your consent. Deletes third-party cookies when you close the browser. Restricts access to first-party cookies that do not have a compact privacy policy so that they can be read only in a first-party context. Per site privacy actions do override these settings.

- **Accept All Cookies:** Permits Web sites to store cookies on your computer. Web sites that create cookies can read them. Per site privacy actions do not override these settings.

Internet Explorer supports the **Platform for Privacy Preferences (P3P)**, which controls how personal information is used by the Web sites that you visit. Personally identifiable information is information that can be used to identify or contact you. You may not want to share your name, e-mail address, home or work address, or telephone number. However, a Web site has access only to the personally identifiable information that you provide, or to the entries you make while visiting a Web site. For example, a Web site cannot determine your e-mail address unless you provide it. A Web site cannot gain access to other information on your computer. If a Web site collects personally identifiable information, it may store the information in a **cookie**, a small file that a Web site saves on your computer.

Import Button

The Import Button permits custom privacy settings from a file on your computer. This permits your organization to standardize privacy settings. Your security team downloads files containing custom privacy settings from privacy organizations or other Web sites on the Internet. You could use these custom privacy settings to keep employees from accessing Web sites containing questionable content.

Advanced Button

The Advanced button displays the Advanced Privacy Settings dialog box, as shown in Figure 5-11. You can override automatic cookie handling for all Web sites in the Internet zone. You should check the Always allow session cookies box. Session cookies are deleted automatically when you close Internet Explorer. This strikes a useful compromise between protecting privacy and letting sites recognize you during your current visit. If sites cannot recognize your users as they go from page to page, your users may not be able to navigate within the Web site.

Figure 5-11   Advanced Privacy Settings dialog box

Edit Button

The Edit button opens the Per Site Privacy Actions dialog box, as shown in Figure 5-12. From this dialog box, you specify how to handle cookies from a specific site. If your users need to store cookies from a site that was excluded by a previous privacy setting, you can permit cookies to be stored from the site to meet a specific business need.

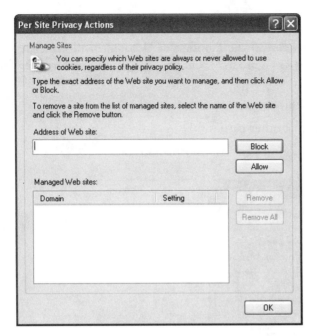

Figure 5-12   Per Site Privacy Actions dialog box

After you configure privacy preferences, Internet Explorer can handle cookies in these ways:

- **Prevent all cookies from being stored:** This setting might prevent you from accessing certain sites.

- **Block first-party cookies** (cookies that are stored by a Web server from the same Internet domain)

- **Block third-party cookies** (cookies that are stored by a Web server from a different domain): Many Web pages that contain advertising obtain the advertising from a third-party site.

- **Allow all cookies to be stored:** Do not notify me when a cookie is stored!

IN THE WORKPLACE

I'm concerned about security. I've installed a personal firewall that controls access to the information on my desktop computer. I felt secure knowing that the firewall blocks Web sites from placing cookies on my computer.

But this security has a price! Preparing to write this text, I wanted to take the 70-272 exam. As I've done on previous occasions before the firewall was installed, I surfed to the *www.2test.com* site to sign-up to take the exam. But without a cookie, Prometric would not permit access to the registration page. Alas, no cookie, no exam!

I shut down the firewall and returned to the Prometric Web site and registered for the exam. Next, I restarted the firewall and felt secure again!

Content Tab

You configure content preferences on the Content tab located in the Internet Explorer properties dialog box, as shown in Figure 5-13. On this tab, you can perform the following activities:

- Configure settings to block questionable Web sites
- Establish the identity of other parties
- Control the transmission of personal information

Figure 5-13   Content tab

The following sections discuss each of the content areas in turn.

Content Advisor Area

At the top of the tab is the Content Advisor. You use the Content Advisor to block access to sites with objectionable material. You can adjust the content ratings in four areas: language, nudity, sex, and violence. For example, your organization might want to block access to Web sites that offer no business value to their employees.

You secure the Content Advisor settings by setting a supervisor password. The first time you configure the Content Advisor, you must specify a supervisor password. This password allows supervisors to turn the Content Advisor on or off and to change Content Advisor settings for users. You can add a hint to help the supervisor to remember the password. Whenever

Internet Explorer prompts for the password, the hint is displayed. You can configure Internet Explorer so that users can access restricted Web pages by typing the supervisor password.

Internet Explorer is installed with a content-based rating system based on the work of the **Internet Content Rating Association (ICRA)**. The ICRA empowers the public, especially parents with young children, to make informed decisions by labeling content. Web authors complete questionnaires describing their content in terms of what is and what is not present. The ICRA provides a small piece of HTML code for the Web authors to include on their Web page.

Content Advisor examines this small piece of code to determine the level. Table 5-2 shows the five levels of the content and describes the content allowed for each level. Level 0 is the most restrictive, preventing users from accessing Web sites that include offensive language, nudity, sex, and violence. Level 4 is the least restrictive, allowing users to access Web sites that present explicit content.

Table 5-2   Content for each level of the Internet Explorer Content Advisor

Level	Language	Nudity	Sex	Violence
0	Inoffensive slang	No nudity	No sexual acts	No violence
1	Mild expletives	Revealing attire	Passionate kissing	Fighting
2	Moderate expletives	Partial nudity	Clothed sexual touching	Killing
3	Obscene gestures	Frontal nudity	Non-explicit sexual touching	Filled with blood and gore
4	Explicit or crude language	Provocative frontal nudity	Explicit sexual activity	Wanton and gratuitous violence

You may set content ratings to any level for each of the four content areas: Language, Nudity, Sex, and Violence. By default, all content ratings are set to Level 0. When Content Advisor is turned on and the rating for a Web site exceeds the rating level you set, Internet Explorer prevents users from accessing the site. You can configure Internet Explorer to allow or prevent access to unrated Web content.

For this rating system to work, the Web page must be rated by the Web author. If the author posts objectionable content, but does not program the page to expose the rating, the Content Advisor may block the page regardless of its content. The Approved Sites feature, which is accessible through the Settings button, can also be helpful in this situation. You may allow or block an approved site.

Activity 5-5: Setting the Content Options for the Internet Explorer

Time Required: 20 minutes

Objective: Configure the Internet Explorer content options settings.

Description: In this activity, you will set the content options settings for Internet Explorer. By configuring the content settings, you protect your users as they surf the Web. You will find this activity useful in your career as a DST because, in order to answer user questions regarding offensive content on Web sites, you will need to have explored configuring the content options in detail.

1. Log on to your computer with the user name **admin01** and password **Password1**.

2. Click **Start**, then click **Internet** in the pinned area to start Internet Explorer.

3. Click **Tools** in the menu bar, click **Internet Options**, then click the **Content** tab to open the Content options.

NOTE   For this lab, you need to start with a disabled Content Advisor. If the Disable button appears, click the **Disable** button. Also, you may be asked to enter a Supervisor password, type **MicrosoftRules** in the Password text box, and click the two **OK** buttons.

4. Click the **Enable** button to turn on the Content Advisor.

NOTE   If you are requested to type a Supervisor password, type **MicrosoftRules** in the Password text box and click the two **OK** buttons.

5. Click the **Settings** button, if it is not grayed out. If necessary, type **MicrosoftRules** in the Password text box, then click the **OK** button.

6. If necessary, click **Language** in the **Select a category to view the rating levels** area.

7. Grasp the slider and drag the slider from Level 0 to Level 4 to view the explanations for the various language levels.

8. Drag the slider to **Level 2: Moderate expletives**, as illustrated in Figure 5-14.

9. Click **Nudity** in the **Select a category to view the rating levels** area.

10. Grasp the slider and drag the slider from Level 0 to Level 4 to view the explanations for the various nudity levels.

11. Drag the slider to **Level 2: Partial nudity**.

12. Click **Sex** in the **Select a category to view the rating levels** area.

13. Grasp the slider and drag the slider from Level 0 to Level 4 to view the explanations for the various Sex levels.

14. Drag the slider to **Level 1: Passionate kissing**.

Figure 5-14   Language set to Level 2

15. Click **Violence** in the **Select a category to view the rating levels** area.

16. Grasp the slider and drag the slider from Level 0 to Level 4 to view the explanations for the various Violence levels.

17. Drag the slider to **Level 3: Killing with blood and gore**.

18. Click the **Apply** button to fix the settings.

19. In your project log, write a brief description of the four content areas and how to set the rating level for each.

20. Click the **Approved Sites** tab.

If this activity has been completed previously, you can remove an existing approved site by clicking **www.linux.com** and clicking the **Remove** button.

NOTE

21. Type **www.linux.com** in the Allow this Web site text box, click the **Never** button, then click the **Apply** button to disallow access to the Linux Web site.

22. Click the **General** tab and check the **Users can see sites that have no rating** check box.

23. If the Create Password button is present, click the **Create Password** button and continue with Step 25.

24. If the Change Password button is present, click the **Change Password** button and continue with Step 25.

25. Type **MicrosoftRules** in the Password text box, press the **Tab** key, type **MicrosoftRules** in the Confirm password text box (if the text box appears), press the **Tab** key, type **MicrosoftRules** in the Confirm new password text box, then type **The Winner is . . .** in the Hint text box.

26. Click the four **OK** buttons.

27. Close the Internet Options dialog box.

28. Type **www.linux.com** in the Address bar and click the **Go** button.

29. Type **MicrosoftRules** in the Password textbox and click the **OK** button.

You will be permitted to view the Linux Web site. You will not be permitted to view any "third-party" Web sites.

NOTE

30. If you are asked an additional time for permission to view the Web site, click the **Cancel** button.

31. Close all of the open windows and log off your computer.

32. In your project log, write a detailed description for use of the Supervisor password related to content management.

Certificates Area

How do you prove who you are? When you present a check in exchange for goods at the store, you may be asked to present your driver's license. The driver's license verifies your identity to the clerk. To verify the identity of your organization and your users on the Web, Internet Explorer deploys industry standard **digital certificates**. Like your driver's license is a viewable credential, digital certificates are electronic credentials. It binds the identity of the certificate owner to a pair of electronic keys (pubic and private). These electronic credentials assure that the keys truly belong to the organization or person. You can use the keys to encrypt and sign information.

You use certificates for user authentication and secure communication with servers on the Web. If you connect to a Web server, a server authentication certificate, issued by a trusted authority, enables you to establish the server's identity. In addition, certificates enable servers to verify your identity. You can expect to assist your users with digital certificates as they access business Web sites to conduct business activities.

Your users will exchange certificates with servers by using a secure transmission protocol. Your users will want to use secure transmission protocols because these protocols provide for privacy, encrypted information, and integrity, unaltered information. When you—or your users—transmit credit card and purchase information, secure channel transmission is typically used.

Messages can be encrypted with the public key and decrypted with the private key. See Figure 5-15 for the process to encrypt the message with the public key, and decrypt the message with the private key, as described in the following list:

1. **Step 1:** The plain text message is encrypted with the public key, which is furnished by the person who will receive the message.

2. **Step 2:** The encrypted message is transferred over the Internet. The encryption process insures that, if intercepted, the message cannot be read.

3. **Step 3:** The cipher text message is decrypted with the private key, which is held by the person who will receive the message.

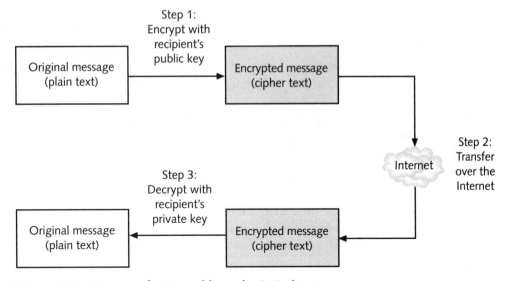

Figure 5-15   Process of using public and private keys

Certificates are issued, authenticated, and managed by a trusted third party called a **Certification Authority (CA)**. A commercial CA must provide services that your organization and users must trust. The primary responsibility of a CA is to investigate the identity of the organizations or persons obtaining certificates. This effort ensures the validity of the identification information contained in the certificate. When a certificate is compromised, the certificate is revoked and added to the Certificate Revocation List (CRL).

Your organization can obtain certificates from a commercial CA. Or the organization can obtain a certificate that permits the issuance of certificates. For use on your intranet, your organization can issue certificates. For customer services on the Internet, your organization might choose a commercial CA.

Activity 5-6: Obtaining and Installing a Digital Certificate

Time Required: 20 minutes

Objective: Obtain a digital certificate from a certificate authority and install the digital certificate.

Description: In this activity, you will obtain a digital certificate from a certificate authority and install the certificate for use by Internet Explorer. With the digital certificate, you can authenticate with Web sites requiring certificates. After obtaining the certificate, you will install the certificate and verify that the certificate is available. You will find this activity useful in your career as a DST because, in order to answer user questions, such as how to obtain a digital certificate, you will need to have explored digital certificates in detail.

1. Log on to your computer with the user name **user01** and password **Password1**.

2. Click **Start**, then click **Internet** in the pinned area to start Internet Explorer.

3. Type **//instructor01/certsrv/** in the Address bar and click the **Go** button. Wait for the Web page, identified by Figure 5-16, to be displayed.

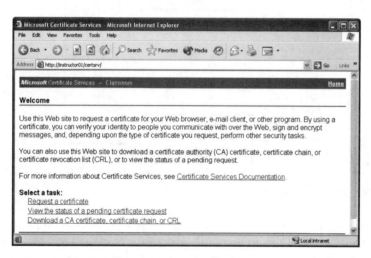

Figure 5-16   Certificate Services Web page

4. Click the **Request a certificate** hyperlink to request a certificate. See Figure 5-17.

5. Click the **User Certificate** hyperlink and click the **Submit** button.

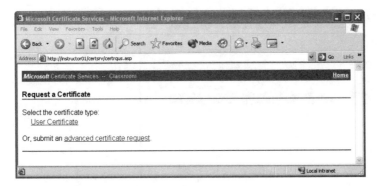

Figure 5-17   Request a certificate Web page

6. Read the **Potential Scripting Violation** warning message and click the **Yes** button. Wait for the server to respond.

7. Click the **Install this certificate** hyperlink.

8. Read the **Potential Scripting Violation** warning message and click the **Yes** button.

9. If necessary, read the **Root Certificate Store** warning message and click the **Yes** button to store the certificate on your computer.

10. Click **Tools** and click **Internet Options**.

11. Click the **Content** tab and click the **Certificates** button. See Figure 5-18 for the installed certificate location.

12. Locate the Certificate and double-click the Certificate. View the Certificate's **Intended purposes**.

13. Click the **OK** button, click the **Close** button, and close any open windows.

14. In your project log, write a detailed description for the process to obtain and store a digital certificate.

Personal Information Area

The Personal Information area is located at the bottom of the Content tab. From this area, you can clear out part of the Internet Explorer History. Also, you can access the settings for information that is transmitted to Web sites.

The first button is the AutoComplete button. By clicking the AutoComplete button, you can modify the AutoComplete settings for Web addresses and forms, as shown in Figure 5-19. By clicking the Clear Forms button, you can clear your History folder of all the entries that you have previously made in Web pages. Also, you can clear your History folder of all username and password entries. Your users should do this periodically so that no other person could use their computer and attempt to view any previously entered private information.

Figure 5-18   Installed certificate located

Figure 5-19   AutoComplete Settings

The second button is the My Profile button. From the My Profile button, you access the **Profile Assistant**, or User Properties dialog box, to maintain your computer's privacy and safety when sharing demographics with a Web site. The User Properties dialog box is shown in Figure 5-20. You store your personal information in a user profile on your computer. Your profile may be shared with Outlook Express. A Web site can ask for information from your profile, but you must provide consent for this access.

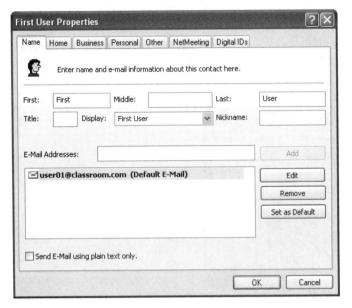

Figure 5-20   Profile Assistant options displayed

When a Web site makes a request, the Profile Assistant dialog box opens. You use the contents of this dialog box to verify what Web site is making the request. You choose what information to share (if any) and view what the Web site intends to do with the information. You should be prepared when your users have questions about how to control personal information that might be transmitted to Web sites.

Table 5-3 summarizes the information displayed in the Profile Assistant dialog box.

Table 5-3   Information in Profile Assistant

Option	Description
"Requestor name" has requested information from you	Displays the name of the requestor
Site	Uniform Resource Locator (URL) of the requesting site
Profile information requested	Clear the check boxes for any items you do not want to send
Always allow this site to see checked items	Add to list of sites for future access to your profile without notifying you
Edit profile	Edit profile information to send this site to make an exception
Privacy	Transfer is encrypted or unencrypted—how the user intends to use the information

Connections Tab

You configure content preferences on the Connections tab located in the Internet Explorer properties dialog box, as shown in Figure 5-21. On the Connections tab, you can set up an Internet Connection and configure LAN settings.

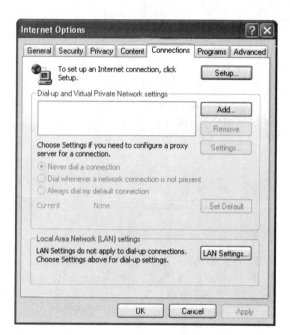

Figure 5-21   Connections tab

Setup Button

From the Setup button, you can configure a dial-up Internet Connection. Clicking the Setup button starts the New Connection wizard. You will learn about Internet Connections in Chapter 10, "Configure and Troubleshoot Devices and Connectivity for Applications."

LAN Settings Button

From the LAN Settings button, you specify LAN connection settings for Internet Explorer. Your network administrators can configure your network so that Internet Explorer is automatically customized the first time it is started. This can help reduce administrative overhead and potentially reduce Help Desk calls about browser settings. Automatic detection of browser settings is supported by both Dynamic Host Configuration Protocol (DHCP) and Domain Name System (DNS). See Figure 5-22 for the Automatic detection settings.

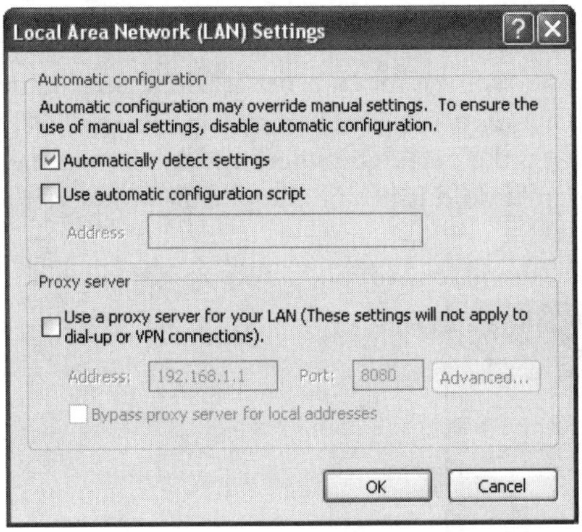

Figure 5-22   Automatic detection selected

As an alternative to automatic configuration, your organization's network administrators can elect to specify manual settings to use for the proxy server. You will enter the address for the proxy server and the port number provided by your network administrator. See Figure 5-23 for an example of the manual settings. Checking Bypass proxy server for local addresses will speed access to Web servers on the local intranet.

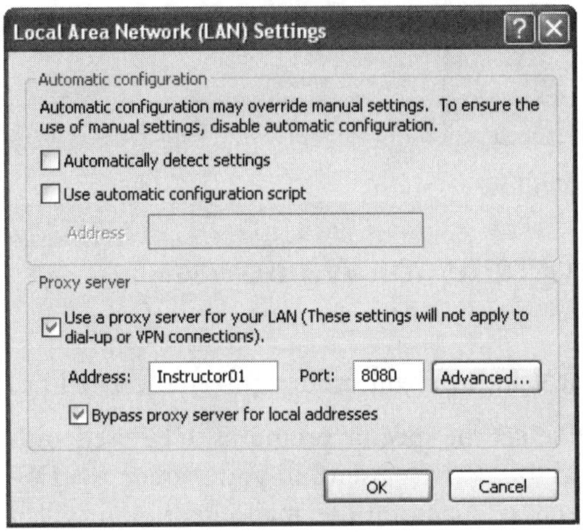

Figure 5-23   Manual proxy server settings

Programs Tab

You can specify what program Windows will use for Internet services. See Figure 5-24 for an example of the settings for such services as e-mail and newsgroups. If you check "Internet Explorer should check to see whether it is the default browser" check box, Internet Explorer will verify that it is the default browser. Should it not be the default browser, it asks if you want it to be the default browser.

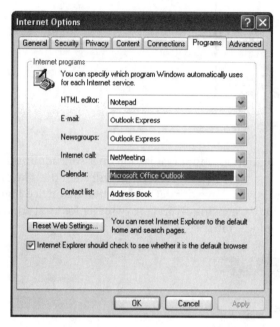

Figure 5-24   Program selection for Windows options

Activity 5-7: Specifying Programs for Windows

Time Required: 15 minutes

Objective: Specify the programs that Windows will use for Internet-related tasks.

Description: In this activity, you will select the specific programs to be used with Windows for Internet-related tasks. You will find this activity useful in your career as a DST because, in order to answer user questions, such as changing the mail client, you will need to be comfortable with specifying Internet programs for Windows.

1. If necessary, log on to your computer with the user name **user01** and password **Password1**.

2. Click **Start**, and click **Internet** in the pinned area to start the Internet Explorer.

3. Click **Tools** in the menu bar, click **Internet Options**, and click the **Programs** tab to open the Program options. See Figure 5-25.

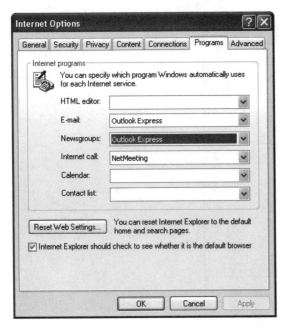

Figure 5-25   Programs tab displayed

4. Click the **HTML editor** drop-down arrow, click **Notepad**, and click the **Apply** button.

5. If necessary, check the **Internet Explorer should check to see whether it is the default browser** check box and the click the **OK** button.

6. Close any open windows and log off the computer.

7. In your project log, write a detailed description for the process to specify the programs to use with Internet Explorer.

Advanced Tab

From the Advanced tab, you can "fine tune" your Internet Options. See Figure 5-26 for an example of the options. You can configure options for accessibility, browsing, HTTP, multimedia, printing, and security.

IN THE WORKPLACE

Take a look at Figure 5-26. What if you wanted a clarification on the finer points of these options? If so, Microsoft provides a Help feature that you may have overlooked. At the upper-right corner of this figure is a question mark. When you click this question mark, the cursor turns to a pointer with a question mark. To access the content of the Help, move the cursor to an item and click. When additional information is available, it will be displayed.

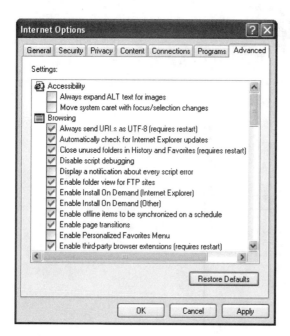

Figure 5-26   Advanced tab

Customizing Browser Features

Note that your organization's network administrators could develop customized versions of Internet Explorer with the **Internet Explorer Administration Kit (IEAK)**. The Internet Explorer could be "preconfigured" and have configuration settings that vary from the settings that you saw in the previous sections. Although you will not be using the IEAK to prepare these packages, you need to know its capabilities to answer your user's questions.

Table 5-4 presents the major features of the IEAK, which save administrators time when deploying Internet Explorer.

Table 5-4   Major customization features

Feature	Description
Customization wizard	Customizes the privacy settings for your users
Privacy	Prevents users from viewing the Privacy tab
Personalizing the toolbar	Gives additional flexibility and design opportunities by personalizing the look and feel of the Internet Explorer toolbar
Policies and Restrictions	Includes new system policies and restrictions that allow preconfigured settings for Internet Explorer 6 features

Table 5-4   Major customization features (continued)

Feature	Description
Custom Components	Chooses when to install custom components
Administrative Privileges	Creates custom packages that will retain administrator privileges after the computer restarts
Outlook Express Links and Icons	Includes Outlook Express in the package and configures the installation so that no links appear to the Outlook Express program

5

INTERNET EXPLORER ERROR REPORTING TOOL

When a program in Internet Explorer stops and cannot recover, the browser displays the Internet Explorer Error Reporting message, as shown in Figure 5-27. The Internet Explorer Error Reporting tool provides fault collection services. It offers to extract information about the problem. You can review the details about the problem then choose to upload the fault information to Microsoft. This information might help Microsoft identify problems that Microsoft needs to fix with future service packs. If a problem known to Microsoft occurs, you may obtain a link to a patch or Knowledge Base article.

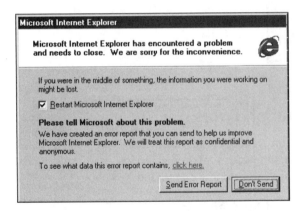

Figure 5-27   Internet Explorer error message

INTERNET EXPLORER ERROR MESSAGES

You may encounter three basic type of errors when working with Internet Explorer:

- Errors that occur during the installation or upgrade of Internet Explorer
- Errors that result because Internet Explorer is not configured properly
- Errors that occur during the use of Internet Explorer

These errors will be discussed in turn in the following sections.

Internet Explorer Installation Errors

This section describes some of the problems that you might encounter when you upgrade Internet Explorer. Explanations of the problems and, where possible, solutions are provided.

Download Server Connection Times Out

Setup can switch servers during an installation to maintain maximum throughput or to recover from a server that is not responding. The switch will occur if Setup detects no throughput or no transfer for two minutes. If Setup cannot reestablish a connection, you will be prompted to cancel or try again.

Cannot Install Internet Explorer Update After Download

When you download Internet Explorer updates, you select the file and download the appropriate version. Because the downloaded files are unique to a particular operating system, you cannot download the files with one operating system and install on another operating system. You will receive a message similar to Figure 5-28.

Figure 5-28   Program error message

Internet Explorer Configuration Errors

This section describes some of the problems, resulting from incorrect Internet Explorer settings, that you or your users might encounter when using Internet Explorer. Explanations of the problems and, where possible, solutions are provided.

Temporary Internet Files Use More Disk Space Than Specified

You might experience these problems with the Temporary Internet Files Folder:

- **Folder uses more space than configured in amount of disk space to use:** You configure a specific amount of space for the Temporary Internet Files and the space is exceeded.

- **Files that are downloaded from Web sites might remain in the folder:** You click the Delete Files button and then observe that files are still present in the Temporary Internet Files Folder.

These problems occur when the content of a Web page is only partially downloaded. For example, you navigate to a page before the browser downloads the page or you interrupt the download by clicking Stop. Activity 5-8 provides the steps to work around these problems.

Disable Third-Party Browser Features

You can install third-party objects that appear in tool bars. These programs run in the same address space as Internet Explorer and can perform any action on the available windows and modules. When you troubleshoot Internet Explorer problems, you may want to disable the third-party tools.

Cannot Connect to the Internet Because a Proxy Server Configuration Is Not Working

If you get a message that the page cannot be displayed, you should check the LAN settings on the Connections tab. You are checking these settings because your organization may choose to use a proxy server to filter access to the Internet. You must configure the proxy server correctly in Internet Explorer. Your network administrators must configure DHCP and DNS correctly for automatic detection to work properly.

Privacy Tab Settings Affect Only the Internet Zone

By design, privacy settings work only in the Internet zone. Internet Explorer automatically accepts all cookies from Web sites in the intranet and Trusted sites zones. Internet Explorer blocks all cookies from the Restricted sites zone.

Existing Cookies Can Still Be Read by Web Sites After Setting Block Option

By design, the Block and Prompt options apply only to new cookies. To protect your privacy, you should click the Delete Cookies on the General tab. You will need to do this after changing the settings on the Privacy tab.

Internet Explorer Usage Errors

This section describes some of the problems that you or your users might encounter when using Internet Explorer. Explanations of the problems and, where possible, solutions are provided.

Privacy Icon Displays Even Though Privacy Settings Allow Cookies

By design, the Privacy icon appears in the status bar each time Internet Explorer restricts a cookie based on your privacy settings or Internet Explorer retrieves a cached file. The Privacy icon may still appear if you change your settings during the current browser session. Press F5 to refresh the Web page, or delete the contents of the Temporary Internet Files folder.

Web Site Reports That You Must Enable Cookies

This occurs when you click the link to another Web site and attempt to access the services of the second, or secondary, Web site. By design, Internet Explorer determines that the secondary site is in the third-party context. The Medium privacy level (the default for the

Internet zone) blocks third-party cookies that do not have a compact policy or third-party cookies that have a compact policy and that provide personally identifiable information that is used without your consent. For your users to connect to the desired Web site, they will need to type the address of the Web site in the Address bar.

Activity 5-8: Cleaning Temporary Internet Explorer Files

Time Required: 20 minutes

Objective: After repeated Web access, clean up the resulting temporary Internet files.

Description: In this activity, you will practice responding to error messages regarding Temporary Internet Files that you might encounter with Internet Explorer. You will practice moving the Temporary Internet Files folder contents to a safe place and moving the contents back to a re-created Temporary Internet Files folder. You will use the Disk Cleanup to remove the files in the Temporary Internet Files folder that are no longer required. You will find this activity useful in your career as a DST because, in order to answer user questions, such as how to gain additional free hard disk space, you will need to have explored cleaning the Temporary Internet Files folder.

1. Log on to your computer with the user name **admin01** and password **Password1**.

2. Click **Start**, click **My Computer**, and double-click **Local Disk (C:)**.

To remove an existing Save folder, right-click the **Save** folder, click **Delete**, and click the **Yes** button.

3. Right-click in the white space, point to **New**, click **Folder**, and type **Save** over the New Folder text. Press **Enter**.

4. Click **Start** and click **Internet** in the pinned area to start the Internet Explorer.

5. Click **Tools** in the menu bar, click **Internet Options**, then if necessary, click the **General** tab.

6. Under **Temporary Internet files**, click the **Settings** button, then click the **Move Folder** button.

7. Expand **Local Disk (C:)**, click the **Save** Folder, as indicated in Figure 5-29, and click the **OK** button.

8. Click the **OK** button, click the **Yes** button. Wait for the logoff to occur.

9. Log on to your computer with the user name **admin01** and password **Password1**.

10. Click **Start**, click **My Computer**, and double-click **Local Disk (C:)**.

11. Double-click the **WINDOWS** folder, then double-click the **Temp** folder.

Figure 5-29 Save folder located

12. Right-click in the white space, point to **New**, click **Folder**, type **Temporary Internet Files** over the New Folder text, and press **Enter**.

13. Click **Start**, then click **Internet** in the pinned area to start the Internet Explorer.

14. Click **Tools** in the menu bar, click **Internet Options**, then if necessary, click the **General** tab.

15. Under **Temporary Internet files**, click the **Settings** button, click the **Move Folder** button, expand **Local Disk (C:)**, expand the **WINDOWS** folder, expand the **Temp** folder, click the **Temporary Internet Files** folder, then click the **OK** button.

16. Click the **OK** button, click the **Yes** button. Wait for the logoff to occur.

17. Log on to your computer with the user name **admin01** and password **Password1**.

18. Click **Start**, click **My Computer**, and double-click **Local Disk (C:)**.

19. Right-click in the white space, click **Properties**, and click the **Disk Cleanup** button. Wait for the analysis to complete.

20. Uncheck the **Temporary Internet Files** check box, as indicated in Figure 5-30.

21. Click the **OK** button and click the **Yes** button. Wait for the cleanup to complete.

22. Close any open windows.

23. In your project log, write a detailed description for the process to move and restore the contents of the Temporary Internet Files folder.

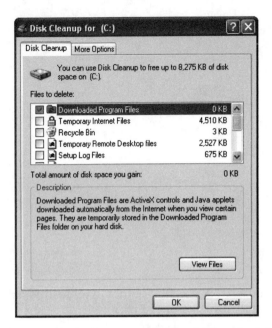

Figure 5-30   Temporary Internet Files check box cleared

WORKING WITH AND REPAIRING OUTLOOK EXPRESS

Outlook Express is automatically preinstalled when you purchase a new computer with Windows XP Home or Windows XP Professional. When you upgrade to Windows XP Professional, Outlook Express is upgraded to version 6. Therefore, if you are using Windows XP Home or Professional, you have Outlook Express available. In Activity 5-9, you will explore repairing Outlook Express.

You follow the same procedure for repairing Outlook Express that you followed for Internet Explorer. To repair an existing copy of Outlook Express, you should run the System File Checker.

NOTE

Activity 5-9: Repairing Outlook Express

ACTIVITY

Time Required: 20 minutes

Objective: Repair Outlook Express.

Description: In this activity, you will repair an installation of Outlook Express by replacing files that may be corrupt or missing. You will find this activity useful in your career as a DST because, in order to repair a failing Outlook Express, you will need to have explored the steps to replace the damaged files.

1. If necessary, log on to your computer with the user name **admin01** and password **Password1**.

2. Insert the Windows XP CD and, if necessary, click the **Exit** link.

3. Click **Start**, click **Run**, type **sfc /scannow**, and click the **OK** button.

4. In your project log, write a brief summary on this process to repair Outlook Express.

5. Close any open windows.

6. Log off the computer.

CONFIGURING OUTLOOK EXPRESS

Although Internet Explorer will access the Internet without configuration, Outlook Express requires that servers be identified. To assist your users with Outlook Express, you must learn how to configure Outlook Express.

Configure Outlook Express with the Internet Connection Wizard

Microsoft anticipated your need for assistance with the configuration of Outlook Express and provided the Internet Connection wizard. In this section, you will learn to use the wizard to perform the initial configuration for Outlook Express.

E-mail Server Types

Before using Outlook Express, you specify the incoming and outgoing server types. In Figure 5-31, the incoming e-mail server is a Post Office Protocol version 3 (POP3) server. In addition to POP3, Outlook Express supports Internet Message Access Protocol (IMAP) and HyperText Transfer Protocol (HTTP) for e-mail. The outgoing server is a Simple Mail Transfer Protocol (SMTP) server.

E-mail Server Accounts

Before you use Outlook Express to send and receive e-mail, you must set up an account. Outlook Express handles multiple accounts. You can have a separate account for each e-mail service that you access. Also, each person using the computer can have his or her own separate account.

When you start Outlook Express the first time, you use the Internet Connection wizard to set up your first e-mail account. You will be asked to provide the items indicated in Table 5-5.

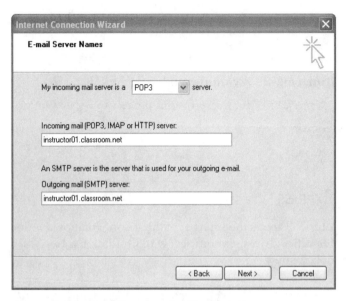

Figure 5-31   E-mail servers for Outlook Express

Table 5-5   Sample Internet Connection Wizard entries

Item	Description	Sample
Display name	Name to appear on the From field of an outgoing message	First User
Account name	E-mail for return mail	user01@classroon.net
Incoming server type	Choose from POP3, IMAP, or HTTP	POP3
Incoming mail server	Name of incoming mail server	instructor01. classroom.net
Outgoing mail server	Name of outgoing SMTP server	instructor01. classroom.net
Account name	Account name on Active Directory	user01
Password	Password in Active Directory	Password1
Log on using SPA	Check the box to use the Active Directory user account	Box checked

You will use the Internet Connection wizard to set up your e-mail account in Activity 5-10.

Web-based E-mail Accounts

The e-mail that you get in a **Hotmail** (Web-based e-mail service owned by Microsoft) account or other Web-based account is kept on the account provider's computer. If you or your users travel, a Web-based account permits access to e-mail over the Internet anywhere in the world.

To use a web-based e-mail, go to the provider's Web site and follow the instructions on the Web site to set up the account. Then set up the e-mail account using Outlook Express's Internet Connection wizard. Figure 5-32 illustrates a setup of a Hotmail server. Notice that there is not an option for the SMTP mail server for Web-based mail when you select HTTP as the e-mail option.

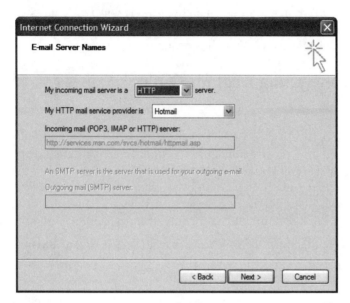

Figure 5-32 Hotmail server setup

IN THE WORKPLACE

Microsoft is taking security seriously!

Microsoft released a service pack for Windows XP. In this service pack, the option to not allow attached files to be saved or opened that could potentially be a virus was enabled by default. Some attachments saved prior to the installation of the service pack could no longer be saved.

These changes have made Outlook Express more secure and this is good. Be prepared to explain to your users why these measures are being taken. I suspect that future changes will "harden" Outlook Express and result in additional opportunities to visit with our users.

Newsgroup Accounts

A newsgroup is where people with common interests can share news and opinions. You can ask questions and get answers. Newsgroups are a lot like e-mail, which explains why newsgroups are accessed from Outlook Express. People correspond by posting messages back and forth. You can read messages anonymously without others knowing. Or you reply when you have an answer. This conversation takes the form of a **thread** or sequence of responses to an initial message posting.

No one owns newsgroups. Most are unmoderated free-for-alls in which every-thing and anything goes. I may get reliable information but I also may get off-the-wall answers, profanity, and other "noise." In a moderated newsgroup, the moderator may filter what appears so that the quality of the news is improved.

You can follow one or more newsgroups. In Activty 5-11, you will configure Outlook Express to use certificates. In Activity 5-12, you will configure Outlook Express to follow the MCDST news on the Microsoft public newsgroup.

Activity 5-10: Configuring Mail for Outlook Express

Time Required: 15 minutes

Objective: Configure Outlook Express to use an e-mail account.

Description: In this activity, you will configure Outlook Express to use an e-mail server located on the Instructor01 server. You will use the Internet Connection wizard to set up the e-mail account. You will test your configuration by sending an e-mail message to yourself. You will find this activity useful in your career as a DST because, in order to add e-mail accounts, you will need to be comfortable with configuring e-mail for Outlook Express.

1. Log on to your computer with the user name **user01** and password **Password1**.

2. Click **Start** and click **E-mail** in the pinned area to start Outlook Express.

If this activity has been completed previously, you can delete an existing account by doing the following: click **Tools**, click **Accounts**, click the **Mail** tab, click the account under **Account**, click the **Remove** button, click the **Yes** button, and click the **Close** button.

3. If the wizard does not start automatically, click **Set up a Mail Account** hyperlink to start the Internet Connection wizard.

4. Type **First User** in the Display name text box and click the **Next** button.

5. Type **user01@classroom.net** in the E-mail address text box and click the **Next** button.

6. Type **instructor01.classroom.net** in the Incoming mail (POP3, IMAP, or HTTP) server text box, type **instructor01.classroom.net** in the Outgoing mail (SMTP) server text box, and click the **Next** button.

7. Type **Password1** in the Password text box, check the **Log on using Secure Password Authentication (SPA)** check box, and click the **Next** button.

8. Click the **Finish** button.

9. Click the **Create a new Mail message** hyperlink, type **user01@classroom.net** in the To text box, type **Test Message** in the Subject text box, type a message of your choice in the message area, and click the **Send** button.

10. Click the **Send/Recv** icon, click the **There is 1 unread Mail message in your Inbox** hyperlink, and double-click the message from First User.

11. Close all open windows.

12. In your project log, write a detailed description for the process to configure Outlook Express to support e-mail.

Activity 5-11: Configuring Outlook Express to Use Certificates

Time Required: 20 minutes

Objective: Configure Outlook Express to use digital certificates.

Description: In this activity, you will configure Outlook Express to use Certificates for e-mail. You will use the Internet Connection wizard to set up the e-mail account. You will test your configuration by sending an e-mail message to yourself. You will find this activity useful in your career as a DST because, in order to help your users use digital certificates, you will need to be comfortable with configuring Outlook Express to use Certificates.

1. If necessary, log on to your computer with the user name **user01** and password **Password1**.

2. Click **Start** and click **E-mail** in the pinned area to start Outlook Express.

3. Click **Tools**, click **Accounts**, and click the **Mail** tab.

4. Click **instructor.classroom.net** under Account, click the **Properties** button, and click the **Security** tab. See Figure 5-33.

5. Click the **Select** button under **Signing certificate**.

6. If necessary, click **First User** under **Issued to**. Click the **OK** button. Figure 5-34 shows the assigned certificate.

7. Click the **Select** button under **Encrypting preferences**.

8. If necessary, click **First User** under **Issued to**. Click the **OK** button.

9. Click the **OK** button and the **Close** button.

10. Click the **Create a new Mail message** hyperlink, type **user01@classroom.net** in the To text box, type **Test Security Message** in the Subject text box, and type a message of your choice in the message area.

11. Click **Tools** and click **Digitally Sign**. View the red icon to the right of the To text box.

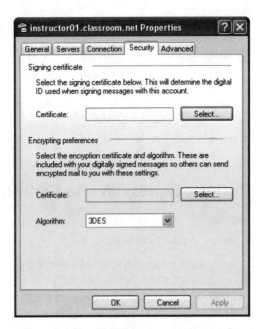

Figure 5-33 Security tab

Figure 5-34 Signing certificate assigned

12. Click **Tools** and click **Encrypt**. View the blue icon to the right of the Cc text box.

13. Click the **Send** button.

14. Click the **Send/Recv** icon, click the **There is 1 unread Mail message in your Inbox** hyperlink folder, and double-click the message from First User.

15. Click the red icon to the right of the From text box. Read the Security message that verifies that the mail was digitally signed and click the **OK** button.

16. Click the blue icon to the right of the To text box. Read the Security message that verifies that the mail was encrypted and click the **OK** button.

17. Close all open windows.

18. In your project log, write a detailed description for the process to use digital certificates with e-mail in Outlook Express.

Activity 5-12: Configuring Newsgroups for Outlook Express

Time Required: 15 minutes

Objective: Configure Outlook Express to use newsgroups.

Description: In this activity, you will configure Outlook Express to use the MCDST Newsgroup from Microsoft. First, you will identify the user of the newsgroup. Next, you will configure the connection to the Microsoft news server and the MCDST news group. You will test your configuration by downloading and reading the news for the MCDST newsgroup. You will find this activity useful in your career as a DST because, in order to assist your users with access to newsgroups, you will need to have explored configuring newsgroups for Outlook Express.

1. If necessary, log on to your computer with the user name **user01** and password **Password1**.

2. Click **Start** and click **E-mail** in the pinned area to start Outlook Express.

To remove an existing news server, right-click **msnews.microsoft.com**, click **Remove account**, and click the **Yes** button.

3. Click **Set up a Newsgroups account** to start the Internet Connection wizard.

4. Type **First User** in the Display name text box and click the **Next** button.

5. Type **user01@classroom.net** in the E-mail address text box and click the **Next** button.

6. Type **msnews.microsoft.com** in the News (NNTP) server text box and click the **Next** button.

7. Click the **Finish** button and click the **Yes** button. Wait for the names of the newsgroups to be obtained.

8. Type **mcdst** in the Display newsgroups which contain text box, click the **Subscribe** button, as indicated by Figure 5-35, and click the **OK** button.

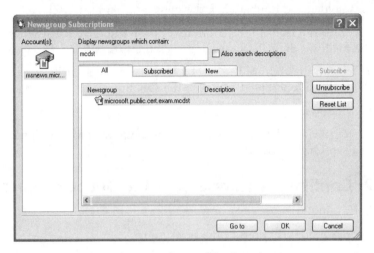

Figure 5-35   Newsgroup selection displayed

9. Click the **microsoft.public.cert.exam.mcdst** folder. Wait for the news to download.

10. Click and read any item of interest.

11. Close all open windows.

12. In your project log, write a detailed description for the process to use newsgroups in Outlook Express.

INTERPRET OUTLOOK EXPRESS ERROR MESSAGES

This section describes some of the problems that your users might encounter when they use Outlook Express. Explanations of the problems and, where possible, solutions are provided.

Preview Pane Does Not Display News Messages

While you are reading news messages, you might receive the message: Press <Space> to display the selected message. Press the spacebar to redisplay the message. If you double-click the message to open it, you might receive the error message: There was an error opening the message. This problem occurs when there is not enough free space on your hard disk to save the news message. Increase the amount of free space on your hard disk by removing any unnecessary files from the hard disk or emptying the Recycle Bin.

The Command Failed to Execute

When you attempt to save a mail attachment to your hard disk in Outlook Express, you might receive the message: The command failed to execute. This problem occurs when there is not enough free space on your hard disk to save the news message. Increase the amount of free space on your hard disk by removing any unnecessary files from the hard disk or empty the Recycle Bin.

CHAPTER SUMMARY

- Internet Explorer is an integral part of the Microsoft Windows XP operating system. Because Windows XP uses components of Internet Explorer to display content on the desktop, it cannot be removed.

- Your users should know how to set their home page and manage the Temporary Internet Files and History. You may want to provide one-on-one training for these tasks.

- Internet Explorer permits you to categorize Web sites in to four zones: Internet, local intranet, Trusted sites, and Restricted sites. You place Web sites in these zones to manage the Web environment.

- Using the privacy features of Internet Explorer, your organization can create a secure environment that protects users' personal information on the Internet. You can configure Internet Explorer's privacy options to protect your users as they surf the Internet.

- You protect the users in your organization from viewing objectionable content by configuring the Content options.

- Your users may use Outlook Express to receive, read, and send e-mail. You must be prepared to answer your users' questions on these two components.

- You use digital certificates to identify yourself to the Internet. Likewise, digital certificates are used to identify other parties and Web sites on the Internet. With digital certificates, personal information and credit card numbers can be encrypted during transmission.

- You can configure LAN connections to meet the requirements of your organization using automatic detection or manual proxy settings.

- You must be prepared to troubleshoot some of the problems that you may encounter with Internet Explorer, including errors that occur during the installation or upgrade of Internet Explorer, errors that result because Internet Explorer is not configured properly, and errors that occur during the use of Internet Explorer.

- You set up Outlook Express to access various types of mail servers. You configure Outlook Express to access news servers.

- You incorporated digital certificates with Outlook Express to permit encryption and signing of messages.

❑ You must be prepared to troubleshoot some of the problems that your users may encounter during the use of Outlook Express.

KEY TERMS

ActiveX controls — A reusable component based on Microsoft's ActiveX Technology. ActiveX components interact with one another in a networked environment.

Certification Authority (CA) — An issuer of digital certificates. A certificate authority may be an external certificate-issuing company or an internal company authority installed on a server.

compact privacy policy — Sent at the time a cookie is set by a Web site and summarizes a Web site's policy with regard to that cookie.

digital certificates — An electronic credential issued by a certification authority to identify a user on the Internet.

first-party cookies — Cookies that are owned or controlled in common by one company.

History — A detailed list of Web sites the computer has visited, which is retained on a computer's hard drive for a predetermined number of Web sites.

Home page — A Web page intended to serve as a starting point for a Web browser.

Hotmail — A Web-based e-mail service owned by Microsoft. Hotmail provides free e-mail accounts.

Internet Content Rating Association (ICRA) — Content-labeling advisory system that empowers parents and consumers to make informed choices about what they and their children experience on the Internet.

Internet Explorer Administration Kit (IEAK) — Microsoft developed the IEAK to provide for the customization and deployment of Internet Explorer packages.

Internet zone — An invisible boundary that prevents certain Web-based applications on the Internet from performing unauthorized actions with a Web browser.

Local intranet zone — An invisible boundary that prevents certain Web-based applications on the company network from performing unauthorized actions with a Web browser.

persistent cookies – A cookie that remains stored on the computer when the browser is closed.

personally identifiable information — Information about a person that is personally identifiable, such as your name, e-mail address, state/country of residence, and picture.

Platform for Privacy Preferences (P3P) — A framework for products and practices that will permit Web users to control the amount of personal information they share with Web sites.

Profile Assistant — Stores personal information and sends this information to Web sites that require it. This information cannot be viewed on your computer or shared with others without your permission. An Internet tool provided with Internet Explorer.

proxy servers — A firewall component that manages Internet traffic to and from the local area network.

Restricted sites zone — An invisible boundary that prevents sites with undesirable Web-based applications on the Internet from performing unauthorized actions with a Web browser.

session cookies — A cookie that is removed from the computer when the browser is closed.

Temporary Internet Files — File located on a computer's hard disk in which a browser stores the Web site data for every Web page that a user visits. When the Web server sends the Web page files to the browser, they are stored in a file so that the next time the user visits the same Web site the browser takes the data from the temporary Internet file.

5

third-party cookies — Cookies that come from Web sites other than the site the user is browsing.

thread — In newsgroups, a series of messages and replies related to a specific topic.

Trusted sites zone — An invisible boundary that permits sites with Web-based applications on the Internet from performing authorized actions with a Web browser.

REVIEW QUESTIONS

1. When you install Windows XP, which of the following Internet Explorer components is installed? (Choose all that apply.)
   a. Internet Explorer
   b. Outlook Express
   c. Windows Media Player
   d. Newsgroup Reader

2. If Outlook Express has corrupt or missing files, you can _____ to solve the problem.
   a. reinstall the Windows XP operating system
   b. uninstall and reinstall Internet Explorer
   c. uninstall and reinstall Outlook Express
   d. purchase and install an upgrade

3. When you display the Properties dialog box for the Internet Options, you will see the _____ tab. (Choose all that apply.)
   a. General
   b. Settings
   c. Privacy
   d. Content

4. From the General tab in Internet Explorer Internet Options, you can
   _____ . (Choose all that apply.)
   a. set the home page
   b. set security levels
   c. manage temporary Internet files
   d. manage the History list

5. A Security Manager uses the _____ zone to set Security levels for Web
   sites that are not trusted.
   a. Local intranet
   b. Approved sites
   c. Busted sites
   d. Restricted sites

6. A(n) _____ acts as a protective boundary between the internal and
   external networks.
   a. zone regulator
   b. firewall
   c. Internet Information Server
   d. file server

7. All sites in the _____ zone are inside the firewall.
   a. Local intranet
   b. Internet
   c. Trusted sites
   d. Restricted sites

8. The _____ Security level provides safe browsing and prompts before
   downloading potential unsafe content.
   a. Low
   b. Medium–Low
   c. Medium
   d. High

9. The _____ Security level is used with untrusted sites.
   a. Low
   b. Medium–Low
   c. Medium
   d. High

10. You can access Web sites by using a(n) _____ . (Choose all that apply.)

    a. DNS name

    b. site name

    c. Internet Protocol (IP) address

    d. e-mail address

11. Internet Explorer supports the Platform for Privacy Preferences, which controls how personal information is used by Web sites. Which of the following is considered personally identifiable information? (Choose all that apply.)

    a. first and last name

    b. e-mail address

    c. home address

    d. work address

    e. telephone number

12. Which of the following is a characteristic of cookies on a computer? (Choose all that apply.)

    a. They are small files saved on the client server.

    b. They remain from session to session.

    c. First-party cookies are stored from servers from the same domain.

    d. They are a pleasant, enjoyable morsel.

13. The _____ privacy level prevents Web sites without a compact privacy policy from storing cookies.

    a. Low

    b. Medium

    c. Medium-High

    d. High

14. By default, the Privacy level for the Internet is _____ .

    a. Low

    b. Medium

    c. Medium-High

    d. High

15. By design, privacy settings work only in the Internet zone. Which of the following is a behavior for the other Security zones? (Choose all that apply.)

    a. They accept all cookies from Web sites in the intranet sites zone.

    b. They accept all cookies from Web sites in the Trusted sites zone.

    c. They block all cookies from the Trusted sites zone.

    d. They block all cookies from the Restricted sites zone.

16. Internet Explorer supports the RSACi content-based system. When the Content Advisor is turned on, which action prohibits a Web page from being displayed? (Choose all that apply.)

    a. The Web page does not have a rating.

    b. The rating level for the Content Advisor exceeds the rating on the Web site.

    c. The rating on the Web site exceeds the Content Advisor rating level.

    d. When the Users can see sites that have the no ratings check box is checked.

17. Which of the following regarding the Content Advisor is true? (Choose all that apply.)

    a. The User's password is used to make changes.

    b. The Supervisor's password is used to make changes.

    c. Web sites with objectionable content may be viewed by entering the user's password.

    d. Web sites with objectionable content may be viewed by entering the supervisor's password.

18. The _____ permits personal information to be maintained for sharing on Web sites.

    a. Personal Assistant

    b. Profile Assistant

    c. Personal Manager

    d. Profile Manager

19. _____ are electronic credentials that bind the identity to the credential.

    a. Certificate Authorities

    b. User passwords

    c. Digital certificates

    d. Software signs

20. The Internet Explorer Administration Kit (IEAK) is used by Network Administrators to _____ . (Choose all that apply.)

    a. customize the privacy settings for users

    b. preconfigure settings for Internet Explorer

    c. include Outlook Express in the package

    d. prevent users from viewing the Privacy tab

21. The Internet Explorer Reporting tool is used to _____ . (Choose all that apply.)

    a. provide error correction services

    b. extract information about a problem

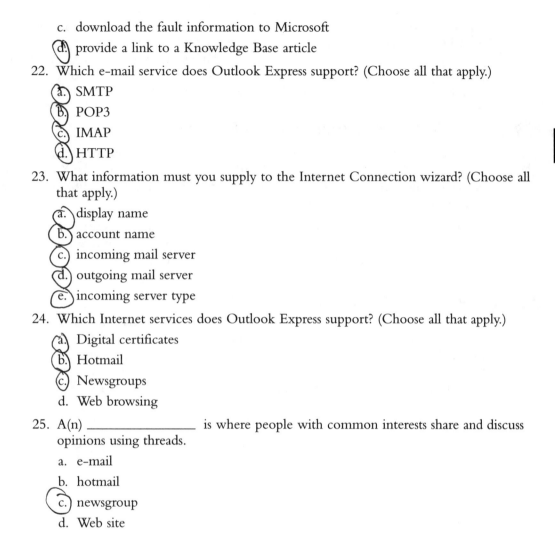

c. download the fault information to Microsoft

d. provide a link to a Knowledge Base article

22. Which e-mail service does Outlook Express support? (Choose all that apply.)

a. SMTP

b. POP3

c. IMAP

d. HTTP

23. What information must you supply to the Internet Connection wizard? (Choose all that apply.)

a. display name

b. account name

c. incoming mail server

d. outgoing mail server

e. incoming server type

24. Which Internet services does Outlook Express support? (Choose all that apply.)

a. Digital certificates

b. Hotmail

c. Newsgroups

d. Web browsing

25. A(n) _____ is where people with common interests share and discuss opinions using threads.

a. e-mail

b. hotmail

c. newsgroup

d. Web site

CASE PROJECTS

CASE PROJECTS

Case 5-1: Installing Internet Explorer and Outlook Express

You are a desktop support technician. Your network consists of a Windows 2003 Active Directory domain with 15 servers and 750 computers running Windows XP Professional.

The Security Manager runs a tight ship regarding security. He has made recommendations in regard to the configuration of Security and Privacy for Internet Explorer. The Network Administrator has used the IEAK to create preconfigured packages for installation on the organization's desktop computers.

You are responding to a question posed by Joseph. He recently purchased a new computer from a major electronics retailer that has Windows XP Home installed. He remarks that the Internet Explorer that he uses at home appears different than the Internet Explorer that he uses at work. How will you explain the reasons for these differences to Joseph? Be sure to express your answer in business terms rather than technical terms.

Case 5-2: Configuring Internet Explorer

You are a consultant working as a desktop support technician for a small nonprofit organization. Their network consists of 10 computers with Windows XP Professional installed. Your users connect to the Internet through a single computer with Internet Connection Sharing (ICS) installed.

The manager is concerned about protecting the privacy of employees when they access Web sites. How will you configure Internet Explorer to meet the manager's concerns? Be sure to express your answer in business terms rather than technical terms.

Case 5-3: Configuring Outlook Express

You are a consultant working as a desktop support technician at the small nonprofit organization described in Case 5-2. Most of the employees travel several days per month and take their laptop computers with them. When in the office, they will access the Internet Service Provider's e-mail server to receive and send messages. When they travel, they need access to Hotmail. How will you configure Outlook Express to meet these requirements?

6

INSTALLING OFFICE 2003

After reading this chapter and completing the exercises, you will be able to:

♦ Install Microsoft Office 2003

♦ Troubleshoot application installation problems using the Setup.exe log file

♦ Troubleshoot application installation problems using the Installer Log file

---

As you are aware, the role of the DST requires that you be prepared to install Microsoft Office 2003 (hereafter called Office). You can expect questions from your users on the installation of the features of Office. Your organization will value your ability to troubleshoot Office installation by using log files.

First, you will learn to install Office using various techniques. Office can be installed from the Office CD-ROM and from images placed on file servers. The installation tools provide for automated installation and repair.

Next, you will learn the process to troubleshoot application installation problems. As Office installs, the activities are logged to files that you can analyze.

INSTALLING MICROSOFT OFFICE 2003

To support Office installations for your users and to answer your users' questions about the installation of Office, you must have the skills to:

- Verify that a particular computer conforms to Microsoft's requirements for Office.
- Use the Setup and Installer programs to install Office.
- Explore the setup sequence for the installation of Office.
- Use local installation sources to install Office and to add features to an existing Office installation.
- Use Microsoft Product Activation antipiracy technology to verify licensing.
- Use the On First Use feature that permits users to install additional features on demand.
- Use the Self-Healing feature to reinstall missing or corrupt program files.
- Add Applications with Add or Remove Programs.
- Use the Rollback feature to remove a failed installation.
- Create an administrative installation point to place the Office program on a server.
- Install Office from a shared image.
- Assist with the installation of Office using Group Policy.
- Create log files.
- Verify the local installation source.

These topics will be discussed in the following sections.

Verifying Installation Requirements

To install Office, you must have a computer that meets the minimum hardware requirements, as shown in Table 6-1. Also, you will have to upgrade the Windows operating system if you or your user's computer is running a **legacy operating system**, such as Windows 95, Windows 98, Windows Millennium, or Windows NT.

Table 6-1   Minimum requirements for Office

Component	Minimum Requirement
Processor	Intel Pentium 233 or faster processor
Memory	128 MB
Hard disk	400 MB + 240 MB for installation files cache
Drive	CD-ROM or DVD Drive

Table 6-1   Minimum requirements for Office (continued)

Component	Minimum Requirement
Display	Super VGA (800 x 600) or higher-resolution monitor
Operating system	Microsoft Windows 2000 with SP3, Windows XP

The Microsoft documentation states that 240 MB is required for installation when using local installation sources. In practice, the space requirement is a bit larger—270 MB to 280 MB.

In order to successfully install Office, you must know the minimum requirements and know how to verify that a desktop computer meets the requirements. You will use the following tools to make this determination (accessing each of these tools is discussed in Activity 6-1):

- **My Computer Properties:** This tool gives you information about processor speed, installed memory (RAM), the Windows operating system, and service packs.

- **Local Disk Properties, General tab:** This tool gives you information about available free space for Office and installation files.

- **Local Disk Properties, Hardware tab:** This tool gives you information about availability of a CD-ROM or DVD drive for the Office CD.

- **Display Properties:** This tool gives you information about screen resolution.

More than once I've been asked to install an application on a substandard personal computer. My advice is: If the computer does not meet the requirements, contact your manager and discuss the problem. Even if you were to succeed at installing the application, your user would not be happy with the results.

Activity 6-1: Verifying Desktop Computer Meets Minimum Requirements for Installation

Time Required: 15 minutes

Objective: Determine if the local computer meets the minimum requirements prior to installation.

Description: In this activity, you will determine the capacities of a local computer and compare the capacities to the basic requirements for the installation of Office. You will find this activity useful in your career as a DST because you can avoid potential installation problems by verifying that the local computer meets the installation requirements.

1. Log on to your computer with the user name **admin01** and password **Password1**.

2. Click **Start**, right-click **My Computer**, and click **Properties**. Locate the items indicated in Figure 6-1.

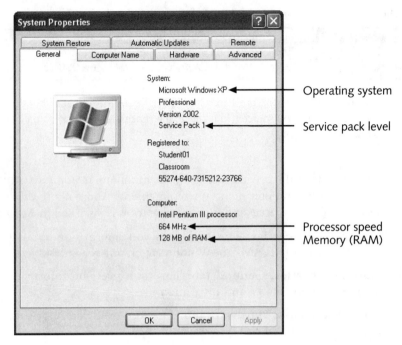

Figure 6-1 My Computer Properties

3. In your project log, write the values for System, Service Pack, Computer processor, and RAM.

4. Click the **Cancel** button.

5. Click **Start**, click **My Computer**, right-click **Local Disk (C:)**, and click **Properties**. Locate the free space, as identified in Figure 6-2.

6. In your project log, write the value for free space.

7. Click the **Hardware** tab. Locate the DVD/CD-ROM, as shown in Figure 6-3.

8. In your project log, write the name of the DVD/CD-ROM drive.

9. Click the **Cancel** button.

10. Right-click on the desktop, click **Properties**, and click the **Settings** tab. Locate the Screen resolution space, as shown in Figure 6-4.

11. In your project log, write the value for the screen resolution.

12. Click the **Cancel** button.

13. In your project log, compare the values that you have written to the requirements in Table 6-1. Indicate your assessment of whether this computer meets the minimum requirements to install Office.

14. Close the My Computer window.

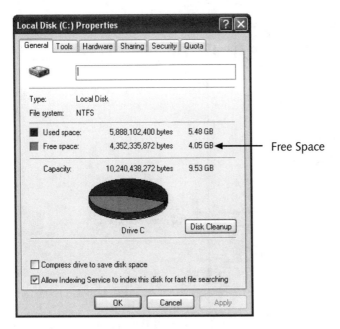

Figure 6-2   Local Disk (C:) Properties

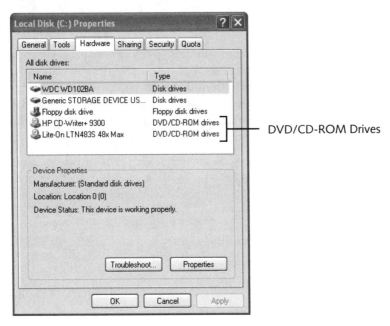

Figure 6-3   Hardware tab showing DVD/CD-ROM

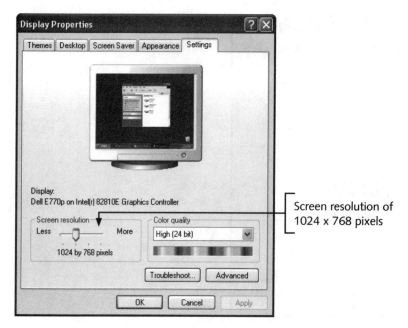

Figure 6-4 Display Properties showing Screen resolution

Using Windows Installer

Most Windows applications include a built-in .msi **package** (a package comprises the information and programs needed to install an application). When you start the installation process, you are deploying the application from this package. **.msi** is the file extension for the Installer package files. Each package (.msi file) contains a relational-type database that stores all the instructions and data to install (or uninstall) a package file. For example, you could use a file called english.msi to install the English application.

The Windows Installer service (hereafter called the Installer), which is a component of the Windows XP operating system, provides you with a standard method for installing applications. The Installer reads a .msi file and performs these installation-related tasks:

- Copying files to the hard disk
- Making additions and updates to the registry
- Creating shortcuts on the desktop
- Displaying dialog boxes to query for user installation preferences

When you use the Installer, you gain these benefits:

- **Transactional operations:** Installation operations are transactional. That is, for each operation the Installer performs, it creates an equivalent undo operation. If a failure occurs, you can use the Installer to return the applications to the original state.

- **Installation on First Use:** Installer supports first use or on-demand installation of features. For example, a feature may not be installed by default, but your user can trigger the on-demand installation of this feature.

- **Self-Healing:** Installer supports the abilities of applications to repair themselves. Applications detect common installation problems at start up and automatically use the Installer to repair the problem.

- **Installation in locked-down environments:** In fully locked-down environments, your users do not have the required privileges to install applications. The Installer runs in an "elevated state" to perform this installation for your user when the user does not have the privileges to install the application.

- **Change or Modify:** Installer permits additional features of the application to be installed. You can add additional features of the application that may not have been selected on the initial installation.

- **Update:** Installer updates the existing application by applying patches to the application. The Installer applies service packs provided by a vendor.

The Installer allows you to choose from among four alternatives:

- **Run from My Computer:** The files are installed on the local hard drive and run locally.

- **Run from CD:** The program files are run from the CD.

- **Installed on First Use:** The feature or application shows up on the menu but is not installed until your user selects the function from the menu.

- **Not installed:** No files are copied and your user is not informed of the option.

In order to keep your users' applications functioning optimally, you will need to remain current with the application of patches and service packs. The application of patches and service packs will be presented in detail in Chapter 13.

Exploring the Setup Sequence for Office

The Office Setup program, located on the Office CD, coordinates the installation process from beginning to end. The basic installation of Office is similar to the installation of other Windows applications: You insert the CD, the Setup program runs, and you follow the on-screen instructions to complete the installation. As an added benefit, when you complete your installation of Office, you do not need to restart your computer.

The files listed in Table 6-2 are often used during the installation of Office. You will find these file names informative as you explore the Setup and Installer technology used to install Office.

Table 6-2   Files used to install Office

File	Description
Setup.exe	Office Setup program. Located in the \ folder.
Setup.ini	Setup settings file. Located in the Files\Setup folder.
Ose.exe	Office source engine. Copies files from the source to the hard drive of the local computer.
Msiexec.exe	The executable for the Installer.
Msi file	The Installer package, which contains the information to install an application.
Mst file	The Installer transform. Used to customize Office.
LogFile_Taskn.txt	The Setup log file. Generated by Setup for each task.

At the start of the install process, Setup performs these tasks:

1. Reads the Setup.ini file and passes this information to the Installer. You can customize the Setup.ini file to control many aspects of the install process.

2. Installs ose.exe to copy the required installation files to the hard disk on the local computer. This step occurs only when you are installing from the Office CD or a compressed CD image on the network.

3. Calls the Installer (Msiexec.exe) to finish the installation. Creates the Setup log file.

The Installer performs these tasks:

1. Reads the contents of the .msi file (such as PRO11N.MSI), for specific information defined for the installation.

2. Reads the contents of the .mst file, which customizes the installation.

3. Completes the installation of the application.

Using Local Installation Sources

When you install from the Office CD or an image of the CD on the network, Setup determines which drive on the local computer has the most free space. Setup then installs the Ose.exe program on that drive. The Ose.exe program then copies a single cabinet (.cab) file to the local computer and extracts the files to a hidden folder. If there is enough space, about 270 MB, the Ose.exe program also copies the entire install source to the local computer. This copying is important. If there is room for the entire install source, your users can install features on demand without requiring the Office CD or a connection to a network share. If there is not enough space, you—or your users—will need the Office CD to add features or additional Office applications.

You can install Office 2003 by running the Setup program from either the Office CD or a compressed image from a network share. You create the compressed image on the network share by copying the files on the Office CD to the network share. You may find it easier to install from a network share. If you install from the network share, you will not need to carry the Office CD from computer to computer. From either the Office CD or the network share, you can still create the local installation source on the local computer.

Activity 6-2: Uninstalling an Existing Copy of Office (Optional)

Time Required: 20 minutes

Objective: Uninstall an existing copy of Office.

Description: In this activity, you will uninstall Office from a desktop computer. When a previous installation has occurred and you need to remove the existing components, you will need to complete this activity so that your computer has a clean platform on which to install the new version of Office. You will find this activity useful in your career as a DST because in order to remove a copy of Office, you must have explored the uninstallation of Office in detail.

1. If necessary, log on to your computer with the user name **admin01** and password **Password1**.

2. Click **Start**, point to **Control Panel**, and click **Add or Remove Programs**.

3. Click **Microsoft Office Professional Edition 2003**, click the Remove button, and click the **Yes** button.

4. Wait for the Installer to remove Office.

5. Close all open windows.

6. In your project log, write a brief summary about the steps to remove Office.

Activity 6-3: Installing Office from the Installation CD

Time Required: 30 minutes

Objective: Install Office from the Installation CD.

Description: In this activity, you will install Office to a desktop computer from a retail edition. You will find this activity useful in your career as a DST because in order to install Office, you must have explored the installation for Office in detail.

1. If necessary, log on to your computer with the user name **admin01** and password **Password1**.

2. Insert the Office CD in the drive.

3. Wait for the CD to autorun and notice the files copied message as shown in Figure 6-5.

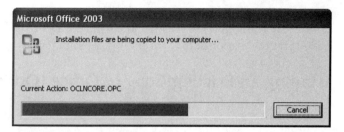

Figure 6-5   Installation files copied to your computer

4. When the Product Key dialog is displayed, as shown in Figure 6-6, enter the 25-character Product Key provided by your instructor. Click the **Next** button.

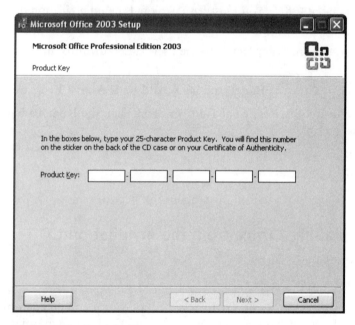

Figure 6-6   Product Key

5. When the User Information window appears, type the user information, as shown in Figure 6-7. Click the **Next** button.

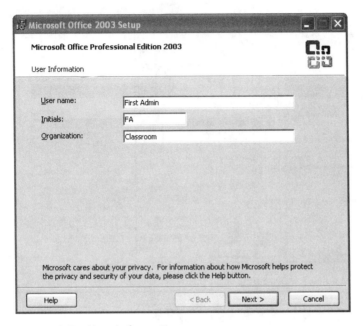

Figure 6-7   User Information

6. When the End-User License Agreement window appears, as shown in Figure 6-8, read the license agreement, and check the **I accept the terms in the License Agreement** check box. Click the **Next** button.

7. When the Type of Installation window appears, as shown in Figure 6-9, click the **Custom Install** option button. Note the Install to location. Click the **Next** button.

8. Uncheck all of the check boxes with the exception of the Word check box. Check the **Choose advanced customization of applications.** check box, as shown in Figure 6-10, and click the **Next** button.

9. Click the **Microsoft Office Excel** drop-down menu, click **Installed on First Use**, as shown in Figure 6-11, and click the **Next** button.

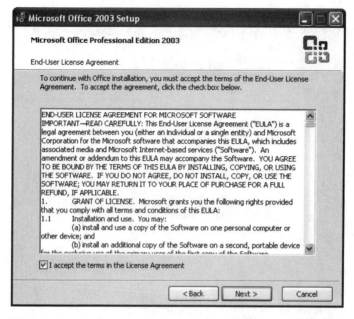

Figure 6-8 End-User License Agreement

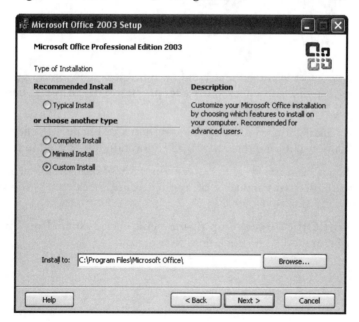

Figure 6-9 Type of Installation

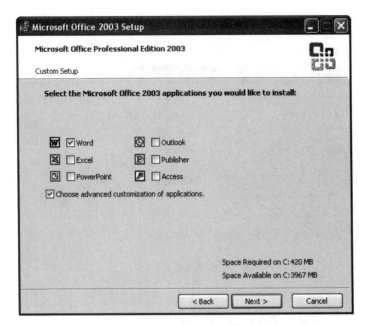

Figure 6-10   Custom Setup

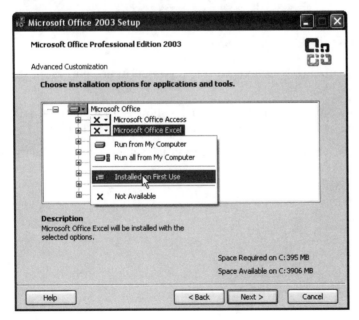

Figure 6-11   Advanced Customization with Excel selected

10. Review the Summary window, as shown in Figure 6-12, and click the **Install** button.

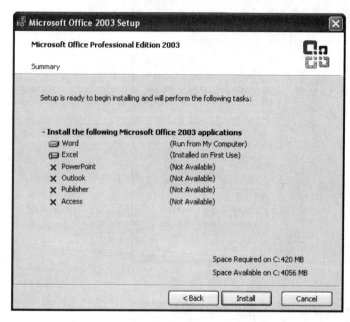

Figure 6-12   Summary window

11. Wait for the installation to complete. During the installation, your screen should resemble Figure 6-13.

12. When the Setup Completed window appears, as shown in Figure 6-14, read the message about the Office Installation files and click the **Finish** button.

13. In your project log, write a list of the steps to install Office. Use the activity as a guide.

14. Leave the Office CD in the drive.

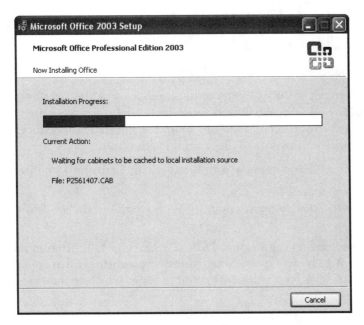

Figure 6-13   Installation progress information

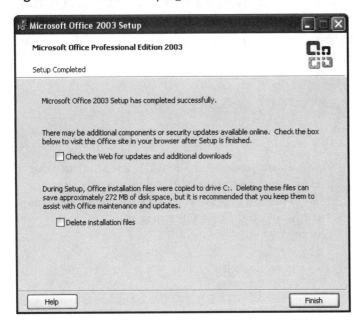

Figure 6-14   Setup Completed window

Activity 6-4: Exploring the Location of Menus and Files for Office

Time Required: 15 minutes

Objective: Explore the location of menus and files for Office.

Description: In this activity, you will explore the locations that the Installer placed the menu items and program files. You will find this activity useful in your career as a DST because in order to answer your users' questions about the installation of Office, you must have explored the location of menus and files for Office in detail.

1. If necessary, log on to your computer with the user name **admin01** and password **Password1**.

2. Click **Start**, point to **All Programs**, point to **Accessories**, and click **Windows Explorer**.

3. Expand **My Computer**, expand **Local Disk (C:)**, expand **Documents and Settings**, expand **All Users**, expand **Start Menu**, expand **Programs**, and click Microsoft Office. In your project log, write a note about which applications are installed.

4. Collapse **Documents and Settings**.

5. Expand **Program Files**, expand **Microsoft Office**, and click **OFFICE11**. In your project log, write a note about the structure of the OFFICE11 folder.

6. Right-click **OFFICE11**, click **Properties**. In your project log, write a note about the size of the OFFICE11 folder.

7. Click the **Cancel** Button.

8. Close the open windows.

Product Activation

Microsoft Product Activation is an antipiracy technology designed to verify that the product has been legitimately licensed. You can activate Office on one computer an unlimited number of times. The activation process generates a **hardware hash** (a nonunique number generated from the PC's hardware configuration) that is used to identify your physical computer and submits this information to Microsoft.

IN THE
WORKPLACE

What items are used to generate the "hardware hash"? It is rumored (Microsoft has guarded the contents) that the following items are used:

- Volume serial number string of the system volume
- Network adapter physical (MAC) address
- CD-ROM drive hardware identification string
- Graphics adapter hardware identification string
- CPU serial number string
- Hard drive hardware identification string
- SCSI host adapter hardware identification string
- IDE controller hardware identification string
- Processor model string hardware identification string
- RAM size

If you change many of these items, you will be required to call Microsoft to reactivate your software.

You must activate Office prior to 50 launches (or program runs). If you do not activate within the 50 launches, you will not be able to create new documents or edit existing documents. However, you can view or print existing documents. Even if you pass the 50-launch mark, your opportunity to activate Office to enable full functionality will never expire.

How do you activate Office? There are two methods:

- **Internet-based:** You first launch the Activation wizard. Then, your Internet connection is detected, a connection to a Microsoft activation server is created, and your installation information is transferred. A confirmation ID is passed back to your computer and Office is activated.

- **Telephone:** You first launch the Activation wizard. You then call the toll-free number on the screen and access a voice-activated service. Using your phone, you key the number on the screen. You listen to the confirmation ID and enter the code to activate Office.

IN THE
WORKPLACE

How difficult is the phone activation process? You are using an automated system in which you speak to a voice response system. You are reading and speaking six digits at a time for nine groups. You can ask that the numbers be confirmed before going on. For the confirmation ID, you are listening to six digits at a time for seven groups. You have an opportunity to ask for the digits to be repeated.

I've activated numerous servers and desktop computers using the phone. Perhaps I've been lucky, but I was able to activate successfully each time.

If a reinstallation of the software is needed, is reactivation required? Not always. If you install the same version of the software and the hard disk is not reformatted prior to reinstalling, the software will remain activated. Reactivation will be required if the hard disk is reformatted and the software is then reinstalled. The reactivation is required because the software's activation status is stored on the hard drive and reformatting the hard drive erases that status.

ACTIVITY

Activity 6-5: Exploring Microsoft Activation

Time Required: 15 minutes

Objective: Explore Microsoft Activation.

Description: In this activity, you start the Word program and activate your installation of Office. You will find this activity useful in your career as a DST because you must explore this activation in detail to answer your users' questions about activating Office.

1. If necessary, log on to your computer with the user name **admin01** and password **Password1**.

2. Click **Start**, point to **All Programs**, point to **Microsoft Office**, and click **Microsoft Office Word 2003**.

3. When the Microsoft Office 2003 Activation wizard screen appears, as shown in Figure 6-15, click the **Next** button.

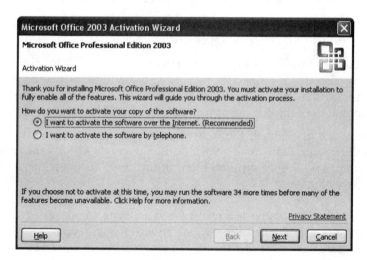

Figure 6-15   Activation wizard

4. In your project log, write a brief description about activation.

5. Close the open windows.

Using the On First Use Feature

Recall that for the On First Use Feature, the feature or application shows up on the menu but is not installed until your user selects the function from the menu. This allows your user to essentially customize the features from an approved list without the intervention of a person with administrator privileges. Your organization may use this feature to permit your users to install features as they are needed.

ACTIVITY

Activity 6-6: Installing Office Excel on First Use

6

Time Required: 15 minutes

Objective: Explore the On First Use option for Office.

Description: In this activity, you will install Excel on first use. You will find this activity useful in your career as a DST because in order to use the On First Use option, you must have explored the option in detail.

1. If necessary, log on to your computer with the user name **admin01** and password **Password1**.

2. Click **Start**, point to **All Programs**, point to **Microsoft Office**, and click **Microsoft Office Excel 2003**.

3. Wait for the installation to complete, as shown in Figure 6-16.

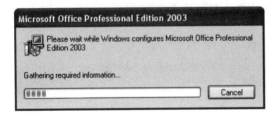

Figure 6-16   Installation progress

4. If the Microsoft Office 2003 Activation wizard dialog box appears, click the **Cancel** button.

5. In your project log, write a brief explanation of the On First Use feature.

6. Close all open windows.

Self-Healing Feature of Office

Office can also automatically repair itself—hence the term "self-healing"—if it detects a corrupt component or application. You can manually repair an application if there is any concern that the current installation of the application is not functioning properly. A library of file names maintained in the registry helps the detection system determine what files should be replaced when a specific application or component cannot be started. If required, Office calls the Installer and reinstalls only the affected files and registry entries. Your organization can use this feature to permit users to automatically repair Office if there was adequate free disk space during the installation to create the Local Installation Source.

Activity 6-7: Exploring the Self-Healing Feature

Time Required: 15 minutes

Objective: Explore the Self-Healing feature of Office 2003.

Description: In this activity, you will delete the Excel.exe program from your hard disk. Then, you will run Excel from the Start menu. You will find this activity useful in your career as a DST because in order to use the Self-Healing feature, you must have explored the Self-Healing feature of Office in detail.

1. If necessary, log on to your computer with the user name **admin01** and password **Password1**.

2. Click **Start**, point to **All Programs**, point to **Accessories**, and click **Windows Explorer**.

3. Expand **My Computer**, expand **Local Disk (C:)**, expand **Program Files**, expand **Microsoft Office**, and click **OFFICE11**.

4. Right-click **EXCEL.EXE**, click **Delete**, and click the **Yes** button.

5. Click **Start**, point to **All Programs**, point to **Microsoft Office**, and click **Microsoft Office Excel 2003**.

6. Wait for the Installer to patch Excel.

7. If the Microsoft Office 2003 Activation wizard dialog box appears, click the **Cancel** button.

8. In your project log, write a brief description about the Self-Healing feature of Office.

9. Close all open windows.

Adding Applications with Add or Remove Programs

Add or Remove Programs helps you manage application programs and Windows components on your computer. You can add programs (such as Microsoft Excel or Word). If the Setup program was able to create the Local Installation Point on your hard disk, the change proceeds without the need of the Office CD. Also, you can use Add or Remove Programs to remove application programs that are no longer needed. To open Add or Remove Programs, click Start, click Control Panel, and then double-click Add or Remove Programs.

ACTIVITY

Activity 6-8: Adding Applications

Time Required: 15 minutes

Objective: Explore the ability to change or modify features of Office.

Description: In this activity, you will add the PowerPoint program. You will find this activity useful in your career as a DST because in order to answer your users' questions about changing the installation of Office, you must have explored the Change feature in detail.

1. If necessary, log on to your computer with the user name **admin01** and password **Password1**.

2. Click **Start**, point to **Control Panel**, and click **Add or Remove Programs**.

3. Click **Microsoft Office Professional Edition 2003** and click the **Change** button.

4. Wait for the Maintenance Mode Options window to be displayed, as shown in Figure 6-17.

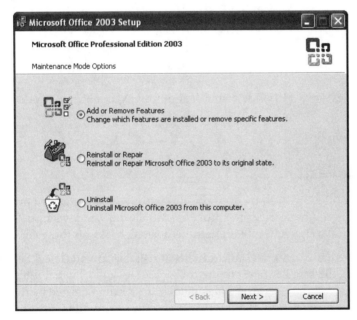

Figure 6-17   Maintenance Mode Options window

5. Click the **Next** button.

6. Check the **PowerPoint** check box, as shown in Figure 6-18, and click the **Update** button.

7. Wait for the installation to complete and click the **OK** button.

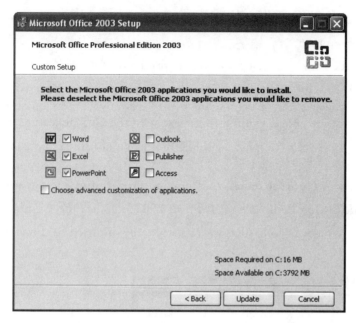

Figure 6-18   Custom setup with PowerPoint selected

8. In your project log, write a brief description about the Maintenance Mode features of Office.

9. Close the open windows.

Using the Rollback Feature

The **Rollback** feature allows you to recover gracefully from a computer or power failure. As each installation action is performed, the process that calls the Windows Installer file into action updates a rollback script and, if files are to be deleted, backs up those files.

When the Rollback feature is activated, and an Office install fails or you cancel Setup before the process is complete, the Installer refers to the rollback script and a hidden folder to undo the installation. This process removes all the files and registry settings created by the Installer, up to the point of the interruption, then reinstalls any files or registry entries that were removed.

Activity 6-9: Exploring the Rollback Feature for Office

Time Required: 15 minutes

Objective: Observe the changes that occur when the Rollback feature is used.

Description: In this activity, you will uninstall Office from a desktop computer. Next, you will start an installation of Office. Then, you will cancel the installation and verify that the files were removed. You will find this activity useful in your career as a DST because in order to use the Rollback feature, you must have explored the feature in detail.

1. If necessary, log on to your computer with the user name **admin01** and password **Password1**.

2. Click **Start**, point to **Control Panel**, and click **Add or Remove Programs**.

3. Click **Microsoft Office Professional Edition 2003**, click the **Remove** button, and click the **Yes** button.

4. Wait for the Installer to remove Office.

5. Close the Add or Remove Programs window.

6. If necessary, insert the Office CD in the drive. If the Office CD is already in the drive, open and close the drive to activate the autorun feature.

7. When the Product Key dialog box appears, enter the 25-character Product Key provided by your instructor. Click the **Next** button.

8. Click the **Next** button.

9. When the End-User License Agreement dialog box appears, check the **I accept the terms in the License Agreement** check box and click the **Next** button.

10. Click the **Next** button and click the **Install** button.

11. Wait until the Current Action states Copying new files. Click the **Cancel** button.

12. When the confirmation message appears, as shown in Figure 6-19, click the **Yes** button.

Figure 6-19 Confirmation message

13. Observe the subsequent rollback information, as shown in Figure 6-20.

14. When the cancellation message appears, as shown in Figure 6-21, click the **OK** button.

15. Remove the Office CD from the drive.

16. In your project log, write a brief description of the Rollback feature of Office.

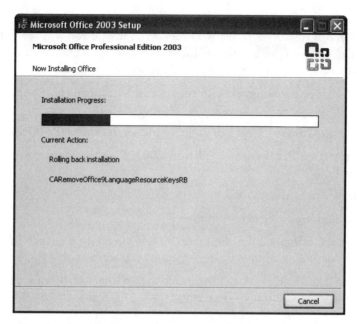

Figure 6-20   Rollback message

Figure 6-21   Microsoft Office 2003 Setup cancellation message

Using Administrative Installation Points

If you are employed at a large organization, most likely your organization uses Administrative Installation Points for the installation of Office. When an Administrative Installation Point is used, the installation bypasses the Setup program and is managed by the Installer. Organizations that use Group Policy (a subject in a later section) use Administrative Installation Points.

When you run Setup with a switch from the Start and Run, you create an Administrative Installation Point. The Administrative Installation Point contains the extracted files from the Office CD. Your users can thus install features on demand without requiring the CDA. However, for this to work, the Administrative Installation Point used for the Install must be available. Your end users will have problems if the Administrative Installation Point has been moved to another file server. Such a move might occur when the network administrators moved the files to balance the space allocation among multiple servers.

NOTE

Only editions of Office acquired through a volume license agreement or academic volume license agreement allow you to create the administrative installation point. If you have a retail version, you cannot use the Administrative Installation Point. You can use only the compressed image on your network or the Office CD.

ACTIVITY

Activity 6-10: Creating the Administrative Installation Point (Instructor Demonstration)

Time Required: 15 minutes

Objective: Create the Administrative Installation Point on the Instructor02 computer.

Description: In this activity, your instructor will run Setup with a switch to expand the Office files and place them in the Office folder. Next, he or she will configure sharing and security for the shared Office folder on the Instructor02 computer. You will find observing this activity useful in your career as a DST because in your organization this task will be performed by the network administration team and you must have observed the steps to answer your users' questions about the installation from the network using Administrative Installation Points.

1. Your instructor logs on to the Instructor02 computer. (For brevity, all subsequent steps are written in the normal second-person singular format.)

2. Insert the Volume License Agreement Office CD into the drive.

3. When the Welcome to Office 2003 Setup dialog box appears, click the **Cancel** button, click the **Yes** button, and click the **OK** button.

4. Click **Start**, click **Run**, type **d:\setup /a** in the Open text box, and click the **OK** button.

5. If you receive the message shown in Figure 6-22, you are not using a volume license edition of Office. You must use the Volume License Agreement Office CD.

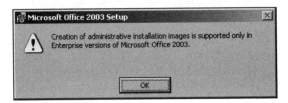

Figure 6-22 Creation of administrative images message

6. When the Administrative Installation page appears (as shown in Figure 6-23), type the Product Key and click the **Next** button.

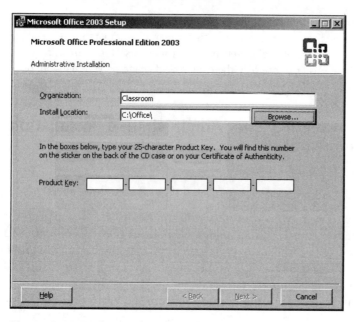

Figure 6-23 Administrative Installation page

7. When the End-User License Agreement dialog box appears, check the **I accept the terms in the License Agreement** check box and click the **Install** button.

8. Wait for the file expansion and copy to complete. Click the **OK** button.

9. Click **Start**, point to **All Programs**, point to **Accessories**, and click **Windows Explorer**.

10. Expand **My Computer**, click **Local Disk (C:)**, click **Office**, click **Files**, click **Setup**, and double-click **setup.ini**.

11. Locate the **;COMPANYNAME=my company** line, remove the semicolon character (;), type **Classroom** over my company, as shown in Figure 6-24, click **File**, click **Save**, and close the Notepad window.

12. In Windows Explorer, click the **Back** button on three subsequent screens, right-click **Office**, click **Sharing and Security**, click the **Share this folder** option button, type **Office 2003 Administrative Installation Point** in the Description text box, as shown in Figure 6-25, and click the **Apply** button.

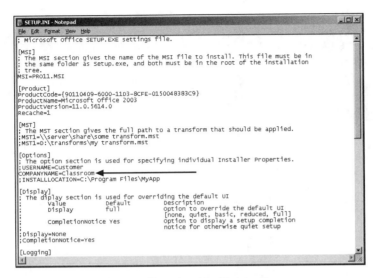

Figure 6-24   Setup.ini file edited in Notepad

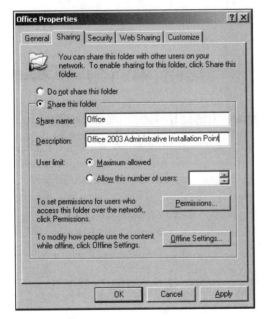

Figure 6-25   Folder sharing configured

13. Click the **Security** tab and click **Users(INSTRUCTOR2\Users)** under Group or user names. View the security settings, as shown in Figure 6-26. Click the **OK** button.

14. Close any open windows.

15. Remove the Office CD from the drive.

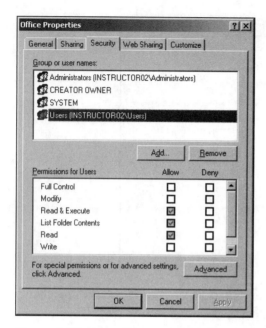

Figure 6-26   Security permissions for Users group

16. In your project log, write a brief description of the steps to create an Administrative Installation Point.

Installing from the Administrative Installation Point

From the Administrative Installation Point, you can run the Installer against the .msi file on the network share. The Installer copies the extracted files directly using the Administrative Installation Point as the source. Your organization would use the Administrative Installation Point to deploy Office to a large number of users. When installing Office from an Administrative Installation Point, the Install on First Use feature automatically returns to the same location for the additional files. This spares the DST a return trip with the Office CD when a user uses one of these new features.

ACTIVITY

Activity 6-11: Installing Office from the Administrative Installation Point

Time Required: 15 minutes

Objective: Install Office from the Office share using the Administrative Installation Point created in Activity 6-10.

Description: In this activity, you will install Office to a desktop computer from an Administrative Installation Point. You will find this activity useful in your career as a DST because in order to install Office from an Administrative Installation Point, you must have explored the installation of Office from an Administrative Installation Point in detail.

1. If necessary, log on to your computer with the user name **admin01** and password **Password1**.

2. Click **Start**, right-click **My Computer**, and click **Map Network Drive**, as shown in Figure 6-27.

Figure 6-27 Map Network Drive dialog box

3. Click the **Browse** button, expand **Classroom**, expand **Instructor02**, click **Office**, as shown in Figure 6-28, click the **OK** button, and click the **Finish** button.

Figure 6-28 Browse For Folder dialog box

4. When the Office on 'Exchange Server (Instructor02)' (Z:) (or the share that your instructor is using) dialog box appears, as shown in Figure 6-29, double-click the **PRO11** icon.

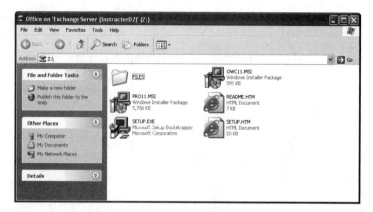

Figure 6-29 Office on 'Exchange Server (Instructor02)' (Z:) dialog box

5. Click the **Next** button on the two subsequent screens, then click the **Install** button.

6. Wait for the installation to complete and click the **Finish** button.

7. Close any open windows.

8. In your project log, write a brief description of the steps to install Office from an Administrative Installation Point.

9. Log off your computer.

Installing Office Using Policy-based Installation

If your organization has a large number of Office installations to complete, your organization will benefit by using **Group Policy** (the policy used by Active Directory to manage the settings on desktop computers). Using Group Policy to deploy Office can be a good choice for the following:

- Small- or medium-sized organizations that have deployed Active Directory

- Organizations that cover a single geographic area

- Organizations with consistent hardware and software configurations on both desktop computers and file servers

In the following sections, these topics will be presented:

- Active Directory

- Organizational Units

- Group Policy

- Installing software with Group Policy

Using Active Directory

By using Active Directory, your organization gains the benefits of centralized administration of users and computers. That is, Active Directory makes it possible for your organization's network administrators to manage all users, computers, and software on the network.

Generally, a Microsoft Windows network will have entities such as the following stored in Active Directory:

- **User accounts:** Contain information about users, such as first name, last name, username, and password
- **Computer accounts:** Contain information about computers, such as computer name, operating system, and description
- **Organizational Units (OUs):** Simplify administration by allowing the organization of objects, such as user accounts or computer accounts
- **Group Policy Objects (GPOs):** Define what a system will look like and how it will behave for a defined group of users or computers

You should be aware of user and computer accounts. OUs and GPOs merit more explanation.

Organizational Units

With OUs, your organization's network administrators can organize user accounts and computer accounts. For example, your organization might place the user accounts for the DSTs in an OU called Desktop Support. The network administrators might create an OU called Human Resources to store all the user accounts for the personnel assigned to the Human Resources department. Not only will this use of OUs make it easier to locate and manage Active Directory objects, but it allows the network administrator to apply Group Policy settings to control events such as software deployment.

Group Policy

Group Policy is a network administrator's tool for defining and controlling how programs, network resources, and the operating system operate for users and computers in an organization. In an Active Directory environment, Group Policy is applied to users or computers on the basis of their membership in containers such as organizational units. Group Policy settings are contained in a GPO that is associated with selected OUs.

Installing software with Group Policy, your organization's network administrators can control the installation of software over the network. A Group Policy Object (GPO) is a collection of Group Policy settings. The GPO is associated with an Active Directory container as indicated by the arrows in Figure 6-30. For example, one type of organizational unit (OU) is an Active Directory container filled with four user accounts. Using a GPO associated with this OU, the installation of software can be controlled for the four users.

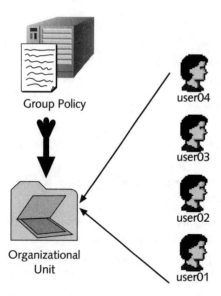

Figure 6-30   Active Directory and Group Policy

As discussed in the sections that follow, there are three ways to install and manage Office applications by policy:

- Assign Office to computers
- Assign Office to users
- Publish Office to users

Assigning Office to computers is the simplest way to use Group Policy. Using this method, Office is installed on the computer the next time the computer starts. These applications appear on the Start menu of all users. When you troubleshoot problems with applications, you will need to know which are assigned.

Assigned applications are resilient. If your user removes an Office application from the computer, the Installer automatically reinstalls the application the next time the computer starts. Your users can repair Office applications on his or her computer, but only an account with administrative privileges can remove installations.

When your organization assigns Office to Users, information about the software is advertised at your users' computers on the Start menu or Windows desktop the next time your user logs on. When your user clicks an Office shortcut, the Installer retrieves the application from a file server, installs the application, and starts the application. If your user clicks on an associated file extension in the Windows Explorer (such as Office Word document or Office Excel worksheet), the Installer automatically installs the corresponding Office application in the same way.

For an assigned installation, the application will be available only to the user installing the application. The application will not be available to other users unless they likewise complete an installation. However, if your users roam from computer to computer, the applications will follow the users and be installed as needed.

Assigned applications are resilient. If your user removes an Office application from the computer, the Installer automatically reinstalls the application the next time the user logs on.

When your organization publishes applications to users, no shortcuts are added to the Start menu. However, published applications, which are available to be installed from the Control Panel, Add or Remove Programs, may be installed by authorized users. Microsoft Visio is an example of an application that might be installed as a published application.

If your organization plans to have users run Office Setup themselves, consider publishing Office to users. Then, your user can install Office from Add or Remove Programs anytime he or she chooses.

TROUBLESHOOTING APPLICATION INSTALLATION PROBLEMS USING LOG FILES

Both the Office Setup and Installer generate log files during the Office install process. Office Setup and the Installer track the progress and post information in the log files on the hard drive. You use these logs to troubleshoot issues that may arise during the installation of Office.

Creating Log Files

In order to use the log files to troubleshoot problems, you must know how to locate the current log files. When you install Office, log files are created automatically. The log files are created in a hidden folder with a name similar to C:\Documents and Settings\admin01\Local Settings\Temp.

The log files have names similar to the two entries in Table 6-3. The Setup creates a log file name similar to what is listed in the first row of the table. Recall that Setup invokes the Installer. Each invocation of the Installer creates a log file name similar to the second line. In this example, the number 0012 represents the twelfth invocation of Setup. This number increases by one each time you run Setup.exe. The task numbers start with one each time you run Setup.exe.

Table 6-3   Sample Log file names

Feature That Creates the Log File	Filename of the Feature	Log file name
Setup	Setup.exe	Microsoft Office 2003 Setup(0012).txt
Installer	Msiexec.exe	Microsoft Office 2003 Setup(0012)_ Task(0001).txt

In order to troubleshoot a problem with the current installation, you would want to locate the log files with the highest number after Setup in the file name. The highest number equates to the latest version.

TROUBLESHOOTING WITH THE SETUP.EXE LOG FILE

You will see in Activity 6-12 that the log file for the Setup.exe file is very short because the number of tasks that Setup.exe performs is limited to tasks such as the following:

1. Read the Setup.ini file.
2. Verify that the correct operating system and service pack are being used.
3. Start Windows Installer.
4. Check for installed beta versions of Office 2003.
5. Check the version of the Tahoma and TahomaBD fonts.

The Setup.exe log files can provide useful information that you can use to troubleshoot failed installations. Some of the items that you will want to check appear in the following sections.

Verifying the Local Installation Source

Recall that if sufficient hard disk space exists on the local computer, Setup creates the local installation source by default. If the user's computer does not have sufficient disk space, Setup caches the installation files for only the selected features.

Setup creates the local installation source in the following hidden folder on your users' computers: C:\Msocache\Downloadcode.

Recall that the amount of free disk space for the Local Installation Source should be greater than 240 MB. This free space is important because you may want to install features on demand or run Setup in maintenance mode to add new features for your users. By default, Setup retains the Local Installation Source after the installation is complete.

You will verify the location of the Local Installation Source and the names of the files copied in Activity 6-12.

TROUBLESHOOTING WITH THE INSTALLER LOG FILE

You will discover that the Installer log file is much larger than the Setup log file. Unfortunately, it might appear to be incomprehensible at first glance. However, the following tips might be useful as you work through its contents:

1. If you receive an error during installation, search for the error in the log file.

2. All log files have one or more errors that can be ignored. For example, you should be able to ignore a message similar to: Info 2898. An internal error has occurred. Contact your Information Technology department for assistance.

3. One thing to search for is the string "Note". You may find the actual resolution for the problem located in a note several lines above the error.

4. Another string to search for in the log file is "Return Value 3". When an action is performed during Setup, the action is noted in the log files. When that action is complete, a return value is noted. If you see a return value of 1, the action was successful; however, if the action failed, you will see a return value of 3.

6

You will search for representative entries of the above in Activity 6-12.

There is a problem with using log files to troubleshoot. You must know what the log file for a successful installation looks like. By comparing the log from a successful installation to the log of a failing installation, you can start to discover what has gone wrong. You might want to consider creating a binder with good logs in preparation for your next adventure in troubleshooting.

Activity 6-12: Exploring the Office Installation Log Files

Time Required: 15 minutes

Objective: Locate information that could be used to troubleshoot a failed installation of Office.

Description: In this activity, you will explore the contents of a set of Office installation log files. You will find this activity useful in your career as a DST because in order to install Office from an Administrative Installation Point, you must have explored this process in detail.

1. Log on to your computer with the user name **admin01** and password **Password1**.

2. Click **Start**, click **My Computer**, and click **Local Disk (C:)**.

3. Click **Tools**, click **Folder Options**. click the **View** tab, click the **Show hidden files and folders** option button, as shown in Figure 6-31, click the **Apply to All Folders** button, click the **Yes** button, and click the **OK** button.

4. Double-click **Local Disk (C:)**.

5. Double-click the **Documents and Settings** folder, double-click the **admin01** folder, double-click the **Local Settings** folder, and double-click the **Temp** folder. Your results should resemble Figure 6-32.

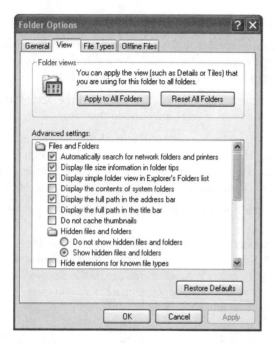

Figure 6-31   View tab with Show hidden files and folders selected

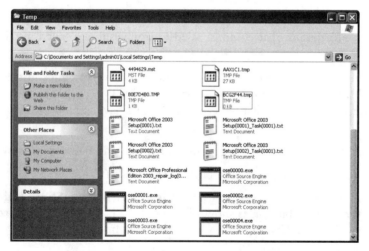

Figure 6-32   Windows Explorer - Temp folder

6. In your project log, write a brief description of the steps to locate the Temp folder.

7. Double-click **Microsoft Office 2003 Setup(0001).txt**. Your results should resemble Figure 6-33

8. Locate the line that reads **Detected Windows Info:**. In your project log, provide the entries in Table 6-4.

Figure 6-33 Notepad with Microsoft Office 2003 Setup(0001).txt file

Table 6-4 Detected Windows Info

Information field	Description	Value
PlatformId	Windows 9X or NT Family	
MajorVersion	Product Family	
MinorVersion	Operating system within product family	
ServicePackLevel	Version of service pack installed for the operating system	

IN THE WORKPLACE

The Detected Windows Info reveals an interesting insight into the internal numbering scheme used within the Windows operating systems. The Platform ID for the NT Family is 2. For Windows 2000 or later, the MajorVersion is 5. The MinorVersions are 0 for Windows 2000, 1 for Windows XP, and 2 for Windows Server 2003. These values are much different from the marketing names with which we are familiar. And then again, would you run out and buy Windows 5.1?

9. Locate the line that reads **Files to Download** and view the files that will be copied by the Office source engine. See Figure 6-34.

10. Locate the line that reads **Local Cache Drive: C:** and determine if enough free space exists to cache all of the cabinet files. See Figure 6-35.

11. In your project log, provide an indication if there was enough free space to cache all of the cabinet files.

Microsoft Office 2003 Setup(0001).txt - Notepad

File Edit Format View Help

```
Files to Download:
File: FILES\WINDOWS\INF\AER_1033.ADM (DW20.ADM_1033)
File: FILES\PFILES\COMMON\MSSHARED\DW\DW20.EXE (DW20.EXE_0001)
File: FILES\PFILES\COMMON\MSSHARED\DW\DWDCW20.DLL (DWDCW20.DLL)
File: FILES\PFILES\COMMON\MSSHARED\DW\1033\DWINTL20.DLL (DWINTL20.DLL_0001_1033)
File: FILES\PFILES\COMMON\MSSHARED\DW\DWTRIG20.EXE (DWTRIG20.EXE)
File: FILES\PFILES\MSOFFICE\OFFICE11\OCLEAN.DLL (OCLEAN.DLL_1033)
File: FILES\PFILES\MSOFFICE\OFFICE11\OCLNCORE.OPC (OCLNCORE.OPC_1033)
File: FILES\PFILES\MSOFFICE\OFFICE11\OCLNCUST.OPC (OCLNCUST.OPC_1033)
File: FILES\PFILES\MSOFFICE\OFFICE11\1033\OCLNINTL.OPC (OCLNINTL.OPC_1033)
File: FILES\PFILES\MSOFFICE\OFFICE11\OFFCLN.EXE (OFFCLN.EXE_1033)
File: FILES\SETUP\OSE.EXE (OSE.EXE)
File: PRO11N.MSI (PRO11N.MSI)
File: FILES\PFILES\MSOFFICE\OFFICE11\1033\PSS100.CHM (PSS100.CHM_1033)
File: FILES\PFILES\MSOFFICE\OFFICE11\1033\PSS10R.CHM (PSS10R.CHM_1033)
File: FILES\PFILES\MSOFFICE\OFFICE11\1033\SETUP.CHM (SETUP.CHM_1033)
File: SKU111.XML (SKU111.XML_0002_1033)
File: A2561408.CAB (A2561408.CAB)
File: A3561408.CAB (A3561408.CAB)
File: A4561408.CAB (A4561408.CAB)
File: AV561404.CAB (AV561404.CAB)
File: CC561401.CAB (CC561401.CAB)
File: CD561401.CAB (CD561401.CAB)
File: CF561401.CAB (CF561401.CAB)
File: CL561401.CAB (CL561401.CAB)
File: CM561401.CAB (CM561401.CAB)
File: CP561401.CAB (CP561401.CAB)
File: CR561401.CAB (CR561401.CAB)
File: CS561404.CAB (CS561404.CAB)
File: E2561412.CAB (E2561412.CAB)
File: E3561406.CAB (E3561406.CAB)
File: E4561412.CAB (E4561412.CAB)
File: EV561406.CAB (EV561406.CAB)
File: G3561412.CAB (G3561412.CAB)
```

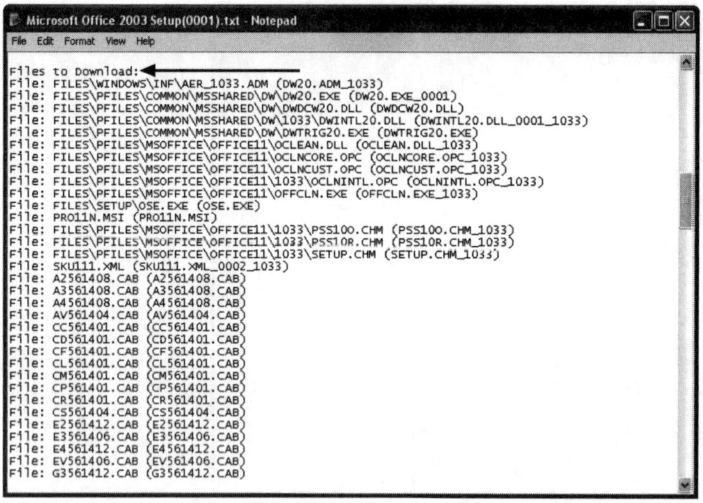

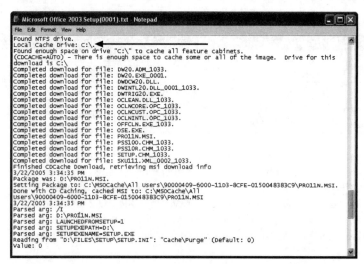

Figure 6-34 Notepad with Microsoft Office 2003 Setup(0001)_Task(0001).txt file

Microsoft Office 2003 Setup(0001).txt - Notepad

File Edit Format View Help

```
Found NTFS drive.
Local Cache Drive: C:\
Found enough space on drive "C:\" to cache all feature cabinets.
(CDCACHE=AUTO) - There is enough space to cache some or all of the image.  Drive for this
download is C:\
Completed download for file: DW20.ADM_1033.
Completed download for file: DW20.EXE_0001.
Completed download for file: DWDCW20.DLL.
Completed download for file: DWINTL20.DLL_0001_1033.
Completed download for file: DWTRIG20.EXE.
Completed download for file: OCLEAN.DLL_1033.
Completed download for file: OCLNCORE.OPC_1033.
Completed download for file: OCLNCUST.OPC_1033.
Completed download for file: OCLNINTL.OPC_1033.
Completed download for file: OFFCLN.EXE_1033.
Completed download for file: OSE.EXE.
Completed download for file: PRO11N.MSI.
Completed download for file: PSS100.CHM_1033.
Completed download for file: PSS10R.CHM_1033.
Completed download for file: SETUP.CHM_1033.
Completed download for file: SKU111.XML_0002_1033.
Finished CDCache Download, retrieving msi download info
3/22/2005 3:34:35 PM
Package was: D:\PRO11N.MSI.
Setting Package to: C:\MSOCache\All Users\90000409-6000-11D3-8CFE-0150048383C9\PRO11N.MSI.
Done with CD Caching, cached MSI to: C:\MSOCache\All
Users\90000409-6000-11D3-8CFE-0150048383C9\PRO11N.MSI
3/22/2005 3:34:35 PM
Parsed arg: /I
Parsed arg: D:\PRO11N.MSI
Parsed arg: LAUNCHEDFROMSETUP=1
Parsed arg: SETUPEXEPATH=D:\
Parsed arg: SETUPEXENAME=SETUP.EXE
Reading from "D:\FILES\SETUP\SETUP.INI": "Cache\Purge" (Default: 0)
Value: 0
```

Figure 6-35 Notepad with Local Cache Drive C:\ located

12. Locate the line that reads **Successfully launched MsiExec** and locate the chained install return code (which should be 0 for a successful execution of the Installer). See Figure 6-36.
13. In your project log, provide an indication if the MSIExec was successful.
14. Close the Notepad window.

Figure 6-36   Notepad with Successfully launched MsiExec located

15. Double-click **Microsoft Office 2003 Setup(0001)_Task(0001).txt**. Your results should resemble Figure 6-37.

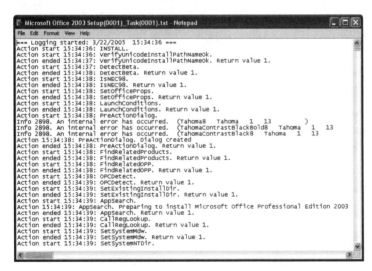

Figure 6-37   Notepad with Microsoft Office 2003 Setup(0001)_Task(0001).txt file

16. Click **Format** and click **Word Wrap**.

17. Click **Edit**, click **Find**, type **Note** in the Find what text box, and click the **Find Next** button.

18. If you did not find a note associated with an error, note that there were no fatal errors. If you got errors, contact your instructor. Click the **Find Next** button.

19. Repeat Step 18 until you get a cannot find "Note" message, click the **OK** button, and click the **Cancel** button.

20. In your project log, provide an indication if there were any errors discovered when searching for "Note".

21. Press Ctrl+Home.

22. Click **Edit**, click **Find**, type **Return value 3** in the Find what text box, and click the **Find Next** button.

23. If you got a message indicating Cannot find "Return value 3", note that there were no fatal errors. If you got errors, contact your instructor. Click the **OK** button.

24. In your project log, provide an indication if there were any errors discovered when searching for "Return value 3".

25. Close any open windows.

26. Log off your computer.

Chapter Summary

❑ Prior to installing Office, you should verify that the desktop computer meets or exceeds the minimum requirements.

❑ The Installer provides you with a standard method for installing Office and other Windows applications.

❑ Where there is an additional free disk space of about 240 MB, Setup will copy the compressed Office files, which will permit changes without needing to insert the Office CD.

❑ You practiced the Office installation from the Office CD.

❑ You practiced uninstalling Office.

❑ You practiced using Installer features:

  ❑ **On First Use:** Install feature on-demand

  ❑ **Self-healing:** Damaged or missing program files are replaced

  ❑ **Rollback:** Automatically remove a failed installation

❑ You activated Office over the Internet. But you could activate by using a telephone.

❑ Your instructor created an Administrative Installation Point from where you installed Office.

- You learned that if your organization has deployed Active Directory they could use Group Policy to trigger the installation of Office:

  - Assign Office to a computer

  - Assign Office to a user

  - Publish Office to a user

- You learned how to troubleshoot failed Office installations with the log files that are created during the installation.

6

Key Terms

First Use — Microsoft technology that permits an application or feature to be installed on demand.

Group Policy — Policy used by Active Directory to manage the settings on desktop computers. Used to trigger the installation of software.

hardware hash — A value created by combining hardware identifiers and applying the hashing algorithm. Used with Microsoft's activation process.

legacy operating system — An operating system that remains in use after an organization installs new operating systems. Operating systems prior to Windows 2000.

msi — File extension for files to be deployed with the Installer.

package — Information and programs needed to install an application.

rollback — Return to a previous stable state.

self-healing — Microsoft technology that permits an application or feature to be reinstalled when a component file is missing or damaged.

Review Questions

1. Which of the following would be considered a legacy operating system? (Choose all that apply.)

   a. Windows 95
   b. Windows 98
   c. Windows Millennium
   d. Windows NT
   e. Windows XP

2. Which of the following can be determined by observing the My Computer Properties dialog box? (Choose all that apply.)

   a. processor speed
   b. installed memory

c. Windows operating system version

d. available free space

e. screen resolution

3. The _____ is a component of the Windows XP operating system that provides a standard method for installing applications.

   a. Windows Program service

   b. Windows MSI service

   c. Windows Installer service

   d. Windows Setup service

4. When Installer uses _____ , it creates an equivalent undo operation for each operation it performs.

   a. transactional operations

   b. On First Use

   c. self-healing

   d. rollback

5. _____ support(s) on-demand installation of features.

   a. Transactional operations

   b. On First Use

   c. Self-healing

   d. Rollback

6. Which alternative does the Installer permit? (Choose all that apply.)

   a. Run from My Computer

   b. Run from CD

   c. Installed On First Use

   d. Not installed

7. About how much free disk space is required to permit the copy of the compressed Office files to a hard drive?

   a. 200 MB

   b. 240 MB

   c. 270 MB

   d. 300 MB

8. Which task is performed by the Installer? (Choose all that apply.)

   a. copying files to the hard disk

   b. making additions and updates to the registry

   c. creating shortcuts on the desktop

   d. displaying dialog boxes to query for user installation preferences

9. Which characteristic describes the On First Use feature? (Choose all that apply.)

   a. application shows up on menu

   b. installed from Add or Remove Programs

   c. installed after clicking on the program shortcut

   d. installed after clicking on the program extension

10. The Installer provides a feature called _____ , which permits an automatic repair when it detects a corrupt component.

   a. transactional operations

   b. On First Use

   c. self-healing

   d. rollback

11. What extension is used to identify Installer packages?

   a. .pck

   b. .ins

   c. .msi

   d. .pk

12. Which of the following is a characteristic of product activation? (Choose all that apply.)

   a. antipiracy technology

   b. activate Office on one computer only once

   c. process generates a hardware hash

   d. can be done over the Internet

   e. can be done by using a telephone

13. The _____ feature allows graceful recovery from a power failure.

   a. Transactional operations

   b. On First Use

   c. self-sealing

   d. rollback

14. Which characteristic describes Administrative Installation Points? (Choose all that apply.)

   a. requires a volume license agreement

   b. started by running Setup with a switch

6

c. stores compressed files on the file server

d. permits installs over a network

15. Under which situations would using Group Policy to deploy Office be a good choice? (Choose all that apply.)

    a. small- or medium-sized organizations that have deployed Active Directory

    b. organizations that compromise a single geographic area

    c. organizations with inconsistent hardware and software configurations on both desktop computers and file servers

    d. organizations with consistent hardware and software configurations on both desktop computers and file servers

16. Organizations use Group Policy to manage software for users who belong to _____ .

    a. Group Policy objects

    b. Group Policy units

    c. Organizational Units

    d. Organizational Objects

17. In what way can you install and manage Office applications by Group Policy? (Choose all that apply.)

    a. assign Office to computers

    b. assign Office to users

    c. publish Office to computers

    d. publish Office to users

18. Assigned applications are _____ , which means the Installer will reinstall an application removed by a user.

    a. flexible

    b. resilient

    c. hardy

    d. pliant

19. The log files created by the installation of Office are stored in the _____ folder for the admin01 user.

    a. C:\Settings\admin01\Local Settings\Temp

    b. C:\Settings\admin01\Local Settings\Temp

    c. C:\Documents and Settings\admin01\Local Settings\Temp

    d. C:\Documents and Settings\admin01\Local\Temp

20. What is the return value for a failed action in the Installer log file?

a. 0

b. 1

c. 2

d. 3

CASE PROJECTS

Case 6-1: Installing Microsoft Office 2003 for the Computers in a Workgroup

You are a consultant working as a desktop support technician for a small nonprofit organization. You are assisting a network technician with the installation of 10 new computers with Windows XP Professional installed in a peer-to-peer network. These computers will meet the requirements for Office 2003. Your users connect to the Internet through a single computer with Internet Connection Sharing (ICS) installed.

You have been tasked to develop a detailed installation plan to meet the varied requirements of these groups of employees and volunteers:

❑ Two managers who require Microsoft Word, Excel, and PowerPoint

❑ One secretary who requires Microsoft Word, Excel, Publisher, and PowerPoint

❑ Three counselors who require Microsoft Word

❑ Twenty-four part-time volunteers who require Microsoft Word

Your installation plan must present all the viable options to install Office for the personnel that will be using these computers. Consider these items in your written plan:

❑ PC requirements

❑ Installer features including On First Use

❑ Local installation sources

❑ CD-ROM versus network compressed images

❑ Activation

Case 6-2: Installing Microsoft Office 2003 for the Computers in a Large Organization

You are a desktop support technician. Your network consists of a Windows 2003 Active Directory domain with 10 servers, including application and database servers and 500 computers running Windows XP Professional. Your users connect to the Internet through a firewall.

You have been tasked to develop a detailed plan to install a common set of Office applications for all employees. Your plan must present all the viable options to install Office for the personnel who will be using these computers. Consider these items in your plan:

- PC requirements
- CD-ROM versus network compressed images versus Administrative Installation Points
- Activation
- Assigning versus publishing

Case 6-3: Troubleshooting Microsoft Office 2003 Installations Using Log Files

You are a desktop support technician. Your network consists of a Windows 2003 Active Directory domain with 10 servers, including application and database servers and 500 computers running Windows XP Professional.

Your supervisor has asked you to develop a list of factors that you consider critical to the process of using log files to troubleshoot Office installation problems. You must provide a comprehensive list of the items to examine.

7

CONFIGURING AND TROUBLESHOOTING OPERATING SYSTEM FEATURES

After reading this chapter and completing the exercises, you will be able to:

♦ Configure operating system features

♦ Troubleshoot with operating system features

Microsoft XP and Microsoft Office 2003 provide a number of features that your users may find useful as they use these two products. To succeed as a DST, you must continually strive to improve your troubleshooting skills.

This chapter starts with the features related to the Windows XP operating system. You must be prepared to assist your users with the capability to backup and restore files, manage the performance settings of the operating system, and configure settings to run older programs.

The chapter closes with a section on troubleshooting. You need to add a number of skills to your troubleshooting tool kit: temporarily log on to a user's computer using an account with the privileges of an administrator, obtain a glimpse into the performance of your computer, and work with Windows File Protection. Microsoft provides a number of troubleshooters to aid in the resolution of known problems. You will need to learn to use these troubleshooters.

RESOLVING ISSUES RELATED TO OPERATING SYSTEM FEATURES

Windows XP provides a number of features that can be used with Microsoft Office 2003. You will be learning how to assist your users with these features.

You might already recognize the importance of backing up files, especially your My Documents folder. By learning how to back up and restore folders and files, you will be able to recover files that were accidentally deleted. When you make changes to your computer, by adding a device or installing software, the computer may malfunction. You may need to recover a computer by restoring a previous state after changes have been made. Your users will expect that you can address their questions regarding the performance of their computers. If you need to run an older program, you may need to know how to "tweak" Windows XP to run the older program.

Backing Up and Restoring Files

The Backup Utility helps you make a copy of the files on your hard disk. In the event of the loss of one or more files, you can use the backup copy to restore the lost or damaged data. You will want to train your users to back up the important files on their hard drive.

To start the Backup Utility, run All Programs, Accessories, System Tools, Backup. The first two buttons, as shown in Figure 7-1, are Backup Wizard (Advanced) and Restore Wizard (Advanced). They back up or restore the files and the configuration of your computer. The third button starts the Automated System Recovery wizard, which prepares a backup of the critical system configuration files that can be activated when the operating system is reinstalled to repair a damaged operating system. Because the use of the Automated System Recovery wizard is beyond the scope of the 70-272 exam, this topic will not be presented. You will learn to use the first two options to protect user and system data.

In the Windows XP Home Edition, the Backup Utility is not installed. You can gain practice in using the Help and Support Center by searching for install xp backup. The installation instructions are located in the Microsoft Knowledge Base article as HOW TO: Install Backup from the CD-ROM in Windows XP Home Edition.

To start the Backup wizard, click the Backup Wizard (Advanced) icon and click the Next button. From the What to Back Up screen (see Figure 7-2), you have three choices:

- **Back up everything on this computer:** Does not permit any choices.
- **Back up selected files, drives, or network data:** Permits a choice on which folders and files to back up.

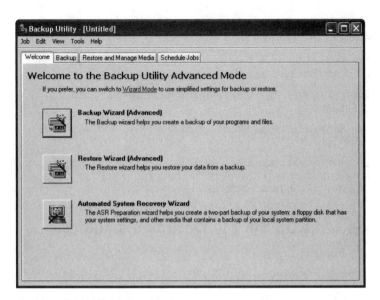

Figure 7-1   Backup Utility

■ **Only back up the System State data:** Backs up all of the data that is relevant to the Windows XP operating system. By checking the System State, you have requested that the Registry, the files under Windows File Protection, and the boot files be backed up. The **Registry** contains the information to configure the system. **Windows File Protection** files are protected system files for the Windows XP operating system. The **boot files** are the files needed to start Microsoft Windows.

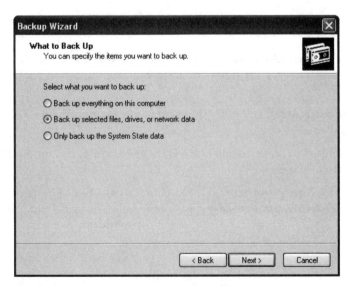

Figure 7-2   Back up selected files, drives, or network data

If your organization does not use magnetic tape for backup, here are a number of effective options that you may want to consider:

- **Removable USB drive:** Functions as a removable hard disk. Removable flash drives are available in capacities up to 1 GB.

- **External hard drive:** Connected by USB with capacities that match the internal hard drives.

- **CD-ROM writer:** Available with capacities to 740 MB. Media has a modest cost.

- **Second internal hard drive:** Available with capacities that match internal hard drives. With costs approaching $1 per GB, my personal choice is a second internal hard drive.

Activity 7-1: Backing Up the My Documents Folder

Time Required: 15 minutes

Objective: Use the Backup Utility to back up the My Documents folder.

Description: In this activity, you will practice backing up a folder on your hard drive. You are practicing using the Backup wizard because you may need to conduct one-on-one training for your users. Also, you may need to answer your users' questions about backing up folders and files.

1. Log on to your computer using the user name **admin01** and password of **Password1**.

2. Click **Start**, point to **All Programs**, point to **Accessories**, point to **System Tools,** and click **Backup**.

3. If needed, uncheck the **Always start in wizard mode** check box and click the **Advanced Mode** link.

4. Click the **Backup Wizard (Advanced)** icon, click the **Next** button, click the **Backup selected files, drives, or network data** option button and click the **Next** button.

5. Check the **My Documents** check box (either one), as shown in Figure 7-3, and click the **Next** button.

6. Click the **Browse** button. If needed, click the **Cancel** button to ignore the Please insert a disk into drive A: message.

7. Double-click the **My Computer** icon, double-click **Local Disk (C:)**, and then type **Backup My Documents** *mm-dd-yyyy* (where *mm-dd-yyyy* is today's date). Your screen should resemble Figure 7-4. Click the **Save** button.

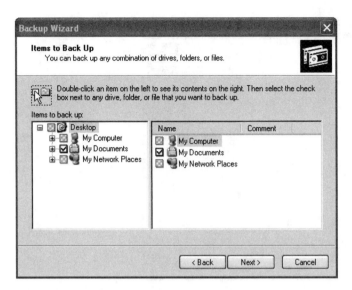

Figure 7-3   Items to Back Up screen

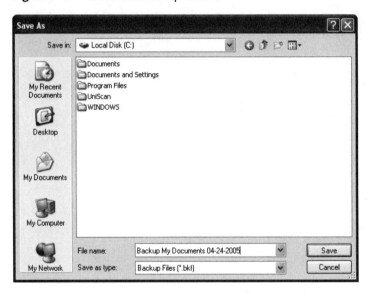

Figure 7-4   Saving a backup

8. Review the drive destination and name, as shown in Figure 7-5, click the **Next** button, and click the **Finish** button.

9. Wait for the backup to complete, as shown in Figure 7-6.

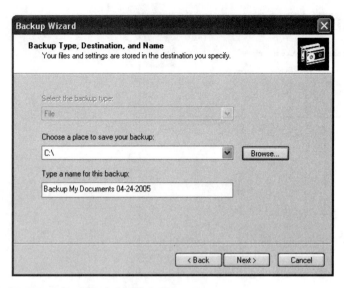

Figure 7-5   Backup job information

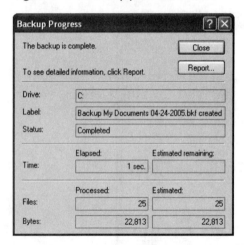

Figure 7-6   Backup progress

10. Click the **Report** button and review the detailed report in Notepad.

11. Close the Notepad window, click the **Close** button, and close the Backup Utility window.

12. Write a brief explanation describing how you might assist a user with folder backups in your project log.

Restoring Files

From the Backup Utility, you can select the Restore Wizard (Advanced) button to start the restore process. You will have the opportunity to select the check boxes for the items that you want to restore, as depicted in Figure 7-7.

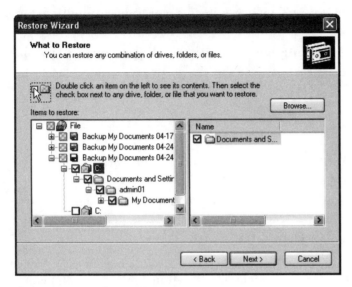

Figure 7-7   What to Restore screen

There are three choices for the destination of the restore:

- **Original location:** Restore to original folder(s). Useful for restoring lost or damaged files.

- **Alternate location:** Restore to a folder you specify with the original folder structure. Useful if you need some of the files but do not want to overwrite the current files.

- **Single Folder:** Restore the files to a folder and ignore the existing folder structure in the backup. Useful when you are searching for a file by content or when you do not know its location.

ACTIVITY

Activity 7-2: Restoring the My Documents Folder to an Alternate Location

Time Required: 15 minutes

Objective: Use the Backup Utility to restore the My Documents folder.

Description: In this activity, you will practice restoring a folder to an alternate location on your hard drive. From the folder, you will be able to see the restored copies of the files. You are practicing using the restore because you may need to conduct one-on-one training for your users. Also, you may need to answer your users' questions about restoring folders and files.

1. If necessary, log on to your computer using the user name **admin01** and password of **Password1**.

2. Click **Start**, click **My Computer**, and click the **My Documents** hyperlink.

NOTE

If the Temp folder exists, right-click the **Temp** folder, click **Delete**, and click the **Yes** button.

3. Right-click in the white space, point to **New**, click **Folder**, type **Temp** over New Folder, and press **Enter**.

4. Click **Start**, point to **All Programs**, point to **Accessories**, point to **System Tools**, and click **Backup**.

5. Click the **Restore and Manage Media** tab.

6. Locate and double-click the **Backup My Documents *mm-dd-yyyy*** (where *mm-dd-yyyy* is the date on which the backup file was created in Activity 7-1) entry under Backup Identification Label.

7. Check the check box next to the C: folder in the left pane.

NOTE

You will be restoring the files to an alternate location. From the alternate location, you would be able to review each file prior to copying over the original.

8. Click the **Restore Files to** drop-down arrow and click **Alternate location**.

9. Click the **Browse** button, expand **My Documents**, click **Temp**, and click the **OK** button.

10. Click the **Start Restore** button and click the **OK** button.

11. Wait for the restore to complete.

12. Click the **Report** button and review the detailed report in Notepad.

13. Close the Notepad window, click the **Close** button, and close the Backup Utility window.

14. Double-click the **Temp** folder, double-click the **Documents and Settings** folder, double-click the **admin01** folder, double-click **admin01**'s **Documents**, then review the documents, which are a copy of the My Documents folder.

15. Close the documents window.

16. Write a brief explanation describing how you might assist a user with folder restores in your project log.

Managing Performance

The visual impact of Windows is enhanced by the various visual effects that are available. Many of these custom options change the aesthetics of the items displayed. For example, you can choose to display shadows under menus, which gives the appearance of a 3-D effect, or smoothes the edges of screen fonts for a laptop display. In addition, Windows automatically allocates processor time and computer memory according to the default settings.

Activity 7-3: Adjusting Visual Effects

Time Required: 15 minutes

Objective: Explore visual effects using Performance options.

Description: In this activity, you will practice selecting the options for visual effects. You will cycle through the various options and observe the visual changes. Before trying the custom changes on your own, you will observe the visual changes for the Show shadows under mouse pointer option. You are practicing customizing the visual effects so that you can answer your users' questions about the default and custom visual effects on their computers.

1. If necessary, log on to your computer using the user name **admin01** and password of **Password1**.

2. Click **Start**, right-click **My Computer**, click **Properties**, click the **Advanced** tab, and click the **Settings** button under Performance. Your screen should resemble Figure 7-8.

3. Click the **Adjust for best appearance** option button. Notice the changes, if any, to the check boxes under Custom.

4. Click the **Adjust for best performance** option button.

5. Notice all of the check boxes under Custom are checked.

6. Click the **Let Windows choose what's best for my computer** option button.

7. Click the **Custom** option button.

8. Uncheck the **Show shadows under mouse pointer** check box and click the **Apply** button. Notice the mouse pointer has changed from a 3-D look.

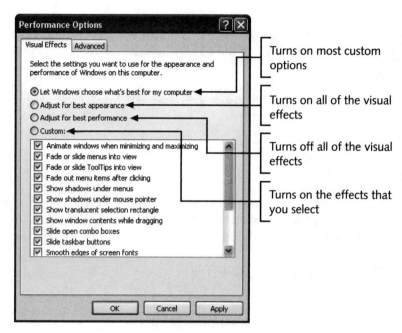

Figure 7-8   Visual Effects tab

9. Check the **Show shadows under mouse pointer** check box and click the **Apply** button. Notice the mouse pointer has changed back to a 3-D look.

10. Repeat this process for any additional items that look interesting.

11. Click the **Let Windows choose what's best for my computer** option button and click the **OK** button.

12. Write a brief description describing how you might assist a user on how to set visual effects in your project log.

13. Close all open windows and log off your computer.

Adjusting Advanced Options

Choosing the Advanced tab of the Performance Options dialog box allows you to balance system performance for the processor, memory usage, and virtual memory, as discussed in the following list:

- **Processor scheduling:** As you may know, programs running as **foreground programs** respond to the actions issued by the user. **Background services**, such as anti-virus programs, operate without user interaction while the user is working on other tasks. If your desktop runs a number of background programs and applications are infrequently accessed from the desktop, choose the Background services option button.

- **Memory usage:** By default, programs use a greater share of memory than the System cache. A **system cache** preloads data from the hard disk in anticipation that the data will be needed, which speeds access to data on the hard drive. If you use the computer to share a large number of folders, perhaps in a workgroup, choose the System cache option button.

- **Virtual memory: Virtual memory** is hard disk space that is used by Windows as if it was additional RAM. Windows normally determines the size of the **paging file**, the area on the hard disk set aside for virtual memory.

Because you and your users run applications, Processor scheduling and Memory usage are optimized when Programs, the default, is selected, as shown in Figure 7-9.

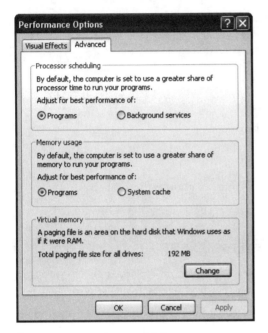

Figure 7-9   Advanced tab

By selecting the Change button, the Virtual Memory dialog box is displayed, as shown in Figure 7-10. If you have multiple physical hard drives, you could gain performance by splitting the paging file across multiple drives.

The default behavior is to permit Windows to set the size of the paging file. For a computer with 128 MB of memory, the default minimum allocation will be 192 MB, or 1.5 times the amount of memory. The default maximum allocation will be 384 MB or 3.0 times the amount of memory. If you add memory to your computer, you may need to adjust these memory settings.

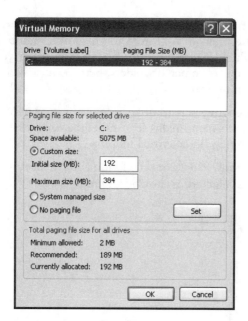

Figure 7-10   Virtual Memory dialog box

There are two additional options available:

- **System managed size:** Let Windows choose the best size.

- **No paging file:** Select to remove the paging file. Use this when the existing paging file is corrupt.

At the bottom of the screen, there is an additional set of entries, as discussed in the following list:

- **Minimum allowed:** Minimum required size is always 2 MB

- **Recommended:** Always approximately 1.5 times the available memory (Always about 3 MB shy)

- **Currently allocated:** Total paging file size for all drives

IN THE WORKPLACE

How much memory do you need? Microsoft recommends a minimum of 128 MB for Microsoft Office 2003. For each office application you intend to run, add 8 MB. However, there are Knowledge Base articles on the Microsoft Web site that suggest 265 MB as a minimum.

At the time this was written, most computers were available with 256 to 512 MB of memory. Computers in this range should run Microsoft Windows XP and Microsoft Office 2003 without any problems.

ACTIVITY

Activity 7-4: Managing Performance with System Properties

Time Required: 15 minutes

Objective: Review the settings for processor scheduling and memory usage, and configure virtual memory.

Description: In this activity, you will practice selecting the options for managing performance. You will observe the default program settings for setting processor scheduling and memory usage. You are practicing customizing the virtual memory so that you can optimize virtual memory settings and answer your user's questions about the use of virtual memory on their computers.

7

1. If necessary, log on to your computer using the user name **admin01** and password **Password1**.

2. Click **Start**, right-click **My Computer**, and click **Properties**.

3. Under Computer, locate and record the amount of memory (RAM) in your project log. _99 GB_

4. Click the **Advanced** tab and click the **Settings** button under Performance. Click the **Advanced** tab.

5. If the Programs option button under Processor scheduling is not selected, click it.

6. If the Programs option button under Memory usage is not selected, click it.

7. Write a brief description on how to set processor scheduling and memory usage in your project log.

8. Calculate 50% of the amount of memory that you wrote down in your project log for Step 3. Add this calculated amount to the amount of memory that you wrote down giving the minimum amount of virtual memory. _1.5 GB_

9. Double the minimum amount of virtual memory giving the maximum amount of virtual memory.

10. Under Virtual memory, click the **Change** button.

11. If necessary, click the **Custom size** option button.

12. Type the minimum amount of virtual memory that you calculated in Step 8 into the Initial size (MB) text box.

13. Type the maximum amount of virtual memory that you calculated in Step 9 into the **Maximum size (MB)** text box.

14. Click the **Set** button, and click the three **OK** buttons.

15. Write a brief description of how you might assist a user to set virtual memory in your project log.

16. Log off the computer.

Making Older Programs Run Using Compatibility Mode

The vast majority of existing programs run properly on Windows XP. To assist your users to run an older game or a program written for an earlier version of Windows, you should configure the settings on the Compatibility tab, as shown in Figure 7-11. The Compatibility tab is functional only for programs that were designed to run with earlier versions of Windows or MS-DOS.

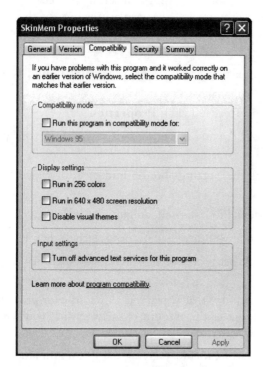

Figure 7-11   Compatibility tab

Let's say that you were having a problem with a program that was originally designed to run on Windows 98. You could set the compatibility mode for the program to Windows 98 and try running the program again. If you are successful, the program will start in that mode each time that you access it.

The Compatibility tab also allows you to try different settings, such as the following:

- **Run in 256 colors:** Sets the display color depth to 256 colors while the program is running. You will want to use this if you are experiencing problems with the colors that are being displayed by the program.

- **Run in 640 x 480 screen resolution:** Adjusts the screen resolution to 640 x 480 pixels. Use this if you are experiencing problems with video display related to the window size.

- **Disable visual themes:** Prevents visual themes from being applied to the program. You will want to use this if you are experiencing problems with menus or with buttons on the title bar.

- **Turn off advanced text services for this program:** Allows advanced text services, such as speech recognition, to be turned off. Use this if the program uses unsupported speech recognition.

Activity 7-5: Configuring Compatibility Mode Settings for a MS-DOS Program

Time Required: 15 minutes

Objective: Set compatibility mode settings for a MS-DOS program.

Description: In this activity, you will configure the compatibility mode settings for a MS-DOS program provided by your instructor. You are practicing using the compatibility mode feature to run an older program so that you can answer your users' questions about making older programs run on Windows XP.

1. If necessary, log on to your computer using the user name **admin01** and password **Password1**.

2. Insert the disk with the MS-DOS program provided by your instructor into the floppy drive.

3. Click **Start**, click **My Computer**, double-click **3½ Floppy (A:)**, right-click the program file, and click **Copy**.

4. Click the **Address** drop-down menu, click **Local Disk (C:)**, right-click the **Program Files** folder, and click **Paste**.

5. Double-click the **Program Files** folder, right-click the program file, click **Properties**, and click the **Compatibility** tab.

6. Check the **Run this program in compatibility mode for** check box and click the **OK** button.

7. Double-click the program file. If you have problems running the program, contact your instructor.

8. Close all open windows.

9. Write a brief explanation of how you could run MS-DOS programs requiring compatibility mode settings in your project log.

Activity 7-6: Configuring Compatibility Mode Settings for a Windows Program

Time Required: 15 minutes

Objective: Set compatibility mode settings for an earlier Windows program.

Description: In this activity, you will configure the compatibility mode settings for a Windows program provided by your instructor. You are practicing using the compatibility mode feature to run an older program so that you can answer your users' questions about making older programs run on Windows XP.

1. If necessary, log on to your computer using the user name **admin01** and password **Password1**.

2. Insert the disk with the Windows program provided by your instructor into the floppy drive.

3. Click **Start**, click **My Computer**, double-click **3½ Floppy (A:)**, right-click the program file, and click **Copy**.

4. Click the **Address** drop-down menu, click **Local Disk (C:)**, right-click the **Program Files** folder, and click **Paste**.

5. Double-click the **Program Files** folder, right-click the program file, click **Properties**, and click the **Compatibility** tab.

6. Check the **Run this program in compatibility mode for** check box and click the **OK** button.

7. Double-click the program file. If you have problems running the program, contact your instructor.

8. Close the program window.

9. Right-click the program file, click **Properties**, click the **Compatibility** tab, check the **Run in 256 colors** check box, and click the **OK** button.

10. Double-click the program file. If you have problems running the program, contact your instructor.

11. Close the program window.

12. Repeat Steps 9 through 11 for **Run in 640 x 480 screen resolution** and **Disable visual themes**.

13. Write a brief explanation of how you could run an older Windows program requiring compatibility mode settings in your project log.

14. Log off the computer.

TROUBLESHOOTING TOOLS

You might know that a troubleshooter is a person trained and skilled in resolving problems. You can enhance your value to your organization by polishing your troubleshooting skills with the following troubleshooting tools:

- **Run as:** Use this tool to run a program with elevated privileges.
- **Task Manager:** Use this tool to manage applications and processes.
- **Windows File Protection:** Use this tool to maintain operating system files at correct versions.
- **Safe Mode:** Use this tool to correct operating system startup problems.
- **Recovery console:** Use this tool to use when Safe Mode fails to correct a problem.
- **Windows XP Troubleshooter:** Use this tool to use to resolve problems known to Microsoft.

7

Using Run As

Sometimes, end users encounter situations in which they are aware that their computer has one or more errors and yet they are unsure as to the exact text of the errors. To help them, you can use the Run As command to access the Event Viewer while they are still signed on. By accessing the Event Viewer, you can determine what errors have previously occurred on their computer. Such determination will lead to the resolution of the conflict that caused the error.

ACTIVITY

Activity 7-7: Using Run As with Administrator Rights

Time Required: 15 minutes

Objective: Run a program requiring administrative rights from an account with limited rights.

Description: In this activity, you will practice using the Run As feature to run a program requiring administrative privileges. By mastering the use of this feature, you will be able to easily troubleshoot your users' problems without needing them to log off their user accounts.

1. Log on to your computer using the user name **user01** and password **Password1**.
2. Click **Start**, click **Control Panel**, double-click **Administrative Tools**, and double-click **Computer Management**.
3. Click **Device Manager**, read the text of the message, and click the **OK** button.
4. Close the Computer Management window.

5. In the Administrative Tools folder, right-click **Computer Management**, and click **Run as**. Your screen should resemble Figure 7-12. Click the **The following user:** option button, type **classroom\admin01** in the User name text box, type **Password1** in the Password text box, and click the **OK** button.

Figure 7-12   Selecting a user

6. Click **Device Manager** and notice that the Device Manager is displayed without the message encountered in Step 3.

7. Close all open windows.

8. Write a brief explanation of how you could run programs requiring administrative rights while logging on to the system with an administrator user account in your project log.

9. Log off your computer.

Managing Tasks with Task Manager

You can use Task Manager to monitor currently running applications and processes on the computer. By using Task Manager, you can selectively stop a hung application or process. This will help you get an end user out of a jam and back into productivity.

You can start Task Manager in one of three ways:

- Press Ctrl+Alt+Delete, and click Task Manager
- Press Ctrl+Shift+Esc
- Right-click an empty area of the taskbar, and click Task Manager

When you open Task Manager, there are four tabs, as shown in Figure 7–13. With these tabs, you can select to control applications and processes as well as view system and network performance.

Figure 7-13 Task Manager

The following sections discuss each in turn.

NOTE A fifth tab, called Users, is available to you so long as the computer system you are working on is in a Windows Workgroup or is a standalone system with no networking capabilities installed. This tab is not available to computer systems in a domain network.

Applications Tab

From the Applications tab, you can determine if a program is not responding or hung. You can kill the program by selecting the program and clicking the End Task button. From the remaining two buttons, you can switch to a listed program or start a new program.

Processes Tab

You can use the Processes tab, as shown in Figure 7-14, to view the names of processes running on the computer and display processor (CPU) and memory usage (Mem Usage). You can use this information to troubleshoot problems with programs. You can sort each column of data by clicking on the column name.

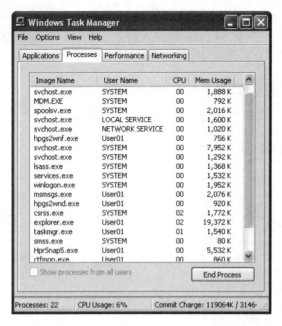

Figure 7-14   Processes tab

To troubleshoot your computer, you could determine which programs were using the most processor or memory. A program with an abnormally high CPU value could be a hung program. Or, a program with an extremely large amount of memory usage might be a program with a **memory leak** (memory usage of a process grows without bound). To stop a process, select the program and click the End Process button.

By killing a process, you could render your computer unstable or lose valuable data in memory!

NOTE

Performance Tab

From the Performance tab, as shown in Figure 7-15, you can get a quick view of your computer's CPU Usage and Page File Usage. Also, you can see a variety of counts on various other items for your computer which are of lesser value for troubleshooting. A high CPU usage, consistently more than 90%, is an indication that the processor speed is inadequate. A high rate of page file activity is an indication that the computer needs additional RAM memory.

Networking Tab

You can use the Networking tab, as shown in Figure 7-16, to view a graph of network activity related to the network card in the computer. The Networking tab is displayed only when a network card is present.

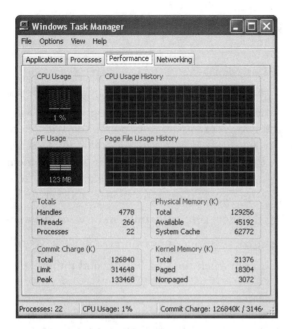

Figure 7-15   Performance tab

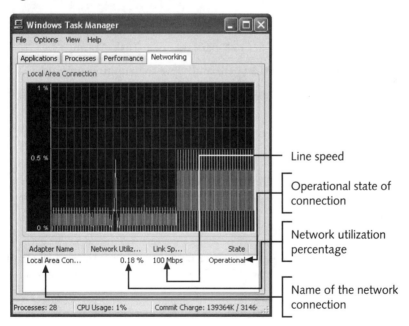

Figure 7-16   Networking tab

Activity 7-8: Controlling Processes with Task Manager

Time Required: 15 minutes

Objective: Manage processes with Task Manager.

Description: In this activity, you will practice controlling processes with the Task Manager. You will start a 16-bit program (winhelp a Windows 3.1 legacy program). You will view the running programs and verify that the two programs are responding. You will determine the relationship between the ntvdm, woewxec, and winhelp programs by terminating the respective processes. You will check the performance of the processor, RAM memory, and network activity. You are practicing using the Task Manager so that you can troubleshoot your user's problems related to applications, processes, performance, and networking.

1. Log on to your computer using the user name **admin01** and password **Password1**.

2. Click **Start**, point to **All Programs**, point to **Accessories**, and click **WordPad**.

3. Click **Start**, click **Run**, type **winhelp**, click the **OK** button, and minimize the Windows Help window.

Running winhelp starts the 16-bit version of Windows Help, an old Help program, which will be viewed as a black window. You will kill the application in a later step.

4. Right-click an empty spot on the task bar and click **Task Manager**.

5. If necessary, click the **Applications** tab and view the running programs.

6. Click the **Processes** tab to view the active processes. Your screen should resemble Figure 7-17.

7. Locate the ntvdm.exe, wowexec.exe, and winhelp.exe processes (circled in Figure 7-17).

The program ntvdm.exe (NT Virtual Machine) creates a virtual DOS machine to run DOS programs. The wowexec.exe (windows on windows executive) program creates the environment that is required to run 16-bit (Windows 3.1) programs.

8. Click the **winhelp.exe** process, click the **End Process** button, read the caution message, and click the **Yes** button. Note that the wowexec.exe and ntvdm.exe processes remain.

9. Click the **ntvdm.exe** process, click the **End Process** button, read the caution message, and click the **Yes** button. Note the wowexec.exe and ntvdm.exe processes were removed.

10. Click the **Performance** tab and view the CPU Usage and CPU Usage History.

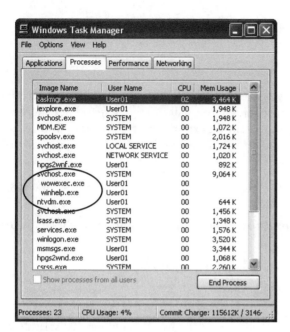

Figure 7-17   Active processes

11. Click the **Windows Task Manager** title bar and drag it with your mouse to another location.

12. Observe the CPU spike when you moved the Windows Task Manager window.

13. Click the **Networking** tab and view the Network Utilization.

14. Close all open windows.

15. In your project log, write a brief explanation of how you could use the Task Manager to kill a program with a memory leak or a program loop. Write a brief explanation of how you could use the Task Manager to determine if a computer had sufficient memory and adequate processor cycles.

Windows File Protection (WFP)

When programs are installed, the Windows system files must not be overwritten. These files are used by the operating system and by application programs. Protecting these files prevents problems with applications and the operating system. Fortunately, Windows File Protection (WFP) prevents application installations from replacing critical Windows system files.

You can use the System File Checker to scan all protected files to verify their versions. If System File Checker discovers that a protected file has been overwritten, it retrieves the correct version of the file from the **cache folder** (folder that holds needed system files) or the Windows CD-ROM and replaces the incorrect file.

ACTIVITY

Activity 7-9: Checking System Files

Time Required: 30 minutes

Objective: Use the System File Checker to verify the integrity of Windows system files.

Description: In this activity, you will practice checking system files to determine if any Windows system files have been overwritten. You will run the System File Checker to build the cache folder and verify that the system files are the correct version. You are practicing running the System File Checker so that you can resolve your users' problems related to overwritten system files.

1. If necessary, log on to your computer using the user name **admin01** and password **Password1**.

2. Click **Start**, point to **All Programs**, point to **Accessories**, and click **Command Prompt**.

3. Type **sfc /scannow** at the command prompt and press **Enter**.

4. Minimize the Command Prompt window.

5. If requested, insert the Windows XP Professional CD-ROM, click the **Retry** button, and click the **Exit** link on the Welcome to Microsoft Windows XP splash screen.

6. Wait for the files to be verified.

7. Close all open windows.

8. In your project log, write a brief description of how you could use the System File Checker to verify that the Windows system files are the correct version.

Using the Windows Advanced Options Menu

Safe Mode allows you to start a computer with only basic files, services, and drivers. The drivers loaded include the keyboard, mouse, monitor, hard drive, and **base video** (video with minimal resolution, 640 x 480 pixels and color depth, 16 colors).

Often, you can resolve or troubleshoot startup problems from Safe Mode. For instance, you can solve these problems:

- Recover from a system crash
- Replace a failing device driver for a display adapter
- Restore the display settings to a viewable resolution when the resolution is not supported by the monitor
- Back out of a misconfigured setting for a network adapter that keeps the computer from starting properly

You can also select a number of useful options to troubleshoot common problems:

- **Safe Mode:** This starts the operating system with only basic files, services, and drivers.

- **Safe Mode with Networking:** This is the same as Safe Mode but adds network support. If the suspected system failure is due to a failed update on a network card driver, this will not be a good choice to make.

- **Safe Mode with Command Prompt:** This is the same as Safe Mode but starts with a command prompt only.

- **Enable Boot Logging:** This creates a log of all startup events in a file.

- **Enable VGA Mode:** This starts the system in 640 x 480 (VGA mode). Use Enable VGA mode when the system display is set to a mode that the monitor cannot display.

- **Last Known Good Configuration (your most recent settings that worked):** This starts your computer using the system configuration that was saved immediately after the logon was completed. Use the Last Known Good Configuration to recover from startup problems. For example, the system appears unstable after a new application or device is added.

- **Start Windows Normally:** This starts Windows XP normally.

- **Reboot:** This restarts the computer.

The Directory Services Restore mode (Windows domain controllers only) and Debugging mode are beyond the requirements for the MCDST examination and will not be presented.

Activity 7-10: Using the Safe Mode Options

Time Required: 15 minutes

Objective: Practice using Safe Mode to recover from system failures.

Description: In this activity, you will practice using the Safe Mode options. You will practice starting your computer with the previous system configuration. You will start your computer in Safe Mode. From Safe Mode, you can correct problems with device drivers. You are practicing using the Safe Mode so that you can resolve your users' problems related to system changes that have rendered the computer unusable.

1. Turn off your computer with the Windows XP CD-ROM in the CD-ROM drive.

2. Power on your computer and wait for the Power On Self-Test (POST) to complete.

3. Prior to the appearance of the Windows XP splash screen as shown in Figure 7-18, press the **F8** key.

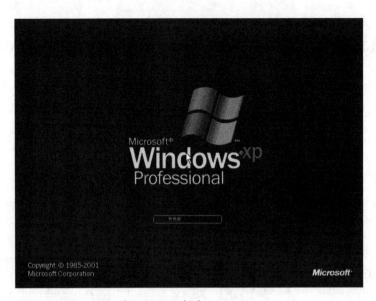

Figure 7-18   Windows XP splash screen

4. Wait for Windows Advanced Options Menu to be displayed, as shown in Figure 7-19.

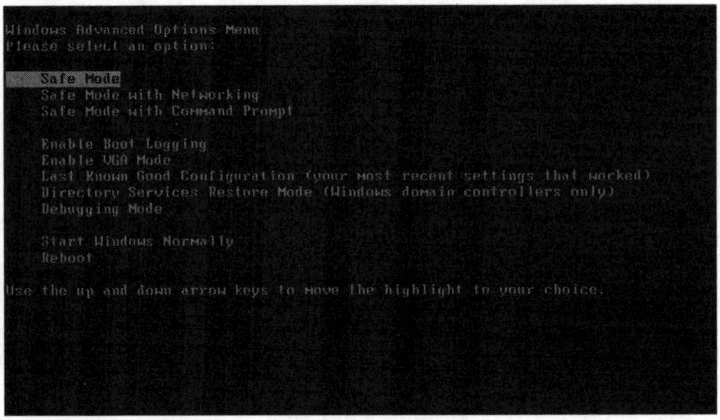

Figure 7-19   Advanced Options Menu screen

5. Press the **up** or **down arrow** until Last Known Good Configuration (your most recent settings that worked) is highlighted and press the **Enter** key.

6. Log on to your computer using the user name **user01** and password **Password1**.

7. Shut down and power off the computer.

8. Power on your computer and wait for the POST to complete.

9. Prior to the appearance of the Windows XP splash screen, press the **F8** key.

10. Wait for Windows Advanced Options Menu to be displayed.

11. If necessary, press the **up arrow** until Safe Mode is highlighted and press the **Enter** key.

12. Log on to your computer using the user name **student** and password **Password1**.

13. Click the **Yes** button. Observe that you are logged on in Basic Video mode with a message displayed in each corner.

14. Log off your computer.

15. In your project log, write a brief description of how you could use the Last Known Good Configuration or Safe Mode to resolve a configuration problem that appeared prior to the next logon.

Using the Recovery Console

With the Recovery Console, you can view disk volumes, format drives, read and write data on a local drive, and perform many other administrative tasks. The Recovery Console is particularly useful if you need to repair your system by copying a file from a floppy disk or CD-ROM to your hard drive. Also, you can reconfigure services or disable devices that might prevent your computer from starting properly.

Activity 7-11: Recovering a Computer with the Recovery Console

Time Required: 20 minutes

Objective: Practice using the Recovery Console

Description: In this activity, you will practice running the Recovery Console. You will boot the Windows XP Installation CD. After starting the Recovery Console, you will practice using various commands. You are practicing running the Recovery Console so that you can resolve your users' problems when Safe Mode has failed.

1. Your computer should be turned off with the Windows XP Professional CD-ROM in the drive.

2. Power on your computer and wait for the POST to complete.

If needed, you can start the Windows Installation from the first installation disk.

3. When Press any key to boot from CD appears, press the **spacebar**. If you miss the Press any key to boot from CD prompt, turn off your computer and try again.

4. Wait for the Windows Setup to load files to memory.

5. When the Welcome to Setup screen is displayed, as shown in Figure 7-20, press the **R** key.

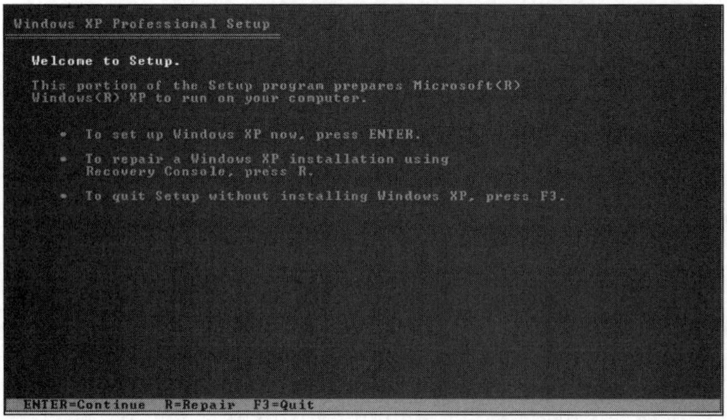

Figure 7-20 Welcome to Setup screen

6. Locate the number of the Windows installation that you are troubleshooting, as shown in Figure 7-21. Type the corresponding number and press the **Enter** key.

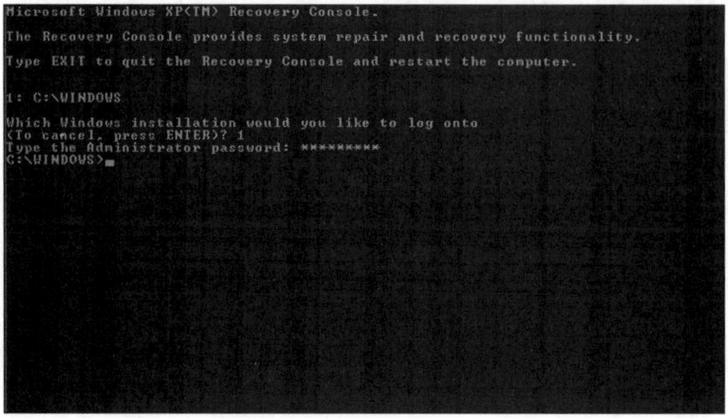

Figure 7-21 Recovery Console

7. Type **Password1** and press the **Enter** key.

8. At the C:\WINDOWS prompt, type **help** and press the **Enter** key. See Figure 7-22.

Figure 7-22   Help in the Recovery Console

9. Press the **Enter** key and notice that one additional line is displayed.

10. Press the **spacebar** and notice that additional lines are displayed.

11. Type **dir /?** and press the **Enter** key. Notice that help for the dir command is displayed.

12. Type **dir** and press the **Enter** key. Notice that the directory is displayed.

13. Press the **spacebar** until the remaining entries are displayed.

14. Type **diskpart /?** and press the **Enter** key.

15. Type **diskpart** and press the **Enter** key. Notice that the volume information is displayed as shown in Figure 7-23. Press the **Esc** key.

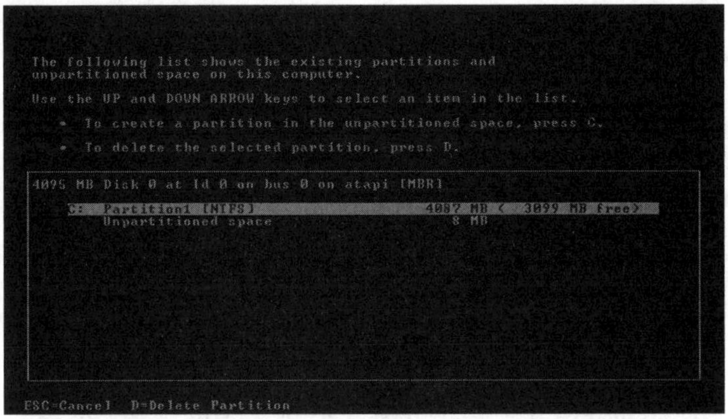

Figure 7-23   Diskpart showing volume information

16. Type **fixboot /?** and press the **Enter** key.

17. Type **fixboot** and press the **Enter** key. Type **Y** and press the **Enter** key. Was the boot sector rewritten?

18. Type *command /?* (where *command* is any command) and press the **Enter** key.

19. Type **exit** and press the **Enter** key.

20. Remove the Windows XP Professional CD-ROM in the drive.

21. When Windows starts, log on using the user name **admin01** and password **Password1**.

22. In your project log, write a brief description of how you could use the Recover Console to resolve a problem in which the computer will not start Windows XP.

Using Windows XP Troubleshooters

Do you need a hand with the resolution of a problem? You should consider the Windows XP troubleshooters. These are wizards that guide you through the steps to diagnose and fix known computer-related problems.

ACTIVITY

Activity 7-12: Troubleshooting with the Windows XP Trouble-shooters

Time Required: 30 minutes

Objective: Explore the use of the XP troubleshooters.

Description: In this activity, you will practice using the XP troubleshooter to resolve a problem with your network. To simulate a network problem, you will remove the network cable. You will proceed through a number of troubleshooter dialog boxes. As you follow the steps, you will discover the solution to the problem. You are practicing using the XP troubleshooter so that you can resolve your users' problems.

1. If necessary, log on to your computer using the user name **admin01** and password **Password1**.

2. Remove the network cable from your computer.

NOTE

If you receive a message asking if you want to work offline, click the **Yes** button.

3. Click **Start**, click **Help and Support**, and click the **Fixing a problem** link. Your screen should resemble Figure 7-24.

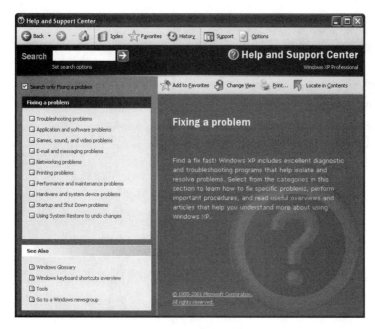

Figure 7-24 Help and Support Center

4. Click the **Networking problems** link and click the **Drives and Network Adapters Troubleshooter** link.

5. Click **the My network adapter does not work** option button, as shown in Figure 7-25 and click the **Next** button.

6. Click the **Yes, my hardware is on the HCL** option button and click the **Next** button.

7. Follow the instructions on the screen starting with To check the status of your device.

8. Click the **No, . . . Device Manager does not show any problem with my device** option button and click the **Next** button.

9. Click the **I want to skip this step and try something else** option button and click the **Next** button.

10. Click the **I want to skip this step and try something else** option button and click the **Next** button.

11. Follow the instructions on the screen starting with **Is your network connection hardware working?**.

12. Did you plug the cable into the network adapter and watch the blinking lights?

13. Close all open windows.

Figure 7-25 Drives and Network Adapters Troubleshooter page

14. In your project log, describe how you might use the Windows XP troubleshooter to resolve a problem for a user.

15. Log off your computer.

Chapter Summary

The Windows XP operating system provides a number of features that you should be prepared to support:

◻ With the Windows Backup Utility, users back up and restore the My Documents folder.

◻ Windows XP provides the performance tool to manage settings of the operating system that you will use to support visual effects and virtual memory.

◻ With compatibility mode, you can make older programs run on Windows XP.

Do not overlook the importance of troubleshooting. To resolve user problems, you will benefit from a troubleshooting strategy. To be effective, you will need to add tools to your troubleshooting tool kit:

◻ Run A permits you to temporarily log on to a user's computer using an account with the privileges of an administrator.

◻ With the Task Manager, you can easily obtain a glimpse into the performance of your computer.

◻ You use Windows File Protection to protect and restore critical system files to the correct version.

◻ By using Safe Mode, you can troubleshoot and correct problems that keep the computer from starting properly.

◻ When Safe Mode fails, you can resort to the Recovery Console to correct startup problems.

◻ The XP troubleshooters provide you with guidance in the resolution of problems known to Microsoft.

Key Terms

background services — Programs that execute during momentary lulls in the foreground processing.

base video — Video settings that are set at the minimum: 640 x 480 pixels and 16 colors. Used when the current settings exceed the capability of the display monitor.

boot files — The files needed to start Microsoft Windows. For Windows XP, they are ntldr, ntdetect.com, and boot.ini.

cache folder — A folder containing files that are stored as needed for frequent access.

foreground programs — One or more programs that currently interact with the user.

memory leak — An error in a program's memory allocation logic that causes it to fail to release unneeded memory, leading to eventual collapse due to memory exhaustion.

paging file — File stored on a hard drive used to implement virtual memory.

Registry — A hierarchical database used to store information needed to configure the system.

system cache — A folder containing files that are stored to speed access to the files.

virtual memory — Memory that appears to an application to be larger than physical memory. Simulated by using secondary storage, such as a hard disk.

Windows File Protection — A process in which the existence and integrity of a file are maintained.

REVIEW QUESTIONS

1. Which capability does the Windows XP backup program provide? (Choose all that apply.)

   a. It can help you install software.

   b. It can help you back up folders and files.

   c. It can help you back up critical system configuration files.

   d. It can help you restore folders and files.

2. From the What to Back Up screen in the Windows XP Backup, what are the choices? (Choose all that apply.)

   a. Back up the My Documents folder

   b. Back up everything on this computer

   c. Back up selected files, drives, or network data

   d. Only back up the System State data

3. Which files does Microsoft Windows use to start the computer? (Choose all that apply.)

   a. Sys.exe

   b. Ntdetect.com

   c. Ntldr

   d. Boot.ini

   e. Win.exe

4. Which of the following devices can the Backup Utility use? (Choose all that apply.)

   a. removable USB drives

   b. external hard drives

   c. internal hard drives

   d. CD-ROM writers

   e. magnetic tape drives

5. Using the Windows XP Backup Utility, to which destination can files be restored? (Choose all that apply.)

   a. original location

   b. My Documents

   c. alternate location

   d. single folder

6. From the System Properties Advanced tab dialog box, which of the following can be managed? (Choose all that apply.)

   a. user profiles

   b. visual effects

   c. processor scheduling

   d. memory usage

   e. virtual memory

7. If a computer had 256 MB of RAM, which of the following would be the correct virtual memory settings? (Choose all that apply.)

   a. minimum of 256 MB

   b. minimum of 384 MB

   c. maximum of 384 MB

   d. maximum of 512 MB

   e. maximum of 768 MB

8. Which of the following programs can you configure using Windows XP compatibility mode? (Choose all that apply.)

   a. utilities written for Windows XP

   b. Microsoft Office 2003

   c. games written for Windows 95

   d. engineering applications written for MS-DOS

   e. accounting applications written for Windows 98

9. Which of the following options can you configure with Windows XP compatibility mode? (Choose all that apply.)

   a. Windows XP support

   b. Windows 98 support

   c. display color depth

   d. screen resolution

10. For which of the following reasons should you use Run As? (Choose all that apply.)

   a. to log on as an administrator

   b. to avoid security risks

   c. to avoid logging off the user

   d. to run administrative programs

   e. to run office applications

7

11. To start Task Manager, which of the following could be used? (Choose all that apply.)
    a. press Ctrl+Alt+Delete and click Task Manager
    b. press Crl+Shift+Esc
    c. right-click an empty area of the taskbar and click Task Manager
    d. right-click an empty area of the desktop and click Task Manager
    e. right-click the My Computer icon and click Task Manager

12. Which tab is in Task Manager when you have a domain network? (Choose all that apply.)
    a. Applications
    b. Processes
    c. Performance
    d. Networking
    e. Users

13. From the Processes tab of the Task Manager, you can see whether _____ have caused a process to fail. (Choose all that apply.)
    a. hung programs
    b. running programs
    c. memory leaks
    d. memory releases

14. Which of the following might be an indication that a computer is inadequate for your user's activities? (Choose all that apply.)
    a. program with abnormally high CPU usage
    b. CPU usage consistently greater than 90%
    c. program with extremely large amount of memory usage
    d. a high rate of paging activity

15. From the Networking tab of the Task Manager, what helpful information can you view? (Choose all that apply.)
    a. adapter name
    b. adapter address
    c. network utilization
    d. link speed
    e. state

16. From the Windows Advanced Options menu, what options can be selected? (Choose all that apply.)
    a. Safe Mode
    b. Safe Mode with Networking

c) Safe mode with Command Prompt

d.) Enable VGA mode

e. Last Known Good Configuration

17. Which driver is loaded when Safe Mode is selected from the Windows Advanced Options menu? (Choose all that apply.)

a) keyboard

b) mouse

c.) monitor

d) hard drive

e. networking

18. What is true about the Last Known Good Configuration on the Windows Advanced Options menu?

a) It starts your computer using the system configuration that was saved after logon.

b. It starts your computer using the system configuration that was saved after shutdown.

c. It starts the computer with only the basic system files.

d. It starts with a command prompt only.

19. Which activity can be performed with the Recovery Console commands? (Choose all that apply.)

a) view disk volumes

b) format drives

c) write files to the hard drive

d) locate problem drivers

e) display Help information

20. For which problem could the Windows XP troubleshooter be used? (Choose all that apply.)

a) application and software

b) games, sound, and video

c) networking

d) printing

e) performance and maintenance

7

CASE PROJECTS

CASE
PROJECTS

Case 7-1: Providing Backups for Critical Documents

You are a self-employed desktop support technician. Your customer operates a small legal office with eight networked computers running Windows XP Professional.

You stop by the legal office to help one of the legal assistants with a configuration problem. After you complete this task, one of the partners expresses a concern. Yesterday, a file for a critical document was accidentally deleted from one of the floppy disks stored at the typist's desk. Although they were able to retype the document, he asked if there was a better way to ensure that documents could be recovered.

What solution will you offer the partner in the legal firm? In your past dealings with this customer, you have determined that he prefers to review a document with at least three alternatives. He expects to see the advantages and disadvantages for each alternative.

CASE
PROJECTS

Case 7-2: Observing Performance with Task Manager

You are a desktop support technician. Your network consists of a Windows 2003 Active Directory domain with 12 servers and 500 computers running Windows XP Professional.

You are responding to a question from Susan regarding the performance of her computer. She has stated that the computer appears "sluggish." How will you use the Task Manager to research her problem? Explain, in detail, the reasons that you used each Task Manager feature.

CASE
PROJECTS

Case 7-3: Using Windows Advanced Options Menu

You are a consultant offering desktop support services for small offices. You are responding to a request to bring a computer back to life.

The user of the computer installed a new document scanner yesterday and the computer fails with a stop message today. How will you use Windows Advanced Options menu to troubleshoot this problem? Explain, in detail, the reasoning behind your choices.

8

RESOLVING ISSUES RELATED TO OFFICE APPLICATION USAGE

After reading this chapter and completing the exercises, you will be able to:

♦ Resolve issues related to customizing and personalizing Office applications

♦ Resolve issues related to using the Office Proofing Tools

♦ Resolve issues related to using the Office System Tools

As you are aware, the role of the DST requires that you be prepared to resolve issues related to Office Application usage. The Office applications provide a wide range of capabilities that can be tailored to meet the work habits of your users. For example, your users can set options to control the appearance of toolbars. Your value to the company will be enhanced by your ability to help make your end users productive.

If your organization creates documents in multiple languages, you will want to learn how to install, configure, and use the Office Proofing Tools. With the Office Proofing Tools, your users will have access to fonts, spelling and grammar checkers, and AutoCorrect lists for foreign languages.

Microsoft Office 2003 provides a number of Office System Tools that expand the capabilities of Microsoft Office 2003. You will be learning how to assist your users with these tools.

CUSTOMIZING AND PERSONALIZING OFFICE APPLICATIONS

Office provides customizable toolbars. Your users will use toolbars when they create and edit Access databases, Word documents, Excel worksheets, and PowerPoint presentations. Many components of the Word interface—menus, toolbars, keyboard shortcuts, and the like—work essentially the same way in the other Office applications. You should be able to translate the skills you learn in customizing Word toolbars into the remaining Office applications.

Office gets personal! Your users can personalize both the menus and toolbars in Office. Your users will have numerous personalization choices that will allow them to tailor Office's menus and toolbars to work the way they choose to interface with Office.

Office corrects and formats text as your users type. Office supplies corrections for misspelled words and applies the appropriate text formatting. These two features and the other text and formatting features will make your users more productive.

Office provides two tools that allow your users greater control and flexibility over formatting. There are two features that you will want to share with your users: Reveal Formatting and the Format Painter.

Working with the Office Toolbars

Toolbars give your users easy access to certain features such as formatting, drawing, and saving files without going to the menu. The graphical nature of Office's toolbars makes it easier to point and click than to open menus and search for commands. Tool buttons, embedded in toolbars, remind your end users what to look for.

Docking Toolbars

The two toolbars used most often and displayed by default are the Standard toolbar and Formatting toolbar, as shown in Figure 8-1. By default, the Standard and Formatting toolbars appear **docked** (fixed to the top, bottom, or side of the window) on a single row, showing the buttons that you use most often. To move a toolbar, drag the **move handle** (which is the button on the toolbar that makes it possible to move a toolbar). For a change in pace, you might want to float a toolbar over the document by dragging a toolbar from the docked position.

IN THE WORKPLACE

I've noticed that some users place the toolbars on the side. When asked, they have usually responded that it was easier to access with the mouse.

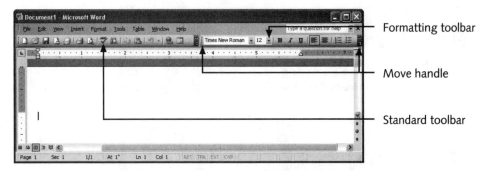

Formatting toolbar

Move handle

Standard toolbar

Figure 8-1 Word toolbars - Docked Standard and Formatting

Stacking Toolbars

Your users may prefer that the toolbars be stacked, as shown in Figure 8-2. To stack the toolbars, you can click the Tools menu, click Customize, and click the Options tab. Under Personalized Menus and Toolbars, select the Show Standard and Formatting toolbars on two rows check box. Of course, your users could drag one of the two toolbars into the "stacked" positions. Microsoft Office frequently provides more than one way to accomplish a task.

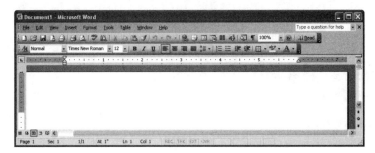

Figure 8-2 Word toolbars - Stacked Standard and Formatting

Modifying Toolbar Buttons

You can arrange the sequence of buttons on a toolbar to fit the way you want to access the buttons. Likewise, you can add or remove buttons. You rearrange and modify buttons by using your mouse. You can win points from your users by showing them how to do this.

To move a button, hold the Alt key and drag the button to a new location on the toolbar. To add more tool buttons to the toolbar, click on the Toolbar Options list arrow at the right edge of the toolbar, click Add or Remove Buttons, and click Standard (or the name of the toolbar you are modifying). You select the desired tool button(s) from the list shown in Figure 8-3. To delete a button, hold the Alt key and drag the button off the toolbar. To duplicate an existing button on another toolbar, hold Alt+Ctrl and drag the button to the new location.

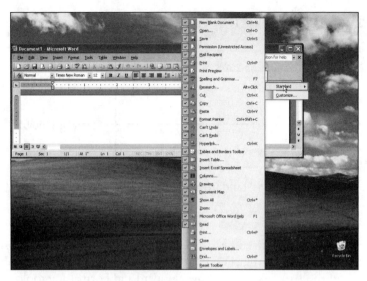

Figure 8-3 Word toolbars - Standard toolbar buttons

Showing and Hiding Toolbars

To show or hide a toolbar, right-click a toolbar, click Customize, click the Toolbars tab, and then, in the Toolbars list, check or uncheck the toolbar, as shown in Figure 8-4.

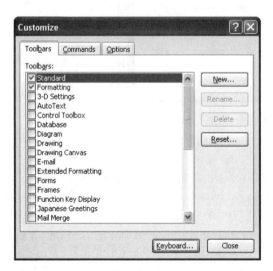

Figure 8-4 Word toolbars - Check to show

Activity 8-1: Customizing Toolbars

Time Required: 15 minutes

Objective: Customize the appearance of the Office toolbar.

Description: In this activity, you will practice customizing the toolbars. You will change the location of the toolbars and manipulate a toolbar button. You are practicing using the toolbars so that you can answer your users' questions about the usage of toolbars in Word and other Office applications.

1. Log on to your computer using the user name **user01** and password **Password1**.
2. Click **Start**, point to **All Programs**, point to **Microsoft Office**, and click **Microsoft Office Word 2003**.
3. Drag the Standard toolbar with the move handle to the left side of the screen.
4. Drag the Formatting toolbar with the move handle to the left side of the screen.
5. Drag the Standard and Formatting toolbars using the move handle back to the top of the screen.
6. Click **Tools**, click **Customize**, click the **Options** tab, check the **Show Standard and Formatting Toolbars on two rows** check box, and click the **Close** button.
7. Hold **Alt** and drag the **Spelling and Grammar** button (ABC letters over check mark) to the right two buttons.
8. Hold **Alt+Ctrl** and drag the **Spelling and Grammar** button to the right.
9. Hold **Alt** and drag the duplicate **Spelling and Grammar** button off of the Standard toolbar.
10. Click **Tools**, click **Customize**, click the **Toolbars** tab, check the **Extended Formatting** check box, and observe the third toolbar is added.
11. Uncheck the **Extended Formatting** check box and observe that the third toolbar is removed.
12. Write a brief description of how you might assist a user to customize the toolbars and toolbar buttons in your project log.
13. Click the **Close** button.

Creating a Custom Toolbar

You should be prepared to show your users the steps to create a custom toolbar. For example, your users frequently need to locate or replace text and would benefit from having a custom toolbar for these activities.

On the Tools menu, click Customize, click the Toolbars tab, and click New. In the Toolbar name box, type the name you want. See Figure 8-5.

8

Figure 8-5   Word toolbars - Creating a custom toolbar

In the Make toolbar available to box, select which template or document to make the toolbar available in, and then click OK. Then, click the Commands tab and do one of the following:

- **Add a button to the toolbar:** Click a category in the Categories box. Drag the command you want from the Commands box to the displayed toolbar.

- **Add a built-in menu to the toolbar:** In the Categories box, click Built-in Menus. Drag the menu you want from the Commands box to the displayed toolbar.

When you have added all the buttons and menus you want, as shown in Figure 8-6, click Close.

Activity 8-2: Creating a Custom Toolbar

Time Required: 15 minutes

Objective: Create a custom Office toolbar.

Description: In this activity, you will practice creating a custom toolbar in Word. You are practicing creating a custom toolbar so that you can answer your users' questions about the creation of custom toolbars in Word and other Office applications.

1. If necessary, log on to your computer using the user name **user01** and password **Password1**.

2. If necessary, click **Start**, point to **All Programs**, point to **Microsoft Office**, and click **Microsoft Office Word 2003**.

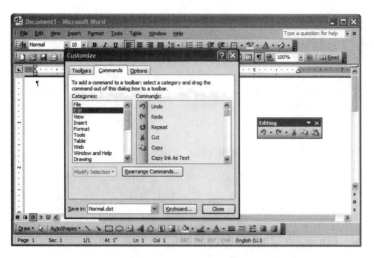

Figure 8-6   Word toolbars - Buttons added to custom toolbar

3. Click **Tools**, click **Customize**, click the **Toolbars** tab, if necessary, click the **New** button, type **Editing** (if this activity has been completed previously, name the Editing toolbar Editing1, Editing2, and so on) in the Toolbar name text box, and click the **OK** button.

4. Click the **Commands** tab, click **Edit** in the Categories box, drag the **Undo** button to the Editing toolbar, and drag the Redo button to the Editing toolbar.

5. Drag **Cut**, **Copy**, **Paste**, and **Paste Special** to the Editing toolbar.

6. Click the **Close** button in the Customize dialog box.

7. Type **Sample Text** in the document and highlight **Sample Text**.

8. Click the **Copy** button on the Edit toolbar, press **Enter** twice, click the **Paste** button twice, and click the **Undo** button to test the Editing toolbar.

9. Write a brief description describing how you might assist a user to create a custom toolbar in your project log.

10. Close any open document windows. If prompted to save the document, click **No**.

Troubleshooting Toolbars

You or your user cannot find a toolbar button. You remember that you were able to access the toolbar button previously. However, you have been using Office for several hours and have been working on multiple documents. To solve this problem, consider one of the following:

- **There may not be enough room to display all of the buttons:** If the toolbar is on the same row as another toolbar, there might not be enough room to display all the buttons. Click Toolbar Options and click the button you need.

- **The Office program window may not be maximized:** Some toolbar buttons may be hidden if your user's program window is not maximized.

- **The button appeared before but is not visible now:** Office stores the buttons that you have used frequently on your toolbar. As you work with Word and select previously hidden tools, Word adds them to the displayed toolbar. When the Always show full menus check box is unchecked, these personalized settings affect the buttons that are shown on a toolbar.

Customizing Menu and Toolbar Behavior

You and your users can control the behavior of the menus and toolbars in Office. For example, your users may want to always see the full menu. On the Tools menu, click Customize and click the Options tab, as shown in Figure 8-7.

Figure 8-7   Word menu and toolbar customizations

From the Options dialog box, you can perform these tasks:

- **Show Standard and Formatting toolbars on two rows:** Change from the default, which has these two toolbars on the same row. Show more buttons on each toolbar.

- **Always show full menus:** Do not use personalized menus.

- **Show full menus after a short delay:** Show full menus after three seconds. Requires that Always show full menus check box is unchecked.

- **Reset menu and toolbar usage data:** Affects the buttons shown on a toolbar only if the toolbar is not wide enough to display all of the buttons.

- **Large icons:** Displays larger icons for the toolbar buttons.

- **List font names in their font:** Display font names using the actual font in Font drop-down list.

- **Show ScreenTips on toolbars:** Show the name of the button when pointed to with the mouse.

- **Show shortcut keys in ScreenTips:** Show the keyboard shortcut key with the ScreenTip.

- **Menu animations:** Choose a menu animation from System default, Random, Unfold, Slide, and Fade.

- **Keyboard button:** Change the shortcut key(s) for a menu command.

IN THE WORKPLACE

Need to know the shortcut keys for a menu command? I've had users who really preferred to drive Office using shortcut keys. By clicking the Keyboard button, I could find the shortcut keys for almost every menu entry.

8

Personalizing Office Features

In addition to the customization of the behaviors located on the dialog box, located at Tools, Customize, Word provides another series of feature personalization options located at Tools, Options. You found a brief set of customization choices on the Customize dialog box in the previous section. In the following sections, you will find the personalization choices on the Options dialog box.

Much of the way that Word works can be personalized. If your users find that a specific feature in Word is bothersome, more often than not the annoyance can be disabled with a check box. For instance, a common feature that users find convenient to disable is Smart Tags. The following sections cover some of the most important features on the Options dialog box.

View Tab

You select options on the View tab (from Options on the Tools menu) to control what appears on the screen, as shown in Figure 8-8. When you create a document, the options for the View tab are applied. If you make a change, these changes will remain in effect when you close and reopen the document. Your users will find the formatting marks helpful. For example, the Tab characters show how text lines up on the screen.

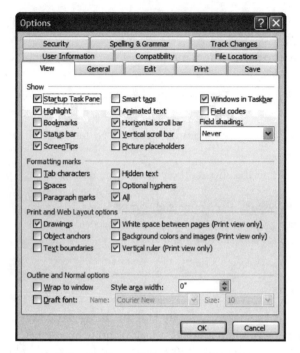

Figure 8-8   Options dialog box - View tab

General Tab

You select various options on the General tab that control the general behavior of an Office application, as shown in Figure 8-9. One option that your users may find useful is to increase the Recently used file list (up to nine). The result of this selection will show up on the File menu when the user needs to locate a document or worksheet that he or she recently worked on.

 Sometimes I become tired of looking at black text on a white background. I switch to white text on a blue background, which is more pleasing to the eye.

IN THE WORKPLACE

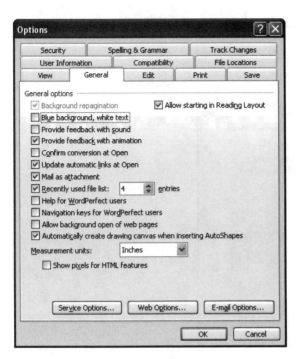

Figure 8-9   Options dialog box - General tab

Edit Tab

You can control how Word reacts when you type text by customizing the Edit tab. See Figure 8-10. For example, the default Typing replaces selection deletes the selected text when you begin to type. You might want to clear this check box and have Word insert new text in front of the selected text and not delete the selected text. End users often choose this option in work situations such as when making a few minor corrections to an existing document or presentation.

Print Tab

In Figure 8-11, you see the default printer settings. If your users need to speed printing and print the document with minimal formatting, your users could select Draft output.

IN THE WORKPLACE

I often type the answers to test questions as hidden text. To print the answer key, I select the Include with document - Hidden text option, which prints all text that has been formatted as hidden. And yes, the students get the test without the hidden text.

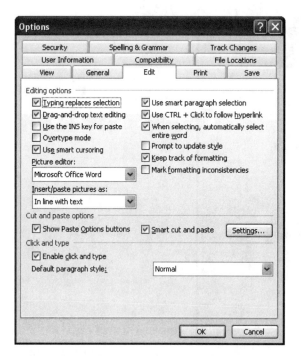

Figure 8-10   Options dialog box - Edit tab

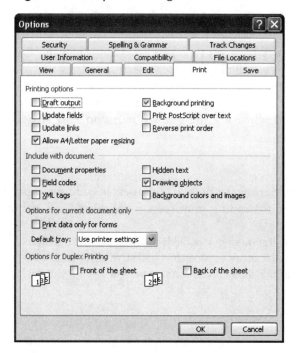

Figure 8-11   Options dialog box - Print tab

Save Tab

On the Save tab, as shown in Figure 8-12, you choose settings for backup copies and **AutoRecovery** (periodically saves files to permit file recovery). Your users may want to select the Always create backup copy option, which creates a backup copy of a document each time you save the document. Each backup copy replaces the previous backup copy. Word applies the .wbk filename extension to all backup copies, and it saves them in the same folder as your user's original document.

Another option that your users may want to select is the Save AutoRecover info every option, which automatically creates a document-recovery file at the interval (1 to 120 minutes) your user specifies in the minutes box. If your user's computer stops responding or loses power unexpectedly, Word opens the AutoRecover file the next time your user starts Word. The AutoRecover file may contain unsaved information that your user would have otherwise lost. Remember that AutoRecover does not replace the Save command. Your user must save the document when he or she finishes working on it.

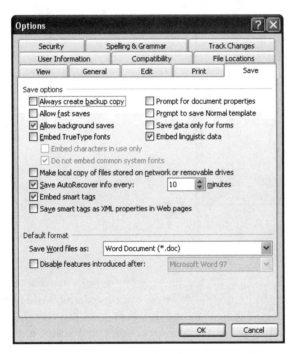

Figure 8-12   Options dialog box - Save tab

User Information Tab

Your users enter personal information, as shown in Figure 8-13, on the User Information tab. Type the name and initials that you want to appear in Word documents. Word uses the name in letters and envelopes to track changes and to mark comments your user inserts into a document. Word uses the initials for marking comments and for several built-in letter and memo elements.

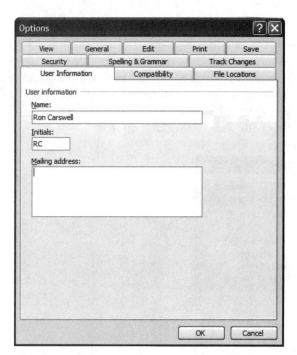

Figure 8-13   Options dialog box - User Information tab

Compatibility Tab

Your users can select options to change his or her display actions to that of a given word-processing program, as shown in Figure 8-14. These options permit Word to resemble an older version of Word or a version of WordPerfect. Also, your users can customize display options for the active document. The options affect a document's appearance only while he or she works on it in Word.

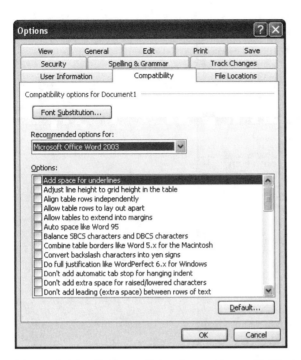

Figure 8-14   Options dialog box - Compatibility tab

File Locations Tab

Figure 8–15 shows the File Locations tab, which lists the default storage location for documents, templates, and other items you create and use in Office. From the File Locations tab, you can change the location that Office uses for these various files. Click the item you want to change, and then click Modify to set a new default location.

The default locations for templates and the Startup folder are treated as trusted locations. If you change these locations, be sure that the new folder is a secure location. For example, placing a template in an unsecured location could result in another user overlaying your template. Overlaying the template could cause future formatting problems in a document.

Security Tab

See Figure 8-16 for the Security options. Office has several built-in features designed to protect the data files used within the Office applications. For example, files can be saved with a password that is required to read the contents of the file. This concept will be presented in further detail in Chapter 12. The default locations for templates and the Startup folder are treated as trusted locations. If you change these locations, be sure that the new folder is a secure location. For example, placing a template in an unsecured location could result in another user overlaying your template. Overlaying the template could cause future formatting problems in a document.

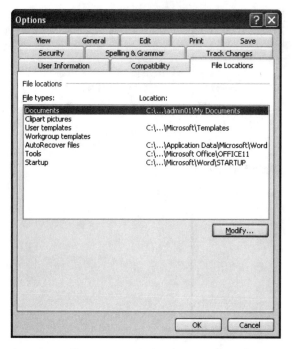

Figure 8-15   Options dialog box - File Locations tab

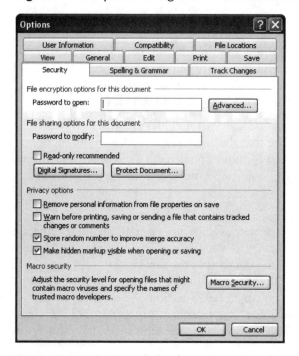

Figure 8-16   Options dialog box - Security tab

Spelling & Grammar Tab

On the Spelling & Grammar tab, as shown in Figure 8-17, you configure the options that control how the spell checking module and grammar checker performs. The spell checking module, which Word shares with the other Office applications, permits personal dictionaries and easy right-click access to suggested spellings for words underlined with the "red wavy line."

If your users find the "red wavy line" annoying and prefer to correct mistakes after they are done typing, uncheck the Check spelling as you type check box. This will permit your user to "power type" and enter text without the interference of the spell checker. However, your users will need to remember to run the batch spell check to have Office check for spelling errors. The easiest way to run this spell check is to press F7 key.

You and your users may consider the grammar checker's advice overly simplistic. Or your users find the "green wavy line" annoying. If so, uncheck the Check grammar as you type check box.

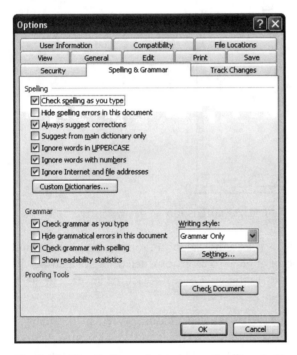

Figure 8-17   Options dialog box - Spelling & Grammar tab

Track Changes Tab

Working on a document as a writer with multiple editors can become chaotic. Your users may prefer to have the changes identified by the person making the change. For example, each person working on the document can have his or her text entries identified with a different color. From the Track Changes tab, as shown in Figure 8-18, you can assist your users to maintain the integrity of the document with revision tracking.

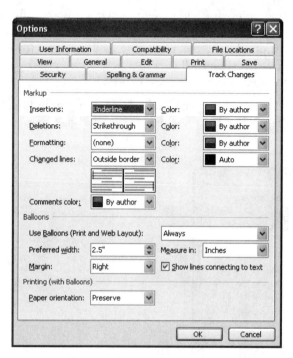

Figure 8-18   Options dialog box - Track Changes tab

You can set the format for markup insertions, deletions, formatting changes, and changed lines. Likewise, you can set the color applied to insertions, deletions, formatting changes, and changed lines. By default, Word uses a different color for each reviewer. The default setting for all options except Changed lines is By author.

Word displays comments and tracks changes in balloons located in the margins of your document. Selecting Never next to "Use Balloons (Print and Web Layout)" places comments and tracked changes in the text of your document. For the Show lines connecting to text option, Word displays a line connecting each balloon to the location of each change or comment in the document.

IN THE
WORKPLACE
When working on the revisions to textbooks, I prefer to have the comments and deletions appear as balloons to the right of the text, which is the default setting or "Always". If I need to see the deletions within the text, I might switch temporarily to "Only for comments/formatting". I've found the third option "Never" just ugly! There is too much to sort through: text, deleted text, format changes, and links to comments.

How Personalized Toolbars and Menus Work

When your users begin working with Office, the Personalized Menus option is enabled. When you click any menu item, you will see only a subset of the choices available under that menu. You can force the full menus to appear by using any of these techniques:

- Click the chevron character (>>) at the bottom of the menu.
- Point and wait about three seconds without making a selection.
- Click a specific top-level menu item twice: The first click displays the short menu. The second click expands it to the full menu.

As you work with an Office application, such as Word, Office attempts to learn your usage patterns. In general, personalized toolbars and menus follow these rules:

- When you first install an Office application, you see a default short selection for menus. If you leave the default for the Standard and Formatting toolbars (on a single row), you will see a default short selection for these two toolbars as well.

- Default menu items remain visible for at least six different Word sessions on six different days in which you use other items on the same menu. If you use Word every day, but you use the Insert menu only once a month, for example, it might be six months before your default choices on the Insert menu change.

- Each time you use a hidden toolbar or menu item, it is promoted to the list of visible entries. Word may hide a button to make room for a newly promoted button.

- Menu items remain visible for at least three different sessions on three different days after you use the items.

- The more you use an item, the longer it appears.

- Office never changes the order of items on toolbars and menus. Menu items always appear in the same relative order.

ACTIVITY
Activity 8-3: Researching the Options to Personalize Office Features

Time Required: 45 minutes

Objective: Discover the options to personalize the features of Office.

Description: In this activity, you will research the options for the features of Office to learn where the customization for each feature is located and how to set the option. You will use the Help in Office to research the various settings for each option. You are researching the features of Office so that you can be prepared to locate the answers to your users' questions about the personalization of Office features.

1. If necessary, log on to your computer using the user name **user01** and password **Password1**.

2. If necessary, click **Start**, point to **All Programs**, point to **Microsoft Office**, and click **Microsoft Office Word 2003**.

3. Click **Tools** and click **Options**.

4. Click the **View** tab.

5. Click on the **Question mark** button on the upper-right corner of the Options dialog box and click the **View** tab on the Microsoft Office Word Help.

6. View each option on the View tab and read the corresponding information in the Microsoft Word Help window.

7. Write a brief explanation of how you might answer a user's questions about the options located on the View tab.

8. Close the Help screen.

9. Repeat Steps 4 through 8 for the remaining tabs.

10. Close any open document windows.

Customizing the Auto Options

AutoCorrect and AutoFormat can be both helpful (saving your users time) and a hindrance (making your users do things they may not want to do). For an example of a helpful intervention, consider the text correcting features that catch and help to repair common misspellings. On the other hand, the replacement of "½" for "1/2" may be annoying when your user is typing a document requiring equations. Your users will expect you to know how to customize these two options and the other "auto options."

 The "auto options" is my term, not Microsoft's. They chose to combine AutoCorrect, AutoText, AutoFormatting, and AutoFormat As You type, and the new feature Smart Tags under AutoCorrect Options. Just to keep things simple, let's call this group "auto options."

The five "auto options" are presented in the following sections.

Customizing AutoCorrect

If you've used Word for any period of time, you have been exposed to AutoCorrect. Recall when you typed "teh" and it was changed to "the". This change occurred because the AutoCorrect engine lurks in the background and watches as you type. Whenever you create a word-ending action (press the spacebar, type a punctuation mark, or press Enter), AutoCorrect looks in the AutoCorrect list for a matching entry to the preceding word. If a match is found, the old text is replaced by the contents of the AutoCorrect entry.

In Figure 8-19, you see the various options for the customization of AutoCorrect.

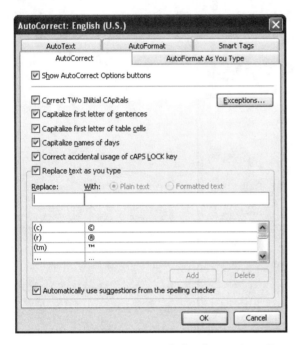

Figure 8-19 AutoCorrect dialog box - AutoCorrect tab

There are a number of customization options from which you can expect questions from users:

- **Correct TWo INitial CAptials box:** Replaces words with two consecutive capitals when the word appears in the AutoCorrect list (or dictionary).

- **Capitalize first letter of sentences:** Assumes you are starting a new sentence when you type the characters period and space.

- **Correct accidental usage of cAPS LOCK key:** Comes into play when you type one lowercase character, press the Caps Lock key, and continue typing. Turns the first character into a capital, makes the other characters lowercase, and turns off the Caps Lock.

- ■ **Automatically use suggestions from the spelling checker:** Consult the spelling checker if the word does not appear in the AutoCorrect list.

Customizing AutoText

Although AutoCorrect automatically corrects as you type, AutoText watches what you type and offers suggestions. This AutoText feature is available only in Word. When you start to type an AutoText entry, after typing the first four characters, Word displays a ScreenTip to alert you that a possible matching entry exists. For example, if you type sept, you will see a ScreenTip suggesting September. Press Enter to accept the ScreenTip.

The AutoText options are shown in Figure 8-20. If you want to use AutoText with AutoCorrect, leave the Show AutoComplete suggestions check box checked.

Figure 8-20   AutoCorrect dialog box - AutoText tab

Another way to use AutoText is to click the Insert menu and Autotext, as shown in Figure 8-21. Pick the category and click your choice. You will learn to add entries to the AutoText list in Activity 8-5.

Figure 8-21   Insert an AutoText entry

Customizing AutoFormat As You Type

You can automatically format a document either as you type or after you've written it. In both cases, you can control which automatic changes Word makes. You can also turn off automatic formatting.

Word analyzes each paragraph to see how it's used in the document—for example, as a heading or as an item in a numbered list—and then applies a style that's appropriate for that item.

Figure 8-22 displays the customizations that are available on the AutoFormat As You Type tab from the menu. Select your preferences by checking or unchecking the appropriate check box.

Customizing AutoFormatting

Figure 8-23 displays the customizations that are available on the AutoFormat tab. You select the formatting preferences that could be applied after you type the text by selecting Format and AutoFormat. Select your preferences by checking or unchecking the appropriate check box.

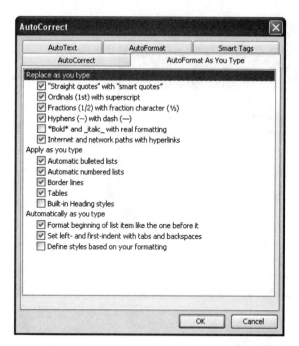

Figure 8-22   AutoCorrect dialog box - AutoFormat As You Type tab

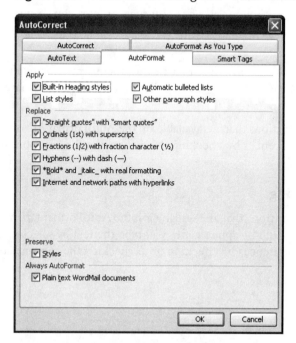

Figure 8-23   AutoCorrect dialog box - AutoFormat tab

Customizing Smart Tags

You enable smart tags by selecting smart tag recognizers from the list, as shown in Figure 8-24. Each smart tag recognizer identifies a type of data, such as names, dates, or telephone numbers, and contains the logic needed to provide one or more actions for each data type. You can select the smart tag recognizers or add additional recognizers from commercial sources marketing Smart Tags, such as ProWrite (mailing labels) or WorldLingo (translation services).

8

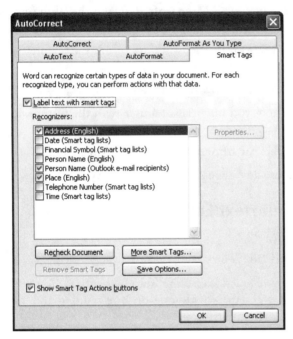

Figure 8-24   AutoCorrect dialog box - Smart Tags tab

Activity 8-4: Customizing AutoCorrect Options

Time Required: 20 minutes

Objective: Customize the options for the AutoCorrect feature.

Description: In this activity, you will practice customizing the features of AutoCorrect. You are practicing customizing the AutoCorrect options because you may need to conduct one-on-one training for your users. Also, you may need to answer your users' questions about adding text to the AutoCorrect list.

1. If necessary, log on to your computer using the user name **user01** and password **Password1**.

2. If necessary, click **Start**, point to **All Programs**, point to **Microsoft Office**, and click **Microsoft Office Word 2003**.

3. Click **Tools**, and if necessary, click the **double chevron (>>)**, and then click **AutoCorrect Options**.

4. View the check boxes for the **AutoCorrect** tab.

5. Click the **Exceptions** button and view the entries on the **First Letter** tab.

6. Click the **INitial CAps** tab and view the entries.

7. Click the **OK** button.

8. Type **msr** in the Replace text box, type **Microsoft Rules** in the With text box, and click the **Add** button.

9. Write a brief description of how you might assist a user with the features located on the AutoCorrect tab.

10. Click on the **AutoFormat As You Type** tab and view the entries.

11. Write a brief description of how you might assist a user with the features located on the AutoFormat as You Type tab.

12. Repeat Steps 10 and 11 for the **AutoFormat** and **Smart Tags** tabs.

13. Click the **OK** button and close any open document windows.

Activity 8-5: Creating AutoText Entries

ACTIVITY

Time Required: 15 minutes

Objective: Create and test an AutoText entry.

Description: In this activity, you will practice creating AutoText entries. You are practicing creating AutoText entries so that you can provide one-on-one training and answer your users' questions about creating AutoText entries.

1. If necessary, log on to your computer using the user name **user01** and password **Password1**.

2. Click **Start**, point to **All Programs**, point to **Microsoft Office**, and click **Microsoft Office Word 2003**.

3. Click the **Show/Hide ¶** button on the Standard toolbar.

4. Type **The information on this Site is provided with the understanding that the authors and publishers are not herein engaged in rendering legal, accounting, tax, or other professional advice and services.** and press **Enter**.

5. Highlight **The information on this Site is provided with the understanding that the authors and publishers are not herein engaged in rendering legal, accounting, tax, or other professional advice and services.** Click **Insert**, point to **AutoText**, and click **New**.

6. Type **lglmsg** in the Please name your AutoText entry text box and click the **OK** button.

7. Click in front of the last paragraph mark in the document.

8. Click **Insert**, point to AutoText, point to **Normal**, and click **lglmsg**.

9. Write a brief description describing how you might assist a user with the creation and use of the features of AutoText.

10. Close any open document windows. If you are prompted to save changes, click **No**.

11. Close the Editing toolbar.

Working with Formatting in Word

Word displays the text on screen as your users would expect to see it on the printed page. Yet, there are situations where the formatting applied may not be exactly what your users expected. You can expect questions from your users about the formatting that Word is applying to a particular area of text. For example, why does Word always try to format my numbered list? There are two features that you will want to learn to use: Reveal Formatting and Format Painter.

Working with Reveal Formatting

You can use the new Reveal Formatting task pane in Word to view a detailed description of any text in your document. You can also use it to modify or clear the formatting, compare the formatting of different selections, or to find blocks of text with similar formatting.

On the Format menu, click Reveal Formatting. Select the text whose formatting you want to review. The formatting information will appear in the Reveal Formatting task pane. At this point, you can do any of the following:

- **Change any formatting properties:** Select the text in the document, and then change any options you want in the task pane.

- **Determine the formatting source:** Select the Distinguish style source check box to discover if the formatting comes from a style.

- **Show formatting marks:** Select the Show all formatting marks check box.

IN THE WORKPLACE

Word is a WYSIWYG, or What You See is What You Get, word processor. This means Word shows you on screen exactly what your document will look like when printed out. This reduces the need for "reveal codes," because you can see the text formatting as you apply and manipulate it. You can use Reveal Formatting, which shows the formats that are applied to study how Word formats paragraphs.

8

Using the Format Painter

The Format Painter is a tool that allows you to copy formats from existing text and apply it to other text in your document. This saves you from having to remember which font, size, color, and so on you need to use. When your users work with Excel worksheets, they can use the Format Painter to apply cell formats. This is a visual tool that you will want to share with your users.

To copy enhancements, select the text containing the enhancements to copy. On the Formatting toolbar, click Format Painter (the button resembles a paint brush) and select the text to be enhanced. The text you selected is formatted with the enhancements you copied.

IN THE WORKPLACE Have you ever wanted to apply the same format to items in different locations in a document? Instead of clicking the Format Painter button on the Standard toolbar every time you want to apply the new format, you can take advantage of the button's "sticky" feature. When double-clicked the Format Painter button becomes "sticky" (stays selected). When you're finished applying the format, click the Format Painter button again or press ESC to release the "sticky" button.

Activity 8-6: Working with Formatting

Time Required: 15 minutes

Objective: Use the Reveal Formatting task pane and the Format Painter.

Description: In this activity, you will practice using the Reveal Formatting task pane. Also, you will practice applying formatting with the Format Painter. You are practicing using the Reveal Formatting task pane and Format Painter button so that you can answer your users' questions about formatting in Office.

1. If necessary, log on to your computer using the user name **user01** and password **Password1**.

2. If necessary, click **Start**, point to **All Programs**, point to **Microsoft Office**, and click **Microsoft Office Word 2003**.

3. Type **This line is exciting** and press **Enter**.

4. Type **This line is boring** and press **Enter**.

5. Highlight **This line is exciting**, then click **Format** and **Reveal Formatting**.

6. Click the **Font** link in the Reveal Formatting task pane, click **Bold** in the Font style list, and click the **OK** button.

7. Click the **Compare to another selection** check box.

8. Highlight **This line is boring** and view the indicated differences in the Reveal Formatting task pane.

9. Highlight the word **exciting**, click the **Format Painter** button, highlight the word **boring**, and observe the change.

10. Write a brief explanation in your project log describing how you might assist a user with formatting using Reveal Formatting and Format Painter.

11. Close any open windows and log off the computer. If you are prompted to save the changes, click **No**.

USING THE PROOFING TOOLS

For your users who read and write in multiple languages, you should consider the Microsoft Office 2003 Proofing Tools, which is an add-in package that contains the proofing tools that Microsoft makes for more than 30 languages. Your users will have access to fonts, spelling and grammar checkers, AutoCorrect lists, AutoSummarize rules (Microsoft Word only), translation dictionaries, and, for Asian languages, Input Method Editors.

With Proofing Tools installed, Word automatically detects the language of the current text by looking for characteristic vocabulary and grammar. It switches language-checking tools on the fly, but your users can use the spelling, hyphenation, and other layout tools throughout the Office suite.

ACTIVITY

Activity 8-7: Installing the Proofing Tools

Time Required: 15 minutes

Objective: Install the Microsoft Proofing Tools add-in.

Description: In this activity, you will install the Microsoft Proofing Tools add-in. You are installing the Microsoft Proofing Tools add-in so that you can resolve issues related to the Microsoft Proofing Tools add-in.

1. Log on to your computer using the user name **admin01** and password **Password1**.

2. Insert the Proofing Tools 2003 CD and wait for the CD to autorun.

3. When the Product key dialog box is displayed, enter the *Product Key* provided by your instructor and click the **Next** button.

4. Verify the User Information and click the **Next** button.

5. Click the **I accept the terms in the License Agreement** check box and click the **Next** button.

6. Click the **Install** button and wait for the installation to complete.

7. Click the **Finish** button.

8. Click **Start**, point to **All Programs**, point to **Microsoft Office**, point to **Microsoft Office Tools**, and click **Microsoft Office 2003 Language Settings**.

9. Wait for Microsoft Office to be configured.

10. When the Microsoft Office 2003 Language Settings dialog box is displayed, click **French (Canada)** in the Available languages list, as shown in Figure 8-25, click the **Add >>** button, and click the **OK** button.

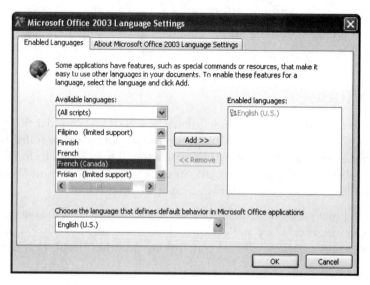

Figure 8-25   Available languages list

11. Write a brief explanation in your project log describing how you might assist a user with the setup of an additional language in the Office Proofing Tools.

12. Log off the computer.

Activity 8-8: Using the Proofing Tools

Time Required: 15 minutes

Objective: Use the spelling and grammar checkers for English and French.

Description: In this activity, you will practice using the proofing tools for text entered in both English and French. You are practicing using the proofing tools so that you can answer your users' questions about using the proofing tools.

1. Log on to your computer using the user name **user01** and password **Password1**.

2. If necessary, click **Start**, point to **All Programs**, point to **Microsoft Office**, and click **Microsoft Office Word 2003**.

3. Type **This is English** and press **Enter**.

4. Type **C'est francais** and press **Enter**.

5. Highlight **C'est francais**, click the **Spelling & Grammar** button, click the **Dictionary language** drop-down list, and click **French (Canada)**.

6. If necessary, click the **Yes** button to install the French dictionary.

7. Click the **Change** button to correct the spelling of **francais**.

8. Click the **No** button.

9. Click in front of the last paragraph mark.

10. Type **C'est une autre phrase en francais** and press **Enter**.

11. Click the **Spelling & Grammar** button and observe that the language was identified as French (Canada), click the **Ignore All** button, and click the **OK** button.

12. Type **This is texn** and press **Enter**.

13. Highlight **This is texn**, click **Tools**, point to Language, click **Set Language**, click **English (U. S.)**, and click the **OK** button.

14. Click the **Spelling & Grammar** button, click the **Change** button, click the **Yes** button, then click the **OK** button.

15. Write a brief explanation in your project log describing how you might assist a user with the checking of spelling in multiple languages.

16. Close any open windows. If you are prompted to save the changes, click **No**.

USING THE OFFICE SYSTEM TOOLS

When you install Office, a submenu is created under Microsoft Office. It is called Office System Tools. The Office System Tools permit access to a number of tools that your users may find helpful. For example, the ability to scan documents is one of the Office System Tools.

Note the following useful facts:

- Your users will be using artwork to improve the effectiveness of written documents and visual presentations. You will need to learn a feature to organize this artwork.

- Another feature backs up your users' application settings and copies the settings to a file. You will learn the steps to back up and restore these settings.

- The third major feature provides the ability to scan documents. You will want to learn this feature to assist your users with this new feature.

- The last major feature is the Office Application Recovery tool. Although Windows XP and Office 2003 are very stable, the possibility exists that an application program might hang. In order to assist your users, you will want to learn how to recover these hung programs.

Organizing Clips

The Microsoft Clip Organizer manages clips. A clip is a single media file, including art, sound, animation, or movies. You can insert clips in presentations, publications, and other Microsoft Office documents.

You can use Clip Organizer to build clip collections, adding clips or cataloging clips in ways that make sense to you. For example, you can create a collection to group the clips you use most frequently. Groups might correlate to the projects that you are working on. Also, Clip Organizer can automatically catalog the media files stored on your hard disk.

Microsoft is one source for Media files. The Microsoft Clip Organizer provides Internet access to online media libraries. Commercial sources for media files include Animation Factory and Hemera.

If people in your organization frequently create PowerPoint presentations, you may want to consider a subscription to a commercial source such as Animation Factory. My wife subscribes yearly to Animation Factory for about $100. Animation Factory's PowerPoint templates and graphic images will add life to that next important business presentation. Another source that she recommends is Hemera (the Greek goddess of light). Hemera specializes in graphic images.

The Microsoft Clip Organizer creates and maintains an index to the media files, which makes searching faster. With the index, you can locate a media file by searching by keyword. This proves useful in situations where you need to locate a special clip art clip in a presentation.

Activity 8-9: Using the Microsoft Clip Organizer

Time Required: 15 minutes

Objective: Resolve issues related to office application support features.

Description: In this activity, you will practice using the Microsoft Clip Organizer. On first use, Microsoft Clip Organizer will build the initial index. Then you will practice searching for a media file. You will learn to obtain and save media files using an online connection to Microsoft. You are practicing using the Microsoft Clip Organizer so that you can answer your users' questions about the Microsoft Clip Organizer.

1. If necessary, log on to your computer using the user name **user01** and password **Password1**.

2. Click **Start**, point to **All Programs**, point to **Microsoft Office**, point to **Microsoft Office Tools**, and then click **Microsoft Clip Organizer**.

3. If needed, check the **Don't show this message again** check box, then click the **Now** button. Wait for the media collection to be created and indexed.

4. Click the **Search** button, type **book** in the Search for text box, then click the **Go** button. Wait for the thumbnails to be displayed as shown in Figure 8-26.

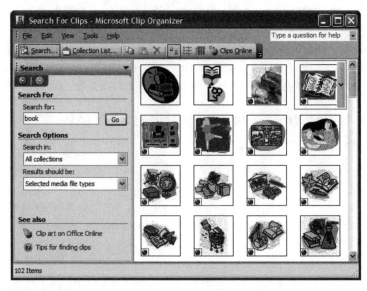

Figure 8-26   My Pictures - Microsoft Clip Organizer

Some of the clip art items have an icon in the lower-left corner. These are available online. See Figure 8-26.

NOTE

5. Click the **Clip art on Office Online** hyperlink, click the arrow next to **All media types** drop-down arrow, click **Clip art**, type **book** in the text box, and then click the **Go** button.

6. Check the check box under an image of your choice, then click the **Download 1 item** hyperlink. If needed, click the **Continue** button after the ActiveX control is downloaded.

7. Click the **Download Now** button. Click the **Open** button.

The clip art is automatically installed and appears in the Collection List beneath "Downloaded Clips" by Category.

NOTE

8. Close the Web browser window and the Microsoft Clip Organizer.

9. Write a brief description of how you might assist a user with the Microsoft Clip Organizer in your project log.

Using the Save My Settings Wizard

The Save My Settings wizard allows you to back up the Microsoft Office 2003 settings to a file. These settings are saved in a profile settings file (.ops file), which is a snapshot of registry settings and related files for the Microsoft Office 2003 configuration.

You can save or restore your configuration settings to the current computer or to another computer. You could use the restore to repair a user's Microsoft Office 2003 configuration. Also, you could use the restore to transport the configuration to a new computer for a user.

ACTIVITY

Activity 8-10: Using the Save My Settings Wizard

Time Required: 15 minutes

Objective: Resolve issues related to office application support features.

Description: In this activity, you will practice backing up and restoring the office profile settings. You will use the Save My Settings wizard to back up the current office profile settings. Then you will practice restoring the office profile settings. You are practicing saving and restoring the office profile settings so that you can resolve your users' problems for the office configuration settings.

1. If necessary, log on to your computer using the user name **user01** and password **Password1**.

2. Click **Start**, point to **All Programs**, point to **Microsoft Office**, point to **Microsoft Office Tools**, and then click **Microsoft Office 2003 Save My Settings Wizard**, as shown in Figure 8-27.

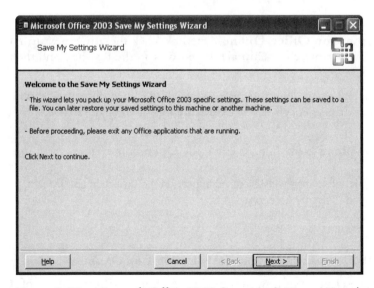

Figure 8-27   Microsoft Office 2003 Save My Settings Wizard screen

3. Click the **Next** button, and if necessary, click the **Save the settings from this machine** option button. Read the explanation below the **Save the settings from this machine** option button, then click the **Next** button.

4. Review the location of the **File to save settings to** text box, then click the **Finish** button.

5. Wait for the backup to complete, and then click the **Exit** button.

6. Click **Start**, point to **All Programs**, point to **Microsoft Office**, point to **Microsoft Office Tools**, and then click **Microsoft 2003 Save My Settings Wizard**.

7. Click the **Next** button, and if necessary, click the **Restore previously saved settings to this machine** option button. Read the explanation below the **Restore previously saved settings to this machine** option button, then click the **Next** button.

8. Review the location of the **File to restore settings from** text box, then click the **Finish** button.

9. Wait for the restore to complete, then click the **Exit** button.

10. Write a brief description describing how you might solve a problem for a user by restoring a previously saved office profile file in your project log.

11. Log off the computer.

Using Office Document Imaging

Microsoft Office Document Imaging actually has three components:

- **Office Document Scanning:** A scanning component that scans paper documents producing a graphics image file and optionally with Optical Character Recognition (OCR) converts the graphics image file into a document file.

- **Office Document Image Viewer:** View scanned documents on the screen.

- **A printer driver:** Save a printed file as a graphics image file.

In Figure 8-28, these three components are illustrated in three boxes. In the top box, you see the scanning component, with a digital scanner, which converts a printed document to an image file. Optionally, Optical Character Recognition converts a scanned image file into an editable document. In the middle box, you see the Image Viewer from which you can view scanned documents on your screen with the Document Imaging Component. In the bottom box, you see the last component, the Printer Driver, takes the printed output of a program and creates an image file.

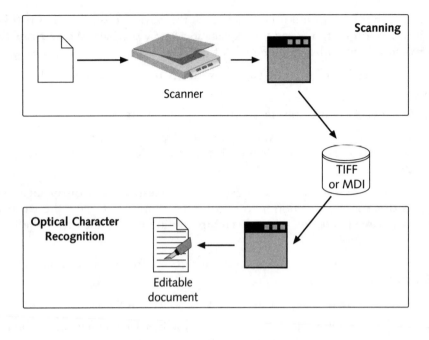

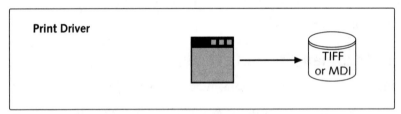

Figure 8-28   Image processing

Use Office Document Scanning

Document scanning is the process of scanning paper documents and converting them to digital images. You can scan paper documents and convert and save them as digital images in two formats:

- **Tagged Image File Format (TIFF):** A high-resolution, tag-based graphics format. TIFF is used for the universal interchange of digital graphics.

- **Microsoft Document Imaging Format (MDI):** A high-resolution, tag-based graphics format. MDI is based on the TIFF used for digital graphics.

The scanning component allows you to scan documents and make them available on your computer by using any installed scanner. Figure 8-29 displays the screen when Microsoft Office Document Scanning is selected from the Start menu.

Figure 8-29   Scan New Document dialog box

On the Scan New Document screen, you will notice a number of entries:

- **Select a preset for scanning:** Select a predefined setting that is optimized for a particular need

- **Scan:** Start a document scan

- **Preset options:** Create a preset from a dialog box

- **Original is double sided:** Select to scan the reverse side

- **Scanner:** Choose a scanner from multiple installed models

- **Prompt for additional pages:** Select to manually insert pages

- **View file after scanning:** Display the image in Microsoft Office Document Imaging

NOTE

You must install a digital scanner with the scanning software to use the scanning feature in Office. If you encounter a problem scanning documents, then the problem is most likely the software that came with the scanner.

Viewing Documents with the Document Imaging Viewer

The imaging component makes it easy for you to view documents on the screen as shown in Figure 8-30. You can select and manipulate recognized text, and rearrange multipage documents. From the imaging component, you can send documents to others by e-mail.

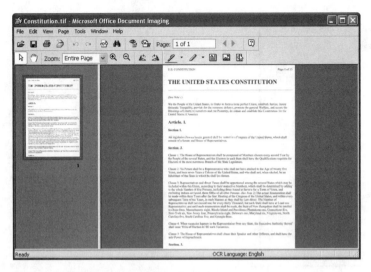

Figure 8-30   Document Imaging viewer

Using the Print Driver

The Microsoft Office Document Image Writer print driver is included with Microsoft Office Document Imaging. You can print to the Document Image Writer and create a TIFF or MDI file. One use of the Microsoft Office Document Image Writer is to create images for Web sites. This component, the Microsoft Office Document Image Writer, appears in the Printers and Faxes folder.

ACTIVITY

Activity 8-11: Performing Office Document Scanning and Imaging

Time Required: 15 minutes

Objective: Resolve issues related to office application support features.

Description: In this activity, you will practice scanning and imaging a document. You will start with a printed document. With a scanner you will create an image file of the document. Next, you will use optical character recognition to convert the image to editable text for a Microsoft Word document. You are practicing scanning and imaging documents so that you can resolve your users' problems and answer questions using the Microsoft Office Document Imaging feature.

1. Log on to your computer using the user name **admin01** and password **Password1**.

2. Place a black-and-white document in the scanner.

3. Click **Start**, point to **All Programs**, point to **Microsoft Office**, point to **Microsoft Office Tools**, and then click **Microsoft Office Document Scanning**.

For the first use of Microsoft Document Scanning, you may be asked to insert the Microsoft Office CD-ROM to install the software, click the OK button, and then wait for the software to be installed. You will need to select the scanner that you will be using from the displayed list.

4. Click the name of the scanner that you will be using, click the **OK** button, verify that the **Black and white** preset is selected, and then click the **Scan** icon.

Your instructor may provide special instructions for the model of scanner that you will be using to scan your documents.

5. Wait for the scanner to complete the scan.

6. Your scanned document will automatically load into the Microsoft Office Document Imaging window.

7. Click the **Close** button to close the Scan New Document window.

8. Click **File**, click **Save As**, type **Sample Document** in the File name text box, and then click the **Save** button.

9. Write a brief description of how you might assist a user to scan a document in your project log.

10. Click **Tools**, click **Send Text to Word**, and then click the two **OK** buttons.

11. Wait for the document image to be converted to text.

12. Verify that you can edit the document in Microsoft Word. This might be an opportunity to "clean up" the document and make it pretty!

13. Click **File**, click **Print**, click the **Name** drop-down list, and if necessary, select **Microsoft Office Document Image Write**. Click the **OK** button, then click the **Save** button.

14. Notice that your converted document is displayed in the Microsoft Office Document Imaging window.

15. Close all open windows and log off the computer.

16. Write a brief description of how you might assist a user to use Microsoft Document Imaging to convert an image file to text using OCR and to create an image file in your project log.

Recovering Office Applications

What do you do when an Office program, such as Word or Excel, stops responding? How do you avoid losing the document or spreadsheet changes since the last file save? You use the Microsoft Office Application Recovery tool. When an Office program stops responding, this tool provides you with a way to potentially recover data. Your end users will thank you many times over for your proficiency in using this tool. To use the Recovery tool, click Start, point to All Programs, point to Microsoft Office, point to Microsoft Office Tools, and then click Microsoft Office Application Recovery, as shown in Figure 8-31.

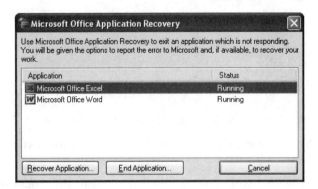

Figure 8-31   Microsoft Office Application Recovery

From the Microsoft Office Application Recovery screen, you can:

- **View the status of running office programs:** Running or Not Responding
- **Recover Application:** Forces the selected Office program to fail and then restart
- **End Application:** Forces the selected program to fail without performing any recovery activities
- **Cancel:** No action is taken with the program that is selected

When an Office application fails, you will be presented with a dialog box indicating that a problem has occurred as illustrated in Figure 8-32. You may want to click the What data does this error report contain? hyperlink and read Microsoft's disclosure statement prior to sending a report. If you desire, you can elect to send the error report to Microsoft by clicking the Send Error Report button and then recover the data. Click the Don't Send button to recover the data without sending the report.

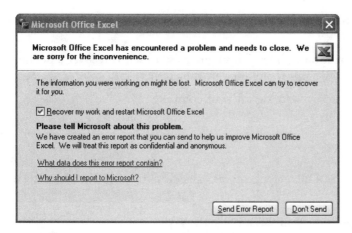

Figure 8-32   Microsoft Office Excel encountered a problem

Activity 8-12: Recovering a Microsoft Office Application

Time Required: 15 minutes

Objective: Resolve issues related to Office application support features.

Description: In this activity, you will practice recovering a Microsoft Office application. You will simulate the failure of Microsoft Excel and complete the recovery of the worksheet. You are practicing recovering a Microsoft Office application so that you can answer your users' questions.

1. Log on to your computer using the user name **user01** and password **Password1**.

2. Click **Start**, point to **All Programs**, point to **Microsoft Office**, and then click **Microsoft Office Excel 2003**.

3. Type **1000** in cell A1 and press **Enter**.

4. Click **File**, click **Save As**, type **Sample Worksheet**, and click the **Save** button. If necessary, click the **Yes** button.

5. Click **Start**, point to **All Programs**, point to **Microsoft Office**, point to **Microsoft Office Tools**, and then click **Microsoft Office Application Recovery**.

6. Click the **Recover Application** button. Wait for the recovery to complete.

7. Click the **Don't Send** button, then wait for the document recovery to be completed.

8. Click **Sample Worksheet.xls** to recover the file and click the **Close** button.

9. Click **File**, click **Save As**, click the **Save** Button, and click the **Yes** button, if necessary.

10. Write a brief description of how you might assist a user to recover a document when Microsoft Word stops responding in your project log.

11. Close any open windows and log off your computer.

CHAPTER SUMMARY

You learned to customize Office applications. Specifically, you learned how to work with Word to:

- Dock and stack toolbars, modify toolbar buttons, and show/hide toolbars
- Create a custom toolbar
- Troubleshoot toolbars

You learned how to customize the personal menus and toolbars to control Word from the following option tabs:

- View: Appears on the screen
- General: Does not fit on other tabs
- Edit: Reacts when you type and edit
- Print: Prints documents
- Save: Saves copies of documents for backup and recovery
- User information: Enter user information
- Compatibility: Behave like previous versions of word processing programs
- File locations: Storage locations for documents
- Security: Location of templates and startup folder
- Spelling and Grammar: Control behavior of Spelling and Grammar
- Track Changes: Identify the person changing a document
- How personalized toolbars and menus work

You learned how to customize the features of automatic text correction and formatting from the following tabs:

- AutoCorrect: Correct text as it's typed
- AutoText: Substitute text when text shortcuts are entered
- AutoFormat As You Type: Apply formatting as you type
- AutoFormatting: Apply formatting after typing the document

□ Smart tags: Recognize data and perform a related action

You learned about the use of the Reveal Formatting task pane, which your users can use to review the formatting applied to a selected area of text. When your users need to format an area of text with the formatting of another area of text, you are prepared to provide one-on-one training on the Format Painter.

You installed and configured the proofing tools to support multiple languages. The Proofing Tools provide features such as spell check and AutoCorrect for documents containing the languages of other countries.

You learned to use the Office System Tools for the following tasks:

□ Organizing Clips: Manage media files

□ Save My Settings wizard: Back up and restore personal Office settings

□ Document scanning: Convert paper documents to formatted, editable documents

□ Viewing documents: View scanned document images

□ Print driver: Convert documents to images

□ Recovering Office applications: Recover documents when Office applications crash

8

Key Terms

AutoRecovery — System feature that periodically saves files to permit file recovery after the occurrence of program crashes or power failures.

docked — Move a toolbar to the edge of an application window.

Microsoft Document Imaging Format (MDI) — Microsoft extension of TIFF file format.

move handle — Button on the toolbar that makes it possible to move a toolbar.

optical character recognition (OCR) — Process in which pattern matching is used to convert scanned images into editable text.

Tagged Image File Format (TIFF) — Common file format used for scanning, storage, and interchange of graphic images.

Review Questions

1. In which Office applications can you use toolbars? (Choose all that apply.)

   a. Access
   b. Excel
   c. PowerPoint
   d. Word

2. Which of the following toolbars is available in Word? (Choose all that apply.)

    a. Standard

    b. Formatting

    c. Drawing

    d. Microsoft

3. By default, the Standard and Formatting toolbars are _____ .

    a. stacked

    b. docked

    c. optional

    d. moved

4. Which of the following techniques forces a full menu to appear?

    a. click the chevron character (>>) at the bottom of the menu

    b. right-click a submenu item

    c. wait about three seconds without making a selection

    d. click a specific top-level menu item twice

5. Which of the following actions will move or copy a button on or to a toolbar? (Choose all that apply.)

    a. click Edit, click Copy, and click Paste

    b. hold Ctrl and drag the button

    c. hold Alt and drag the button

    d. hold Alt+Ctrl and drag the button

6. What are the correct steps to create a custom toolbar? (Choose all that apply.)

    a. click the Tools menu and click Customize

    b. click the Toolbars tab and click New

    c. drag a command to the new toolbar

    d. drag a button to the new toolbar

7. Which of the following is a possible reason that you cannot find a button on a toolbar? (Choose all that apply.)

    a. not enough room on the toolbar

    b. program window not maximized

    c. button not recently used

    d. button marked as hidden

8. You can select the _____ tab to control what appears on the screen.
   a. General
   b. Edit
   c. View
   d. Print

9. You can select the _____ tab to control how Word reacts when you type text.
   a. General
   b. Edit
   c. View
   d. Print

10. Which of the following actions is considered a word-ending action for AutoCorrect? (Choose all that apply.)
    a. pressing the spacebar
    b. pressing the period [.] key
    c. pressing the question mark [?] key
    d. pressing Enter

11. Which of the following is a customization that can be set for AutoCorrect? (Choose all that apply.)
    a. correct TWo INitial CAptials box
    b. capitalize first letter of sentences
    c. correct accidental usage of cAPS LOCK key
    d. automatically use suggestions from the spelling checker

12. To review formatting, select _____ from the Format menu.
    a. Show Formatting
    b. List Formatting
    c. Apply Formatting
    d. Reveal Formatting

13. Which task can you accomplish with the Format Painter? (Choose all that apply.)
    a. copy a font size from one Excel cell to another
    b. copy the font color from one Excel cell to another
    c. copy text from one Word document to another
    d. copy text from one Excel cell to another

8

14. Which feature is supplied when Microsoft Proofing Tools are installed? (Choose all that apply.)
    a. spell checkers
    b. grammar checkers
    c. fonts
    d. AutoCorrect lists

15. The Microsoft Clip Organizer builds clip collections for which type of clips? (Choose all that apply.)
    a. art
    b. sound
    c. animation
    d. movies
    e. documents

16. The Save My Settings wizard saves a copy of settings in a(n) _____ file.
    a. TIFF
    b. MDI
    c. OPS
    d. SMS
    e. SWS

17. Microsoft document scanning saves images in which type of file? (Choose all that apply.)
    a. TIFF
    b. MDI
    c. OPS
    d. SMS
    e. SWS

18. With Microsoft Document Imaging, you can _____ . (Choose all that apply.)
    a. perform optical character recognition
    b. view converted documents
    c. convert a TIFF or MDI file into an editable document
    d. edit documents
    e. edit graphics files

19. The Microsoft Document Image Writer can be used to _____ image files.

   a. print

   b. scan

   c. edit

   (d) create

   e. view

20. From the Microsoft Office Application Recovery screen, you can _____ . (Choose all that apply.)

   (a) view the status of running programs

   b. cancel an application

   (c) recover an application

   (d) cancel the recovery attempt

CASE PROJECTS

Case 8-1: Customizing Office Applications

You are a desktop support technician. Your network consists of a Windows Server 2003 Active Directory domain with 10 servers, including application and database servers and 500 computers running Windows XP Professional.

You are responding to a question posed by George. He wants to know how he can use the toolbars in Word more effectively. What advice will you be giving George? Include information about docking and stacking toolbars, showing toolbars, and building custom toolbars.

Case 8-2: Personalizing Office Applications

You consult as a desktop support technician. Your customer's network consists of five computers configured as a workgroup.

Your customer has expressed that "Word does not work the way I want it to." What advice will you give to your customer? How will you determine what changes need to be made?

CASE
PROJECTS

Case 8-3: Using Microsoft Office Imaging

You are a desktop support technician. Your network consists of a Windows Server 2003 Active Directory domain with 12 servers and 500 computers running Windows XP Professional.

You are responding to a question by Susan regarding document imaging. She wants you to explain how document imaging could be used to trade documents between the legal group and the corporation's external legal office. What will you tell Susan about document scanning and imaging?

9

CONFIGURE, CUSTOMIZE, AND MIGRATE TO OUTLOOK

After reading this chapter and completing the exercises, you will be able to:

- ◆ Describe how to use the advanced features and capabilities of Outlook
- ◆ Configure and personalize Outlook features
- ◆ Integrate Outlook Express and Outlook
- ◆ Restore data and repair corrupted data

As you are aware, the role of the DST requires that you be prepared to resolve issues related to Microsoft Office Outlook 2003 (hereafter called Outlook for brevity). Outlook provides a wide range of capabilities that can be tailored to meet the message and collaboration needs of your users.

Your users expect that you will be prepared to assist them with the configuration and customization of Outlook features. You will be learning how to answer your users' questions about these Outlook features. You will be learning how to help your users migrate to Outlook from Outlook Express or perhaps, use both e-mail clients.

Your users expect you to possess the skills to restore and repair their e-mail files. One technique that you will need to learn is e-mail archival.

Using the Features of Outlook

Before you can work with Outlook, you will need to establish a connection to the Exchange Server. Following this connection, you will be ready to work with the folders in Outlook.

Your users expect that you will be ready to answer their questions about the features of Outlook. Here is a list of questions that you might hear from your users:

- What do I need to do to connect to the Exchange Server?
- How will I use the various Outlook folders?
- How do I surf the Internet without leaving Outlook?
- Are there some ways I can organize my data?
- Where can I locate the e-mail addresses for other people at work?
- How do I create a list to send e-mail to the members of my project team?
- How can I locate specific e-mail messages in my Inbox?
- Are there ways to have my incoming e-mail placed in folders automatically?
- When I'm working at home, how can I access my e-mail from the office?

The sections that follow will prepare you to answer these and additional potential questions. Before you can work with Outlook folders, you will need to establish a connection to the Exchange Server.

Connecting to an Exchange Server

To compete successfully in today's fast-paced world, your users must find ways to communicate and collaborate more efficiently. E-mail is currently the most widely used collaborative technology. Your organization may deploy Outlook to work with Exchange Server to meet the requirements for these e-mail and collaboration services.

Exchange Server is Microsoft's premium messaging and enterprise collaboration server. Exchange's primary role is as an electronic mail message storage but it can also store calendars, task lists, contact details, and other data included in Outlook.

ACTIVITY

Activity 9-1: Connecting Outlook to an Exchange Server

Time Required: 15 minutes

Objective: Connect the Outlook client to an Exchange Server.

Description: In this activity, you will create a connection for Outlook to use Microsoft Exchange Server. You will find this activity useful in your career as a DST because, in order to answer users' questions about connecting Outlook to Exchange Server, you will need to have explored creating this connection in detail.

NOTE

You will need to use the user01 (First User) e-mail account or the assigned e-mail account your instructor has created on the Instructor01 server.

1. Log on to your computer with the user name **user01** and password **Password1**.

2. Click **Start**, click **Control Panel**, double-click **Mail**, and click the **E-mail Accounts** button.

3. If this activity has been completed previously and if the View or change existing e-mail accounts option button is selected, click the **Next** button, click the **Remove** button, click the **Yes** button, click the **Finish** button, and click the **E-mail Accounts** button.

4. Click the **Next** button, click the **Microsoft Exchange Server** option button, as shown in Figure 9-1, and click the **Next** button.

9

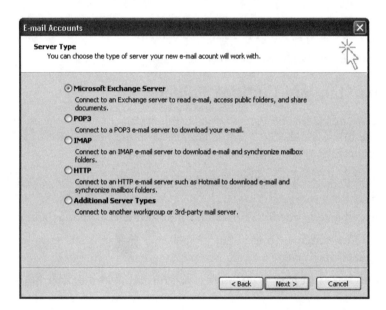

Figure 9-1   Server Type with Microsoft Exchange selected

5. Type **instructor02** in the Microsoft Exchange Server text box, uncheck the **Use Cached Exchange Mode** check box, type **user01** in the User Name text box, as shown in Figure 9-2, click the **Check Name** button, and click the **Next** button.

6. If necessary, click the **Yes** button. Click the **Finish** button and click the **Close** button.

7. Write a brief description in your project log explaining how you might assist a user to connect Outlook to an Exchange Server.

8. Close the Control Panel window.

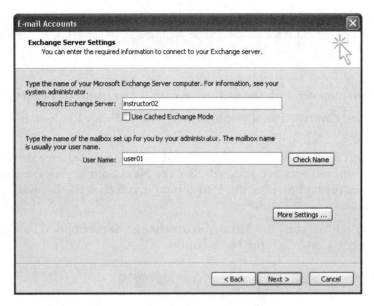

Figure 9-2   Microsoft Exchange Server settings

Working with the Standard Outlook Folders

Your users will use a standard set of folders to organize their data. In order to assist your users and answer their questions, you should become familiar with the purpose for each Outlook folder in the following list:

- **Inbox:** Holds in-coming e-mail. Your users will have a separate inbox for each e-mail account.

- **Calendar:** Manages schedules, including appointments, meetings, and events.

- **Contacts:** Stores information about people, such as name, address, phone numbers, and additional items.

- **Tasks:** Lists tasks that have been assigned to you and tasks that have been assigned to subordinates.

- **Notes:** Stores and organizes notes.

- **Outbox:** Stores outgoing messages until they are picked up for delivery.

- **Sent Items:** Stores a copy of messages that you have sent.

- **Deleted Items:** Stores deleted Outlook items and can contain items of various types (for example, messages, contacts, and tasks).

- **Drafts:** Holds unfinished drafts of messages and other items. Your users will use this folder for messages that are not yet completed for example, when your user discovers that he or she needs an additional tidbit of information to complete the message.

In the sections that follow, you learn about the configuration of the four top-level folders that you may expect your users to use when working with Outlook. After studying about these four Outlook folders, you should be able to extend the learned skills to the remaining folders.

Using the Inbox Folder

The Inbox displays messages from your default message store. For most organizations, this default store will be from the Exchange Server. As shown in Figure 9-3, the Inbox view shows the header for each message. While the header contains such information as sender, subject, date, and time, these columns may not all be visible. The Reading pane on the right hides many of these columns of data. If you move the Reading pane to the bottom, you can view the message header columns.

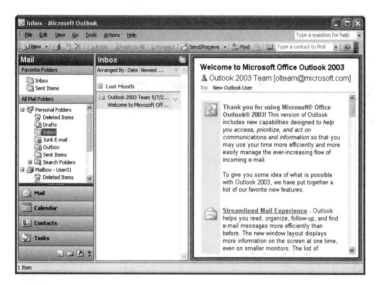

Figure 9-3   Outlook Inbox folder

To sort messages, click on the column header. To switch the sort sequence, such as descending for ascending, click the column header a second time.

Activity 9-2: Customizing the Inbox View

Time Required: 15 minutes

Objective: Customize and use the Inbox view.

Description: In this activity, you will customize the Inbox folder. You will find this activity useful in your career as a DST because, in order to answer users; questions about customizing the Inbox folder, you will need to have explored the customization of the Inbox folder in detail.

1. If necessary, log on to your computer with the user name **user01** and password **Password1**.

2. Click **Start**, point to **All Programs**, point to **Microsoft Office**, and click **Microsoft Office Outlook 2003**.

3. Click **Inbox** under Personal Folders and, if necessary, read the generated message from Outlook.

4. If you get the **Would you like to AutoArchive...** message, click the **Don't prompt me about this again** check box and click the **No** button.

5. Click the **New** button, type **user01@classroom.net** in the To text box, type **Test Message** in the Subject text box, type **Test of Exchange Server** in the message area, and click the **Send** button.

6. If necessary, click the **Send/Receive** button. Wait for the message to be transferred, and click on the message from User01 (First User).

7. Click **View**, point to **Arrange By**, and view the options as shown in Figure 9-4.

Figure 9-4   Outlook Inbox folder - Arrange By options

8. Click **View**, click **Navigation Pane**, and note that the Navigation pane is removed.

9. Click **View**, click **Navigation Pane**, and note that the Navigation pane has returned.

10. Click **View**, point to **Reading Pane**, click **Bottom**, and note that the Reading pane is positioned below the headers.

11. Click **View**, click **AutoPreview**, and note that the first part of each message is displayed.

12. Click the **Received** column header and note that the message sequence has changed.

13. Write a brief description in your project log explaining how you might assist with the customization of the Inbox folder.

14. Leave Outlook open for the next activity.

Using the Calendar Folder

In the Calendar folder, your user will see his or her schedule in several convenient ways. By default, the calendar is displayed as the current day, as shown in Figure 9-5. From the Date Navigator, located in the upper-right corner, your user can select another date to view. To see the details of a scheduled event, double-click the entry.

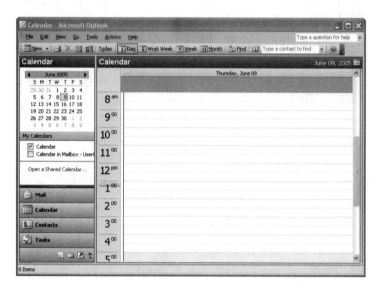

Figure 9-5 Outlook Calendar folder

To add an entry, you user will need to complete one of the following actions:

- Double-click the time slot for the start time. This will open an Appointment form.
- Right-click a time slot and pick the type (appointment, meeting, or event).
- Select a time and select File and then New.
- Click the down-arrow beside New on the Standard toolbar and select the type.

My wife uses the Calendar view to track birthdays, anniversaries, and so on. Because of her Outlook calendar, she frequently sends me e-mail messages that start "Do you know that you are about to miss another...". I'm sure that my kids think that I'm really a cool dad who never forgets.

ACTIVITY

Activity 9-3: Configuring the Calendar View

Time Required: 15 minutes

Objective: Customize and use the Calendar view.

Description: In this activity, you will customize the Calendar folder. You will find this activity useful in your career as a DST because, in order to answer users' questions about customizing the Calendar folder, you will need to have explored the customization of the Calendar folder in detail.

1. If necessary, log on to your computer with the user name **user01** and password **Password1**.

2. If necessary, Click **Start**, point to **All Programs**, point to **Microsoft Office**, and click **Microsoft Office Outlook 2003**.

3. Click **Calendar** in the Navigation pane, and double-click on the Calendar at 2:00 PM.

4. Type **Project Meeting** in the Subject text box, click the **Label** drop-down list arrow, and click **Important**.

5. Click the **End time** drop-down list arrow and click **3:00 PM**.

6. Type **First project meeting** in the message area and click the **Save and Close** button.

7. Click **View**, click **Work Week**, and note that Monday through Friday is shown.

8. Click **View**, click **Week**, and note that Monday through Sunday is shown.

9. Click **View**, click **Month**, and note that a monthly calendar is shown.

10. Click **View**, click **Day**, and note that a calendar for one day is shown.

11. Click **View**, click **TaskPad**, and note that the TaskPad pane is shown and the Monthly calendar was moved to the right.

12. Double-click in the TaskPad pane, type **Agenda** in the Subject text box, click the **Due date** drop-down list arrow and select a date before today's date, click the **Start date** drop-down list arrow, and select a date before the Due date.

13. Type **First project meeting** in the message area and click the **Save and Close** button.

14. Click **View**, point to **Arrange By**, point to **Current View**. See Figure 9-6.

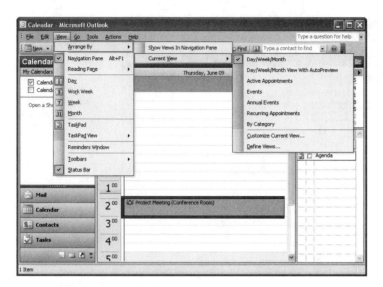

Figure 9-6 Outlook Calendar folder - Arrange By options

15. Write a brief description in your project log explaining how you might assist with the customization of the Calendar folder

16. Leave Outlook open for the next activity.

Using the Contacts Folder

The Contacts folder stores contact information. By default, Outlook displays the Address Card view, as shown in Figure 9-7. This view shows the name for each contact with other fields selected by your user, such as address and phone number.

Your users can issue the following commands to customize the view:

- **Address Card:** Displays the name of each contact with other selected fields.
- **Detailed Address Cards:** Increases the amount of fields displayed for each contact.
- **Phone List:** Displays the contacts as a phone list.
- **By Category:** Groups contacts by their assigned categories.
- **By Company:** Groups contacts by organization.
- **By Location:** Groups contacts by region or country.
- **By Follow-up Flag:** Groups contacts by the status of the assigned follow-up flag.

To add a contact entry to the Contacts folder, open and complete a contact form. To open a contact form, right-click on an empty space on the screen and click New Contact or click the New button on the toolbar.

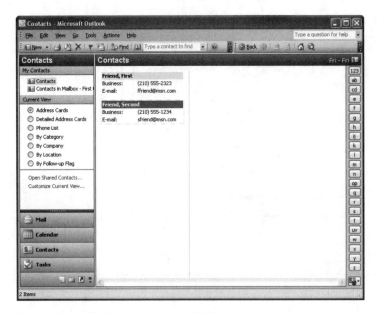

Figure 9-7 Outlook Contacts folder

Activity 9-4: Customizing the Contacts View

Time Required: 15 minutes

Objective: Customize and use the Contacts view.

Description: In this activity, you will customize the Contacts folder. You will find this activity useful in your career as a DST because, in order to answer users' questions about customizing the Contacts folder, you will need to have explored the customization of the Contacts folder in detail.

1. If necessary, log on to your computer with the user name **user01** and password **Password1**.

2. If necessary, Click **Start**, point to **All Programs**, point to **Microsoft Office**, and click **Microsoft Office Outlook 2003**.

3. Click **Contacts** in the Navigation pane.

4. Double-click on the Contacts pane and create a contact for yourself by completing the appropriate fields (be sure to specify an e-mail address).

5. Click the **Save and Close** button.

6. Double-click on the Contacts pane and create a contact for another student (be sure to specify an e-mail address).

7. Click the **Save and Close** button.

8. Click the **Detailed Address Cards** option button under Current View and note the additional information that is displayed for each contact.

9. Click the **Phone List** option button under Current View and note a phone list is displayed.

10. Click the **By Category** option button under Current View and note the contacts are sorted by the assigned categories.

11. Click the **By Company** option button under Current View and note the contacts are sorted by the company.

12. Click the **By Location** option button under Current View and note the contacts are sorted by the location (state and country).

13. Click the **By Follow-up Flag** option button under Current View, right-click in the Follow-up flag column for a contact, click **Follow Up**, click the **Flag to** drop-down list arrow, click **Send E-mail**, and click the **OK** button.

14. Click the **Address Cards** option button under Current View, and click **View**, point to **Reading Pane**, and click **Bottom**.

15. Write a brief description in your project log explaining how you might assist with the customization of the Contacts folder.

16. Leave Outlook open for the next activity.

Using the Tasks Folder

Your user will use the Outlook Tasks folder to maintain his or her list of tasks. The default view, as shown in Figure 9-8, is a simple list with subject, due date, and status. The task list shows tasks that your user has assigned to others, as well as those assigned to him or her. For detailed information about a task, double-click on a task entry.

To add a task, double-click on a blank task entry to open the new task form, where your user completes the task definition.

Your users can choose View, Arrange By, Current View, and then one of the following commands to change the Tasks Folder view:

- **Simple List:** Shows whether the task has been completed, task name, and due date.
- **Detailed List:** Shows the information in the Simple List and adds status, percent complete, and categories.
- **Active Tasks:** Shows tasks that are active.
- **Next Seven Days:** Displays tasks for the next seven calendar days.
- **Overdue Tasks:** Displays incomplete tasks with due dates that were missed.
- **By Category:** Organizes the tasks by the assigned categories.
- **Assignment:** Shows the tasks assigned to specific people.

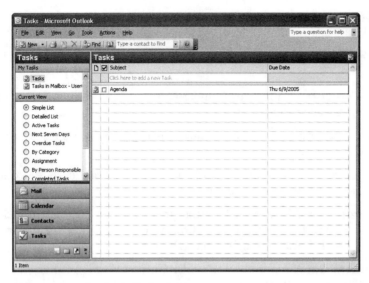

Figure 9-8 Outlook Tasks folder

- **By Person Responsible:** Groups the tasks according to the person responsible for each task.

- **Completed Tasks:** Shows the completed tasks.

- **Task Timeline:** Displays a time line of all tasks.

Activity 9-5: Customizing the Tasks View

Time Required: 15 minutes

Objective: Customize and use the Tasks view.

Description: In this activity, you will customize the Task View folder. You will find this activity useful in your career as a DST because, in order to answer users' questions about customizing the Task View folder, you will need to have explored the customization of the Task View folder in detail.

1. If necessary, log on to your computer with the user name **user01** and password **Password1**.

2. If necessary, Click **Start**, point to **All Programs**, point to **Microsoft Office**, and click **Microsoft Office Outlook 2003**.

3. Click **Tasks** in the Navigation pane.

4. Click **View**, point to **Arrange By**, and point to **Current View**. See Figure 9-9.

Figure 9-9   Outlook Tasks folder - Arrange By options

5. Click the **Detailed List** option button and note the changes to the Task pane.

6. Repeat Step 5 for the remaining entries under Current View.

7. Write a brief description in your project log explaining how you might assist with the customization of the Tasks folder.

8. Close the Outlook window.

Using Outlook on the Web

Outlook includes several features to integrate with the Internet. The sections that follow discuss this integration between Outlook and the Internet.

Browsing the Web from Outlook

Your users can browse the Web without leaving Outlook. This feature is handy when your users need to view online documents or retrieve a file without starting Internet Explorer. Outlook's integration with Internet Explorer allows your users to continue working in Outlook without having to open a second program, which allows them to avoid switching between applications.

By adding the Web toolbar, as shown in Figure 9-10, you can click on the Start Page button to access your Start page. To return to Outlook, select the folder you need from the folder list.

Figure 9-10   Outlook showing Web access

Accessing Your Mail with a Web Browser

When you—or your users—are out-of-town, you might want to access your organization's e-mail with a Web browser. For example, you might need to review information about the project that you are working on. Or perhaps, your user might need to check his or her calendar for the details of tomorrow's meeting. Whatever the situation, Exchange Server supports access to your Exchange Server with Outlook Web Access.

I'm really in love with the ability to read my e-mail from a Web browser. From home, I can check e-mail for the project on which I'm working and zip off a response to a question.

**IN THE
WORKPLACE**

ACTIVITY

Activity 9-6: Using a Web Browser to Access an Exchange Server Mailbox

Time Required: 15 minutes

Objective: Use a Web browser to access an Exchange Server mailbox.

Description: In this activity, you will use Internet Explorer to access your e-mail on the Exchange Server. You will find this activity useful in your career as a DST because, in order to answer users' questions about using a Web Browser to Access an Exchange Server Mailbox, you will need to have explored these steps in detail.

1. If necessary, log on to your computer with the user name **user01** and password **Password1**.

2. Click **Start** and click **Internet Explorer** in the pinned items area.

3. Type **Instructor02\exchange\user01** in the Address bar and press **Enter**.

4. Click the **New** button, type **User01** in the To text box, type **Test Web Mail** in the Subject text box, type **Test** in the message area, and click the **Send** button.

5. Click the **Inbox** folder. Your screen resembles Figure 9-11.

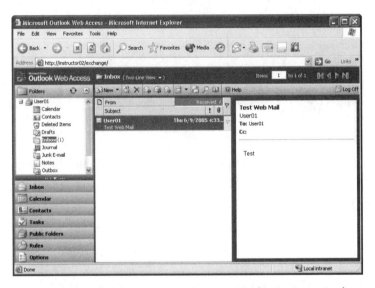

Figure 9-11   Internet Explorer showing Web access to Exchange Server

6. Write a brief description in your project log explaining how you might assist a user with accessing an Exchange Server from a Web browser.

7. Close the Internet Explorer window.

Connecting to Exchange Server with HTTP

A new feature of Outlook adds support for connecting to Exchange Server with HTTP, the standard protocol used for Web access. This feature is not the same as the technique that was presented in the previous section. If your users frequently access the organization's network from remote sites, your organization may have deployed this feature. Contact the network administration team to determine if this feature is in use.

Using Categories with E-mail

One of the primary functions of Outlook is to help your users organize their data. To make things easier, your users can assign categories, which are words or phrases, to Outlook items. For example, they may choose to assign the category Personal to e-mail from family members.

What can your users do with categories? After assigning categories to Outlook items, the users can search, organize, and sort by categories. For example, categories can be assigned to find items associated with a specific project. Of course, to make categories work, your users must be diligent in the assignment of categories to Outlook items. If they start to waver in their commitment to assigning categories, they will find that they may not be able to organize their e-mails.

NOTE

Your users can use the categories provided by Outlook or add their own.

IN THE WORKPLACE

I like to assign a particular category to a template. When a template is selected for an e-mail message, the category is automatically assigned.

Your users will use one of these methods to display the Categories dialog box, depending on the type of Outlook item they are creating:

- **Message:** Click Options and click Categories.
- **Calendar, contact, or task item:** Click the Categories button at the bottom.
- **Note:** Add the note, click the note icon, and click Categories.

ACTIVITY

Activity 9-7: Using Categories with E-mail Messages

Time Required: 15 minutes

Objective: Use categories with e-mail messages.

Description: In this activity, you will add a new category to the Master Categories List. Next, you will create a new e-mail message and assign the category. Then, you will search for messages assigned to the category. You will find this activity useful in your career as a DST because, in order to answer users' questions about using categories, you will need to have explored these steps in detail.

1. If necessary, log on to your computer with the user name **user01** and password **Password1**.

2. Click **Start**, point to **All Programs**, point to **Microsoft Office**, and click **Microsoft Office Outlook 2003**.

3. Click **Mail** in the Navigation pane, and click **Inbox** under Personal Folders.

4. Click the **New** button list arrow and click **Mail Message**.

5. Type **user01@classroom.net** in the To text box, type **Second Test Message** in the Subject text box, and type **Test of Categories** in the message area.

6. Click the **Options** button, and click the **Categories** button.

7. Check the **Master Category List** button, type **Test** in the New category text box, click the **Add** button, and click the **OK** button.

8. Check the **Test** check box and click the **OK** button.

9. Click the **Close** button and click the **Send** button.

10. If necessary, click the **Send/Receive** button. Wait for the message to be transferred, and click on the message from User01 (First User).

11. Click **Tools**, point to **Find**, click **Advanced Find**, click the **More Choices** tab, type **Test** the **Categories** text box, and click the **Find Now** button.

12. Double-click the message located in the search list at the bottom of the dialog box.

13. Write a brief description in your project log explaining how you might assist a user to use categories with e-mail messages.

14. Close the mail message and Advanced Find window.

15. Leave Outlook open for the next activity.

Managing Address Books and Distribution Lists

In order to send an e-mail message, your user must indicate the address of the recipient. When you use Exchange Server, there is an address list—the **Global Address List (GAL)**. The GAL resides on the Exchange Server and contains the addresses for mailboxes created on the Exchange Server. In addition to containing the list of mailboxes on the Exchange Server, the GAL contains distribution groups that permit addressing to a group of individuals.

As you have seen, you can create addresses in one or more contact folders. Outlook consolidates your contact folders into the **Outlook Address Book (OAB)**. With a new installation of Outlook, the OAB contains only the Contacts folder. As you add other contact folders these folders appear in the OAB.

You can create a **Personal Address Book (PAB)**, which Outlook stores separate from the address book associated with the Outlook data store. The entries in the PAB do not contain as many fields as the OAB. However, you can use the PAB to store information isolated from your other Outlook data.

I recently used a Personal Address Book to hold the e-mail addresses for a charity organization with which I was working. This enabled me to send e-mail without placing individuals in my Outlook Address Book.

Activity 9-8: Using Address Books and Distribution Lists

ACTIVITY

Time Required: 15 minutes

Objective: Use Address Books and addressing options.

Description: In this activity, you will use an Address Book entry to send a message. Also, you will create a distribution list. You will find this activity useful in your career as a DST because, in order to answer users' questions about using the Address Book, you will need to have explored these steps in detail.

1. If necessary, log on to your computer with the user name **user01** and password **Password1**.

2. If necessary, click **Start**, point to **All Programs**, point to **Microsoft Office**, and click **Microsoft Office Outlook 2003**.

3. Click **Tools**, and click **Address Book**. Your screen resembles Figure 9-12.

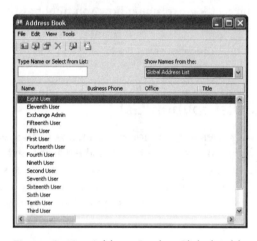

Figure 9-12   Address Book - Global Address List

4. Click **First User** in the Name column, and click the **New Message** button (it is the last button on the toolbar).

5. Type a message to yourself, and click the **Send** button.

6. Close the Address Book window.

7. In your project log, write a brief summary that describes how you could assist a user to send an e-mail message using the Global Address List.

8. Click **Tools**, click **Address Book**, click the **Show Names from the** drop-down list arrow, and click **Contacts**.

9. Click the **New Entry** button (first button on toolbar), click the **In the** drop-down list arrow, click **Contacts**, click **New Distribution List**, and click the **OK** button.

10. Type **Best Friends** in the Name text box, click the **Select Members** button, click the **Show Names from the** drop-down list arrow, and click **Contacts**.

11. Highlight the contacts that you created in Steps 4 through 7 in Activity 9-4, and click the **OK** button.

12. Click the **Categories** button, check the **Personal** check box, and click the **OK** button.

13. Your completed Distribution List entry resembles Figure 9-13. Click the **Save and Close** button.

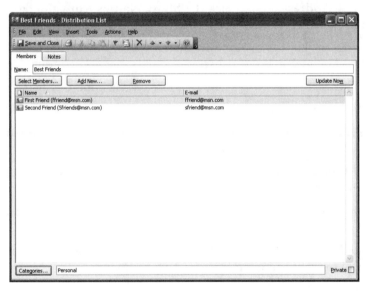

Figure 9-13   Best Friends - Distribution List window

14. Write a brief description in your project log explaining how you might assist a user to send an e-mail message using a Distribution List.

15. Close the Address Book window.

16. Click **Contacts** in the Navigation pane, right-click **Best Friends** in the Contacts pane. Click **New Message to Contact**, type a short message to your peers, and click the **Send** button.

Only one PAB is permitted per e-mail account. If this activity has been previously completed, you will not be able to complete Steps 17 through 19.

NOTE

17. Click **Start**, click **Control Panel**, and double-click the **Mail** icon.

18. Click the **E-mail Accounts** button, click the **Add a new directory or address book** option button, click the **Next** button, select the **Additional Address Books** option button, and click the **Next** button.

19. Click **Personal Address Book**, click the **Next** button, click the two consecutive **OK** buttons, and click the **Close** button.

20. Close all open windows.

21. Click **Start**, point to **All Programs**, point to **Microsoft Office**, and click **Microsoft Office Outlook 2003**.

22. Click **Tools**, click **Address Book,** click the **Show Names from the** drop-down list arrow, and click **Personal Address Book**.

23. Click the **New Entry** button, click the **In the** drop-down list arrow, click **Personal Address Book**, click the **Internet Address**, and click the **OK** button.

24. Complete the entries on the SMTP - General tab, and click the **OK** button.

25. Close the Address Book window.

26. Click the **Address Book** button (resembles a book), click the **Show Names from the** drop-down list arrow, and click **Personal Address Book**.

27. Click the **Find Items** button (second button), type the first letter of the Display name from Step 24, and click the **OK** button.

28. Double-click the entry in the Search Results, view the entry information and update as needed, and then click the **OK** button.

29. Write a brief description in your project log explaining how you might assist a user to send an e-mail message using the Personal Address Book.

30. Close the Address Book window.

31. Leave Outlook open for the next activity.

Managing E-mail Messages

Your users will expect you to help them manage their e-mail messages. For example, you can expect questions similar to the following:

- How do I search for e-mail messages that were sent to a specific person?
- How can I organize e-mail from certain individuals or for a particular project?
- How can I have e-mails placed in a particular folder?
- How can I have Outlook notify persons sending me e-mail when I'm out of the office?

Answers to these items and others will be presented in the sections that follow.

Using E-mail Search Folders

Outlook provides features that permit your users to find specific e-mail. In addition, your users can use Search Folders to search for a set of messages that meet a certain criteria, such as all of the e-mail messages for a particular project. A Search Folder is not really a folder, but a view that behaves much like a separate folder.

Your users might want to "flag" outgoing messages as a means of including special instructions with a message. For example, you could mark a message with a review reminder as you send a message to your manager. By including the flag in the message header, you could reduce the chances that the message requiring review would be missed.

Activity 9-9: Searching for E-mail Messages

Time Required: 15 minutes

Objective: Locate e-mail messages with Search Folders.

Description: In this activity, you will use Search Folders to identify e-mail messages meeting specific requirements. Also, you will practice placing a reminder flag on a message. You will find this activity useful in your career as a DST because, in order to answer users' questions about using Search Folders, you will need to have explored these steps in detail.

1. If necessary, log on to your computer with the user name **user01** and password **Password1**.

2. If necessary, click **Start**, point to **All Programs**, point to **Microsoft Office**, and click **Microsoft Office Outlook 2003**.

3. Click **Mail** in the Navigation pane.

4. Click **Tools**, click **Options**, click the **Mail Format** tab, uncheck the **Use Microsoft Office Word 2003 to edit e-mail messages** check box, and click the **OK** button.

5. Click **New**, type **user01** in the To text box, and type **Test Flag** in the Subject text box.

6. Click **Actions**, point to **Follow Up**, click **Add Reminder**, click the **Flag to** drop-down list arrow and click **Review**, click the **Due by** drop-down list arrow and click the **Today** button, and then click the **OK** button.

7. Click the **Send** button.

8. If the Reminder dialog box is displayed, click the **Click Snooze to be reminded again in** drop-down list arrow and click **1 hour**, and then click the **Snooze** button.

9. In the Navigation pane, under All Mail Folders, expand **Search Folders**, and note the default Search Folders as shown in Figure 9-14.

10. Click **Unread Mail**, and read any unread messages.

11. Click **File**, point to **New**, and click **Search Folder**.

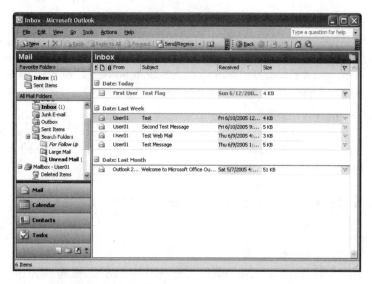

Figure 9-14   Search Folders windows

12. Click **Mail sent directly to me**, and click the **OK** button.

13. Click the **Sent Directly to Me** folder and locate the e-mail sent directly to me.

14. Click **File**, point to **New**, and click **Search Folder**.

15. Scroll and click **Create a custom Search Folder**, click the **Choose** button, type **Test Messages** in the Name text box, click the **Criteria** button, type **Test** in the Search for the word(s) text box, click the three **OK** buttons and note the headers that contain the word **Test**.

16. Write a brief description in your project log explaining how you might assist a user to use Search Folders for select e-mail.

17. Leave Outlook open for the next activity.

Using Rules to Organize E-mail

You—and your users—are often swamped by the volume of daily e-mail messages. What is needed is an automated process to analyze these messages and place the critical ones in one or more Personal folders. Your users will find the ability to filter incoming e-mail useful. For example, e-mail from their supervisor could be moved into a Personal folder called Boss.

You create rules to specify to Outlook how to identify a message (conditions) and what to do with the message (actions). These conditions might include the person sending the message, message size, the priority assigned, or a variety of other conditions. For actions, you could place the message in a special folder, respond to the message with an existing message, or play a sound.

Rules are all created the same way—the Outlook Rules wizard. Activity 9-10 presents the general steps to create rules. With the Rules wizard, you should not have problems creating rules.

When your users are away from their offices, they will want to use the Out of Office wizard to automatically generate replies to incoming messages. For example, when a user is out of town on a business trip, he or she can easily create a short message indicating when he or she will return.

The Out of Office Assistant works only with e-mail accounts on the Exchange Server. Because the Out of Office Assistant works on the Exchange Server, your out-of-office messages will be sent even if you are not running Outlook.

CAUTION

You are aware that when your users are not available for whatever reason, they can create e-mail messages that are sent automatically to anyone who sends them an e-mail. However, the use of these messages can be abused. Here are a few tips that you can pass along to your users to minimize the abuse potential:

IN THE WORKPLACE

- Keep the message short.
- Keep the messages up-to-date.
- Turn-off the rule when you return.

Activity 9-10: Creating E-mail Rules

ACTIVITY

Time Required: 15 minutes

Objective: Create Outlook rules to analyze and process e-mail messages.

Description: In this activity, you will use the Rules wizard to create an e-mail processing rule. In addition, you will create an out-of-office rule. You will find this activity useful in your career as a DST because, in order to answer users' questions about using Outlook Rules, you will need to have explored these steps in detail.

1. If necessary, log on to your computer with the user name **user01** and password **Password1**.
2. If necessary, click **Start**, point to **All Programs**, point to **Microsoft Office**, and click **Microsoft Office Outlook 2003**.
3. Click the **Inbox** folder, click **Tools**, and click **Rules and Alerts**, as shown in Figure 9-15.
4. If the Test rule exists, click the **Delete** button and click the **Yes** button.
5. Click the **New Rule** button, click the **Move messages with specific words in the subject to a folder**, as shown in Figure 9-16, and click the **Next** button.

9

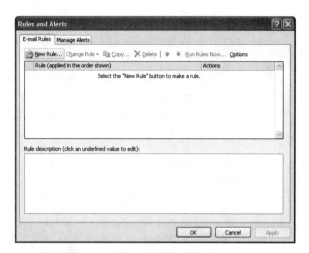

Figure 9-15   Rules and Alerts

Figure 9-16   Rules wizard

6. Click the **specific words** link under Step 2: Edit the rule description (click an underlined value).

7. Type **Test** in the Specific words or phrases to search for in the subject text box, click the **Add** button, and click the **OK** button.

8. Click the **specified** link under Step 2: Edit the rule description (click an underlined value).

NOTE If this activity has been completed previously, you will name the folder in Step 9 as Test1, Test2, and so on.

9. Click the **New** button, type **Test** in the Name text box, and click the **OK** button.

10. Click the **OK** button. Your screen should resemble Figure 9-17.

Figure 9-17   Created rule

11. Click the **Next** Button. Review the conditions as shown in Figure 9-18.

Figure 9-18   Rule conditions

12. Click the **Next** Button. Review the actions as shown in Figure 9-19.

Figure 9-19   Rule actions

13. Click the **Next** Button. Review the exceptions as shown in Figure 9-20.

Figure 9-20   Rule exceptions

14. Click the Next button, check the **Run this rule now on messages already in "Inbox"** check box, as shown in Figure 9-21, and click the **Finish** button.

Figure 9-21   Finishing the rule setup

15. Wait for the rule to be processed and click the two **OK** buttons.

16. Click the **Test** folder and view the filtered e-mails.

17. Write a brief description in your project log explaining how you might assist a user to create an e-mail rule with the Rules wizard.

18. Click the **Inbox** folder, click **Tools**, and then click **Out of Office Assistant**.

19. Type **I will be out of the office until Monday. I will be checking my mail during my absence.** in the AutoReply only once to each sender with the following text text box, as shown in Figure 9-22.

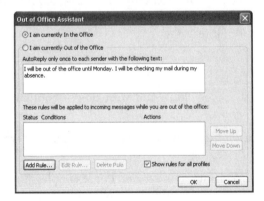

Figure 9-22   Out of Office Assistant

20. Click the **I am currently Out of the Office** option button and click the **OK** button.

21. Click the **New** button, type **user01@classroom.net** in the To text box, type **Test Out of Office** in the Subject text box, type **Test** in the message area, and click the **Send** button.

22. If necessary, click the **Send/Receive** button. Wait for the message to be transferred, and click on the message from User01 (First User).

23. Click **Tools**, click **Out of Office Assistant**.

24. Click the **I am currently In the Office** option button and click the **OK** button.

25. Write a brief description in your project log explaining how you might assist a user to set up an out-of-office message.

26. Leave Outlook open for the next activity.

CONFIGURING AND PERSONALIZING OUTLOOK FEATURES

Because Outlook is a complex application with many features, your users have many options for controlling the way it looks and functions. They will also have many questions. For example, your users might ask the following about tailoring Outlook:

- How do I identify and manage junk e-mail?

- How do I use a message editor other than Microsoft Word?

- How do I protect my system against viruses and worms?

- How do I mark messages as read when I preview them?

Each of the following sections describes a tab in Outlook's Options dialog box. (To open the Options dialog box, click Tools and Options.) It is with the options on these tabs that your users will configure and personalize Outlook features.

Preferences Tab

The Preferences tab, shown in Figure 9-23, lets you—and your users—configure general settings for all of Outlook's primary functions.

Each section on the Preferences tab controls how a specific Outlook component works. The following list helps you locate the specific settings:

- **E-mail:** Specify how Outlook handles messages. For example, Junk E-mail specifies options for identifying and managing unwanted messages.

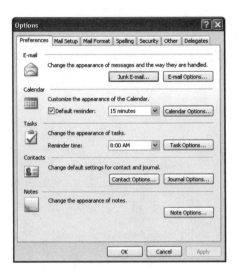

Figure 9-23   Options dialog box - Preferences tab

9

- **Calendar:** Control the look of Outlook's calendar. For example, the days of the work week and holidays.

- **Tasks:** Set the color for completed and overdue tasks, and set up reminders for tasks with due dates.

- **Contacts:** Specify naming preferences for new contacts.

- **Notes:** Specify the font style, color, and size used in notes.

Mail Setup Tab

From the Mail Setup tab (see Figure 9-24), you will find settings that control e-mail accounts. For example, you can add or remove e-mail accounts or control the frequency that e-mail is retrieved.

The following list provides information about the settings to be configured in each section of the Mail Setup tab:

- **E-mail Accounts:** Add, remove, or change an e-mail account.

- **Send/Retrieve:** Define the settings to specify the frequency that e-mail is sent or retrieved.

- **Data Files:** Control settings for the Personal folders.

- **Dial-up:** Configure settings that determine how Outlook handles dial-up connections when sending or receiving messages.

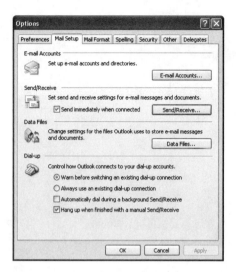

Figure 9-24   Options dialog box - Mail Setup tab

Mail Format Tab

With the settings on the Mail Format tab (see Figure 9-25), your users control how messages look and how to compose messages. For example, your users may want to know how to choose from among plain text, rich text, and HTML formats for composing text messages.

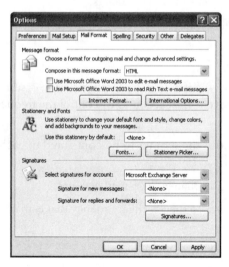

Figure 9-25   Options dialog box - Mail Format tab

The following list presents the sections on the Mail Format tab:

- **Message format:** Specify the format for outgoing messages. Specify the default e-mail editor.

- **Stationery and Fonts:** Set the background for composed messages.

- **Signatures:** Select the signature text for each e-mail account.

Spelling Tab

From the Spelling tab (see Figure 9-26), your users will specify how spelling should be checked for text composed in Outlook.

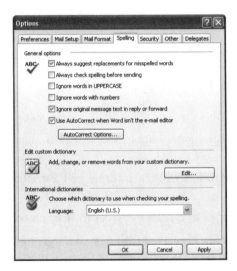

Figure 9-26   Options dialog box - Spelling tab

The following items summarize by section the settings available on this tab:

- **General options:** Set general outlines for the spelling checker. Outlook, like Word, supports AutoCorrect and permits options to be configured.

- **Edit custom dictionary:** Add, change, or remove words from your custom dictionary.

- **International dictionaries:** Specify the language to use with the spelling checker.

Security Tab

Your users will use the Security tab, as shown in Figure 9-27, to configure a wide range of security options. For example, your users will be able to validate their identity to others and protect their system against viruses and worms.

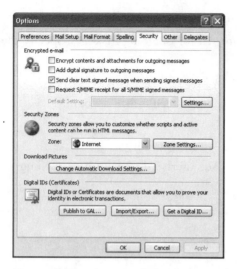

Figure 9-27   Options dialog box - Security tab

The Security tab contains the following sections:

- **Encrypted e-mail:** Encrypt outgoing messages. Add a digital signature to a message.

- **Security Zones:** Set the security zone setting to Internet or Restricted sites. Set individual zone settings.

- **Download Pictures:** Block pictures in e-mail messages to help protect privacy.

- **Digital IDs (Certificates):** Manage digital certificates and signatures. Publish your digital certificate so others can send you an encrypted e-mail message. Obtain a digital certificate from a Certificate Authority.

Other Tab

The Other tab (see Figure 9-28) provides a selection of settings that permit various settings for Outlook.

This tab contains the following sections:

- **General:** Specify other general settings. Determine how to process deleted items.

- **AutoArchive:** Control how Outlook archives data.

- **Reading Pane:** Determine how messages are processed in the Reading pane. For example, mark items read when viewed for five seconds.

- **Person Names:** Enable and configure MSN Messenger access from Outlook.

Figure 9-28   Options dialog box - Other tab

Delegates Tab

The Delegates tab (see Figure 9-29) lets your user specify other users, such as assistants or other team members, who can access his or her folders. Optionally, these users can send messages on behalf of your user.

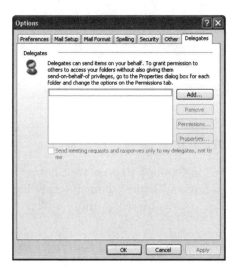

Figure 9-29   Options dialog box - Delegates tab

From this tab, your users can manage the aspects of delegation to assistants. They can add or remove assistants, grant permissions to an assistant, and block responses for messages sent by delegates.

Activity 9-11: Explore the Options for Outlook Features

Time Required: 45 minutes

Objective: Explore the options to personalize the features of Outlook.

Description: In this activity, you will practice exploring the features of Outlook to learn where the customization for each feature is located. Also, you will use the Help in Outlook to research the various options and settings. You are exploring the features of Outlook so that you can answer your users' questions about the personalization of Office features.

1. If necessary, log on to your computer using the user name **user01** and password **Password1**.

2. If necessary, click **Start**, point to **All Programs**, point to **Microsoft Office**, and click **Microsoft Office Outlook 2003**.

3. Click **Tools**, and click **Options**.

4. Click the **Preferences** tab.

5. Click on the **Help** button on the title bar of the Options dialog box, and click the **Preferences** tab link on the Microsoft Office Outlook Help.

6. View the options on the Preferences tab and select each to review the information in Help.

7. Write a brief description of how you might assist a user with the features located on the Preferences tab.

8. Close the Help screen.

9. Repeat Steps 4 through 8 for the remaining tabs.

10. Close the Options dialog box.

11. Leave Outlook open for the next activity.

INTEGRATING OUTLOOK EXPRESS AND OUTLOOK

You should be prepared to integrate Outlook and Outlook Express. Recall that you learned about Outlook Express in Chapter 5, "Configure and Troubleshoot Internet Explorer and Outlook Express." In this part of the chapter, you will learn to move address books and messages between the two e-mail clients.

Information about integrating two e-mail clients can be useful if your users are switching from Outlook Express to Outlook. Or perhaps, a user wants to use Outlook Express for a short period of time on a notebook computer. Learning how to access e-mail from Outlook Express when traveling will be useful in this situation as well.

Copying Addresses and Messages to Outlook

When migrating from Outlook Express to Outlook, you copy information from Outlook Express for use in Outlook. These items include:

- **Address Book:** Export the Address Book to an Outlook PAB.
- **Messages:** Import one or more folders to Outlook.

How Outlook Express Stores Addresses

Outlook Express uses the **Windows Address Book (WAB)** to store addresses. The WAB file has the same name as your logon name with a WAB file extension, such as, User01.WAB. For User01, the file is stored in the C:\Documents and Settings\User01\Application Data\Microsoft\Address Book folder.

You will not need to know where the WAB is located to migrate from Outlook Express to Outlook. However, you will need to know where the file is located to move between two computers. You can use the Search to find the *.WAB files.

How Outlook Express Stores Messages

Outlook Express stores messages grouped into database files. Each database file represents an Outlook Express folder. The Outlook Express Inbox is stored in the Inbox.dbx file. The remaining folders reside in other .dbx database files.

You will not need to know where Outlook Express folders are located to migrate from Outlook Express to Outlook. However, you will need to know where the files are located to move between two computers. You can use the Search feature located on the Start menu to find the *.dbx files. Because these files are in hidden folders, you will need to check the Search hidden files and folders check box in the View tab of the Folder Options dialog box to see them.

Exporting Addresses from Outlook Express

Because you used a Personal Address Book in Outlook for Activity 9-8, you can export the addresses directly from Outlook Express to the PAB. Without the PAB, you could import the WAB into the Contacts folder. Importing the WAB to the Contacts folder of Outlook results in those addresses being mingled with your contacts, which is something you may not want to do.

Activity 9-12: Export the Windows Address Book (WAB)

Time Required: 15 minutes

Objective: Export the WAB into an Outlook Personal Address Book.

Description: In this activity, you will practice exporting the Windows Address Book. You will find this activity useful in your career as a DST because, in order to answer users' questions about exporting the Windows Address Book, you will need to have explored these steps in detail.

1. If necessary, log on to your computer using the user name **user01** and password **Password1**.

2. If necessary, Click **Start**, point to **All Programs**, point to **Microsoft Office**, and click **Microsoft Office Outlook 2003**.

3. Click **Tools**, and click **Address Book**.

4. Click **Tools**, click **Options**, click the **Keep personal addresses in** drop-down list arrow, click **Personal Address Book**, as shown in Figure 9-30, click the **OK** button, and close the Address Book window.

Figure 9-30   Addressing options

5. Click **Start**, point to **All Programs**, and click **Outlook Express**.

6. If the Outlook Express is not currently your default mail client message appears, click the **No** button.

7. Click **File**, point to **Export**, and click **Address Book**.

8. Click **Microsoft Exchange Personal Address Book**, and click the **Export** button.

9. When the Confirm Replace dialog box appears, as shown in Figure 9-31, click the **No to All** button.

10. Wait for the Address Book to be exported and click the **OK** button.

11. Click the **Close** button to close the Outlook Express window.

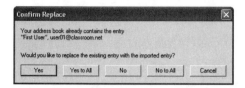

Figure 9-31   Confirm Replace dialog box

12. Write a brief description in your project log explaining how you might assist a user with exporting a Windows Address Book.

13. Leave Outlook open for the next activity.

Importing Messages into Outlook

If you—or your users—are migrating to Outlook from Outlook Express, you will need to import the messages into Outlook. To do so, you can use the File, Import and Export commands as detailed in Activity 9-13.

ACTIVITY

Activity 9-13: Importing Messages Into Outlook

Time Required: 15 minutes

Objective: Import messages into Outlook from Outlook Express.

Description: In this activity, you will practice importing messages into Outlook from Outlook Express. You will find this activity useful in your career as a DST because, in order to answer users' questions about importing messages into Outlook, you will need to have explored these steps in detail.

1. If necessary, log on to your computer using the user name **user01** and password **Password1**.

2. If necessary, click **Start**, point to **All Programs**, point to **Microsoft Office**, and click **Microsoft Office Outlook 2003**.

3. Click **File**, and click **Import and Export**.

4. Click **Import Internet Mail and Addresses**, as shown in Figure 9-32, and click the **Next** button.

5. Click **Outlook Express 4.x, 5.x, 6.x**, uncheck the **Import Address book** check box, as shown in Figure 9-33, and click the **Finish** button.

6. Wait for the import to complete and click the **Save in Inbox** button.

7. Write a brief description in your project log explaining how you might assist a user with importing messages from Outlook Express.

8. Leave Outlook open for the next activity.

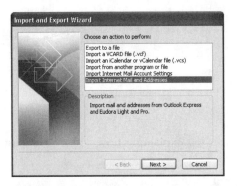

Figure 9-32   Import and Export wizard

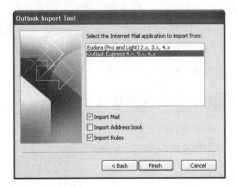

Figure 9-33   Outlook Import Tool

Copying Addresses and Messages to Outlook Express

In addition to copying addresses and messages from Outlook Express to Outlook, you can copy them the other way. Your users may do this when they are going to use a notebook computer in a remote office and do not want to install Outlook on the notebook.

You must run Outlook and Outlook Express on the same computer to copy addresses. First, import the addresses from the Outlook PAB to Outlook Express. Then, copy the appropriate WAB file to the notebook.

Copying Addresses from an Outlook Personal Address Book to Outlook Express

You can copy addresses from an Outlook PAB to your Outlook Express Address Book, the Windows Address Book. Your users may do this when they are going to use a notebook computer in a remote office and do not want to install Outlook on the notebook.

Activity 9-14: Import the Personal Address Book

Time Required: 15 minutes

Objective: Import the Outlook Personal Address Book into Outlook Express.

Description: In this activity, you will practice importing the Outlook PAB. You will find this activity useful in your career as a DST because, in order to answer users' questions about importing the PAB, you will need to have explored these steps in detail.

1. If necessary, log on to your computer using the user name **user01** and password **Password1**.

2. Click **Start**, point to **All Programs**, and click **Outlook Express**.

3. Click **File**, click **Import**, and click **Other Address book**.

4. Click **Microsoft Exchange Personal Address book**, and click the **Import** button.

5. When the import process has completed, click the **OK** button, then the Close button.

6. Write a brief description describing how you might assist a user with importing addresses from Outlook.

7. Leave Outlook and Outlook Express open for the next activity.

Copying Messages from Outlook to Outlook Express

Messages may be imported from Outlook to Outlook Express with a wizard provided with Outlook Express. Outlook Express imports from your default message store, which for most organizations will be the Inbox within the Personal Folders.

Activity 9-15: Importing Messages from Outlook

Time Required: 15 minutes

Objective: Import the Outlook Inbox into Outlook Express.

Description: In this activity, you will practice importing the Outlook Inbox into Outlook Express. You will find this activity useful in your career as a DST because, in order to answer users' questions about importing the Inbox, you will need to have explored these steps in detail.

1. If necessary, log on to your computer using the user name **user01** and password **Password1**.

2. Click **Start**, point to **All Programs**, and click **Outlook Express**.

3. Click **File**, click **Import**, and click **Messages**.

4. Click **Microsoft Outlook**, and click the **Next** button.

9

5. Click the **Selected folders** option button, click the **Inbox** folder, as shown in Figure 9-34, and click the **Next** button.

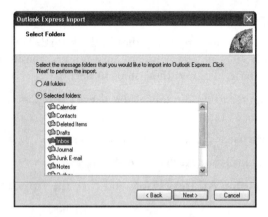

Figure 9-34   Outlook Express Import - Selected folders

6. When the import process has completed, click the **Finish** button.

7. Write a brief description of how you might assist a user with importing messages from Outlook.

8. Close the Outlook Express window.

9. Leave Outlook open for the next activity.

RESTORING DATA AND REPAIRING DATA

Your users expect you to possess the skills to restore and repair their e-mail files. One technique that you will need to learn is to configure the Outlook AutoArchive. With the AutoArchive files, you can restore your users' e-mail data. This will be useful if, for example, the Inbox becomes damaged and needs to be replaced.

In addition to the AutoArchive, you will learn about the Inbox Repair tool in the following sections.

Cleaning Up and Archiving Outlook Information

From time to time, your users will want to set aside some of the inactive data stored in their personal folders. Because they may need the data for a future project, they will not be willing to delete the data. By archiving the data, your users can preserve the data without having the data in their personal folders.

In the sections that follow, you learn about archiving the data in Personal folders. Also, you learn to repair Personal folders by restoring archived data.

Archiving Items Automatically

By default, Outlook reviews your **Personal Folders File (PST)** every 14 days to locate items that are more than six months old. The Personal Folders File holds the contents of folders for the Personal Folders. When items exceed the age limits, the items are automatically moved to an archive file. Your users will find this feature helpful. For example, your users can keep a copy of the items that they have sent so that the items can be referred to at a later date. They may not want the older items to stay with the newer items. In this situation, they would use the AutoArchive feature, as shown in Figure 9-35, to move out the older items. If it is determined later that the items were needed, the items could be restored.

Figure 9-35 Selecting to use default settings

Configuring Automatic Archival

The Outlook AutoArchive feature archives automatically using the settings that you configure. If your user's volume of e-mail is large, he or she may decide to set the AutoArchive to run more often than the default of every 14 days and to archive messages before the default of six months, as shown in Figure 9-36.

The following list will help you to choose the configuration settings for the AutoArchive:

- **Run AutoArchive every** _____ **days:** Specify the per-day cycle. For example, to run every other day set it to run every two days.

- **Prompt before AutoArchive runs:** Display a message before the Archive occurs. The message includes a Cancel button so that you can cancel for that day.

- **Delete expired items (e-mail folders only):** Delete messages that are older than a specified period of time. The default is six months, but you can set this value from one day to 60 months.

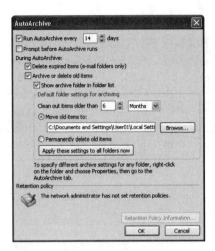

Figure 9-36 AutoArchive settings

- **Archive or delete old items:** Archive or delete old Outlook items. Set the amount of time that should elapse before old items are archived or deleted. . The default is six months, but you can set this value from one day to 60 months.

- **Show archive folder in folder list:** Select if you want Outlook to display the archive folder. From the archive folder, you can easily restore an entry back to a personal folder.

- **Clean out items older than:** Number of days before items are archived or deleted specified in days, week, or months.

- **Move old items to:** Specify the PST file where the archive is stored.

- **Permanently delete old items:** Delete items during AutoArchive session. This would not be a good idea if you need to retain information for longer periods of time.

- **Apply these settings to all folders now:** Apply your choices for this folder to all folders. If you wish, you can apply alternate settings to individual folders.

Activity 9-16: Configuring AutoArchive

Time Required: 15 minutes

Objective: Configure AutoArchive settings.

Description: In this activity, you will practice configuring the AutoArchive settings. Next, you will perform a manual archive of a personal folder. You will find this activity useful in your career as a DST because, in order to answer users' questions about using the AutoArchive, you will need to have explored these steps in detail.

1. If necessary, log on to your computer using the user name **user01** and password **Password1**.

2. If necessary, Click **Start**, point to **All Programs**, point to **Microsoft Office**, and click **Microsoft Office Outlook 2003**.

3. Right-click **Sent Items** under All Mail Folders, click **Properties**, click the **AutoArchive** tab, and click the **Archive items in this folder using default settings** option button.

4. Click the **Apply** button and click the **Default Archive Settings** button.

5. Check the **Run AutoArchive every days** check box and set the Run AutoArchive every day spin box to **1** day.

6. Set the Clean out items older than spin boxes to **1 Months**.

7. Click the two **OK** buttons.

8. Click **File**, and click **Archive**. See Figure 9-37.

Figure 9-37   Archive settings

9. Click the **Browse** button, and note the name and location for the PST file.

10. Click the two **OK** buttons.

11. Write a brief description in your project log explaining how you might assist a user with archiving Personal folders in Outlook.

12. Leave Outlook open for the next activity.

Restoring Data Using the Archive File

Your user has worked on a project for a year. You configured Outlook to use the default AutoArchive settings—run every 14 days to locate items that are more than six months old. Your user returns from a trip to work on the project and discovers that the notebook has crashed and Outlook has lost all of the data. How do you get the data back for the user? Simple! You restore the missing items by importing the archived PST file, as shown in Activity 9-17.

Activity 9-17: Restoring Items with the AutoArchive File

Time Required: 15 minutes

Objective: Restore items from the AutoArchive file to replace a PST.

Description: In this activity, you will practice restoring items to replace a damaged PST. You will find this activity useful in your career as a DST because, in order to restore a PST, you will need to have explored these steps in detail.

1. If necessary, log on to your computer using the user name **user01** and password **Password1**.

2. If necessary, Click **Start**, point to **All Programs**, point to **Microsoft Office**, and click **Microsoft Office Outlook 2003**.

3. Click **File** and click **Import and Export**.

4. Click **Import from another program or file** and click the **Next** button.

5. Scroll and click **Personal Folder File (.pst)** and click the **Next** button.

6. Click the **Browse** button, double-click the **archive** icon, and click the **Next** button.

7. Click the **Sent Items** folder, and click the **Finish** button.

8. Write a brief description in your project log explaining how you might assist a user with restoring a folder for a PST file.

9. Close the Outlook window.

Repairing a Damaged Personal Folder File

If you cannot open a Personal Folders file (PST) or you suspect that the PST is corrupt, you can use the Inbox Repair tool. The Inbox Repair tool (Scanpst.exe) can be used to diagnose and repair errors in the file.

If your user has a corrupt or otherwise damaged PST file, you will perform the steps in Activity 9-18 to correct the problem.

Activity 9-18: Running the Inbox Repair Tool

Time Required: 15 minutes

Objective: Run Scanpst.exe to diagnose and repair a PST file.

Description: In this activity, you will run the Inbox Repair Tool to diagnose and repair a damaged PST file. You will find this activity useful in your career as a DST because, in order to repair a user's PST file, you will need to have explored these steps in detail.

1. If necessary, log on to your computer using the user name **user01** and password **Password1**.

2. Click **Start**, click **Run**, click the **Browse** button, navigate to **C:\Program Files\Common Files\System\MSMAPI\1033\SCANPST.EXE**, and click the **OK** button.

 If you are using a version of Office with a LocaleID other than 1033, replace the value of 1033 in the path with the LocaleID for the installation of Microsoft Office.

NOTE

3. In the Inbox Repair Tool window, click the **Browse** button, navigate to **C:\Documents and Settings\User01\Local Settings\Application Data\Microsoft\Outlook\Outlook**, and click the **Open** button.

4. Click the **Start** button.

5. If errors occurred, click the **Repair** button.

6. Click the **OK** button.

7. Write a brief description in your project log explaining how you might assist a user with running the Inbox Repair tool to repair a PST file.

9

CHAPTER SUMMARY

You learned your way around Outlook. Specifically, you learned how to:

▫ Determine the purpose for each of the nine standard Outlook views or folders

▫ Connect to an Exchange Server

▫ Use and customize the Inbox, Calendar, Contacts, and Tasks folders

▫ Use Outlook to surf the Web

▫ Access the Exchange Server with a Web browser

▫ Use categories to organize outgoing mail

▫ Manage Address Books and Distribution Lists

▫ Use Search folders to locate qualifying e-mail messages

▫ Create rules to organize e-mail

You explored personalization options for these items:

▫ Preferences

▫ Mail Setup

▫ Mail Format

❏ Spelling

❏ Security

❏ Other

❏ Delegates

You learned how to make Outlook and Outlook Express work together. Specifically, you learned these items:

❏ How Outlook Express Stores messages

❏ How to import messages from Outlook Express to Outlook

❏ How Outlook Express stores addresses

❏ How to export addresses from Outlook Express into Outlook

❏ How to import the Addresses from the Outlook PAB to Outlook Express

❏ How to import messages from Outlook to Outlook Express

You learned to manage the restoration and repair of data in Outlook. You learned how to perform these tasks:

❏ Configure the AutoArchive

❏ Create a manual archive

❏ Restore data from an archive

Key Terms

Exchange Server — Microsoft e-mail server designed to meet the messaging and collaboration needs for businesses of all sizes.

Global Address List (GAL) — Contains mailboxes, distribution lists, and public folders in an organization. Specific to Microsoft Exchange Server.

Outlook Address Book (OAB) — Contains mailboxes and distribution lists for an individual using Outlook. Specific to the Contacts folder.

Personal Address Book (PAB) — Contains mailboxes, and distribution lists for an individual using Outlook.

Personal Folders file (PST) — Permits an individual to store messages locally in personal folders. Restricted to 2 GB of data.

Windows Address Book (WAB) — Contains mailboxes and distribution lists for an individual using Outlook Express.

REVIEW QUESTIONS

1. Which of the following e-mail servers is supported by Outlook? (Choose all that apply.)

   a. Microsoft Exchange Server

   b. POP3

   c. IMAP

   d. HTTP

2. Which of the following buttons is available on the Navigation pane? (Choose all that apply.)

   a. Inbox

   b. Calendar

   c. Contacts

   d. Tasks

3. The _____ folder includes names, addresses, and phone numbers.

   a. Inbox

   b. Calendar

   c. Contacts

   d. Tasks

4. The _____ folder includes appointments, meetings, and events.

   a. Inbox

   b. Calendar

   c. Contacts

   d. Tasks

5. _____ is Microsoft's premium messaging and enterprise collaboration server.

   a. ccmail

   b. Exchange

   c. POP3 server

   d. SMTP server

6. Which of the following items does the header information in the Inbox folder contain? (Choose all that apply.)

   a. sender

   b. subject

   c. date

   d. time

9

7. Which of the following actions will add a Calendar entry? (Choose all that apply.)
   a. Double-click the time slot for the start time. This will open an appointment form.
   b. Right-click a time slot and pick the type (appointment, meeting, or event).
   c. Select a time and select File and then select New.
   d. Click the down arrow beside New on the Standard toolbar and select the type.

8. Which of the following commands will customize the Contacts view? (Choose all that apply.)
   a. Address Card
   b. Phone List
   c. By Category
   d. By Company

9. Which of the following fields is displayed in the simple task list? (Choose all that apply.)
   a. Subject
   b. Due Date
   c. Status
   d. Next Seven Days

10. Which of the following commands will customize the Tasks view? (Choose all that apply.)
   a. Detailed List
   b. Overdue Tasks
   c. By Category
   d. Completed Tasks

11. You can use _____ to access e-mail from the Internet.
   a. Outlook
   b. Outlook Express
   c. Internet Explorer
   d. Windows Explorer

12. To make things easier to organize in Outlook, you can use _____ , which are words or phrases.
   a. items
   b. flags
   c. categories
   d. assignments

13. Which of the following Address Books can be used with Outlook? (Choose all that apply.)

    a. GAL

    b. OAB

    c. PAB

    d. WAB

14. You create _____ to specify to Outlook how to identify a message.

    a. priorities

    b. actions

    c. rules

    d. tasks

15. When you are away from the office, you use _____ to notify e-mail senders that you are away from your office.

    a. out rules

    b. away rules

    c. out of office rules

    d. office rules

16. From the Rules wizard, which selections permit rules to be tailored? (Choose all that apply.)

    a. conditions

    b. actions

    c. exceptions

    d. tasks

17. Which spelling options can be set on the Spelling tab? (Choose all that apply.)

    a. Ignore words in UPPERCASE

    b. Ignore words in lowercase

    c. Ignore words with numbers

    d. Ignore original message text in reply or forward

18. Use the _____ tab to specify other users that can access your folders.

    a. Assistants

    b. Delegates

    c. Peers

    d. Managers

9

19. Outlook Express stores addresses in the _____ .

    a. GAL

    b. OAB

    c. PAB

    d. WAB

20. By default, the AutoArchive reviews the PST every _____ .

    a. day and archives items that are over 30 days in age

    b. 14 days and archives items that are more than 6 months old

    c. day and archives items that are more than 6 months old

    d. 30 days and archives items that are more than 6 months old

CASE PROJECTS

CASE PROJECTS

Case 9-1: Managing E-mail Messages

You are a desktop support technician. Your network consists of a Windows Server 2003 Active Directory domain with 10 servers, including Microsoft Exchange Server and 500 computers running Windows XP Professional and Outlook.

You are responding to a question posed by Jill. Jill is not sure which to use: e-mail Search folders or e-mail rules. She receives from 20 to 50 messages each day. Some of these messages are related to the five ongoing projects that she works on. The e-mail messages for projects will have the project title in the subject line.

Table 9-1 summarizes the relationships among the five projects and the persons assigned to the projects. Notice that people frequently work on multiple projects.

Table 9-1   Projects with assigned individuals

Project	Assigned Individuals
Master	Alice, Bob, Carl, David, Eddie, Fred, George, Howard, Irene, Joan, Karl, Leo
Restructure loans	Bob, Carl, David, George, Howard, Irene, Leo
Production results	Alice, David, Eddie, Fred, George, Irene, Joan
New product	Alice, Leo
Customer relations	Alice, George, Howard, Irene, Karl, Leo

What solution will you offer to Jill? Will you use Search Folders? Will you use rules? Both? Jill expects a detailed solution to her problem.

Case 9-2: Integrating Outlook Express and Outlook

You are a desktop support technician. Your network consists of a Windows Server 2003 Active Directory domain with 10 servers, including Microsoft Exchange Server and 232 desktop computers running Windows XP Professional and Outlook Express. In addition, there are 62 remote users with Windows XP Professional and Outlook Express.

Your task is to configure the desktop computers to use Outlook with the new Exchange Server while continuing to use Outlook Express with the remote users. Explain in detail how you will achieve these two objectives.

Case 9-3: Archiving E-mail Messages

You are a desktop support technician. Your network consists of a Windows Server 2003 Active Directory domain with 16 servers, including Microsoft Exchange Server and 965 desktop computers running Windows XP Professional and Outlook.

You have been asked to develop recommendations for cleaning up and archiving Outlook Information. With the aid of a programmer, you have determined the following information, as shown in Table 9-2, concerning the age of e-mail messages on a sample of the desktop computers.

Table 9-2   Percentage of e-mail messages at specified age spans

Age of E-mail Messages	Percentage
Less than 10 days	10
More than 10 days and less than 21 days	15
More than 20 days and less that 31 days	25
More than 30 days and less than 61 days	28
More than 60 days and less than 91 days	12
More than 90 days	10

What will you recommend as a run interval? As a clean-out interval?

10

CONFIGURE AND TROUBLESHOOT DEVICES AND CONNECTIVITY

After reading this chapter and completing the exercises, you will be able to:

♦ Identify and troubleshoot problems with locally attached devices

♦ Describe networking components and interconnectivity

♦ Identify and troubleshoot network connectivity problems

As you are aware, the role of the DST requires that you be prepared to identify and troubleshoot locally attached devices including printers. You will need to learn to manage device drivers with the Device Manager.

Prior to resolving problems with networking components, you must first learn to describe the functions and capabilities of these components. Networking components that you will see in your organization include network cables, network interface cards, switches, and routers.

Your users expect that you are ready to identify and troubleshoot network connectivity problems. You will need to learn about the various utilities that are available to assist with troubleshooting network connectivity.

This chapter will cover the listed topics.

IDENTIFYING AND TROUBLESHOOTING PROBLEMS WITH LOCALLY ATTACHED DEVICES

To identify and troubleshoot locally attached devices, you will need to develop proficiency with the Device Manager. As a DST, you will be called upon to install and troubleshoot storage devices and printers, and the Device Manager will prove useful to you during these tasks.

The sections that follow will prepare you to perform these tasks and more.

Resolving Driver Issues with Device Manager

The Device Manager provides you with information about how the hardware on your computer is installed and configured, and how the hardware interacts with your computer's programs. One quick way to access the Device Manager is to click the Start menu, right-click My Computer, and then click Properties. This string of actions will display the System Properties dialog box. From the System Properties dialog box, click the Hardware tab. Clicking the Device Manager button on the Hardware tab opens the Device Manager.

The Device Manager provides a graphical view of the hardware installed on the computer. From the Device Manager (see Figure 10-1), you can locate the device that you want to maintain, configure, or troubleshoot.

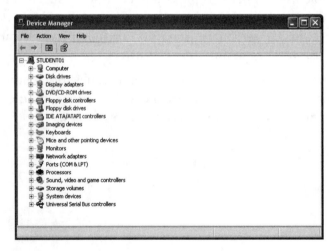

Figure 10-1   Device Manager window

To view the properties for a device, double-click the device entry in the Device Manager window. Also, you could right-click the device entry and click Properties. For an example of the device properties of a graphics card, see Figure 10-2.

Figure 10-2   Device properties for a graphics card

You previously learned about using the Device Manager as a tool in Chapter 1, "Introduction to Supporting Users." In this chapter, you will continue your exploration of the Device Manager. Note that your users expect that you will be ready to identify and troubleshoot problems with devices. Here is a list of tasks that you will be expected to accomplish for your users:

- View device driver properties
- Update an existing driver to fix a problem
- Roll back a driver to a previous version
- Uninstall an existing driver
- Configure driver signing

Viewing Driver Properties

The Driver tab of the Properties dialog box displays information about the device driver for a particular device. Why is device driver trivia important to a DST? You will need to know the driver details when troubleshooting driver problems and updating drivers.

As you'll recall, a **device driver** is a program that controls a device. Every device, whether it is a printer, disk drive, or keyboard, must have a driver program. Many device drivers, such as the keyboard driver, come with the operating system. For other devices, you may need to load a new driver when you connect the device to your computer. In Figure 10-3, you will see some properties for a driver, as follows:

- **Driver Provider:** Name of the company that provided the default device drivers for this device
- **Driver Date:** Date of the device driver for this device

- **Driver Version:** Version of the driver
- **Digital Signer:** Name of the company that digitally signed the device driver

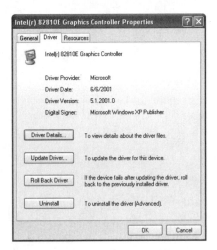

Figure 10-3   Device driver properties for a graphics card

 What does the 5.1.2001.0 mean in Figure 10-3? Microsoft codes the version number of the driver in this format: [*major version*].[*minor version*].[*build number*].[*sub-build number*]. So the driver version in the figure was for major version 5 and minor version 1. The build number was 2001 (this is an ordinal number, not a date) and the sub-build number was 0.

To view the driver details, as shown in Figure 10-4, click the Driver Details button. The names of the driver files are listed at the top of the dialog box. Notice that the Intel Corporation developed, as version 5.13.01.2753.1 (Intel uses a different versioning scheme than Microsoft), the device driver and provided it to Microsoft. Microsoft Windows XP Publisher digitally signed the driver and shipped it with Windows XP Professional.

 Sometimes it is necessary to delete a driver from Device Manager and then restart the computer. This gives Microsoft Windows XP another chance to automatically choose the correct driver. This is commonly necessary when upgrading the drivers for the system board.

Activity 10-1: Viewing Device Driver Properties

Time Required: 15 minutes

Objective: View the device driver properties for the graphics adapter.

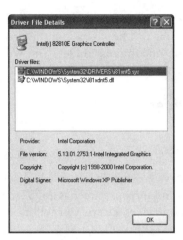

Figure 10-4   Driver details of the driver for a graphics card

10

Description: In this activity, you will view the device driver properties for an installed device such as the graphics adapter. You will find this activity useful in your career as a DST because, in order to determine the device driver properties, you will need to have explored this in detail.

1. Log on to your computer with the user name **admin01** and password **Password1**.

2. Click **Start**, point to **Control Panel**, and click **System**.

3. Click the **Hardware** tab and click the **Device Manager** button.

Contact your instructor for additional instructions for the devices in your computer.

NOTE

4. Expand **Display adapters**, double-click the graphics controller, and click the **Driver** tab.

5. Click the **Driver Details** button and view the Driver File Details.

6. Click the two **OK** buttons.

7. Write a brief description in your project log explaining how you might determine the driver properties for a device.

8. Close any open windows.

Updating a Device Driver

Manufacturers frequently update the device drivers to provide new capabilities or fix problems. You should go to the manufacturer's Web sites to check for the availability of new drivers. Read the manufacturer's instructions about downloading the driver files. Frequently, the files for the drivers are zipped (compressed into a self-executing file). You will need to run the self-executing file on the computer where you will be upgrading the driver. Make a note of the location of the folder that contains the uncompressed files. You will need to know this location when you update the device driver.

Activity 10-2: Updating a Device Driver

Time Required: 15 minutes

Objective: Updating the device driver properties for a device such as the graphics adapter.

Description: In this activity, you will update the device driver for an installed device such as the graphics adapter. You will find this activity useful in your career as a DST because, in order to answer users' questions about updating the device drivers, you will need to have explored these in detail.

1. If necessary, log on to your computer with the user name **admin01** and password **Password1**.

2. Click **Start**, point to **Control Panel**, and click **System**.

3. Click the **Hardware** tab and click the **Device Manager** button.

Contact your instructor for additional instructions for the devices in your computer.

NOTE

4. Expand **Display adapters**, double-click the graphics controller, and click the **Driver** tab.

5. Click the **Update Driver** button and click the **Install from a list or specific location (Advanced)** option button, as shown in Figure 10-5.

Figure 10-5   Hardware Update wizard - Welcome to the Hardware Update Wizard page

6. Click the **Next** button, uncheck the **Search removable media (floppy, CD-ROM...)** check box, and check the **Include this location in the search** check box, as shown in Figure 10-6.

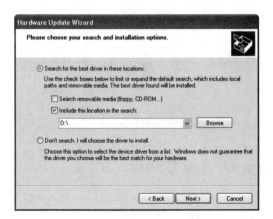

Figure 10-6　Hardware Update wizard - Please choose your search and installation options. page

The path shown in Figure 10-6 may vary depending on previous system settings.

7. Click the **Browse** button, expand **My Computer**, expand **Local Disk (C:)**, click *Video Driver* (or the folder name that your instructor provided), click the **OK** button, and then click the **Next** button.

Your instructor may provide more specific instructions for the installation of the graphics driver.

NOTE

8. If you receive a Cannot Continue the Hardware Update wizard message, skip to Step 10.

9. Click the **Next** button and wait for the Hardware Update Wizard to complete the driver installation.

10. Click the **Finish** button, and click the **Close** button.

11. If needed, click the **Yes** button and wait for the system to restart.

12. Write a brief description in your project log explaining the steps to update a device driver.

13. Close any open windows.

10

Rolling Back a Driver

If you install a new driver and encounter a problem, you will need to replace the driver with the previous driver. Such problems include faulty device operation or error messages when you start Windows. Windows XP facilitates this reinstallation of the previous driver by permitting a device driver roll back.

Does the roll back always work? Yes and no. If the device driver worked before and was not removed, the roll back should allow a return to the previous state for the device.

IN THE WORKPLACE

If the device driver did not function before the roll back, it will not work after the roll back. Once a nonworking driver always a nonworking driver!

Activity 10-3: Rolling Back a Device Driver

ACTIVITY

Time Required: 15 minutes

Objective: Roll back a device driver to a previously installed device driver.

Description: In this activity, you will roll back a device driver to a previously installed device driver. You will find this activity useful in your career as a DST because, in order to repair driver problems, you will need to have rolled back a device driver.

1. If necessary, log on to your computer with the user name **admin01** and password **Password1**.

2. Click **Start**, point to **Control Panel**, and click **System**.

3. Click the **Hardware** tab and click the **Device Manager** button.

Contact your instructor for additional instructions for the devices in your computer.

NOTE

4. Expand **Display adapters**, double-click the graphics controller, and click the **Driver** tab.

5. Click the **Roll Back Driver** button and click the **Yes** button when the message, as shown in Figure 10-7, is displayed.

Intel(R) 82810E Graphics Controller

Are you sure you would like to roll back to the previous driver?

Yes   No

Figure 10-7   Confirmation message

6. Wait for the driver to be rolled back.

7. Click the **Close** button, click the **Yes** button, and wait for the system to restart.

8. Write a brief description in your project log explaining the steps to roll back a device driver.

Uninstalling a Driver

If you will no longer need a device, you can uninstall the device driver. Click the Uninstall button on the Driver tab. You will be asked to confirm this decision before Windows continues with the device removal. You may need to do this is if you are going to remove a device from a system prior to installing a replacement device.

Configuring Driver Signing

How can you be sure that the device driver that you are installing will be compatible with Windows XP? Microsoft attaches digital signatures to Windows device drivers to let you know that the device driver you are installing is compatible. Microsoft states that "the digital signature ensures that this driver has met a certain level of testing, and that the file has not been altered or overwritten by any other installation program since it was signed."

IN THE WORKPLACE

Should you install an unsigned driver? It's all a matter of trust. Do you trust the manufacturer to produce a driver that will be compatible with Windows XP? More than once, I've gone to a manufacturer's Web site to obtain a new device driver and was confronted with instructions to ignore Microsoft's warning and install the driver.

Of course, this override will not work if the driver signing option was set to block. You will need to set the driver signing option to warn or ignore. Install the driver and set the option back to block.

To configure driver signing, click the Driver Signing button located on the Hardware tab. Figure 10-8 shows the three driver signing options. If you logged on with an account with administrator privileges, you can make this setting the default for all users.

Using Storage Devices

With storage devices, you can store programs and data files. In addition to hard drives and network drives, storage devices that you may encounter include floppy drives, CD-ROMs, and more. Removable storage devices use the **Universal Serial Bus (USB)**. A USB permits up to 127 mice, printers, and storage devices to be connected to a single serial bus. Review the following list to compare storage devices:

- 3½ Floppy drive: Provides unreliable portable storage with 1.44 MB. This is the basis for "**sneaker net**," or "floppy net," which is the transfer of files by physically carrying disks from one computer to another.

10

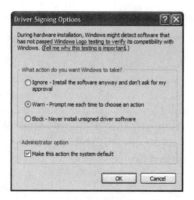

Figure 10-8 Driver Signing Options dialog box

- **CD-R:** Abbreviation for Compact Disc-Recordable. CD-R discs are write-once until media is used. They cannot be erased or re-recorded on. Maximum storage capacity is 650 MB.

- **CD-RW:** Abbreviation for Compact Disc-Rewritable. CD-RW discs are rewritable and can be erased and re-recorded on over and over again. Maximum storage capacity is 650 MB.

- **Zip Drive:** A high-capacity floppy disk drive developed by Iomega Corporation. Zip disks are slightly larger than conventional floppy disks and about twice as thick. They can hold 100 or 250 MB of data.

- **DVD+R:** Abbreviation for DVD+Recordable. DVD+R is write once. Maximum storage capacity is 4.37 GB.

- **DVD-R:** Abbreviation for DVD-Recordable. Often called "minus R", the format is write once. Maximum storage capacity is 4.37 GB.

- **DVD+RW:** Abbreviation for DVD+ReWritable. DVD+RW is a ReWritable media format of the DVD+R standard. Maximum storage capacity is 4.37 GB.

- **DVD-RW:** Abbreviation for DVD-ReWritable. Often called "minus RW", the format is rewritable. Maximum storage capacity is 4.37 GB.

- **USB Removable drive:** Also known as a flash drive or keychain drive. When the user plugs the device into his or her USB port, the computer's operating system recognizes the device as a hard drive. Available in capacities ranging from 8 MB to 2 GB.

- **USB Mobile hard drive:** A hard drive in a mobile case. When the user plugs the device into his or her USB port, the computer's operating system recognizes the device as a hard drive. Available in capacities ranging from 40 GB to 250 GB.

- **Hard drive:** Contains operating system files as well as local data. Available in capacities ranging from 40 GB to 250 GB. Some computers may have more than one hard drive.

■ **Network drive:** Provides storage on a hard drive or drives located on another computer on the network. Space is shared with multiple users.

It's easy to get RAM and hard disk space confused. When people get an "out of memory" error message from their computer, they often think their hard drive is too full, when in reality, the RAM (memory) is getting too full.

In the two sections that follow, a USB storage device will be installed and troubleshooting suggestions for USB devices will be presented.

Installing a USB Storage Device

For most USB devices, installing the USB device on computers running Windows XP is easy! If needed, power on the device. Plug the device or device cable into a USB port. The device will be detected and the proper device drivers installed. Most of the time, that's it! (Of course, however, it is wise to read over the manufacturer's instructions prior to taking the previous actions. This is particularly true when you receive a CD-ROM with the device. You never know when the manufacturer has thrown an extra twist into the mix.)

10

Activity 10-4: Installing a USB Removable Drive

Time Required: 15 minutes

Objective: Install a USB removable drive.

Description: In this activity, you will install a USB removable drive. You will find this activity useful in your career as a DST because, in order to answer users' questions about using USB removable drives, you will need to have installed a USB removable drive.

To complete this activity, you will need a USB removable drive.

1. If necessary, log on to your computer with the user name **admin01** and password **Password1**.

2. Insert the USB removable drive in the USB port.

3. If this is the first insertion, a message similar to Figure 10-9 is displayed. Close the pop-up message.

Figure 10-9   Found new hardware message

4. If this is the first insertion, a message similar to Figure 10-10 is displayed. Close the pop-up message.

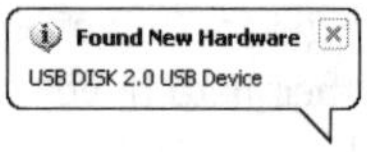

Figure 10-10   Found new hardware message

5. When a window that resembles Figure 10-11 is displayed, the USB removable drive is available for use.

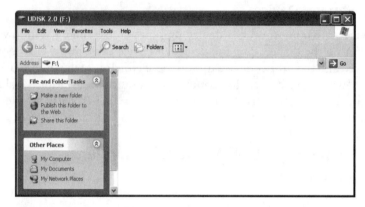

Figure 10-11   Windows Explorer window for removable drive

6. Click the **Safely Remove Hardware** button (green arrow over gray removable drive symbol).

7. When the message shown in Figure 10-12 appears, close the message balloon.

Figure 10-12   This message appears after clicking the Safely Remove Hardware button

8. When the message in Figure 10-13 is displayed, close the message window.

Figure 10-13   Safe To Remove Hardware balloon

9. Remove the USB removable drive.

10. Write a brief description in your project log explaining the steps to install a USB removable drive.

11. Close any open windows.

Troubleshooting Local Storage Device Problems

There are a number of messages that you may see as a DST. This section presents some of those messages and suggested solutions.

One message that you may see when using a USB removable drive is the message that is shown in Figure 10-14. This occurs because you have inserted a USB 2.0 device (480 Mbits/sec speed) into a USB computer port designed for a slower speed (12 Mbits/sec). The message asks you to click to see a solution for this problem of mismatched speeds.

Figure 10-14 HI-SPEED USB Device Plugged into non-HI-SPEED USB Hub message

In Figure 10-15, you see the answer to the problem—install a card with a faster USB port.

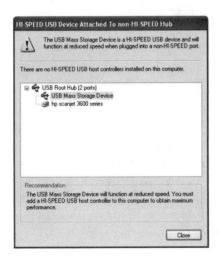

Figure 10-15 Dialog box in which to correct the USB problem

Another problem that you may encounter is the message shown in Figure 10-16. This occurs when Windows detects that the USB removable drive is still active. You may solve this problem by closing the application that is accessing the folder or file.

10

Figure 10-16   Problem Ejecting USB Mass Storage Device dialog box

When Windows detects that 200 MB or less free space is available on the volume used by the operating system, you will see the message shown in Figure 10-17. The message asks you to click to see a solution for this disk space problem.

Figure 10-17   Low Disk Space balloon

In Figure 10-18, you see additional information and a request to continue by accessing the Add or Remove Programs dialog box. As you will see in Activity 10-5, the Disk Cleanup is a safer alternative to deleting programs.

Figure 10-18   Low Disk Space dialog box

When you are working with a storage device (3½-inch floppy drive in this case), you may not be able to store a file from an application because the device is full. You will see a message that resembles Figure 10-19. Do as the message says—free some space on this drive or store the file on another storage device.

Figure 10-19   The disk is full

No discussion of storage devices would be complete without mentioning Disk Cleanup. You use Disk Cleanup to assist with freeing up space on your hard drive. Disk Cleanup searches your drive, then shows you files such as temporary files or unnecessary program files that you can safely delete. After reviewing the suggested file list, you can direct Disk Cleanup to delete some or all of those files.

Activity 10-5: Cleaning up a Local Storage Drive

Time Required: 15 minutes

Objective: Practicing using Disk Cleanup to increase the amount of free space on a hard drive.

Description: In this activity, you will practice using Disk Cleanup to recapture free space on your hard drive. You will find this activity useful in your career as a DST because, in order to assist your users' questions about hard drive space, you will need to have explored Disk Cleanup in detail.

1. If necessary, log on to your computer with the user name **admin01** and password **Password1**.

2. Click **Start**, point to **All Programs**, point to **Accessories**, point to **System Tools**, and click **Disk Cleanup**.

3. Select the drive to clean up, if necessary, and click the **OK** button.

4. Wait for the analysis to complete.

5. Click the **Recycle Bin** (avoid the check box) list entry and check the **View Files** button.

6. View the list of files that are in the Recycle Bin.

7. Right-click a file, click **Delete**, and click the **Yes** button to remove the file from the Recycle Bin.

8. Close the Windows Explorer window.

9. If necessary, check the **Recycle Bin** check box, as shown in Figure 10-20, and click the **OK** button.

10. Click the **Yes** button and wait for the cleanup to be completed.

11. Write a brief description in your project log explaining the steps to cleanup a local hard disk drive.

Working with Printers

For most printers, you can let Windows XP install the printer using Plug and Play. However, should Plug and Play not work, you can use the Add Hardware wizard. As a DST, your users expect you to be able to resolve problems with their printers. You will learn about installing and troubleshooting printers in this section.

10

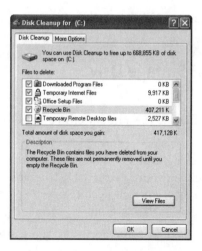

Figure 10-20 Disk Cleanup for (C:) dialog box

Installing Local Printers

With USB and PNP (**Plug and Play**), installing a new printer is a snap! Power on the printer. Plug in the USB cable between the printer and the computer. Wait for Plug and Play to install the printer. As with USB devices, you will see a message similar to Figure 10-21.

Figure 10-21 New hardware has been found balloon

Shortly afterward, you will see a message indicating that the device is ready for use, as shown in Figure 10-22.

Figure 10-22 New hardware is ready for use balloon

Should PNP fail to install the printer, you can always resort to the Add Printer wizard. With the Add Printer wizard, you have more control over the printer installation process.

Activity 10-6: Installing a Local Printer with Add Printer Wizard

Time Required: 15 minutes

Objective: Install a local printer using the Add Printer wizard.

Description: In this activity, you will use the Add Printer wizard to install a printer. You will find this activity useful in your career as a DST because, in order to install printers for your users, you will need to have explored this in detail.

Note: You will need a locally attached printer to complete this activity.

NOTE

1. If necessary, log on to your computer with the user name **admin01** and password **Password1**.

2. If this activity has been completed previously and it is necessary to delete the printer, click **Start**, click **Printer and Faxes**, right-click the installed printer, click **Delete**, click the **Yes** button, and close the Printers and Faxes window.

Your instructor may provide more specific instructions for the installation of the printer.

NOTE

10

3. Click **Start**, click **Printer and Faxes**, click the **Add a printer** link, and click the **Next** button. See Figure 10-23.

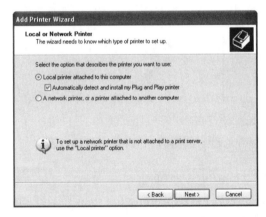

Figure 10-23   Add Printer wizard - Local or Network Printer page

4. If necessary, click the **Local printer attached to this computer** option button.

5. Click the **Next** button. Wait for the printer to be detected. Figure 10-24 shows a completed detection.

Figure 10-24   Add Printer wizard - New Printer Detection page

6. Click the **Next** button, read the summary page (See Figure 10-25), and click the **Finish** button.

Figure 10-25   Add Printer wizard - Completing the Add Printer Wizard page

7. Click the **OK** button and review the printed test page.

8. Write a brief description in your project log explaining the steps to add a local printer using the Add Printer wizard.

Troubleshooting Printers and Print Jobs

As a DST, you will be called upon to resolve problems with printers and print jobs. Some general printer troubleshooting items are appropriate for most but not all printer problems.

Here is a list of items that you will want to check at the printer:

- **Power:** Verify that the printer is turned on and has power. Trace the power cable to a known source of power.

- **Connectivity:** Check the cable connections to both the printer and the computer.

- **Online:** Verify that the printer light indicates that the printer is online.

- **Hardware:** Verify that no hardware problem indicators are lit or flashing.

- **Paper:** Verify that you do not have a paper jam. Verify that there is paper in the paper tray.

- **Manual print:** If available, print a test page using the printer setup.

If the items in the previous list all checked out OK, proceed with the following items at the computer:

- **Print driver:** Verify that the printer has a proper driver.

- **Test page:** Print a test page from the printer properties dialog box.

- **Printer dialog box:** Verify that no print jobs are held.

- **Test print:** Print a short message from Notepad. Notepad text is not formatted.

- **Test application:** Print a document from another application.

Troubleshooting Printing at the Application Level

Your users may identify some common printing problems when using Office applications. They will expect you to assist with problems such as these:

- When a user prints a Word document, nothing happens.

- When a user prints a document, each page has a few (perhaps four to six) characters at the top of each page.

- When a user prints a document, an extra blank page appears at the end of each print job.

- Word stops responding when printing.

Do you need a hand with the resolution of a printing problem? You should consider the Windows XP troubleshooters. These are wizards that guide you through the steps to diagnose and fix known computer-related problems.

IN THE WORKPLACE

Why would Microsoft create the Windows XP troubleshooters? Could it be to reduce telephone support costs for repetitive calls to their help lines?

It appears that the troubleshooters resemble a script that could be used to resolve a problem that was called in. The troubleshooters nearly always arrive at a solution. However, the steps do not always appear the most intuitive.

Figure 10-26 presents a list of the Windows XP troubleshooters. To work through this feature of Windows XP, the following discussion will illustrate how to resolve a particular printing problem.

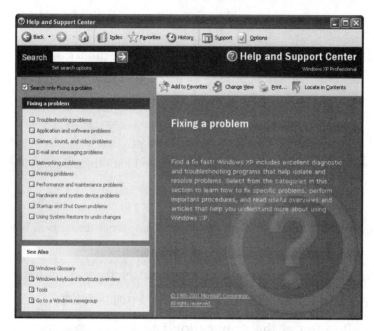

Figure 10-26 Help and Support Center - Fixing a problem page

If you click the Printing problems link on the left side of Figure 10-26, you will see Figure 10-27, which provides a starting point for the resolution of the printing problem. The process to resolve other problems follows similar steps.

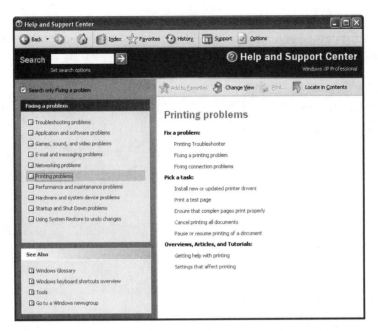

Figure 10-27   Help and Support Center - Printing problems page

In Figure 10-28, a series of questions are presented. You select the condition that matches your problem and select Next to continue. By matching the questions to the problem, you work through to the solutions.

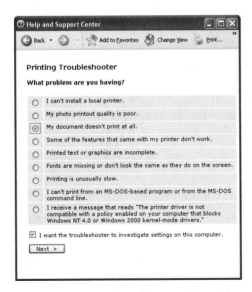

Figure 10-28   A list of potential problems

10

Figure 10-29 is representative of the steps that you will undertake to resolve the problem. You are asked to what degree you were successful. And you continue until the problem is resolved or you exhaust the steps in the troubleshooter.

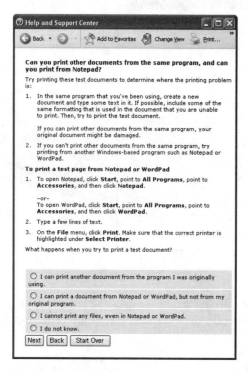

Figure 10-29   Additional questions in the troubleshooting wizard

DESCRIBING NETWORKING COMPONENTS AND INTERCONNECTIVITY

Simply stated, a network is a series of computer devices or nodes interconnected by communication paths. Network size can grow from a pair of computers in the den of your home to thousands of computers for a multinational corporation.

In the following sections, network terminology will be presented. This terminology is important because of the following:

- Your organization uses networked computers.
- You must have a working knowledge of networking concepts to effectively help your end users.
- You need the background to answer questions on the MCDST exam.
- Networking is fun!

Clients and Servers

The client/server model has become one of the central ideas of networking. Client/server describes the relationship between two computers in which the desktop computer, the client, makes a service request of another computer, the server, which fulfills the request.

Clients Use Network Resources

A desktop computer that accesses, or makes use of, network resources is a **client**. The client computer is a complete personal computer as opposed to a "dumb" terminal. A dumb terminal is a device (usually with display monitor and keyboard) with little or no software of its own that relies on a mainframe computer for its "intelligence."

Servers Provide Network Resources

In networking, a **server** is a computer that provides network resources to other computers and their users. A small network may have a single server—a file server that awaits and fulfills requests from client computers for data files. This single file server, with an attached printer, may provide print capabilities for the users of the network.

A corporate network could have dozens of servers. In addition to file servers, your organization's network could have servers that provide a range of services: network management, Web servers, Internet access, and so on.

Peer-to-Peer Networks

An example of a peer-to-peer network is the **Small Office Home Office (SOHO)** network that serves the needs of the small or home office environment. A peer-to-peer network employs desktop computers that are peers (or equals capable of being both clients and servers). The home entrepreneur can purchase a minimum amount of equipment and enjoy the benefits of the SOHO network. In Figure 10-30, the components for the SOHO are pictured. At the top of figure, there is the DSL/cable modem, which connects to the Internet. The router secures the local network and provides connectivity for the two computers. Of course, the printer provides print capability for the network.

Client/Server Networks

If your organization is larger, you may be working with client/server networks. The client/server will have additional desktop computers and more servers to support the increased number of users.

Figure 10-31 shows an example of a client/server network. Starting at the center of the diagram and working outward, you can see that the backbone segment links other segments through routers. A network of this size typically uses a few different types of network media. The backbone network that is used to connect to the different networks and host servers can use 1000 Mbps or GB Ethernet.

10

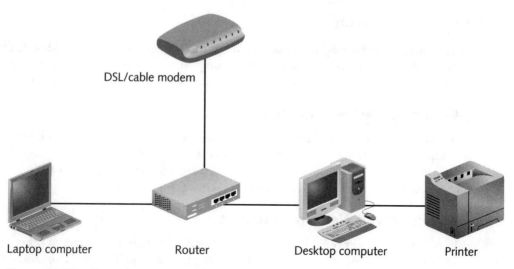

DSL/cable modem

Laptop computer   Router   Desktop computer   Printer

Figure 10-30   Peer-to-peer network

At the top of the diagram, you see remote users connected to the network through a remote access server. On both sides of the diagram, you see the routers that connect to the backbone segment one or more segments populated with desktop computers through switches. Continuing clockwise, you see Internet access secured with a firewall. For speed and efficiency the servers are attached to the backbone segment.

LANs, MANs, and WANs

Computer networks come in many different sizes and configurations. In an attempt to define sensible categories for the major types of network designs, the networking industry has coined terms like "LAN" and "WAN." The concept of "area"—which is represented by the "A" in the acronyms—makes good sense, because a key distinction of the three categories involves the physical distance that the network spans. From small spans to large spans, you will find LANs, MANs, and then WANs.

These three categories of network designs will be presented in the following sections.

Local Area Networks (LANs)

A LAN is a group of computers and other network devices that share a common communications line or wireless link. The scope of the network is limited to a small geographic area (for example, within an office building). Usually, applications and data storage are provided by one or more servers that are shared by multiple computer users. A local area network may serve as few as two or three users (for example, in a SOHO network) or as many as hundreds of users.

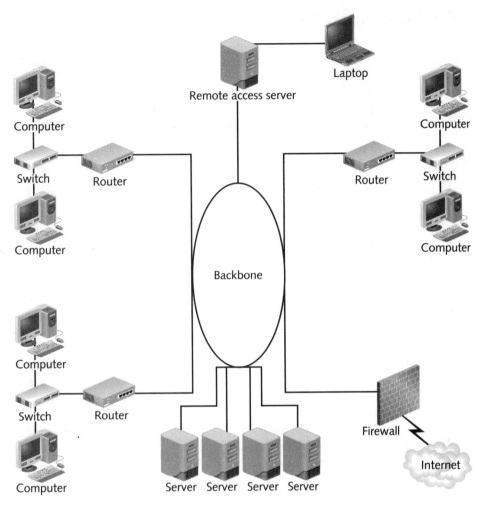

Figure 10-31   Client/server network

Metropolitan Area Networks (MANs)

A MAN is a network that interconnects users and computer resources in a geographic area larger than that covered by even a large local area network. The term is applied to the interconnection of networks in a city into a single larger network. For example, a medical organization with multiple interconnected clinics conforms to the definition of a MAN.

This term is also used to mean the interconnection of several local area networks by routing over communication lines. Because this networking model first appeared on a university campus, it is sometimes referred to as a campus network.

10

Wide Area Networks (WANs)

A WAN is a geographically dispersed telecommunications network. The term distinguishes a broader telecommunication structure from a local area network. A WAN may be privately owned or rented, but the term usually connotes the inclusion of public (shared user) networks. Companies incorporate carrier lines rented from telephone companies and other communication providers. As an alternative to carrier lines, frame relay provides connectivity using shared communication resources.

Network Hardware

Cables, NICs, hubs, switches, routers—such is the language of networking hardware. In order to assist the network administration group in the resolution of your users' problems, you will want to have a clear picture of where each of these fit into the networking picture. In this section you will learn about networking hardware.

Network Wiring

You are probably familiar with the **LAN cable**, or copper patch cable, that connects your computer to the "network." This network connection could be to a socket in the wall or to a wall-mounted network switch. There are a number of network wiring types, each with specific characteristics: cable type, speed, length limitations, and other restrictions. Your organization may use one type of wiring in one area of the building and something different in another area. If you are not sure, it's best to ask someone in the network administration group.

Besides copper wire, the network might use forms of "wiring" such as optical fiber. Or perhaps wireless—no wire at all.

NOTE

Network Interface Cards (NICs)

You plug your LAN cable into a LAN connector on the back of your computer. Many newer models of computers come with an on-board LAN connector (or RJ-45 connector). If your computer does not have an on-board LAN connector, you will need to locate the preinstalled **Network Interface Card (NIC)**. Or perhaps, you will need to install a NIC. Every client or server must have at least one NIC. Servers, for example, might have more than one NIC to connect to more than one LAN segment.

Network Equipment

Your organization will use network equipment to tie numerous servers and even more desktop computers together. Each computer will have one or more NICs and be connected to the network equipment with patch cables. The network equipment that you might encounter in your organization is as follows:

- **Hubs:** Copies frames from a single input port to the other ports so that all devices on the segment can see all the frames. In networking terms, network switches operate at layer one.

- **Switches:** Channels incoming frames from any of multiple input ports to the specific output port on the segment. In networking terms, network switches sometimes operate at layer three but typically operate at layer two.

- **Routers:** A router forwards packets from one network segment to the next network segment. In networking terms, network routers operate at layer three.

Figure 10-32 illustrates one possible relationship between hubs, switches, and routers. Starting at the bottom, you will see the hubs that copy the frames to and from the switches and computers. Working upward, you will see two switches. The switches channel frames to the two hubs connected to each switch. To speed communications, the servers are connected to the switches. At the top, you will see a router. The router forwards packets from the left network segment to the right network segment and back.

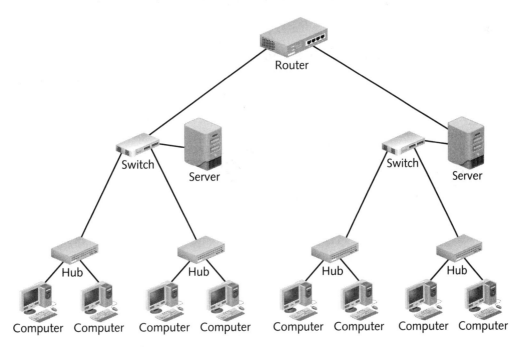

Figure 10-32   Network equipment

Network Printers

It makes good economic sense to share a printer. By sharing a printer on the network, your organization makes the printer available to several users. Network administrators "share" printers on the network. As a DST, you will be assisting your users in connecting their computers to network printers.

Activity 10-7: Connecting a Network Printer with the Add Printer Wizard

Time Required: 15 minutes

Objective: Install a network printer using the Add Printer wizard.

Description: In this activity, you will use the Add Printer wizard to install a network printer. You will find this activity useful in your career as a DST because, in order to install network printers for your users, you will need to have explored this in detail.

1. If necessary, log on to your computer with the user name **admin01** and password **Password1**.

2. If this activity has been completed previously and it is necessary to delete the printer, click **Start**, click **Printer and Faxes**, right-click the installed printer, click **Delete**, click the **Yes** button, and close the Printers and Faxes window.

3. Click **Start**, click **Printer and Faxes**, click the **Add a printer** link, and click the **Next** button.

4. Click the **A network printer, or a printer attached to another computer** option button and click the **Next** button.

5. Click the **Connect to this printer...** option button, type **\\instructor01\ printer01** in the Name text box, as shown in Figure 10-33, and click the **Next** button.

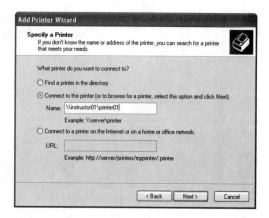

Figure 10-33 Specifying a network printer

6. Wait for the printer to be detected and click the **Next** button.

7. View the Completing the Add Printer wizard summary and click the **Finish** button.

8. Write a brief description in your project log explaining the steps to add a network printer using the Add Hardware wizard.

9. Close any open windows.

Networking Software

An operating system, such as Windows XP Professional, provides an interface to the user while controlling the resources of the desktop computer. In contrast, a **network operating system (NOS)** includes special functions for connecting computers and devices into a local area network (LAN).

The network infrastructure team has the responsibility of configuring the servers running the NOSs on the network. The team installs and configures a range of services for network servers including:

- **Domain Controller (DC):** Manages access to network resources
- **File and print services:** Stores data files and provides print support
- **Domain Name System (DNS):** Resolves computer names into Internet addresses

As indicated in Chapter 1, your knowledge of the Microsoft networking environment permits you to interrelate the desktop with the networking environment. For example, you can visualize the relationship between the desktop computer and the other computers on the network. You use this visual image to troubleshoot the desktop computers that connect to the network.

As a desktop support technician, you may need to contact the network administration group to resolve a desktop problem related to the network. For example, your user may need assistance connecting to a printer located on the network or the user is unable to store a file on a network file server.

10

IDENTIFYING AND TROUBLESHOOTING NETWORK CONNECTIVITY PROBLEMS

Your users expect that you will be ready to identify and troubleshoot problems with network connectivity. When necessary, you will work side by side with the members of the network administration group to resolve your users' network problems.

As a DST, you may be the main contact for your users in the resolution of problems in the following categories:

- Hardware including network interface cards and modems
- TCP/IP addressing including the configuration of IP addressing
- Name resolution including DNS and NetBIOS name resolution
- Remote connection including dial and authentication
- Network security including ICF

The sections that follow will prepare you to perform these tasks and more.

Troubleshooting Hardware Problems

As a DST, you will be called upon to resolve problems with network interface cards and modems. For example, your user may be having problems with a modem when dialing to a vendor's remote site to place a critical order. You will want to respond quickly and resolve the problem with this balky modem.

Troubleshooting Network Interface Cards

When resolving problems with network interface cards, start with the most obvious problem, which is the physical connection between the network cable and the NIC.

Here is a list of items that you will want to check physically at the desktop computer:

- Is the network cable damaged?
- Is the network cable securely plugged in?
- Are the link lights flashing?

If the physical check does not reveal the solution to the problem, you should turn to the software tools available within the Local Area Connection properties. From this dialog box, you can determine if a NIC is operating properly in the computer.

Knowing the number of packets sent from your NIC and received by your NIC can be useful when troubleshooting network connectivity to the LAN. How can you find that information? You can do one or both of the following:

- Monitor activity for the current session by displaying sent and received packet counts.
- Enable the status monitor each time the connection is active by displaying an icon with two blinking blue screens in the notification area.

ACTIVITY

Activity 10-8: Validating Proper NIC Operation

Time Required: 15 minutes

Objective: Determine if a NIC is operating properly.

Description: In this activity, you will determine if a NIC is operating properly in the computer. You will find this activity useful in your career as a DST because, in order to determine the proper operation of a NIC for your users, you will need to have explored this in detail.

1. If necessary, log on to your computer with the user name **admin01** and password **Password1**.

2. Click **Start**, point to **Control Panel**, point to **Network Connections**, and click **Local Area Connection**.

3. Click the **Properties** button, view the Local Area Connection properties, check the **Show icon in notification area when connected** check box, and click the **OK** button.

4. Click the **Local Area Connection is now connected** balloon. Observe the Local Area Connection button in the notification area (the screens should blink to indicate traffic to/from the computer).

5. Click the **Disable** button and notice that the Local Area Connection button in the notification area was removed.

6. Click **Start**, point to **Control Panel**, point to **Network Connections**, and click **Local Area Connection**.

7. Wait for the Local Area Connection to be enabled, click the **Local Area Connection is now connected** balloon and click the **Close** button.

8. Double-click the **Local Area Connection** icon in the notification area of the taskbar.

9. Observe the Bytes Sent and Bytes Received items in the Activity section and click the **Close** button.

10. Write a brief description in your project log explaining the steps to verify that a NIC is working properly.

IN THE WORKPLACE

The icon for the Local Area Connection button that is displayed in the notification area has two computer screens. When a packet is sent or received, the screens blink in blue to indicate this activity.

Which screen is which? The screen in the front is the send; the one in the back is the receive. If nothing else, this fact might be a discussion starter at the next party—"I noticed two blinking screens at the bottom of my Windows desktop. Does anyone know what this means?"

Troubleshooting Modems

Because your user's computer's network access may be made through a modem (for example, a dial-up modem, cable modem, or ISDN), you need to look for issues that resemble the ones for troubleshooting a NIC. One of your first tasks should be to verify that modem has power (assuming that the modem is an external modem). Next, you would want to check the cable connections.

You should use the modem diagnostics to further test the modem. To access this feature, navigate from Start, Control Panel, to Phone and Modem Options applet to open the Modems tab. From the Modems tab, select the modem to be tested, click the Properties button, click the Diagnostics tab, and click the Query Modem button. In a few seconds, you will see the diagnostics, which will resemble Figure 10-34.

10

Figure 10-34 Modem diagnostics

Troubleshooting TCP/IP Problems

What is TCP/IP? TCP/IP is a suite of protocols developed to allow cooperating computers to communicate across a network, including the Internet. The name is misleading, however, because Transmission Control Protocol (TCP) and Internet Protocol (IP) are only two of dozens of protocols that compose the suite. Nonetheless, its name comes from these two protocols.

Why is the TCP/IP protocol important to the DST? There are a number of reasons the DST should learn to work with the TCP/IP protocol:

- It's installed by default when Windows XP is installed.
- You will need to configure and troubleshoot TCP/IP configurations.
- Your users will have questions related to TCP/IP settings.
- You will need to learn to use the TCP/IP troubleshooting commands provided with Windows XP.
- There are questions on TCP/IP on the MCDST exam!

In the sections that follow, you will learn to troubleshoot IP addressing, use the ping and ipconfig commands, and troubleshoot Automatic Private IP Addressing (APIPA).

Troubleshooting IP Addressing

Just as a street address includes a block and house number, an IP address includes a network ID and a host ID. Here is a list of items to consider regarding network IDs and host IDs:

- All nodes on the same physical network segment must have the same network ID. The network ID should not duplicate another network ID.

- Each node is assigned a host ID. The host address cannot duplicate another host address within the network ID.

- You may consider routers as defining the gateways for off-segment communication.

An IP address consists of 32 binary digits. However, because it is difficult to work with binary numbers, the address is segmented into four 8-bit segments called octets, which are represented by a decimal number in the range 0 to 255. The Internet uses three address classes to accommodate networks of varying sizes. You probably will support networks with class A, B, and C addresses assigned to hosts. The class of address defines which bits of an IP address are used for the network ID and which bits are used for the host ID. It also defines the possible number of networks and the number of hosts per network.

For more information on address classes, I recommend searching for IP address classes on the following Web site: http://computer.howstuffworks.com/

NOTE

10

Activity 10-9: Validating Proper TCP/IP Addressing

ACTIVITY

Time Required: 15 minutes

Objective: Validate proper TCP/IP addressing.

Description: In this activity, you will determine if the TCP/IP address configuration is correct for a NIC. You will find this activity useful in your career as a DST because, in order to validate the proper IP address configuration, you will need to have explored IP address configurations in detail.

1. If necessary, log on to your computer with the user name **admin01** and password **Password1**.

2. Click **Start**, point to **Control Panel**, point to **Network Connections**, right-click **Local Area Connection**, and click **Status**.

3. Click the **Support** tab. View the IP address configuration. If the configuration appears wrong, contact your instructor.

4. Click the **Details** button, view the Network Connection details, note the date and time of the lease in your project log, and click the **Close** button.

5. Click the **Repair** button. Wait for DHCP to provide a new lease and click the **OK** button.

6. Click the **Details** button, view the Network Connection Details, compare the date and time of the lease to the values written in your project log, and click the two **Close** buttons.

7. Write a brief description in your project log explaining the steps to determine if the TCP/IP address configuration is correct.

Using Ping to Test Connectivity

For desktop connectivity issues, you should use the Ping utility. With the ping command, you can determine if a desktop can send packets and receive packets from an adjacent desktop, server, or network device. By default, the ping command will send four packets to the destination device.

The output of the ping command provides useful information about the time required for the destination device to respond. A long response time might indicate a heavily loaded network or congestion. If not all packets were received, this fact will be indicated by a high percentage loss value.

When you have a network connectivity problem, you will need to contact the network administration group for the resolution of the problem. They will ask you if you have run the ping command to test connectivity. Personally, I like to complete the ping commands from the desktop outward.

IN THE WORKPLACE

Here is an example of the outward tests that I'm recommending:

- Test the hardware and software on the desktop computer: At the local host, ping 127.0.0.1

- Test connectivity to a node on the local network segment: At the network gateway, ping 192.168.0.1

- Test connectivity to a node on a remote network segment: At the remote DNS server, ping 192.168.0.250

Activity 10-10: Testing TCP/IP Connectivity with Ping

ACTIVITY

Time Required: 15 minutes

Objective: Test TCP/IP connectivity with ping.

Description: In this activity, you will test TCP/IP connectivity with the ping command. You will find this activity useful in your career as a DST because, in order to test TCP/IP connectivity, you will need to have explored the ping command.

1. If necessary, log on to your computer with the user name **admin01** and password **Password1**.

2. Click **Start**, point to **All Programs**, point to **Accessories**, and click **Command Prompt**.

3. Type **ping instructor01** and press **Enter**. Wait for the ping command to send four packets. See Figure 10-35.

4. Type **ping 192.168.0.250** and press **Enter**. Wait for the ping command to send four packets.

5. Type **ping –a 192.168.0.250** and press **Enter**. Wait for the ping command to send four packets.

Figure 10-35   Command Prompt window - ping command

6. Write a brief description in your project log explaining the results that you obtained with the three ping commands.

7. Close the Command Prompt window.

Using the ipconfig Command to Verify IP Configurations

10

For desktop IP configuration issues, you should use the ipconfig command. For example, you use the ipconfig /all command to obtain a detailed listing of the desktop configuration information.

If the IP address or subnet mask is 0.0.0.0, ipconfig is indicating that an error has occurred. Typical problems that you may encounter are as follows:

- Duplicate address encountered with another computer on the network.

- NIC is installed improperly.

- DHCP server is not available.

IN THE WORKPLACE

I have found that if the Local Area Connection Properties dialog box and the ipconfig command show different addresses, then the ipconfig command is the correct one. The discrepancy happens about 1% of the time. I suppose that the ipconfig command is modeled after the UNIX ifconfig command and actually queries the protocol stack for its settings, instead of reading only what they should be, like the Local Area Connection Properties dialog box does.

Activity 10-11: Verifying TCP/IP Configuration with ipconfig

Time Required: 15 minutes

Objective: Verify TCP/IP configuration with ipconfig.

Description: In this activity, you will verify the TCP/IP configuration with the ipconfig command. You will find this activity useful in your career as a DST because, in order to verify TCP/IP configurations, you will need to have explored the ipconfig command.

1. If necessary, log on to your computer with the user name **admin01** and password **Password1**.

2. Click **Start**, point to **All Programs**, point to **Accessories**, and click **Command Prompt**.

3. Type **ipconfig** and press **Enter**. Wait for the ipconfig to display the configuration. See Figure 10-36.

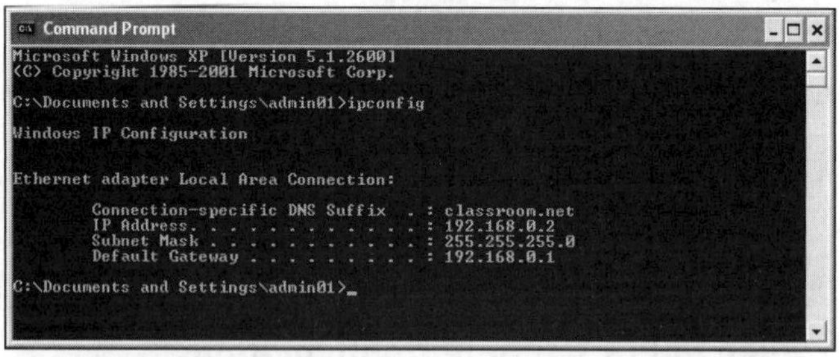

```
Command Prompt                                                    _ □ ×
Microsoft Windows XP [Version 5.1.2600]
(C) Copyright 1985-2001 Microsoft Corp.

C:\Documents and Settings\admin01>ipconfig

Windows IP Configuration

Ethernet adapter Local Area Connection:

        Connection-specific DNS Suffix  . : classroom.net
        IP Address. . . . . . . . . . . . : 192.168.0.2
        Subnet Mask . . . . . . . . . . . : 255.255.255.0
        Default Gateway . . . . . . . . . : 192.168.0.1

C:\Documents and Settings\admin01>_
```

Figure 10-36   Command Prompt window - ipconfig command

4. Type **ipconfig /all** and press **Enter**. Wait for the ipconfig to display the configuration, as shown in Figure 10-37.

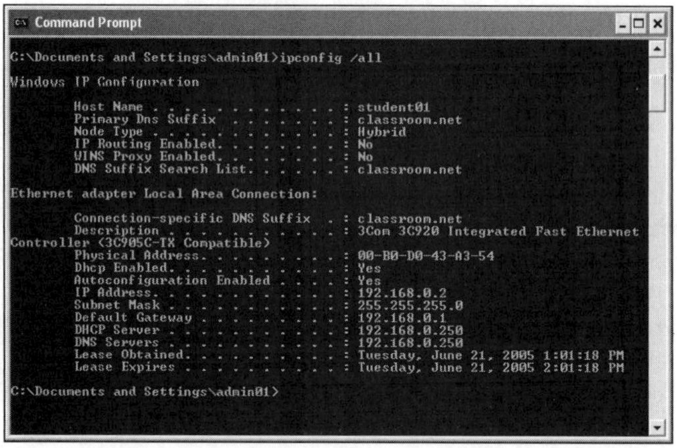

```
Command Prompt                                                    _ □ ×
C:\Documents and Settings\admin01>ipconfig /all

Windows IP Configuration

        Host Name . . . . . . . . . . . . : student01
        Primary Dns Suffix  . . . . . . . : classroom.net
        Node Type . . . . . . . . . . . . : Hybrid
        IP Routing Enabled. . . . . . . . : No
        WINS Proxy Enabled. . . . . . . . : No
        DNS Suffix Search List. . . . . . : classroom.net

Ethernet adapter Local Area Connection:

        Connection-specific DNS Suffix  . : classroom.net
        Description . . . . . . . . . . . : 3Com 3C920 Integrated Fast Ethernet
Controller (3C905C-TX Compatible)
        Physical Address. . . . . . . . . : 00-B0-D0-43-A3-54
        Dhcp Enabled. . . . . . . . . . . : Yes
        Autoconfiguration Enabled . . . . : Yes
        IP Address. . . . . . . . . . . . : 192.168.0.2
        Subnet Mask . . . . . . . . . . . : 255.255.255.0
        Default Gateway . . . . . . . . . : 192.168.0.1
        DHCP Server . . . . . . . . . . . : 192.168.0.250
        DNS Servers . . . . . . . . . . . : 192.168.0.250
        Lease Obtained. . . . . . . . . . : Tuesday, June 21, 2005 1:01:18 PM
        Lease Expires . . . . . . . . . . : Tuesday, June 21, 2005 2:01:18 PM

C:\Documents and Settings\admin01>
```

Figure 10-37   Command Prompt window - ipconfig /all command

5. Write a brief description in your project log explaining the steps to determine if the TCP/IP address configuration is correct.

6. Close the Command Prompt window.

Troubleshooting APIPA Addressing

Microsoft introduced **Automatic Private IP Addressing (APIPA)** to permit computers to self-assign IP address configurations. It is enabled by default on Windows XP. When troubleshooting IP addressing problems, you will encounter APIPA addresses that are unaffectionately known as 169.254's after the network that is automatically assigned. In most cases, APIPA is a nuisance that you will want to work around.

DHCP clients are able to self-assign an IP address in these situations:

- No DHCP server is available on the network.
- A DHCP client is unable to contact a DHCP server.
- A DHCP client attempts to renew an IP address leased from a DHCP server.

In these cases, the client assigns itself an address in the range 169.254.0.1 through 169.254. 255.254. With the ipconfig command, you can verify that APIPA is enabled and an IP address in the APIPA range was assigned. With the ipconfig /renew command, you can ask the computer to request an IP address.

In most organizations, you should not use APIPA. Clients using APIPA can communicate only with other computers using APIPA. There are other problems with APIPA:

- Clients cannot communicate with computers on other subnets.
- Clients do not receive the configuration parameters (such as, default gateway, and DNS server IP address)
- Clients cannot access the Internet.

IN THE WORKPLACE
Here is one situation where APIPA would prove useful: You go to your local electronics superstore and purchase 10 desktop computers, each with built-in network ports, network cables, and a 16-port network switch. You cable the computers to the network switch and turn on the 10 computers. The computers will self-assign via APIPA and are able to communicate with each other.

Troubleshooting Name Resolution Problems

In this section of the chapter, you will learn the basics of troubleshooting name resolution problems. Before you jump into the meat of the discussion, however, it's important to know the following facts:

- When you install Windows XP Professional, you are asked to specify the computer name during the installation process. The name you entered had to conform to the naming rules that your organization uses.
- A **fully qualified domain name (FQDN)** is the name that uniquely defines a host on the IP network, such as the Internet. A FQDN consists of a host name, domain name, and a top-level domain, including the dot (.) for the root domain. For example, www.course.com. is a fully qualified domain name: www is the host

name, .course is the second-level domain, .com is the top-level domain, and the dot at the end is for the root domain. The default host name is the computer name specified during installation.

- **Network Basic Input Output System (NetBIOS)** is an application programming interface (API), which is used by programmers to access services on a LAN. Examples of these services are name management and session management. In addition, NetBIOS provides services to send datagrams between nodes on a LAN. NetBIOS names are always 15 characters in length. Recall that the computer name is 15 characters and that you can specify these characters. The NetBIOS name is the computer name specified during installation.

- DNS servers, with a distributed database of host names, are used to provide name resolution for larger networks. Each DNS server is responsible for maintaining a database of host names for its local area of the network.

- To provide faster host name resolution, the **DNS resolver** places entries in a DNS resolver cache on the local computer. For a period of time, defined as the Time to Live (TTL), any names previously resolved by DNS are added to the DNS resolver cache. The DNS resolver supports negative caching of unresolved or nonvalid DNS names. These entries are added by the DNS resolver in response to a negative answer from a DNS server for a queried name. The DNS resolver places an entry for the host with a message that indicates that no records matched the DNS query.

IN THE WORKPLACE

Why is the DNS client called a resolver? The DNS resolver facilitates the resolution of host names for the TCP/IP applications executed on the client computer.

Now that you know the ins and outs of naming computers, we can begin our detailed discussion of troubleshooting.

Troubleshooting DNS Name Resolution

Recall that DNS is required to resolve host names or fully qualified domain names to IP addresses. Two name resolution problems that you may encounter are:

- A user receives no response when using an application that needs to resolve a host name because a DNS server is not available to resolve the host name.

- The user's application receives a response from the DNS server but the information returned is incorrect because a record at the DNS server was entered incorrectly.

Activity 10-12: Verifying Name Resolution

Time Required: 15 minutes

Objective: Verify name resolution.

Description: In this activity, you will use the netsh diag ping dns command to verify name resolution. This skill will be useful to you as a DST.

1. If necessary, log on to your computer with the user name **admin01** and password **Password1**.

2. Click **Start**, point to **All Programs**, point to **Accessories**, and click **Command Prompt**.

3. Type **netsh diag ping dns** and press **Enter**. Wait for the netsh to display the ping to the dns server. See Figure 10-38.

Figure 10-38   Command Prompt window - netsh diag ping dns command

4. Type **nslookup instructor01** and press **Enter**. Wait for the nslookup to display the configuration, as shown in Figure 10-39.

Figure 10-39   Command Prompt window - nslookup instructor01 command

5. Write a brief description in your project log explaining the steps to determine connectivity to the DNS server and to verify the name of a remote computer.

6. Close the Command Prompt window.

10

Troubleshooting NetBIOS

When your computer starts up, it registers a unique NetBIOS name with a service indicator (a 16th character, which indicates the NetBIOS service the computer is supporting). When a computer needs to use a NetBIOS service with another computer, a NetBIOS name to an IP address resolution must occur. For example, when you attempt to make a network connection to a file share by name, a NetBIOS name resolution occurs.

As DNS maps host names to IP addresses, Windows Internet Naming Service (WINS) maps NetBIOS names to IP addresses. WINS manages the association of NetBIOS names with IP addresses without an administrator having to be involved in each configuration change. WINS automatically creates a NetBIOS name-IP address mapping entry in a database, ensuring that the name is unique and not a duplicate of someone else's computer name. When a computer needs to know the IP address that corresponds to a NetBIOS name, the computer contacts the WINS server. Your users might find WINS mentioned in some network-related programs or system messages.

 Do computers running Windows XP need to use WINS? Well, actually, WINS is no longer needed in pure Windows Server 2003 and Windows XP networks. This is because DNS can handle the name resolution and find all the resources that Windows XP will need. In many organizations, WINS provides services only for legacy systems (such as Windows 9x and Windows NT).

To speed reoccurring NetBIOS name resolutions, previous resolutions are retained in name caches. You can use the nbtstat command to view the contents of these name caches. You will need to verify the contents of the caches on your computer or a remote computer to resolve NetBIOS names to IP addresses.

 Here's a useful trick. As a network administrator, I've needed the hardware address for the NIC in another computer. With the nbtstat -a command, I see the name cache of the other computer and the hardware or MAC address. This is much quicker than walking to the other computer. Plus you won't spill your soda while doing it!

Activity 10-13: Verifying NetBIOS Name Resolution

Time Required: 15 minutes

Objective: Verify NetBIOS name resolution.

Description: In this activity, you will work with the nbtstat command. You will find this activity useful in your career as a DST because you will need this command to look up local name caches.

1. If necessary, log on to your computer with the user name **admin01** and password **Password1**.

2. Click **Start**, point to **All Programs**, point to **Accessories**, and click **Command Prompt**.

3. Type **nbtstat –c** and press **Enter**. Wait for the nbtstat command to display the local name cache. If this computer has accessed another computer recently, your command prompt resembles Figure 10-40.

Figure 10-40   Command Prompt window - nbtstat –c command

4. Type **nbtstat –a instructor01** and press **Enter**. Wait for the nslookup to display the name cache. Your Command Prompt window should resemble Figure 10-41.

10

Figure 10-41   Command Prompt window - nbtstat –a instructor01 command

5. Write a brief description in your project log explaining the steps to determine the local NetBIOS name cache and the NetBIOS name cache of another computer.

6. Close the Command Prompt window.

Troubleshooting Remote Connection Issues

You will need to be prepared to resolve connections to remote access servers. Your users may dial up to these remote access servers. One of the problems that you may encounter is dialing through a modem. Also, you may need to assist with the resolution of authentication problems. Both are discussed in this section of the chapter.

Resolving Dial Problems

You or your users may encounter problems when dialing through a modem. The attempted connection might be to a remote access server or to an ISP. In the event that the connection cannot be completed, work through the following troubleshooting items:

1. Modem is working and is properly configured.

2. Phone line has a dial tone (use a phone handset).

3. Phone number dialed.

4. There are available ports on the remote access server (contact the network infrastructure team).

Resolving Authentication Problems

You or your user may encounter problems when authenticating to remote server. Authentication requires that credentials (a user name and a password) be exchanged with the remote server. In the event that the authentication cannot be resolved, use the following troubleshooting tips:

1. Verify the credentials of the user.

2. Check to see if the remote access server is enabled and started (contact the network administration group).

3. If remote access policies are being used on the remote access connection, contact the network administration group to verify that a remote access policy is not prohibiting the connection.

Identify and Troubleshoot Network Security Components

Internet Connection Firewall (ICF) is Microsoft's implementation of a stateful packet firewall. It allows your users to connect safely to the Internet. Once connected to the Internet, ICF inspects each packet flowing to or from the Internet connection. This inspection occurs to block unwanted packets, such as those packets possibly sent by a person attempting to gain access to the private network from the Internet.

If ICF finds that an inbound packet that was not preceded by an outbound packet, the packet is dropped. For example, if a packet arrives out of the blue and ICF is not aware that the packet is in response to an outbound packet, ICF drops the packet. Otherwise, if you request a page from a Web site (that is, you send an outbound packet), when the information from the Web site arrives (that is, when you receive the inbound packet), the packet is allowed.

At the core of ICF is the stateful packet filter. A stateful packet filter bases its decisions on both a packet state and the context information of a session. To do this, ICF maintains a state table of connection flows. Using the state table, ICF uses three action rules to determine which packets to allow or drop:

- Any packet that matches an entry in the state table is forwarded.

- Any outbound packet that does not match an entry in the state table will create an entry in the state table and the packet is forwarded.

- Any inbound packet that does not match an entry in the state table is dropped.

Your users expect you to be prepared to troubleshoot ICF. Your users may use remote assistance through ICF connections and you should be prepared to troubleshoot the interaction of these two features. Another important concern for the DST is virus detection and prevention. All three of these elements will be discussed in the subsequent sections of this chapter.

Troubleshooting ICF

Because many small organizations using SOHO networks are implementing firewalls to secure their network, you must be ready to troubleshoot ICF. That is, you need to be familiar with common configuration problems:

- When you establish ICF, existing Internet applications may not work through the firewall. The problem is service definitions configured for ICF. You will need to create or modify a service definition that supports the application.

- When ICF is established, your remote users and customers may not be able to connect to Web servers on the private network. To make the Web server available to your Internet users, you must add a service definition that permits access to the Web server.

- If your users have problems browsing the network to locate computers and file shares, check to see if ICF has been configured on the internal network. ICF should be configured only on the network that is connected to the Internet.

To correct these common ICF configuration problems, you will need to access the network configuration from the Network Connections folder. To open the Network Connections folder, click the Start menu, point to Control Panel, point to Network Connections, right-click the appropriate network connection (Local Area Connection or the name typed when the Internet connection was created), and click Properties. To start the configuration of ICF, click the Advanced tab. To turn on/off the Internet Connection Firewall, check/uncheck the Protect my computer... check box.

You can perform advanced configuration for ICF by clicking the Settings button on the Advanced tab. From the Services tab, you can add or edit a Services definition for the common protocols (FTP, SMTP, POP3, HTTP, HTTPS, and Remote Desktop) that a SOHO might use.

Troubleshooting Remote Assistance and ICF

The Remote Assistance connection is dependent on the configuration of the firewall. Both inbound and outbound connections must be permitted on port 3389. If your users cannot establish Remote Assistance connections through ICF, verify that a service definition exists for the Remote Desktop from the Services tab.

10

Virus Detection

You may have heard about the impact of the latest virus. To be a successful DST, you must be prepared to assist your organization with the prevention of intentional intrusions into your users' computers by viruses. You will want to follow these tips to help prevent outbreaks:

- Educate your users about viruses and how they are commonly spread. Your users can unwittingly bring viruses into their computers or your organization's network by loading a file from a source such as the Internet.

- Make your users aware of the common signs of viruses: unusual messages that appear on the screen, decreased system performance, and missing data. If they notice any of these problems on their computer, your users should run their virus-detection software immediately to minimize the chances of losing data.

- You should install at least one commercial virus-detection program on your users' computers. They should use it regularly to check their computers for viruses. Because new viruses are created every day, they should obtain the latest virus signature files when they are available.

- Programs on removable storage devices may also contain viruses. Scan all removable storage devices before copying or opening files from them.

CHAPTER SUMMARY

You learned to identify and troubleshoot problems with devices:

- To resolve issues with Device Manager: view driver properties, update a device driver, roll back a device driver, and use driver signing

- To use storage devices: install storage devices, troubleshooting storage devices, and how to use Disk Cleanup

- To resolve print issues: install local and network printers, troubleshoot local printers, and troubleshoot printers at the application level

You learned to describe network components and interconnectivity:

- Terminology for clients and servers: Clients use network resources; servers provide network resources, peer-to-peer networks, and client/server networks.

- Categories for major types of network designs, Local Area Networks (LANs), Metropolitan Area Networks (MANs), and Wide Area Networks (WANs)

- Definitions and uses for network hardware: network wiring (cabling and cables), network interface cards (NICs), hubs (level 1), switches (level 2 and sometimes 3), and routers (level 3)

- Networking software

You also learned about troubleshooting and identifying network connectivity problems:

❑ Troubleshooting hardware problems with NICs and modems

❑ Troubleshooting LAN problems: IP addressing, status support (two blinking screens, APIPA addressing (169.254.0.x network), and commands (ping and ipconfig)

❑ Troubleshooting name resolution problems with commands (netsh diag ping dns, nslookup, and nbtstat)

❑ Troubleshooting remote connection problems by resolving dial and authentication problems

❑ Identifying and troubleshooting network security components: Internet Connection Firewall (ICF), interaction with Remote Assistance, and virus detection

KEY TERMS

10

Automatic Private IP Addressing (APIPA) — DHCP clients can automatically self-configure an IP address and subnet mask when a DHCP server isn't available. The IP address range is 169.254.0.1 through 169.254.255.254.

client — Computer that accesses shared network resources provided by another computer (server).

device driver — Program that controls a device. Every device must have a driver program.

DNS resolver — Program that facilitates the resolution of host names for the TCP/IP applications executed on the client computer.

fully qualified domain name (FQDN) — Name that uniquely defines a host on an IP network, such as the Internet.

hubs — Devices that join multiple clients by means of a single link to the rest of the LAN.

LAN cable — Cable connecting desktop computer to hub or switch. Sometimes called a patch cable.

Network Basic Input Output System (NetBIOS) — Application programming interface (API), which is used by programmers to access services on a LAN.

Network Interface Card (NIC) — Expansion card or other device used to connect a computer to the network.

network operating system (NOS) — An operating system installed on a server in a network that provides network services to the network.

Plug and Play — A set of specifications developed by Intel that permits a desktop computer to automatically work with peripherals.

routers — Devices that determine the next network point to which a data packet should be forwarded en route toward its destination.

server — Computer that shares network resources that are used by another computer (client).

Small Office Home Office (SOHO) — Network that serves the needs of the small or home office environment.

sneaker net — Transfer of files by physically carrying disks from one computer to another.

switches — Devices that join multiple computers together by means of a single link to the rest of the LAN. Network switches look nearly identical to hubs, but a switch generally contains more "intelligence" than a hub.

Universal Serial Bus (USB) — External bus standard that supports Plug-and-Play installation and hot plugging. A single USB port can be used to connect up to 127 peripheral devices, such as mice, modems, and keyboards.

REVIEW QUESTIONS

1. From the device driver Properties dialog box, which details can be viewed? (Choose all that apply.)

   a. Driver Provider

   b. Driver Date

   c. Driver Version

   d. Digital Signer

2. What is the reason that a manufacturer might update a device driver? (Choose all that apply.)

   a. Provide new capabilities

   b. Compress files into packages

   c. Fix problems

   d. Uncompress files into a folder

3. If you encounter a problem with a failing driver, you might need to _____ the driver to the previous version.

   a. download

   b. install

   c. roll back

   d. update

4. Which of the following is a driver signing option? (Choose all that apply.)

   a. Ignore

   b. Restrict

   c. Warn

   d. Block

5. Which of the following devices is considered a storage device? (Choose all that apply.)

   a. CD-R

   b. DVD+RW

   c. printer

   d. USB removable drive

6. Which of the following physical items on the printer will you want to check when troubleshooting a printer?

   a. Power switch

   b. Printer cable

   c. Printer light

   d. Paper tray

7. Which of the following tasks will you want to perform when troubleshooting a printer? (Choose all that apply.)

   a. Verify the printer has the proper print driver.

   b. Print a test page.

   c. Print a test message with Notepad.

   d. Print a test message with another application.

10

8. A _____ is a desktop computer that makes use of network resources.

   a. switch

   b. client

   c. router

   d. server

9. A _____ is a computer that provides network resources.

   a. switch

   b. client

   c. router

   d. server

10. A _____ is a network component that joins network segments together.

   a. switch

   b. client

   c. router

   d. server

11. The networking device called a switch _____ .

   a. copies frames from a single input port to the other ports

   b. channels incoming frames from any of multiple input ports to the specific output port on the segment

   c. forwards packets from one network segment to the next network segment

   d. switches data from one network segment to the next network segment

12. In networking terms, a router works at level _____ .

   a. 1

   b. 2

   c. 3

   d. 4

13. Which of the following items should you check when troubleshooting a NIC? (Choose all that apply.)

   a. Is the network cable damaged?

   b. Is the network cable securely plugged in?

   c. Are the link lights flashing?

   d. Is the device functioning in the Device Manager?

14. Which of the following is a characteristic of IP addresses for desktop computers? (Choose all that apply.)

   a. consists of 32 bits

   b. consists of 8 octets

   c. octet is in range of 0–255

   d. classes are A, B, C

15. To test connectivity of one computer to another computer, use the _____ command.

   a. ping

   b. ipconfig

   c. nslookup

   d. nbtstat

16. To determine the IP address for the computer at which you are seated, use the _____ command.

   a. ping

   b. ipconfig

   c. nslookup

   d. nbtstat

17. To determine the MAC or NIC hardware address for one computer while you are sitting at another, use the _____ command.

   a. ping

   b. ipconfig

   c. nslookup

   d. nbtstat

18. Assume that you are sitting at computer A. To determine if a host address can be resolved for computer B, you can use the _____ command from your current computer.

   a. ping

   b. ipconfig

   c. nslookup

   d. nbtstat

19. To view the NetBIOS name cache for one computer while you are sitting at another, use the _____ command.

   a. ping

   b. ipconfig

   c. nslookup

   d. nbtstat

20. Which of the following items should you check when resolving a remote connection issue? (Choose all that apply.)

   a. Modem is working and is properly configured.

   b. Phone line is operational and has a dial tone.

   c. Correct phone number dialed.

   d. Correct username and password.

10

CASE PROJECTS

HANDS-ON PROJECTS

Case 10-1: Resolving Driver Issues with Device Manager

You consult as a desktop support technician. Your customer's network consists of eight computers configured as a workgroup.

Two of your customers have raised an issue about the quality of the images displayed on their monitors. They asked you to improve the quality of the displayed graphics images. And they would like to accomplish this without replacing the graphics cards.

Describe in detail the steps that you would take to remedy the problem. Also, consider what you will do if your solution fails.

Case 10-2: Resolving Network Printer Issues

You are a desktop support technician. Your network consists of a Windows Server 2003 Active Directory domain with 10 servers, including application and database servers and 500 computers running Windows XP Professional.

You are responding to a ticket assigned by the Help Desk. George is unable to print to the printer65 network printer. Describe in detail the steps that you will take to resolve the problem. Include every action that you take including communications with George and Help Desk.

Case 10-3: Resolving Network Connectivity Issues

You are a desktop support technician. Your network consists of a Windows Server 2003 Active Directory domain with 10 servers, including application and database servers and 680 computers running Windows XP Professional.

Susan's computer cannot access the network resources. When you use the proper command, you will determine that the IP address of her computer is 169.254.45.76. Describe in detail the steps to resolve the connectivity problem with Susan's computer.

11

RESOLVE FOLDER AND FILE ISSUES

After reading this chapter and completing the exercises, you will be able to:

♦ Configure and troubleshoot access using simple file sharing

♦ Configure and troubleshoot access to Local or Network folders and files

♦ Manage hard disk storage with quotas

♦ Configure and troubleshoot access to Offline files

As you are aware, the role of the DST requires that you be prepared to configure and troubleshoot access using simple file sharing, which permits folders to be shared. You should be prepared to answer your users' questions on the five levels of simple file sharing for standalone computers or computers in a SOHO workgroup.

As an alternative to simple file sharing, you should be prepared to support users who are using local or network folders and files that require more advanced methods for securing access. You will need to be ready to resolve problems with permissions related to this access.

Your organization may elect to manage hard drive space with disk quotas. You will need to be able to answer your users' questions regarding the controlled availability of disk space.

For your mobile users with laptop computers, you will need to be ready to assist them with the use of offline files. One issue that you will want to study in detail is synchronization.

This chapter will cover the preceding issues.

Configuring and Troubleshooting Access to Simple File Sharing

As mentioned, **simple file sharing** is a feature that permits folders to be shared for use by other users on a network. Your users expect that you will be ready to identify and troubleshoot problems with simple file sharing. Here is a list of tasks that you will be expected to accomplish for your users:

- Select a file system
- Select from one of the five levels for simple file sharing
- Configure sharing and security settings
- Troubleshoot access problems when simple file sharing is used

The sections that follow will prepare you to perform these tasks and more

Selecting a File System

With Windows XP, you have several choices for a file system when formatting a partition: FAT and FAT16, FAT32, and NTFS. These file systems will be presented in the following sections.

FAT and FAT16

The **File Allocation Table (FAT)** keeps track of the location of files on the disk. FAT12 is a relatively simple design originally intended for 320 KB floppies with 512-byte clusters. Filenames were limited to 11 characters in the 8.3 format (8 characters for the filename and 3 characters for the file extension).

FAT12 (which uses 12-bit cluster numbers) is the main file system developed for use in the first version of MS-DOS. A **cluster** is the logical unit of file storage on a hard disk that is managed by an operating system. Any file stored on a hard disk takes up one or more clusters of storage. A file's clusters can be scattered among different locations on the hard disk. The clusters associated with a file are kept track of in the FAT. When you read a file, the entire file is obtained for you and you aren't aware of the clusters in which it is stored.

To support demands for hard disks that permitted larger storage amounts, FAT16 (which uses 16-bit cluster numbers) was created. FAT16 was used by MS-DOS and the first version of Windows. A FAT16 partition with the minimum-sized 512-byte clusters can store up to 32 MB. By increasing the cluster size to the maximum cluster size of 32,768 bytes, a hard disk could store 2 GB (which is small when compared to today's hardware). With the implementation of Windows 95, a new version called **Virtual File Allocation Table (VFAT)** was created, which supported long filenames (255 characters). However, VFAT still used 16-bit cluster numbers.

FAT32

Because of demand for larger hard drives pushing storage technology, Microsoft implemented a 32-bit version of FAT. FAT32, which was first used in Windows 95 OSR2 (Operating System Release 2 was available only with new computers) and Windows 98, handles cluster sizes much better than FAT16. FAT32 (which actually uses only 28-bit cluster numbers) permits partitions to be as large as 32 GB. Also, FAT32, like VFAT, permits the use of long filenames.

 IN THE WORKPLACE Windows XP and today's newer BIOSs, which support 28-bit clusters, will permit up to 137 GB on IDE disk controllers. However, Windows XP supports only partitions as large as 32 GB when FAT32 is used. When partitions larger than 32 GB are needed, NTFS is a better alternative.

NTFS

In another part of the Microsoft campus, **NTFS (New Technology File System)** was created to meet some of the shortcomings of the various FAT file systems. NTFS, with 64-bit cluster numbers, permits partitions up to 256 TB (1 TeraByte = 1024 GB). The maximum individual file size is 16 TB. You can also use long filenames.

Here is a list of the features available in the NTFS implementation in Windows XP:

- **Fault Tolerance:** NTFS repairs hard disk errors automatically. (A **hard disk error** is an error that occurs when a computer attempts to write to the hard disk and fails.) Because this repair occurs in the background, you will not see an error message. When Windows XP writes a file to an NTFS partition, it keeps a copy of the file in memory. It then checks the file to make sure it matches the copy stored in memory. If the copies don't match, Windows XP marks that section of the hard disk as bad and won't use it again. Windows XP then uses the copy of the file stored in memory to rewrite the file to an alternate location on the hard disk. If the error occurred during an attempt to read information from the hard disk, NTFS returns a read error to the calling program, and the data is lost.

- **Security:** You can grant various permissions to directories and to individual files. These permissions protect files and directories locally and remotely.

- **Encrypting File System (EFS):** EFS uses public key security to encrypt files on an NTFS volume, preventing unauthorized users from accessing those files. Encryption ensures that only the authorized users and designated recovery agents of that file or folder can access it. EFS is not available in the Windows XP Home Edition.

- **File Compression:** The NTFS compression offers you the opportunity to compress individual files and folders of your choice. Because compression is implemented within NTFS, any Windows-based application can read and write compressed files; there is no need to manually uncompress the file(s) first.

11

- **Disk Quotas: Disk quotas** allow administrators to manage the amount of disk space allotted to individual users. Windows XP enforces quotas on a per-user and per-volume basis. Disk quotas are transparent to the user. When a user views the available disk space for the volume, the system reports only the user's available quota allowance. If the user exceeds this allowance, the system indicates that the disk is full.

There is a problem with disk quotas. Disk quotas can be controlled only at the volume or individual user level. There is no way to control disk quotas for a group of users who are sharing a set of folders. Hopefully, this will be corrected in a new version of Windows—maybe "Longhorn."

Choosing from Among FAT, FAT32, and NTFS

This is really an easy choice. There's only one reason not to choose NTFS—if you have installed multiple operating systems on your computer and an older operating system can't read NTFS (such as Windows 95 or MS-DOS). With **multiboot**, you can start one of several installed operating systems when you start your computer. The legacy operating system (such as Windows 95 or MS-DOS) should be installed first and will require a FAT partition.

If you want to access an NTFS drive across a network, any operating system can access the NTFS partition. When installing Windows XP on a hard disk with a volume greater than 32 GB, you must use NTFS.

Activity 11-1: Verifying the File System in Use

Time Required: 15 minutes

Objective: Determine the file system in use on a particular computer.

Description: In this activity, you will determine the file system in use. You will find this activity useful in your career as a DST because, in order to answer users' questions about file systems, you will need to be able to determine the file system in use on a particular computer.

1. Log on to your computer with the user name **user01** and password **Password1**.

2. Click **Start**, click **My Computer,** and click **Local Disk (C:)**.

3. If necessary, click the **double chevron (>>) Details** link. Read the entry after File System.

4. In your project log, write a brief summary that describes the steps to determine the file system in use.

5. Close any open windows.

6. Log off the computer.

Using Simple File Sharing

With Windows XP, your users can share files with other users on their local computers or with users in the workgroup. To access simple file sharing from the My Documents folder, click Start, right-click My Documents, click Properties, and click the Sharing tab. From this dialog box, as shown in Figure 11-1, you can configure sharing at the folder level.

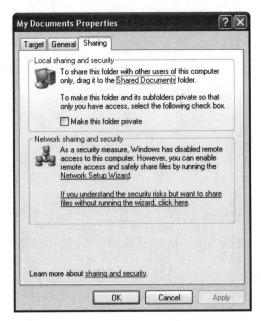

Figure 11-1   Sharing on the local computer

These permissions apply to the folder and all the files and folders within the folder. You can configure five different levels of simple file sharing:

1. My Documents (Private)

2. My Documents (Default)

3. Files in Shared Documents available to local users

4. Shared files on the network (Readable by Everyone)

5. Shared files on the network (Readable and Writeable by Everyone)

By default, files that are stored in the My Documents folder are at Level 2. Files shared at Levels 1, 2, and 3 are available only to users who are sitting at the computer and logged on locally. Files shared at Levels 4 and 5 are available both to users who log on locally and to remote users from the network.

IN THE WORKPLACE Why was simple file sharing developed? I suppose that Microsoft wanted to provide a simple means for multiple users of home computers to share files on a single computer. You do not need to know the ins and outs of sharing and file permissions to use simple file sharing. This concept was extended to SOHO networks of multiple computers.

To implement the sharing of files with other computer users in your network—which can mean you are working at Level 4 or 5—you must run the Network Setup wizard. To do this, you will click the Network Setup Wizard link shown in Figure 11-1. You will practice running this wizard in Activity 11-4.

With Windows XP, your users can share files with other users in the workgroup. From the Properties dialog box, as shown in Figure 11-2, you can configure sharing at the folder level for network users.

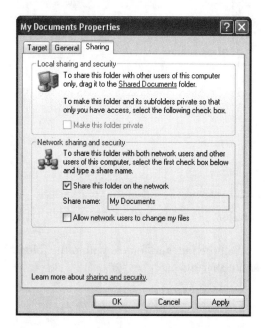

Figure 11-2   Sharing on the network

You will learn about these various check boxes in the sections that follow.

Level 1: Making Your Personal Folders Private

You—and your users—can make the personal folders private. This option is available for personal folders only when the drive is formatted with NTFS. These personal folders include My Documents and its subfolders, Desktop, Start Menu, Cookies, and Favorites. If you do not make these folders private, they are available to everyone who uses your computer. When you make a folder private, all of its subordinate subfolders are private as well. For example, when you make My Documents private, you also make My Music and My Pictures private.

Level 2: Using the My Documents Folder

You are aware that the My Documents folder provides an easy way for your users to store and share their personal files. My Documents, My Pictures, and My Music folders are created for each user of the computer running Windows XP Home. By default, the files in these folders are available to all users who access the computer by logging on locally.

Level 3: Using the Shared Documents Folder

If there is more than one user on your computer, the My Documents folders contain a link to their shared counterparts: Shared Documents, Shared Pictures, and Shared Music. These shared folders provide a place for your users to store files, pictures, and music that everyone on their computer can access.

If you want to share your personal files with other people who use your computer, you can copy or move them from your personal folders to the Shared Documents, Pictures, or Music folders located in Other Places. For example, Susan can put her homework in Shared Documents so that Dad can check her work. And Mom can put digital pictures from the family vacation in Shared Pictures so that the whole family can see them. Unlike your personal folders, shared folders cannot be made private. The contents of these folders are always available to anyone who uses your computer.

NOTE   If you are connected to a network domain, the Shared Documents, Shared Pictures, and Shared Music folders are not available.

Level 4: Shared Files on the Network (Readable by Everyone)

You may need to share folders and files with other users within your workgroup (or family members). For example, assume that you have created a series of "How to" articles that you want to make available, but you want your users to be able only to read—as opposed to changing the contents of—the folder. To facilitate this, you place the articles in a folder called Howto and set the sharing options to share the folder as read-only.

Level 5: Shared Files on the Network (Readable and Writeable by Everyone)

Your user may need to create a folder where he or she can receive the weekly status reports from other users within your workgroup. To do this, you—or your end user—must set the folder as both readable and writeable. The settings are similar to Level 4 but the folder is also writeable.

Configure Sharing and Security Settings

To configure a folder and all files in the folder to Level 1, 2, 4, or 5, you would right-click the My Documents folder, click Properties, click the Sharing tab, and set the check boxes as indicated in Table 11-1. To configure a folder and all files in the folder to Level 3, start Windows Explorer, then move or copy the file or folder to the Shared Documents folder.

Table 11-1   Check box settings for Access Levels 1, 2, 4, or 5

Access level	Make this folder private	Share this folder on the network	Allow network users to change my files
Level 1	Checked	N/A	N/A
Level 2	Unchecked	Unchecked	N/A
Level 4	N/A	Checked	Unchecked
Level 5	N/A	Checked	Checked

Simple file sharing masks from the user the actual sharing permissions and folder permissions that are being set. In Table 11-2, you will see the sharing and folder/file permissions for each of the five levels.

Table 11-2   Permissions at each level

Access level	Sharing permissions	Folder/File permissions
Level 1	N/A	N/A
Level 2	N/A	N/A
Level 3	N/A	Everyone Read
Level 4	Everyone Read	Everyone Read
Level 5	Everyone Full Control	Everyone Change

Troubleshooting Sharing and Security Settings

To troubleshoot simple file sharing for your users, you need to first be aware of which circumstances can and cannot use simple file sharing:

- For Windows XP Home Edition–based computers, simple file sharing is always turned on.

- By default, simple file sharing is turned on for Windows XP Professional–based computers that are joined to a workgroup.

- When Windows XP Professional computers join a domain, simple file sharing can not be used. These computers must use the classic File Sharing and Security tabs on the Folder Property dialog box.

If other users have problems working with files and folders that are shared with simple file sharing, you will need to verify these three check boxes on the Sharing page:

- **Make this folder private:** If your user discovers that others are accessing files that should be private, check the Make this folder private check box.

- **Share this folder on the network:** If other users cannot access a folder, check the Share this folder on the network check box.

- **Allow network users to change my files:** If your user does not want others to update the files in a shared folder, uncheck the Allow network users to change my files check box.

Another item you may need to check is the Internet Connection Firewall. You cannot access files from the network if the Internet Connection Firewall is enabled on the network interface that your users are using for the local area network. To check to see if the Internet Connection Firewall is enabled on the local network interface, click Start, point to Control Panel, point to Network Connections, right-click Local Area Connection, and click Properties. Click the Advanced tab and verify that the Protect my computer... check box is unchecked. The Internet Connection Firewall should be enabled only on the connection to the Internet.

11

Activity 11-2: Placing a Computer in a Workgroup

Time Required: 15 minutes

Objective: Change the membership of a computer from a domain to a workgroup.

Description: In this activity, you will remove a computer from the classroom domain and place it in the WORKGROUP workgroup. You will find this activity useful in your career as a DST because, in order to use simple file sharing, the computer must be moved from a domain to a workgroup and you will need to have explored the steps to accomplish this task.

1. Log on to your computer with the user name **admin01** and password **Password1**.

2. Click **Start**, right-click **My Computer**, click **Properties**, and click the **Computer Name** tab.

3. Click the **Change** button. Under the Member of, click the **Workgroup** option button, type **WORKGROUP** in the Workgroup text box, then click the **OK** button.

4. Type **admin01** in the User name textbox, type **Password1** in the Password text box, and click the **OK** button.

5. Wait for the **Welcome to the WORKGROUP workgroup.** message to be displayed and click the three consecutive **OK** buttons and the **Yes** button.

6. Wait for the computer to restart.

7. In your project log, provide the reason that you removed the computer from a domain and placed it in a workgroup.

Activity 11-3: Configuring Simple File Sharing for Local Folders

Time Required: 15 minutes

Objective: Configure simple file sharing for Local folders.

Description: In this activity, you will move the My Pictures folder to Shared Folders making it available for public use. Next, you will configure the My Documents folder for private use. You will find this activity useful in your career as a DST because, in order to answer users' questions about using simple file sharing with Local folders, you will need to have explored this in detail.

1. Log on to your computer with the user name **user01** and password **Password1**.

2. Click **Start**, point to **All Programs**, point to **Accessories**, and click **Windows Explorer**.

3. Expand **My Computer** and expand the **Shared Documents** folder.

NOTE

If this activity has been previously completed and if it is necessary to replace the My Pictures folder, expand the **Shared Pictures** folder, right-click the **My Pictures** folder, and click **Cut**. Right-click the **My Documents** folder and click **Paste**.

4. Right-click the **My Pictures** folder and click **Cut**.

5. Right-click the **Shared Pictures** folder and click **Paste**.

6. If the This folder is shared and won't be after moving it. message appears, click the **Yes** button.

7. In your project log, write a brief summary that describes the steps to make files available to other local users.

8. Right-click **My Documents**, click **Properties**, and click the **Sharing** tab.

9. If necessary, uncheck the **Share this folder on the network** check box.

10. Check the **Make this folder private** check box and click the **OK** button.

11. In your project log, write a brief explanation of the steps to configure simple file sharing including public and private folders.

12. Close any open windows.

Activity 11-4: Configuring Simple File Sharing for Network Folders

Time Required: 15 minutes

Objective: Configure simple file sharing for Network folders.

Description: In this activity, you will share the My Documents folder with other network users and permit only that the contents be read. Next, you will share the My Pictures folder with other network users and permit the other users to change the files. You will find this activity useful in your career as a DST because, in order to answer users' questions about using simple file sharing with Network folders, you will need to have explored this in detail.

 Note that you will be working with a partner on this activity. The first computer, Student01, of the pair will be used to create the network file share and the second, Student02, will be used to connect to the network file share. You and your partner will want to observe the activities on both computers.

For this activity, the student should substitute Studentxx for Student01 (the sharing computer) and userxx for user01. Substitute Studentyy (the connecting computer) for Student02 and Useryy for User02.

1. If necessary, log on to the **Student01** computer with the user name **user01** and password **Password1**.

2. Click **Start**, right-click **My Documents**, and click **Properties**.

3. If this activity has been previously completed, click the **Sharing** tab and then continue with Step 13.

4. Click the **Sharing** tab and click the **Network Setup Wizard** link.

5. Click the two consecutive **Next** buttons.

6. If necessary, click the **This connects to the Internet through another computer...** option button.

7. Click the three consecutive **Next** buttons.

8. Type **WORKGROUP** in the Workgroup name text box and click the **Next** button.

9. Review the network settings and click the **Next** button.

10. Wait for the configuration to be completed.

11. Click the **Just finish the wizard...** option button and click the **Next** button.

12. Click the **Finish** button.

13. If necessary, uncheck the **Make this folder private** check box.

14. Check the **Share this folder on the network** check box, if necessary, type **My Documents** in the Share name text box, if necessary, uncheck the **Allow network users to change my files** check box, and click the **OK** button.

15. In your project log, write a brief summary that describes the steps to make files available to be readable by other network users.

16. Click **Start**, right-click the **My Pictures** folder, and click **Properties**.

17. Click the **Sharing** tab, check the **Share this folder on the network** check box, if necessary, check the **Allow network users to change my files** check box, and click the **OK** button.

18. In your project log, write a brief summary that describes the steps to make files available to be read and updated by other network users.

19. Close any open windows.

Activity 11-5: Testing Simple File Sharing for Network Folders

Time Required: 15 minutes

Objective: Test simple file sharing for Network folders.

Description: In this activity, you will connect to the folder shared in Activity 11-4. You will find this activity useful in your career as a DST because, in order to answer users' questions about using simple file sharing with network folders, you will need to have explored this in detail.

 You will be working with a partner on this activity. The first computer, Student01, of the pair will be used to create the network file share and the second, Student02 will be used to connect to the network file share. You and your partner will want to observe the activities on both computers.

For this activity, the student should substitute Studentxx for Student01 (the sharing computer) and userxx for user01. Substitute Studentyy (the connecting computer) for Student02 and Useryy for User02.

1. If necessary, log on to your partner's **Student02** computer with the user name **user02** and password **Password1**.

2. Right-click **Start**, click **Properties**, click the **Customize** button, click the **Advanced** tab, scroll and check the **My Network Places** check box, and click the two consecutive **OK** buttons.

3. Click **Start**, click **My Network Places**, and click the **Add a network place** link.

4. Click the **Next** button, if necessary, click **Choose another network location**, and click the **Next** button.

5. Click the **Browse** button, expand **Entire Network**, expand **Microsoft Windows Network**, expand **Workgroup**, expand **Student01**, expand **My Documents**, click **user01's Pictures**, and click the **OK** button.

6. Click the **Next** button, type **Pictures under My Documents on user01** in the Type a name... text box, click the **Next** button, and click the **Finish** button.

7. Click **Start**, click **My Pictures**, double-click **Sample Pictures**, right-click **Water lilies**, and click **Copy**.

8. Return to the **Pictures under My Documents on user01** window, right-click within the **Pictures under My Documents on user01** window, and click **Paste**.

9. You should get the error message as shown in Figure 11-3.

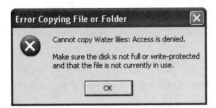

Figure 11-3   Error Copying File or Folder message box

10. In your project log, write a brief explanation for the error message that you obtained.

11. Click the **OK** button and close the open windows.

12. Click **Start**, click **My Network Places**, and click the **Add a network place** link.

13. Click the **Next** button, if necessary, click **Choose another network location**, and click the **Next** button.

14. Click the **Browse** button, expand **Entire Network**, expand **Microsoft Windows Network**, expand **Workgroup**, expand **Student01**, click **My Pictures**, and click the **OK** button.

15. Click the **Next** button, type **My Pictures on user01** in the Type a name... text box, click the **Next** button, and click the **Finish** button.

16. Click **Start**, click **My Pictures**, double-click **Sample Pictures**, right-click **Water lilies**, and click **Copy**.

17. Return to the **My Pictures on user01** window, right-click on **My Pictures on user01**, and click **Paste**.

18. In your project log, write a brief explanation indicating why you were able to copy the file to the folder.

19. Close any open windows and log off the Student2 computer.

IDENTIFY AND TROUBLESHOOT PROBLEMS WITH FOLDERS

Your users expect that you will be ready to identify and troubleshoot problems with access to Local and Network folders and files when more advanced techniques than simple file sharing are deployed. Here is a list of tasks that you will be expected to accomplish for your users:

- Justify the use of the NTFS file system
- Implement local user groups
- Assign share permissions
- Assign NTFS permissions
- Combine share and NTFS permissions
- Analyze combined share and NTFS permissions
- Move and copy files and determine the resultant permissions
- Troubleshoot access problems when share and NTFS permissions are used

The sections that follow will prepare you to perform these tasks and more

NTFS File System Required

If you—or your users—are planning to share folders and files with other network users, you should use the NTFS file system. While FAT and FAT32 permit folders to be shared, these two file systems do not provide the required permissions to properly secure the files. Only NTFS permits user accounts and user groups to be linked to the folder and file permissions, which are required to implement the required security.

Using Local User Groups

As an administrator, you can use local user groups to simplify the management of authorization to network resources. You will want to create groups that define sets of user accounts that have common resource-access requirements. For example, the persons conducting sales activities could be placed in the Sales group. If a new salesperson were hired you could place the new user account in the Sales group. The salesperson could then access the network resources just like any other salesperson. Likewise, if a person changed career assignments from Sales to Advertising, removing the user account from the Sales group would remove access from the network resources. Of course, you would need to add the user account to the Advertising group.

Activity 11-6: Placing a Computer in a Domain

Time Required: 15 minutes

Objective: Return a computer to the classroom domain.

Description: In this activity, you will return a computer to the classroom domain from the WORKGROUP workgroup. You will find this activity useful in your career as a DST because, in order to prepare for and use Share and NTFS permissions in a domain, the computer must be moved from a workgroup to a domain and you will need to have explored the steps to accomplish this task.

1. Return to the Student01 computer. If necessary, log on to your computer with the user name **student** and password **Password1**.

2. Click **Start**, right-click **My Computer**, click **Properties**, and click the **Computer Name** tab.

3. Click the **Change** button. Under the Member of, click the **Domain** option button, type **classroom** in the Domain text box, and click the **OK** button.

4. Type **admin01** in the User name textbox, type **Password1** in the Password text box, and click the **OK** button.

5. Wait for the Welcome to the classroom domain message to be displayed and click the three consecutive **OK** buttons and the **Yes** button.

6. Wait for the computer to restart.

7. In your project log, write a brief explanation for the reason you returned your computer to the classroom domain.

Activity 11-7: Creating Local User Groups

ACTIVITY

Time Required: 15 minutes

Objective: Create a local user group.

Description: In this activity, you will create a local user group consisting of the domain user accounts. You will find this activity useful in your career as a DST because, in order to answer users' questions about using local user groups, you will need to have explored this in detail.

1. Log on to your computer with the user name **admin01**, password **Password1**, and domain **classroom**.

2. Click **Start**, point to **Control Panel**, and click **User Accounts.**

3. Click the **Advanced** tab, click the **Advanced** button, and click **Groups** in the left pane, which displays the window shown in Figure 11-4.

If this activity has been completed before and the Students user group needs to be deleted, right-click **Students** in the right pane, click **Delete**, and click the **Yes** button.

NOTE

4. Right-click **Groups**, click **New Group**, type **Students** in the Group name text box, and type **Local User Group for Users** in the Description text box.

5. Click the **Add** button, click the **Advanced** button, type **user** in the Name text box, click the **Find Now** button, click on the first user listed, hold the **Shift** key, scroll and click the last user listed, and click the two consecutive **OK** buttons.

6. Click the **Create** button and the **Close** button.

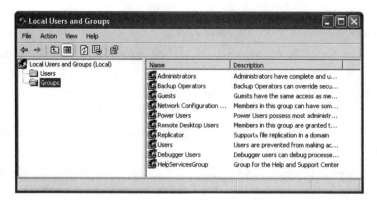

Figure 11-4   Local Users and Groups window

7. In your project log, write a brief description of the steps to create a local user group.

8. Close any open windows.

Assigning Shared Folder Permissions

When sharing a folder with users on the network, you—or your users—must specify the level of access that you are willing to assign to specific users. As you assign shared folder permissions, you must balance security with functionality by allowing access to appropriate resources and prohibiting unauthorized access. To support this granting of shared access, Windows XP Professional provides the shared folder permissions that are listed in Table 11-3.

Table 11-3   Windows XP shared folder permissions

Share Permission	Definition
Read	Display folders and files within the shared folder. Execute programs contained in the folder.
Change	All of the permissions associated with the Read permission. Add folders and files to the shared folder. Append to or delete existing files.
Full Control	All of the permissions associated with the Change permission. Change the file permissions and take ownership of the file resources (requires proper NTFS permissions).

Be careful assigning share permissions. Only give permissions that reflect the required business objectives of specific users. After you give access to a share, access can be blocked only by using NTFS permissions.

IN THE WORKPLACE

Activity 11-8: Assigning Share Permissions

Time Required: 15 minutes

Objective: Assign Share permissions to a folder.

Description: In this activity, you will create a folder and share the folder with appropriate permissions. You will find this activity useful in your career as a DST because, in order to answer users' questions about using share permissions, you will need to have explored this in detail.

1. If necessary, log on to your computer with the user name **admin01**, password **Password1**, and domain **classroom**.

2. Click **Start**, point to **All Programs**, point to **Accessories**, and click **Windows Explorer**.

3. Expand **My Computer**, expand **Local Disk (C:)**, and click **Local Disk (C:)**.

If this activity has been completed before and the Project folder needs to be deleted, right-click the **Projects** folder, click **Delete**, and click the **Yes** button.

NOTE

4. Right-click in the right pane, point to **New**, click **Folder**, type **Projects** over New Folder, and press **Enter**.

5. Right-click the **Projects** folder, click **Sharing and Security**, click the **Share this folder** option button, and click the **Permissions** button.

6. Click the **Add** button, click the **Locations** button, click **Student01**, click the **OK** button, type **Students** in the Enter the object names... text box, click the **Check Names** button, (your results should resemble Figure 11-5), and click the **OK** button.

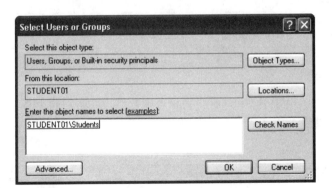

Figure 11-5   Folder sharing permissions

7. Click the **Everyone** group, click the **Remove** button, and click the two consecutive **OK** buttons.

8. In your project log, write a brief description of the steps to create a share and assign a local user group.

9. Close any open windows.

Assigning NTFS Permissions

As an administrator, you secure the folders and files on an NTFS volume. It is worth repeating—*You must be using the NTFS file system to use NTFS permissions.* If your user does not have any permission assigned to his user account or he is not a member of a group with a permission assigned, he will not be able to access the file. It does not matter if he is sitting at the computer or accessing the computer over the network.

Using Folder Permissions

You assign folder permissions to control access to folders and the files contained in these folders. Table 11-4 lists the NTFS permissions that can be assigned to a folder.

Table 11-4   NTFS folder permissions

Permission	Description
List Folder Contents	See the names of subfolders and files.
Read	See the files and subfolder names and view folder attributes, ownership, and permissions.
Read and Execute	Gives the rights assigned by the List Folder Contents and Read permissions. Gives the user the ability to traverse folders.
Write	Create new files and subfolders within the folder. Change folder attributes and view ownership and permissions.
Modify	Delete the folder. Perform the actions permitted by Write and Read and Execute.
Full Control	Change permissions, take ownership, delete subfolders and files, and perform the actions granted by the other permissions.

Using File Permissions

You assign file permissions to control your users' access to files. Table 11-5 lists the NTFS permissions that can be assigned to a file.

Table 11-5   NTFS file permissions

Permission	Description
Read	Read a file and view file attributes, ownership, and permissions.
Read and Execute	Run applications. Perform the actions permitted by the Read permission.

Table 11-5 NTFS file permissions (continued)

Permission	Description
Write	Overwrite an existing file. Change file attributes and view ownership and permissions.
Modify	Modify and delete a file. Perform the actions permitted by Write and Read and Execute.
Full Control	Change permissions, take ownership, delete files, and perform the actions granted by the other permissions.

Multiple NTFS Permissions

Permissions can be assigned to individual user accounts. However, it is more effective to assign permissions to user groups. It is possible for your users to be assigned to multiple user groups.

Being a member of a local user group entitles the user to the same permissions as the other members of the group. If your user has memberships in multiple groups, the permissions associated with each group are combined. And yet there is one exception: Deny. When Deny appears for a permission, such as Read, it overrides any other Read permission. Think of the Deny as "No means No."

NTFS permissions are assigned to all of the files on the NTFS volume. When determining a user's effective permissions, you must examine the permissions assigned to the particular resource. You need to remember that permissions assigned at the file level override the permissions assigned at the folder level.

Permission Inheritance

When you create or copy a subfolder, the subfolder inherits the permissions of the parent folder. Likewise, a file copied or created inherits the permissions of the parent folder. Permission inheritance is the default behavior for subfolders of files that are created or copied under the parent folder, as shown in Figure 11-6. After the Accounting folder was created, the indicated permissions were assigned. When the General Ledger folder was created subordinate to the Accounting folder, the permissions were inherited from the Accounting folder. Likewise, the Accounts Receivable inherited the permissions of the General Ledger folder.

You can prevent subfolders and files from inheriting the permissions of the parent. You may want to do this if you do not want changes to the parent folder to affect the subfolders and files. When you elect to prevent inheritance, you must choose one of these options:

- Copy the inherited permissions from the parent folder
- Remove the inherited permissions and retain only the permissions that you assigned

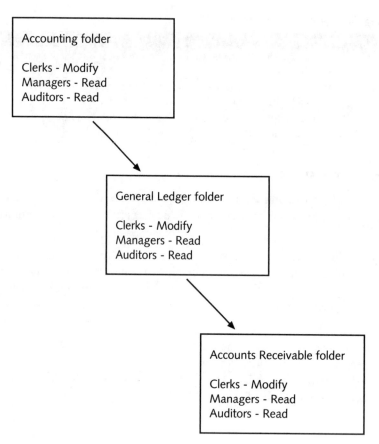

Figure 11-6   Permission inheritance

 How will you know when you need to prevent permission inheritance? When I'm working with the permissions and encounter a grayed out permissions check box, I know that I will need to prevent inheritance. In nearly every instance, I have copied the inherited permissions from the parent. It is so much easier to remove the unneeded permissions than to start from scratch.

Combining Shared Folders and NTFS Permissions

You use share permissions to grant access to resource access over the network. In a previous section, you encountered shared folder permissions. Shared folder permissions provide very limited security. Also, shared folder permissions provide access to the entire directory structure from the shared folder down into the subfolders. For these reasons, you will seldom use shared folder permissions without also using NTFS permissions.

By combining shared folder permissions and NTFS permissions, you gain the highest level of security and control. To effectively use both shared folder permissions and NTFS permissions, you must be able to combine these two types of permissions to control access to network resources.

You can use shared folder permissions to grant access to folders over the network. Then you can use NTFS permissions to secure the resources in your file system. NTFS offers the most flexible level of control and can be assigned to resources on an individual basis.

To determine your users' effective permissions for a given network resource, you need to complete these three steps:

1. **Combine the shared folder permissions.** Recall that Deny means no and overrides that permission.

2. **Combine the NTFS folder permissions.** Recall that Deny means no and overrides that permission.

3. **Determine which is the most restrictive.** The one that is the most restrictive is the effective permission.

Figure 11-7 shows an example illustrating these three steps. For the shared folder permissions, you have a combined permission of Full Control. For the NTFS permissions, Read, Write, and Modify combine as Modify. Between Full Control and Modify, the most restrictive is Modify.

IN THE WORKPLACE

I've demonstrated these three steps for numerous classes. I write the shared folder permissions on the left side of the board, the NTFS permissions on the right. Standing at the board, I make a trickling motion for the shared folder permissions and wait for a response indicating the combined shared folder permissions. I repeat the trickling motion for the NTFS permissions and again wait for the response indicating the combined NTFS permissions. I join my hands together and wait for the most restrictive response. This demonstration must work as I see students in the hallway going through these same motions as they discuss permissions with their peers.

Moving and Copying Files

What happens to the permissions when you move a file? Copy a file? As a DST, you must possess the answers to these two questions to properly move or copy files with permissions on NTFS volumes.

When you are copying or moving files and folders within or between NTFS volumes, remember this key concept: Whenever Windows XP must create a file or folder as a result of a copy or move action, the file or folder will inherit permissions from the destination folder. When a file or folder is moved within an NTFS partition, the file or folder doesn't need to be re-created. Thus, the files and folders retain the original permissions after they are moved.

11

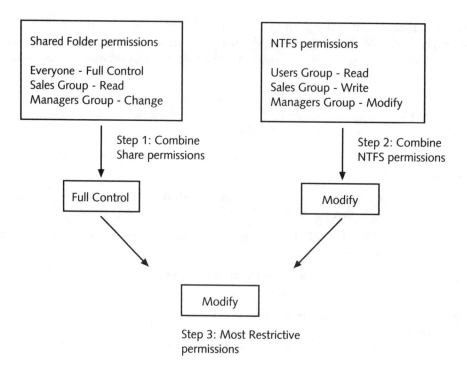

Figure 11-7   The result of combining shared folders and NTFS permissions

However, when a file or folder is copied within or between NTFS volumes, Windows must create a copy of the file or folder being copied. Thus, copying a file or folder results in that copied file or folder inheriting permissions from the destination folder.

The same is true for files or folders being moved between NTFS volumes. When moving a file or folder between NTFS volumes, the moved file or folder must be created on the destination volume, which means the moved file or folder will inherit the destination folder's permissions.

You need to be aware of one more fact: Neither the FAT16 nor FAT32 file systems support NTFS permissions. NTFS is required to support NTFS permissions. Likewise, NTFS permissions are removed when a file or folder is moved or copied to a FAT16 or FAT32 formatted partition.

Table 11-6 summarizes the permission inheritance for move and copy actions on the same or different volumes. Notice that the move on the same volume is the exception—this is the only option that retains the permissions.

Table 11-6   Summary for move and copy actions

Action/Target	Same volume	Different volume
Move	Retain	Inherit
Copy	Inherit	Inherit

Why is the move different from the copy on the same volume? Microsoft's programmers realized that by changing a pointer in the file table they could implement the move. This requires fewer computing resources than a copy followed by a delete.

IN THE WORKPLACE

Activity 11-9: Assigning NTFS Permissions

ACTIVITY

Time Required: 15 minutes

Objective: Assign NTFS permissions to a folder.

Description: In this activity, you will assign NTFS permissions for a folder. You will find this activity useful in your career as a DST because, in order to answer users' questions about using NTFS permissions, you will need to have explored this in detail.

1. If necessary, log on to your computer with the user name **admin01**, password **Password1**, and domain **classroom**.

2. Click **Start**, point to **All Programs**, point to **Accessories**, and click **Windows Explorer**.

3. Expand **My Computer**, expand **Local Disk (C:)**, and click **Local Disk (C:)**.

4. Right-click the **Projects** folder, click **Sharing and Security**, click the **Security** tab, and click the **Advanced** button.

5. Review the NTFS permissions, as shown in Figure 11-8, and click the **OK** button.

11

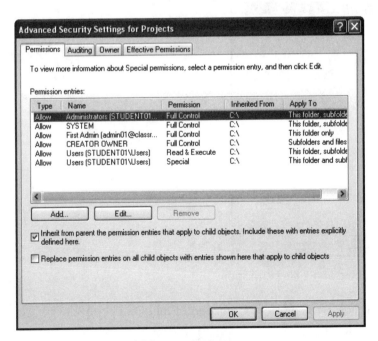

Figure 11-8   NTFS folder permissions

6. Click the **Add** button, click the **Locations** button, click **Student01**, click the **OK** button, type **Students** in the Enter the object name... text box, click the **Check Names** button, click the **OK** button, check the **Allow Modify** check box, and click the **Apply** button.

7. Click the **Advanced** button, uncheck the **Inherit from parent...** check box, and click the **Copy** button.

8. Click the **Users(STUDENT01\Users)** name, click the **Remove** button, and click the two consecutive **OK** buttons.

9. In your project log, write a brief description of the steps to place NTFS permissions on a folder.

10. Double-click the **Projects** folder, right-click in the right pane, point to **New**, click **Text Document**, and press **Enter**.

11. Right-click **New Text Document**, click **Properties**, click the **Security** tab, click **Students (STUDENT01\Students)**, and review the inherited permissions, as shown in Figure 11-9.

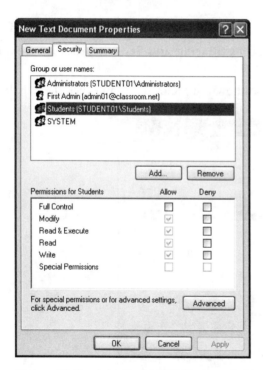

Figure 11-9   Inherited NTFS file permissions

12. In your project log, write a brief explanation of inherited permissions.

13. Close any open windows.

14. Log off the computer.

ACTIVITY

Activity 11-10: Analyzing Share and NTFS Permissions

Time Required: 10 minutes

Objective: Analyze share and NTFS permissions to determine the effective permissions.

Description: In this activity, you will combine the share permissions, combine the NTFS permissions, and determine the effective permission for a given scenario. You will find this activity useful in your career as a DST because, in order to answer users' questions regarding security, you will need to have explored share and NTFS permissions in detail.

1. Using Figure 11-10 and Table 11-7 as guides, specify in your project log the combined permissions and the effective permission for this scenario: Sally is a member of the Everyone, Executive, and Finance groups.

```
Share permissions                      NTFS permissions

Everyone - Full Control                Everyone - Read
Accounting - Deny all access           Accounting - Modify
Executive - Read                       Executive - Read
Finance - Change                       Finance - Modify
Marketing - Read                       Marketing - Write
```

Figure 11-10   Combining share and NTFS permissions

Table 11-7   Combined permissions and effective permission

Combined Share permission	Combined NTFS permission	Most Restrictive permission

2. Using Figure 11-10 and Table 11-8 as guides, specify in your project log the combined permissions and the effective permission for this scenario: Bob is a member of the Everyone, Executive, and Accounting groups.

Table 11-8   Combined permissions and effective permission

Combined Share permission	Combined NTFS permission	Most Restrictive permission

3. Using Figure 11-10 and Table 11-9 as guides, specify in your project log the combined permissions and the effective permission for this scenario: Roger is a member of the Everyone, Executive, and Marketing groups.

11

Table 11-9 Combined permissions and effective permission

Combined Share permission	Combined NTFS permission	Most Restrictive permission

4. Using Figure 11-10 and Table 11-10 as guides, specify in your project log the combined permissions and the effective permission for this scenario: Susan is a member of the Everyone, Accounting, Executive, and Finance groups.

Table 11-10 Combined permissions and effective permission

Combined Share permission	Combined NTFS permission	Most Restrictive permission

5. Using Figure 11-10 and Table 11-11 as guides, specify in your project log the combined permissions and the effective permission for this scenario: George is a member of the Everyone, Finance, and Marketing groups.

Table 11-11 Combined permissions and effective permission

Combined Share permission	Combined NTFS permission	Most Restrictive permission

Troubleshooting Share and NTFS Permissions

To resolve most access problems, you must determine if you have one of the following two problems:

1. The file or folder has the wrong settings. A file or folder can have the incorrect share or NTFS permissions due to inheritance, lack of inheritance, moving a file, or simple human error.

2. The user account has the wrong group memberships. A user account can have incorrect permissions due to improper share or NTFS permissions, improper group membership, or human error.

To resolve problems such as these, follow these steps:

1. Determine what the proper access should be for the user.

2. Inspect the user's group memberships.

3. Inspect the file or folder permissions for the users' groups with special attention to Allow or Deny.

4. Attempt to access other files and folders with the same user account on the same computer.

5. Attempt to access other files and folders with the same user account from another computer.

6. Attempt to access the same files and folders with the administrator account on the same computer.

7. Attempt to access the same files and folders with the administrator account from another computer.

MANAGING DISK STORAGE WITH QUOTAS

Disk quotas permit your administrators to manage disk space usage by your users on critical volumes. You should be prepared to assist your users with their management of this limited disk space. The following sections will discuss this concept in detail.

Implementing Disk Quotas

Disk quotas track and control disk space usage for NTFS volumes. Disk quotas are managed from the Quota tab on the Disk Properties dialog box. As an administrator, you check the Enable quota management check box to start the configuration of quota management, as shown in Figure 11-11.

11

Figure 11-11   Local Disk (C:) Properties dialog box, Quota tab

By checking the Deny disk space to users exceeding quota limit check box, you "turn on" the quota policy that is defined on the remainder dialog box. If you need only to track disk quotas, leave the check box unchecked.

You can use the Do not limit disk usage option button to prevent limiting disk space to future volume users. You might use this option to retain the previous quota limits for existing users and not establish quotas for new users. In practice, this scenario is unlikely but this is how it works!

When you enable disk quotas, you can set two values: the disk space quota limit and the disk space quota warning level. For example, you can set a user's disk quota limit to 600 MB, and the disk quota warning level to 500 MB as shown in Figure 11-12.

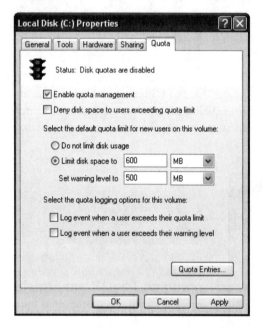

Figure 11-12 Quotas to limit disk space

Recall that you check the Deny disk space to users exceeding quota limit check box to "turn on" the quota policy that you just defined. In this case, the user can store no more than 600 MB of files on the volume.

If you are studying, but not enforcing quota limits, leave the Deny disk space to users exceeding quota limit check box unchecked. Enabling quotas and not limiting disk space use are useful when you do not want to deny users access to a volume but want to track disk space use on a per-user basis.

You can also specify whether to log an event when users exceed either their quota limit or their quota warning level. For example, if the user stores more than 500 MB of files on the volume, you can configure the disk quota system to log a system event. Event Viewer keeps a chronological record of users who exceed their quota or warning level. However, it does not provide information about which users are currently over their quota warning level.

You cannot use file compression to prevent users from exceeding their quota limits because compressed files are tracked based on their uncompressed size. For example, if you have a 50 MB file that is 40 MB after it is compressed, Windows XP counts the file's original 50 MB size toward the quota limit.

Conversely, Windows XP tracks the volume usage for compressed folders and calculates the quota limit based on the compressed size. For example, if you have a 500 MB folder that is 300 MB after it is compressed, Windows XP counts only 300 MB toward the quota limit.

For example, if the folder "Accounting" contains a compressed file, the quota will be calculated based on the size of the uncompressed file. However, if the entire "Accounting" folder is compressed, then quota is calculated based on compressed size.

ACTIVITY

Activity 11-11: Configuring Volume Quotas for Local Disk Usage

Time Required: 15 minutes

Objective: Configure quotas for local disk usage.

Description: In this activity, you will set the volume quotas for disk space. Next, you will enable logging for quota limits and warning levels. You will find this activity useful in your career as a DST because, in order to answer users' questions about using disk quotas, you will need to have explored this in detail.

1. Log on to your computer with the user name **admin01** and password **Password1**.

2. Click **Start**, click **My Computer**, right-click **Local Disk (C:)**, click **Properties**, and click the **Quota** tab.

3. If this activity has been previously completed, click the **Do not limit disk usage** option button.

4. Check the **Enable quota management** check box.

5. Click the **Limit disk space to** option button, type **600** in the Limit disk space to text box, click the drop-down list menu, and click **MB**.

6. Type **500** in the Set warning level to text box, click the drop-down list menu, and click **MB.**

7. In your project log, write a brief summary that describes the steps to configure quota limits.

8. Check the **Log Event when a user exceeds their quota limit** check box.

9. Check the **Log Event when a user exceeds their warning level** check box.

10. Click the **OK** button.

11. In your project log, write a brief summary that describes the steps to configure logging options for quotas.

12. Close any open windows.

Using Individual Disk Quotas

In the previous discussion, you established disk quota limits for all users. If you need to provide disk quota limits to individuals, click the Quota Entries button. You might need to do this for a user with a business need to store more files than other users. For example, assume that John, the accountant, creates fairly large worksheets and will need 1 GB of disk space. The resulting entry for John in the Quota Entries dialog box is shown in Figure 11-13.

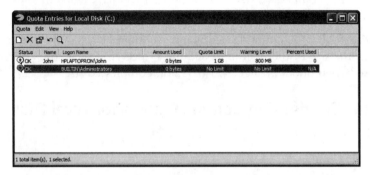

Figure 11-13   Quota Entries for Local Disk (C:) window

You will see that the administrator user account is basically exempt from quota limits. This occurs because the administrator "owns" the system files and should not be denied the ability to create files and folders on the desktop computer.

In the Quota Entries window, you can view each user's quota limit, warning level, and quota usage. You can also change the quota limit and warning level for individual users who need more disk space than the default quota.

IN THE WORKPLACE

What will your users see when disk quotas are being used? Nothing special, because disk quotas are transparent to your user. When a user views the available disk space for the volume, Windows XP reports only the user's available quota allowance. If the user exceeds this allowance, the system indicates that the disk is full.

Troubleshooting Disk Quotas

To resolve disk quota–related problems for your users, you must be aware of a number of items related to troubleshooting disk quotas:

- Because disk quotas can be set only on volumes formatted with the NTFS file system, you will not see a Quota tab for volumes formatted with one of the FAT file systems.

- You cannot delete a quota entry for an individual user until all of the files that the user owns have been deleted from the volume. An alternative solution is to have another user take ownership of the files.

- To obtain more disk space after exceeding the quota allowance, your user must do one of the following:

  - Delete files

  - Reduce the size of existing files

  - Have the administrator increase the quota allowance

ACTIVITY

Activity 11-12: Configuring Individual Quotas for Local Disk Usage

Time Required: 15 minutes

Objective: Configure quotas for individuals that limit local disk usage.

Description: In this activity, you will set the individual limits for disk space. Next, you will enable logging for quota limits and warning levels. You will find this activity useful in your career as a DST because, in order to answer users' questions about using disk quotas, you will need to have explored this in detail.

1. If necessary, log on to your computer with the user name **admin01** and password **Password1**.

2. Click **Start**, click **My Computer**, right-click **Local Disk (C:)**, click **Properties**, and click the **Quota** tab.

3. Click the **Quota Entries** button.

4. If an entry for user01 exists, double-click **user01**, and continue with Step 7.

5. Click the **Quota** menu and click **New Quota Entry**.

6. Type **user01** in the Enter the object names to select text box, click the **Check Names** button, and click the **OK** button.

7. Type **500** in the Set warning level to text box, click the drop-down list menu, and click **KB**, as shown in Figure 11-14.

8. Click the **OK** button. Wait for the Logon Name column to be displayed with logon names.

9. Verify that a warning appears for user01 in the Status column.

10. In your project log, write a brief summary that describes the steps to configure quota limits for an individual.

11

Figure 11-14 Quota Settings for user01 dialog box

11. Close any open windows.

12. Click **Start**, point to **All Programs**, point to **Accessories**, and click **Notepad**.

13. Type a short message in Notepad, click the **File** Menu, click **Save As**, type **test** in the File name text box, and click the **Save** button.

14. Click **Start**, point to **Control Panel**, point to **Administrative Tools**, click **Event Viewer**, and click **System** in the left pane.

15. Locate and double-click the first entry with **ntfs** in the Source column. See Figure 11–15 for a representative example.

16. Click the **OK** button.

17. In your project log, write a brief summary that describes the steps to view messages when an individual exceeds a warning level.

18. Click **Start**, click **My Computer**, right-click **Local Disk (C:)**, click **Properties**, and click the **Quota** tab.

19. Click the **Quota Entries** button, double-click **user01**, click the drop-down list menu for Set warning level to, click **MB**, and then click the **OK** button.

20. Close any open windows and log off the computer.

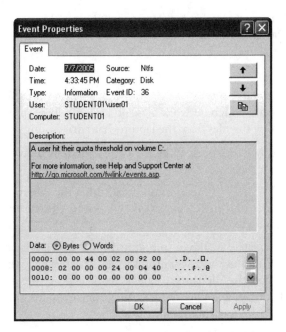

Figure 11-15   A user has hit the threshold

CONFIGURING AND TROUBLESHOOTING ACCESS TO OFFLINE FILES

When using laptop computers, your users can operate their laptop as either a standalone computer or as a networked computer. When your mobile users are not connected to a network, most likely they are working offline. They may still need access to files that are on the network. Windows XP Professional includes an Offline Files feature that enables your users to access files while not attached to the network. With the Offline Files feature, your users can have copies of the same files on the laptop and the network.

In the following sections, you will learn the skills to assist your users with offline files.

Offline Files and Mobile Users

After working offline, some of the files they have used may need to be updated on the network. If a group of your users is sharing files on the network, they may have updated one or more files while your user was working offline. Keeping these files synchronized—keeping the networked and offline versions the same—can be a difficult and time-consuming task for your users. Your users will need to guard against overwriting a new file with an older version. Fortunately, Windows XP Professional takes care of problems such as this accidental overwriting of files. Windows XP Professional keeps track of the original locations of available offline files, tracks which files have been modified, and updates files with the newer versions.

11

The Offline Files feature is not supported in the Windows XP Home Edition. When using Windows XP Professional, you must disable Fast User Switching to use the Offline Files feature.

NOTE

Your organization's network administrator must make the files available for offline use. First, the network administrator must specify which network files and folders will be shared in this way. Then, your user will have to copy the files from the laptop's hard drive using these steps:

1. From My Computer or My Network Places, select the desired network file or folder.

2. Click the Make Available Offline option button (from either the File menu or file or Folder Properties). The files or folder will be copied to your users' Offline Files folder on their hard drive.

Offline files are marked with an indicator, as shown in Figure 11-16, which lets your users know that the file is available for offline use and synchronization. When your users display the menu for a file by right-clicking the filename, a check mark appears next to Make Available Offline. If they decide that they no longer need to synchronize the file, they should remove the check mark from the Make Available Offline.

Sample Offline Document

Figure 11-16   Offline Files indicator

Offline Files Options

Offline Files options are set on the Offline Files tab of the Folder Options dialog box, as shown in Figure 11-17. On this tab, you can choose from these options:

- **Enable Offline Files:** Network files will be available to you while you work offline.

- **Synchronize all offline files when logging on:** All of the network files will be brought up to the most recent versions when you log on.

- **Synchronize all offline files before logging off:** All of the network files will reflect your most recent changes when you log off.

- **Display a reminder every:** Reminder balloons appear in the notification area when you go offline.

- **Create an Offline Files shortcut on the desktop:** Shortcut to the Offline Files folder is placed on the desktop.

- **Encrypt offline files to secure data:** Encrypt the copy of the network file.

- **Amount of disk space to use for temporary offline files:** Amount of disk space on your hard drive to set aside for Offline files.

- **Delete Files button:** Only selected files will be deleted from your hard drive. Network files will not be deleted.

- **View Files button:** View a list of files that will be available offline.

- **Advanced button:** Set up how your computer will behave when a connection to a server is lost. Notify and work offline. Force a reconnection to the server.

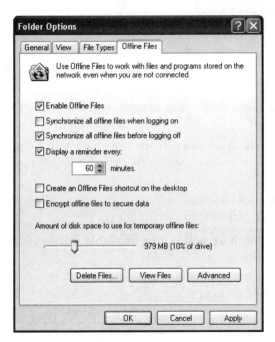

Figure 11-17   Offline Files tab

Offline Files and Servers

Your organization's network administrator will need to configure a shared folder for use as an offline folder. This offline folder will accept the files from your users when they synchronize their offline files with the server. As a DST, you need to know how the network administrator configures the share for the offline files. Your instructor will demonstrate the steps to do this in Activity 11-13. After creating a shared folder, the network administrator will click on the Offline Settings button and make choices from the Offline Settings page, as shown in Figure 11-18.

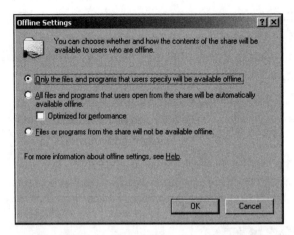

Figure 11-18   Offline settings on the server

Your network administrator chooses whether and how the offline files will be available to users by selecting from these options:

- **Only the files and programs that users specify will be available online:** The default, users have control over which files to synchronize.

- **All files and programs that users open from the share will be automatically available offline:** Files users open from the shared resource will be automatically available online.

- **Optimized for performance:** Automatically cache program files locally. Used when programs are executed from the file server.

- **Files or programs from the share will not be available offline:** Prevent users from storing files offline.

Troubleshooting Offline Files

One special area you need to investigate when troubleshooting offline files is synchronization. If only one user accesses particular files through the Offline Files feature, that user probably won't encounter a problem with synchronization. However, that situation is unlikely in the larger organization. Files and folders usually are available for offline access to multiple users, in which case synchronization becomes more complicated. Here are some scenarios that you are likely to encounter.

Network Files Have Changed

When another user modifies the network copy of a file while your user is working on the same file offline, a situation called file conflict occurs. Windows XP prompts your user to decide how he wants to save the modified file. During synchronization, your user receives a Resolve File Conflict dialog box, which offers three choices for resolving the conflict:

- Write the local version of the file to the network, replacing the changed file.

- Keep the network version of the file, replacing the user's local copy.

- Keep both versions by entering a new filename for the user's local file before copying it to the network.

Network Files Have Been Deleted

When your user tries to synchronize an offline file for which the network copy has been deleted, your user receives an error message that no matching file exists on the network. Your user can copy the file's local version to the network or can delete the file from the local computer.

Removing a File from the Offline Files Folder

When your user deletes an offline file from the local computer, the local system doesn't remove the file from your system. Instead, it simply changes the file's status to reflect that the file was deleted locally. Your user must toggle off the Make Available Offline option prior to deleting the file.

11

ACTIVITY

Activity 11-13: Creating the Offline Folder on a File Server (Instructor Demonstration)

Time Required: 15 minutes

Objective: Create the offline folder on the Instructor01 computer.

Description: In this activity, your instructor will create a folder and configure the folder to support offline files. You will find observing this activity useful in your career as a DST, because in your organization this task will be performed by the network administration team and you must have observed the steps to answer your users' questions about storing offline files on a file server.

1. Your instructor logs on to the **Instructor01** computer. (For brevity, all subsequent steps are written in the normal second-person singular format.)

2. Click **Start**, point to **All Programs**, point to **Accessories**, and click **Windows Explorer**.

3. Expand **My Computer**, click **Local Disk (C:)**, right-click in the right pane, click **New**, click **Folder**, type **Offline**, and press **Enter**.

4. Right-click the **Offline** folder, click **Sharing and Security**, click the **Share this folder** option button, click the **Permissions** button, check the **Allow Full Control** check box, and click the **OK** button.

5. Click the **Offline Settings** button and click the **OK** button.

6. Click the **Security** tab, click the **Add** button, click the **Advanced** button, type **Students** in the Name text box, click the **Find Now** button, click on **Students Global Group**, and click the two consecutive **OK** buttons.

7. Check the **Allow Modify** check box and click the **OK** button.

8. In your project log, write a brief explanation of the steps to create an offline folder on a file server. Include an explanation of the sharing and NTFS permissions.

9. Close any open windows.

Activity 11-14: Specifying Offline Files to Synchronize

ACTIVITY

Time Required: 15 minutes

Objective: Specify the files to synchronize with the file server.

Description: In this activity, you will create a connection to share the Offline Files folder you created in Activity 11-13. Then you will create a file and specify that the file be synchronized. You will find this activity useful in your career as a DST because, in order to answer users' questions about using offline files, you will need to have explored this in detail.

1. Log on to your computer with the user name **user01** and password **Password1**.

2. Click **Start**, click **My Network Places**, and click the **Add a network place** link.

3. Click the **Next** button, if necessary, click **Choose another network location**, and click the **Next** button.

4. Click the **Browse** button, expand **Entire Network**, expand **Microsoft Windows Network**, expand **Classroom**, expand **Instructor01**, click **Offline**, and click the **OK** button.

5. Click the two consecutive **Next** buttons and click the **Finish** button.

6. Click the **Tools** menu, click **Folder Options**, click the **Offline Files** tab, check the **Synchronize all offline files when logging on** check box, check the **Create an Offline Files shortcut on the desktop** check box, and click the **OK** button.

7. In your project log, write a brief explanation of the steps to link to an offline folder on a file server.

8. Right-click in the right pane, point to **New**, click **Text Document**, type **User01**, and press **Enter**.

9. Double-click **User01**, type a brief message of your choosing, click the **File** menu, click **Save**, and close the window.

10. Right-click **User01**, click **Make Available Online**, click the two consecutive **Next** buttons, and click the **Finish** button.

11. Wait for the synchronization to complete.

12. Log off the computer.

13. Wait for the synchronization to complete.

14. Log on to your computer with the user name **user01** and **Password1**.

15. Wait for the synchronization to complete.

16. Double-click the **Shortcut to Offline Files** icon.

17. Double-click **User01,** type an additional brief message of your choosing, click the **File** menu, click **Save**, and close the window.

18. Click the **Tools** menu and click **Synchronize**.

19. Wait for the synchronization to complete.

20. In your project log, write a brief explanation of the steps to synchronize a file with in an offline folder on a file server.

21. Close any open windows and log off the computer.

CHAPTER SUMMARY

- You learned about FAT, FAT32, and NTFS so that you could choose a file system.

- Simple file sharing provides an easy means to share and control data resources for one of five levels:

    - My Documents (Private)

    - My Documents (Default)

    - Files in Shared Documents available to local users

    - Shared files on the network (readable by everyone)

    - Shared files on the network (readable and writeable by everyone)

- You learned some techniques to troubleshoot problems with simple file sharing.

- Windows XP provides an alternative to simple file sharing, which provides granular control over folders and files. To use this feature, you must be prepared to use:

    - Local user groups

    - Shared Folder permissions

    - NTFS Folder permissions

    - Inheritance

    - Combined Shared Folder and NTFS permissions

- You learned some techniques to troubleshoot problems with shared folder and NTFS permissions.

❑ Your organization may elect to manage disk storage on critical volumes with volume and individual disk quotas.

❑ Offline files are a boon to your mobile users and you learned how to assist your users with this feature.

KEY TERMS

cluster — Disk-storage unit consisting of a fixed number of sectors that Windows XP uses to read or write information.

disk quotas — Limit amount of disk space that can be used by an individual user.

File Allocation Table (FAT) — Windows XP creates this data structure on the disk when a disk is formatted.

hard disk error — Error that occurs when a computer attempts to write to the hard disk and fails.

multiboot — Startup capability that allows users to choose from two or more installed operating systems for the current session.

NTFS (New Technology File System) — Advanced file system created by Microsoft and first introduced with Windows NT. Supports long filenames, full security access control, file system recovery, and extremely large storage volumes.

simple file sharing — Feature that permits folders to be shared for use by other users on a network.

Virtual File Allocation Table (VFAT) — File system first used with Windows 95.

REVIEW QUESTIONS

1. Which of the following file systems is supported on Windows XP?(Choose all that apply.)
   a. FAT16
   b. FAT32
   c. NTFS
   d. HPFS

2. _____ is the preferred file system on a Windows XP computer.
   a. FAT16
   b. FAT32
   c. NTFS
   d. HPFS

3. Which of the following is a level within simple file sharing? (Choose all that apply.)

a. My Documents (Private)

b. My Documents (Default)

c. Shared files on the network (readable by everyone)

d. Shared files on the network (readable and writeable by everyone)

4. To configure Level 1 – My Documents (Private) for simple file sharing, you check the_____ check box in the Folder Properties dialog box.

a. Make this folder private

b. Make this folder public

c. Share this folder on the network

d. Allow network users to change any files

5. Which check box do you select to configure Level 4 – Shared files on the network (readable by everyone) for simple file sharing? (Choose all that apply.)

a. Make this folder private

b. Make this folder public

c. Share this folder on the network

d. Allow network users to change any files

6. If you are planning to share folders and files over the network and require the permissions to properly secure the folders and files, you should use the _____ file system.

a. FAT16

b. FAT32

c. NTFS

d. HPFS

7. Which of the following is a shared folder permission? (Choose all that apply.)

a. Read

b. Change

c. Modify

d. Full Control

8. Which of the following is an NTFS folder permission? (Choose all that apply.)

a. List Folder Contents

b. Read and Execute

c. Write

d. Full Control

11

9. Which of the following is an NTFS file permission? (Choose all that apply.)

   a. List Folder Contents

   b. Read and Execute

   c. Write

   d. Full Control

10. When you create or copy a folder, the subfolder _____ the permissions of the parent folder.

    a. assumes

    b. receives

    c. inherits

    d. takes

11. Which of the following can you choose when you elect to prevent inheritance? (Choose all that apply.)

    a. Copy the inherited permissions from the parent folder

    b. Remove the inherited permissions and retain only the permissions that you assigned

    c. Remove the inherited permissions from the parent folder

    d. Copy the inherited permissions and retain only the permissions that you assigned

12. Which of the following is a step that is used to combine shared folder permissions and NTFS permissions? (Choose all that apply.)

    a. Combine the shared folder permissions

    b. Ignore the shared folder permissions

    c. Combine the NTFS folder permissions

    d. Determine which is the most restrictive

13. The _____ file system is required to implement disk quotas.

    a. FAT16

    b. FAT32

    c. NTFS

    d. HPFS

14. Which value can be set when you enable quota limits? (Choose all that apply.)

    a. Time interval between quota resolutions

    b. Percentage override for administrative users

    c. Limit disk space

    d. Set warning level

15. Which check box would you check to study the usage of various users on a volume? (Choose all that apply.)

    a. Enable quota management

    b. Deny disk space to users exceeding quota limit

    c. Log event when the user exceeds his quota limit

    d. Log event when the user exceeds his warning level

16. Which action can you complete from the Quota Entries window? (Choose all that apply.)

    a. View the Status

    b. View the Amount Used

    c. View the Quota Limit

    d. View the Warning Limit

17. Which action can your user take when a user exceeds his or her Quota Limit?

    a. Delete files

    b. Reduce the size of existing files

    c. Have the administrator increase the quota allowance

    d. Have another user take ownership for the files

18. At which times can Offline files be synchronized? (Choose all that apply.)

    a. At machine startup

    b. At logon

    c. At logoff

    d. At machine shutdown

19. Which option is available to a network administrator when configuring the Offline share on a file server? (Choose all that apply.)

    a. Only the files and programs that users specify will be available online

    b. All files and programs that users open from the share will be automatically available offline

    c. Optimized for performance

    d. Files or programs from the share will not be available offline

20. Which action can user A take when user B modifies the network copy of a file while user A is working on the same file offline?

    a. Write the local version of the file to the network, replacing the changed file.

    b. Keep the network version of the file, replacing the user's local copy.

    c. Keep the local version of the file, replacing the network copy.

    d. Keep both versions by entering a new filename for the user's local file before copying it to the network.

CASE PROJECTS

Case 11-1: Implementing Simple File Sharing

You consult as a desktop support technician for a nonprofit organization. Your customer's network consists of five computers configured as a workgroup.

The Volunteer computer is used by the various volunteers of the organization. Each Volunteer is provided a user logon ID. They store their working documents in the My Documents folder. They have asked you to set up a Templates folder for all the volunteers to access. The Templates folder was created by the Supervisor account. How will you implement their request with simple file sharing?

The remaining four computers need to be able to read and update files in the Weekly folder on the Supervisor's computer. How will you implement their request with simple file sharing?

Case 11-2: Analyzing Share and NTFS Permissions

You are a desktop support technician. Your network consists of a Windows 2003 Active Directory domain with 10 servers, including application and database servers and 500 computers running Windows XP Professional.

You have been asked by the Help Desk to assist the network administrator with a network access problem for Bob. Bob is in the Managers, Everyone, and User global groups. Bob must be able to read files and folders in the Accounting, Finance, and Marketing shares. The network administrator has asked that you determine which permissions are correctly configured.

The relative permissions are presented in Tables 11-12 through 11-17.

Table 11-12 Everyone Group Share folder permissions

Share	Folder permissions
\\Server\Accounting	Deny all access
\\Server\Finance	Full Control
\\Server\Marketing	Read

Table 11-13 Everyone Group NTFS folder permissions

NTFS	Folder permissions
\\Server\Accounting	Read and Execute
\\Server\Finance	Read
\\Server\Marketing	Modify

Table 11-14   Users Group Share folder permissions

Share	Folder permissions
\\Server\Accounting	Deny all access
\\Server\Finance	Read
\\Server\Marketing	Change and Read

Table 11-15   Users Group NTFS folder permissions

NTFS	Folder permissions
\\Server\Accounting	Read and Execute
\\Server\Finance	Modify
\\Server\Marketing	List Folder Contents

Table 11-16   Managers Group Share folder permissions

Share	Folder permissions
\\Server\Accounting	Read
\\Server\Finance	Read
\\Server\Marketing	Read

Table 11-17   Managers Group NTFS folder permissions

NTFS	Folder permissions
\\Server\Accounting	Full Control
\\Server\Finance	Modify
\\Server\Marketing	Read

CASE PROJECTS

Case 11-3: Implementing Offline Files

You are a desktop support technician. Your network consists of a Windows 2003 Active Directory domain with 10 servers, including application and database servers, and 500 computers running Windows XP Professional. Of the 500 computers running Windows XP, 32 computers are laptop computers.

Your laptop users need to have access to the current product prices while they are on the road. Product costs are made available when they have their weekly sales meetings at headquarters. They connect their laptops to the network before going to the sales meeting.

How will you configure their laptops to get the current product cost worksheets? How will the laptop user pick up the updated product prices? How will the cost accounts make the data available? How will the network administrator configure the file server?

CONFIGURE APPLICATION SECURITY

After reading this chapter and completing the exercises, you will be able to:

♦ Configure Office application security settings

♦ Configure local security settings

♦ Identify and troubleshoot policy issues

♦ Identify and respond to security incidents

As you are aware, the role of the DST requires that you be prepared to join the Information Technology organization's efforts to maintain the security of the network. Network security is a joint, coordinated effort of all members of the Information Technology teams. Also, you will need to be prepared to answer your users' varied questions on security.

The Office applications have security settings that are independent of the Windows XP operating system. Your users will expect that you can assist them with this independent file and program security.

Security settings can be applied at various levels within your organization. For example, as an administrator, you can configure security policies for the computers in a workgroup. In larger organizations, you will be working with other Information Technology teams to implement and troubleshoot security policies.

You are aware of the negative effects of viruses. You must be prepared to protect your organization from the consequences of rampant viruses.

You will learn about all of these security issues in this chapter.

CONFIGURING OFFICE APPLICATION SECURITY SETTINGS

Office has several built-in features designed to protect the data files used within the Office applications. For example, files can be saved with a password, which is required to read the contents of the file.

Office applications are capable of executing small programs that enhance your users' interaction with a given Office program. However, these small programs result in a security risk—used by hackers to take detrimental actions against your users' computers. Your users will expect you to assist them to avoid these risks.

Configuring Password and Encryption Protection

Your users may need to protect the contents of Excel worksheets, PowerPoint presentations, and Word documents. For example, assume that your user is developing a presentation that will be presented at the quarterly board meeting. If this information leaks out prematurely, the results could be detrimental to the organization. You will need to be ready to assist your users to protect the contents of critical files.

Office programs offer several features to restrict access through the use of passwords or encryption. These file-level security measures are separate from the security options used by Windows XP. To use passwords, your users may set and remember a password. You may want to review the information on strong passwords presented in Chapter 4, "Configure User-related Issues."

NOTE   Besides password protection for access to files, your users may use file encryption.

Encryption is provided by various cryptographic methods available in Office from the File menu, Save As, Tools menu, General or Security Options, and the Advanced button. Figure 12-1 lists a number of encryption types. These types are shown in the following list:

- **Weak Encryption (XOR):** This type can be easily broken and should not be used.

- **Office 97/2000 Compatible:** This is the default encryption type that is not recommended and is provided for usage with legacy files.

- **RC4:** This is a series of encryption routines built on programs first designed by Ron Rivest in 1987. One of these types should be used.

NOTE   The various details of the RC4 encryption routines are beyond the scope of the MCDST exam. If you want additional information on the RC4 encryption routines, search the Microsoft Web site for Microsoft Office Encryption.

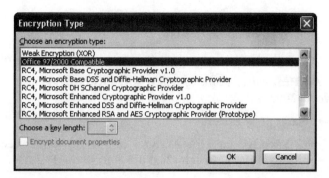

Figure 12-1   Encryption options for Office files

Which encryption option should you use? The Microsoft Enhanced DSS and Diffie-Hellman Cryptographic Provider is a good choice. It was first offered with Windows 2000. The others have existed since Windows 95. Also, this choice uses a longer key length, which provides greater security.

The methods to secure Office files are presented in the following sections.

Protecting Word Documents

Your users have three levels of document file protection to choose from when a Microsoft Word file is saved. They can use these options together or separately:

- **Password to open:** Requires your user to enter a password to open the document.

- **Password to modify:** Requires your user to enter a password to open the document with read/write access.

- **Read-only recommended:** Prompts your user to open the document as read-only. If your user clicks no at the prompt, Word opens the document with read/write access unless another password choice is enabled as well. This is provided to protect an original document from being overwritten.

Your users should encrypt the document when the document contains sensitive information. Encryption is provided by various cryptographic methods available in Office. Again, the default is Office 97/2000 Compatible, which is not recommended. Your users should select the RC4 type recommended by your organization's security officer.

Activity 12-1: Protecting Word Documents

Time Required: 15 minutes

Objective: Configure Word to protect a document.

Description: In this activity, you will configure the Word security settings to protect the contents of documents. You will find this activity useful in your career as a DST because, in order to configure the Word security settings to protect the contents of documents, you will need to have explored the steps to accomplish this task.

1. Log on to your computer with the user name **user01** and password **Password1**.

2. Click **Start**, point to **All Programs**, point to **Microsoft Office**, and click **Microsoft Office Word 2003**.

3. Type **A Secret Message** and press **Enter**.

4. Click the **File** menu, click **Save As**, and type **Activity** (if this activity has been previously completed, then use **Activity1**, **Actvity2**, and so on) in the File name text box.

5. Click the **Tools** menu button, click **Security Options**, and type **Password1** in the Password to open text box.

6. Click the **Advanced** button, click **RC4**, **Microsoft Enhanced DSS and Diffie-Hellman Cryptographic Provider**, as shown in Figure 12-2, and click the two consecutive **OK** buttons.

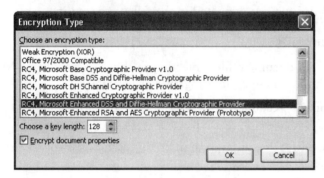

Figure 12-2   Encryption type dialog box

7. Type **Password1** in the Reenter password to open textbox, click the **OK** button, and click the **Save** button.

8. Close the Microsoft Word application window.

9. Click **Start**, point to **All Programs**, point to **Accessories**, and click **Notepad**.

10. Click the **File** menu, click **Open**, click the **Files of type** drop-down list, and click **All Files**.

11. Double-click **Activity** (with the Word icon). See Figure 12-3 for the encrypted document.

12. Close the Notepad window.

13. In your project log, write a brief explanation of the Password protection and encryption features for Word documents.

Figure 12-3   Encrypted Word Document opened in Notepad

Protecting Excel Workbooks

Your users have three levels of workbook file protection to choose from when a file is saved. They can use these options together or separately:

- **Password to open:** Requires your user to enter a password to open the workbook.

- **Password to modify:** Requires your user to enter a password to open the workbook with read/write access.

- **Read-only recommended:** Prompts your user to open the workbook as read-only. If your user clicks no at the prompt, Excel opens the workbook with read/write access unless another password choice is enabled as well. This is provided to protect an original worksheet from being overwritten.

Your users will want to use encryption when the workbook contains sensitive financial data. Your users should select the RC4 type recommended by your organization's security officer.

Activity 12-2: Protecting Excel Workbooks

Time Required: 15 minutes

Objective: Configure Excel to protect a workbook.

Description: In this activity, you will configure the Excel security settings to protect the contents of workbooks. You will find this activity useful in your career as a DST because, in order to configure the Excel security settings to protect the contents of workbooks, you will need to have explored the steps to accomplish this task.

1. If necessary, log on to your computer with the user name **user01** and password **Password1**.

2. Click **Start**, point to **All Programs**, point to **Microsoft Office**, and click **Microsoft Office Excel 2003**.

3. Type **12345** in cell A1 and press **Enter**.

4. Click the **File** menu, click **Save As**, and type **Activity** (if this activity has been previously completed, then use **Activity1**, **Actvity2**, and so on) in the File name text box.

5. Click the **Tools** menu button and click **General Options**.

6. Type **Password1** in the Password to open text box, click the **Advanced** button, click **RC4, Microsoft Enhanced DSS and Diffie-Hellman Cryptographic Provider**, and click the **OK** button.

7. Type **Password2** in the Password to modify text box and click the **OK** button.

8. Type **Password1** in the Reenter password to proceed text box, click the **OK** button, type **Password2** in the Reenter password to modify text box, click the **OK** button, and click the **Save** button.

9. Close the Microsoft Excel – Activity window but keep Microsoft Excel open for the next step.

10. Click the **File** menu and click **Activity** in the Recently used list.

11. Type **Password1** in the Password text box, as shown in Figure 12-4, and click the **OK** button.

Figure 12-4 Password entry dialog box

12. Type **Password2** in the Password text box, as shown in Figure 12-5, and click the **OK** button.

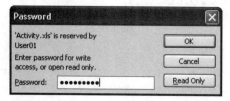

Figure 12-5 Password entry dialog box

13. Type **12345** in cell A2 and press **Enter**.

14. Click the **File** Menu and click the **Save** button.

15. In your project log, write a brief explanation of the Password protection and encryption features for Excel Worksheets.

16. Close the Excel window.

Protecting PowerPoint Presentations

Your users have two levels of presentation file protection. Your user who creates a presentation has read/write access to the presentation and controls the protection level. The two levels of presentation protection are:

- **Password to open:** Requires your user to enter a password to open the presentation.

- **Password to modify:** Requires your user to enter a password to open the workbook with read/write access.

Your users will want to use encryption when the presentation contains sensitive data. You will want to assist your users with selection of the RC4 type recommended by your organization's security officer.

ACTIVITY

Activity 12-3: Protecting PowerPoint Presentations

Time Required: 15 minutes

Objective: Configure PowerPoint to protect a presentation.

Description: In this activity, you will configure the PowerPoint security settings to protect the contents of presentations. You will find this activity useful in your career as a DST because, in order to configure the PowerPoint security settings to protect the contents of presentations, you will need to have explored the steps to accomplish this task.

1. If necessary, log on to your computer with the user name **user01** and password **Password1**.

2. Click **Start**, point to **All Programs**, point to **Microsoft Office**, and click **Microsoft Office PowerPoint 2003**.

3. Click **Click to add title**, type **Activity**, and press **Enter**.

4. Click the **File** menu, click **Save As**, and, if necessary, type **Activity** (if this activity has been previously completed, then use **Activity1**, **Actvity2**, and so on) in the File name text box.

5. Click the **Tools** menu button, then click **Security Options**.

6. Type **Password1** in the Password to open text box, click the **Advanced** button, click **RC4, Microsoft Enhanced DSS and Diffie-Hellman Cryptographic Provider**, and click the **OK** button.

7. Type **Password2** in the Password to modify text box and click the **OK** button

8. Type **Password1** in the Reenter password to open text box, click the **OK** button, type **Password2** in the Reenter password to modify text box, click the **OK** button, and click the **Save** button.

9. Close the Microsoft PowerPoint - [Activity] window but keep Microsoft PowerPoint open for the next step.

12

10. Click the **File** menu and click **Activity** in the Recently used list.

11. Type **Password1** in the Enter password to open file text box, click the **OK** button, and click the **Read Only** button, as shown in Figure 12-6.

Figure 12-6   Password entry dialog box

12. Click the **File** menu and observe that the Save commands are grayed out.

13. In your project log, write a brief explanation of the Password protection and encryption features for PowerPoint presentations.

14. Close the PowerPoint window.

Configuring Macro Security Settings

What is a macro? Originally, a macro was a mini-program consisting of a fixed sequence of keystrokes that could be activated by a simple menu selection or a single keystroke combination. These macros were designed to eliminate the need for repetitive typing of frequently used text or formatting commands. The macro could be recorded to perform a repetitive task, such as, formatting and printing a predefined range of cells in a worksheet.

Today, a **macro** is defined as any program that can be attached and embedded in a worksheet, presentation, document, or e-mail message. This program could be an ActiveX control, COM object, or OLE object. When using Outlook, Publisher, or FrontPage, the term *macro* refers to a macro written in Visual Basic for Applications.

You—and your users—configure macro security by selecting from one of four security settings, as shown in Figure 12-7. Table 12-1 summarizes the four security settings and provides the result for each choice.

NOTE

When you have antivirus software installed, you will see an extra line located at the bottom of the Macro Security dialog box, shown in Figure 12-7, "Virus scanner(s) installed." This indicates that a virus scanner is installed that is compatible with the Microsoft antivirus API.

Figure 12-7   Macro Security dialog box

Table 12-1   Security settings

Option	Security result
Very High	VBA macros can run only if the macros are stored in a specific trusted folder on the user's hard drive.
High	Executables must be signed by an acknowledged trusted source to run. This is the default.
Medium	Users are prompted to enable or disable executables the first time the document is opened. If the executable was previously accepted, the executable runs without prompting the user.
Low	Executables are run without restrictions. This setting is not recommended.

ACTIVITY

Activity 12-4: Configuring Macro Security for Word Documents

Time Required: 15 minutes

Objective: Configure Word Macro Security for Word documents

Description: In this activity, you will configure the macro security settings to protect the contents of documents. You will find this activity useful in your career as a DST because, in order to configure the macro security settings to protect the contents of documents, you will need to have explored the steps to accomplish this task.

1. If necessary, log on to your computer with the user name **user01** and password **Password1**.

2. Click **Start**, point to **All Programs**, point to **Microsoft Office**, and click **Microsoft Office Word 2003**.

3. Click **Tools**, point to **Macro**, and click **Security**.

4. If necessary, click the **Medium** option button, and click the **OK** button.

5. In your project log, write a brief explanation of the steps to set macro security for Word.

6. Close any open windows and log off the computer.

USING LOCAL SECURITY POLICY FOR COMPUTERS IN WORKGROUPS

Group Policy provides control over privileges, permissions, and capabilities of both users and computers. Group Policy simplifies the management of computers for your organization's network administrators. You saw an example of the use of Group Policy in Chapter 6 in the section on Installing Office Using Policy-Based Installation.

There is a Local Security Policy (or Local Group Policy) that can be managed on each computer running Windows XP. Local security settings are important to the DST because the DST should be prepared to answer users' questions related to the local security settings.

You will need to know about these items to answer questions from your users:

- Setting password policies
- Setting account lockout policies
- Disabling the default username
- Adding a security warning message
- Disabling the Shutdown button

In the following sections, you will learn about these items.

Viewing the Local Security Settings Window

You view the Local Security Settings window by navigating from Start, Control Panel, Administrative Tools, and then double-clicking Local Security Policy. From the Local Security Settings window, as shown in Figure 12-8, you can view security settings in these general areas:

- **Account Policies:** Password Policy determines the settings for passwords such as enforcement and lifetimes. Account Lockout Policy determines the circumstances and the length of time a user could be locked out of the computer.

- **Local Policies:** Audit Policy determines if security events are logged. User Rights Assignment specifies which rights or privileges a user has on the computer. Security Options enables or disables security settings for the computer.

- **Public Key Policies:** Allows the user to use digital certificates.

- **Software Restriction Policies:** Allows the **sandboxing** (preventing applications from accessing key resources and causing damage) privileges of folders, applications, and users.

- **IP Security Policies on Local Computer:** Establish policies for secure communication with other computers.

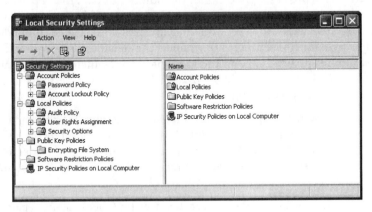

Figure 12-8   Local Security Settings

NOTE

You cannot view the security settings for a computer running Windows XP Home.

Setting Password and Account Lockout Policy

As a DST, you should be prepared to set the account policy for your users in workgroups. Proper use of passwords is your organization's first defense against unwarranted computer usage. Account Lockout Policy thwarts attempts to break into a computer by guessing passwords. You will learn to protect your users' computers by setting Password Policy and Account Lockout Policy.

Setting Password Policy

Password Policy defines the restrictions on passwords which reduce the likelihood of a successful password attack. You will want to create password policy that controls the complexity and lifetime of passwords to protect your users in workgroups. You will configure these items in Password Policy:

- **Enforce password history:** Determines the number of unique new passwords associated with a user account before an old password can be reused. The value for this setting must be between 0 and 24 passwords. The default value for Windows XP is 0 passwords. You will want to set this to 24 passwords.

- **Maximum password age:** Defines how long your user can use a password before it expires. The more frequently the password is changed the less opportunity an attacker has to use a cracked password. However, the lower this value is set, the higher the potential for an increase in calls to the Help Desk. The default value for this setting is 42 days and is appropriate.

- **Minimum password age:** Determines the number of days that a password must be used before your user may change it. The range of values for this setting is between 1 and 998 days. However, you can allow password changes immediately by setting the value for this setting to 0, which is the default value. You will want to set the Minimum password age to the value of 2 days, which is appropriate when the setting is used in conjunction with a similar short time period value for the Enforce password history setting.

- **Minimum password length:** Determines the least number of characters that make up a password for a user account. This text has advocated the use of pass phrases. Recall that "Micro$oftDesktopSupportTechsare#1" is considerably stronger than an 8- or 10-character string of random numbers and letters, and yet is easier to remember.

- **Password must meet complexity requirements:** Checks all new passwords to ensure that they meet basic requirements for strong passwords. Recall, that when your users use weak passwords, the passwords can be broken within hours. Your users should use strong passwords.

- **Store passwords using Reversible Encryption...:** Determines whether the operating system stores passwords using reversible encryption. Storing passwords using reversible encryption is essentially the same thing as storing clear text versions of the passwords. For this reason, this policy should never be enabled unless required by a communications application.

Setting Account Lockout Policy

Account Lockout Policy is a security feature that locks a user account after a number of failed logon attempts that occur within a specified period. For example, you configure the number of attempts allowed and the time period. Computers track logon attempts and you can configure settings to respond to this type of potential attack by disabling the account for a preset period. (A user cannot log on to a locked account.)

You will want to create account lockout settings that protect your users in workgroups. You will configure these items in Account Lockout Policy:

- **Account lockout duration:** Determines the length of time that must pass before an account is unlocked and your user can try to log on again. You specify the number of minutes a locked out account will remain unavailable. If you configure the Account lockout duration setting as 0, locked out accounts will remain locked out until an administrator unlocks them. The Windows XP default value for this setting is not defined. To reduce the number of calls to the Help Desk, while also providing security, you should set the value for the Account lockout duration setting to 30 minutes.

- **Account lockout threshold:** Determines the number of attempts that your user can make to log on to an account before it is locked. Your users can lock themselves out of an account by mistyping their password or by remembering it incorrectly. To avoid locking out your users, you should set the account lockout threshold to a high number (such as, 10 invalid logon attempts). The default value for this setting is 0 invalid logon attempts, which means that an administrator must unlock the account when the user mistypes the password.

- **Reset account lockout counter after:** Determines the length of time before the account lockout threshold resets to 0. The default value for this setting is not defined. If the Account lockout threshold is defined, then this reset time must be less than or equal to the value for the Account lockout duration setting. You will want to set the Reset account lockout counter to 30 minutes.

ACTIVITY

Activity 12-5: Placing a Computer in a Workgroup

Time Required: 15 minutes

12

Objective: Change the membership of a computer from a domain to a workgroup.

Description: In this activity, you will remove a computer from the classroom domain and place it in the WORKGROUP workgroup. You will find this activity useful in your career as a DST because, in order to configure Local Security Policy, the computer must be moved from a domain to a workgroup and you will need to have explored the steps to accomplish this task.

1. Log on to your computer with the user name **admin01** and password **Password1**.

2. Click **Start**, right-click **My Computer**, click **Properties**, and click the **Computer Name** tab.

3. Click the **Change** button. Under Member of, click the **Workgroup** option button, type **WORKGROUP** in the Workgroup text box, and click the **OK** button.

4. Type **admin01** in the User name textbox, type **Password1** in the Password text box, and click the **OK** button.

5. Wait for the **Welcome to the WORKGROUP workgroup.** message to be displayed and click the three consecutive **OK** buttons and the **Yes** button.

6. Wait for the computer to restart.

7. In your project log, provide the reason that you removed the computer from a domain and placed it in a workgroup.

ACTIVITY

Activity 12-6: Setting Local Security Policy

Time Required: 15 minutes

Objective: View and configure Local Security Policy settings.

Description: In this activity, you will view and configure Local Security Policy settings. You will find this activity useful in your career as a DST because, in order to view and configure Local Security Settings, you will need to have explored the steps to accomplish this task.

1. Log on to your computer with the user name **student** and password **Password1**.

2. Click **Start**, click **Control Panel,** double-click **Administrative Tools**, and double-click **Local Security Policy**.

3. Expand **Account Policies** and click **Password Policy**.

4. Double-click **Enforce password history**, type **24** in the password remembered spin box, as shown in Figure 12-9, and click the **OK** button.

Figure 12-9   Enforce password history properties

5. Double-click **Minimum password age**, type **2** in the days spin box, and click the **OK** button.

6. Double-click **Minimum password length**, type **8** in the characters spin box, and click the **OK** button.

7. Double-click **Password must meet complexity requirements**, click the **Enabled** option button, and click the **OK** button.

8. Click **Account Lockout Policy**, double-click **Account lockout threshold**, type **10** in the invalid logon attempts spin box, and click the **OK** button.

9. If necessary, click **OK** to accept the Suggested Value Changes, as shown in Figure 12-10.

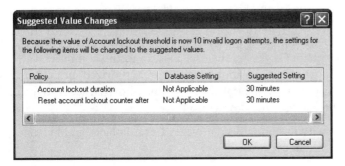

Figure 12-10   Suggested Value Changes

10. In your project log, write a brief explanation of the steps to set Password Policies and Account Lockout Policies.

11. Keep the Local Security Settings window open for the next activity.

Customizing the Logon Process

An administrator can alter the appearance of the default logon process. For example, a security warning message could be displayed. For a computer that is available in an open area, automating the logon or disabling the Shutdown button might be advisable because this reduces the computer's exposure to illicit activities.

You will want to learn to customize the logon process security settings so that you can configure these settings for computers in workgroups. To work with the Local Security Settings, the computer should be a member of a workgroup. You will need the privileges of an administrator to change the Local Security Settings.

The most relevant ways to customize the logon process are presented in the sections that follow.

Disabling the Default Username

By default, Windows XP displays the user account name of the last user to log on. If the same user always logs on to the same machine, this is convenient. However, for computers available in an open area, you may not want to display the user account name as this provides a key piece of information to someone who might want to break in to the machine.

IN THE WORKPLACE

I've discovered another reason to disable the default username. When multiple users share a common computer, I've seen that there is a higher rate of logon password failures. This occurs when users fail to enter their username or assume that they were the last user of the computer. If there is not a default username, they must type their username.

Adding a Security Warning Message

Your organization's security officer may have created a written security policy that requires that warning messages must appear before the user logs on to the computer. U.S. laws exist that state if you intend to prosecute an individual for unauthorized entry, then you must warn the user about the following: usage is monitored, unauthorized access is forbidden, and unauthorized users might be liable for prosecution.

Two entries in Local Security Settings, located under Local Policies and Security Options, are involved:

- **Interactive logon:** Message text for users attempting to log on
- **Interactive logon:** Message title for users attempting to log on

These two settings appear backward to most students. Your normal tendency is to type the windows title first and then type the message text. However, the key for the title appears second in Local Security Settings. So remember, text—then title!

Disabling the Shutdown Button

By default, Windows XP enables a logoff button on the logon dialog box. This option has the potential of encouraging unwanted shutdowns for computers in open areas. If a person has access to the keyboard and mouse, he can shut down the computer. The entry in Local Security Settings, located under Local Policies and Security Options, is Shutdown: Allow system to be shut down without having to log on.

If the power button is accessible, disabling this option might cause more problems than it solves. A computer running Windows XP has a better chance of starting when the computer was shut down through the operating system rather than just being powered off.

Activity 12-7: Customizing the Logon Process

Time Required: 15 minutes

Objective: Customize the logon process.

Description: In this activity, you will customize the logon process. You will find this activity useful in your career as a DST because, in order to customize the logon process for your end users, you will need to have explored the steps to accomplish this task.

1. If necessary, log on to your computer with the user name **student** and password **Password1**.

2. If necessary, click **Start**, click **Control Panel**, double-click **Administrative Tools**, and double-click **Local Security Policy**.

3. If necessary, expand **Local Policies** and click **Security Options**.

4. Double-click **Interactive logon: Do not display last user name**, click the **Enabled** option box, and click the **OK** button.

5. Double-click **Interactive logon: Message title for users attempting to log on**, type **Warning: Use of this system is restricted!**, and click the **OK** button.

6. Double-click **Interactive logon: Message text for users attempting to log on**, type **This system is for use of authorized users only. Individuals using this system without authority, or in excess of their authority, are subject to having their activities on this system monitored and recorded by system personnel.**, and click the **OK** button.

7. Double-click **Shutdown: Allow system to be shut down without having to log on**, click the **Disabled** option box, and click the **OK** button.

8. In your project log, write a brief explanation of the steps to customize the logon process.

9. Close any open windows and log off the computer.

IDENTIFYING AND TROUBLESHOOTING DOMAIN POLICY ISSUES

12

Although you can configure Local Security Policy for computers in a workgroup, Group Policy settings for computers in domains are the joint responsibility of several Information Technology teams. For instance, the security officer and his team establish the security directives for the organization. In addition, the network administration group configures the settings for Group Policy.

As a DST, you will be called upon to assist the other teams with the resolution of problems. To prepare to assist the other teams, you must know about these items:

- The various levels that Group Policies are set

- The sequence that Group Policies are applied

- How Group Policies are viewed

- How to troubleshoot Group Policy issues

Domain Security Policies

Computers running Windows XP Professional can use security policies as a standalone system, in a workgroup, or participate in a domain. When using centralized domain policies, Group Policies can be defined for sites, domains, and organizational units (OUs). Recall that OUs were discussed in Chapter 6. Here are definitions for these three items:

- **Site:** Represents the physical structure of your organization's network. Sites are defined by network administrators and match one or more of the TCP/IP subnets used in the organization.

- **Domain:** Groups computer systems, servers, and other hardware that share a common Active Directory database. Windows Server 2003 Domains are the core unit of the logical structure in Active Directory.

- **Organizational unit:** Organizes objects within a domain. An OU can contain objects such as user accounts, groups, computers, printers, applications, file shares, and other OUs from the same domain. Your network administrators use OUs to group objects into a logical hierarchy that best suits the needs of your organization.

Figure 12-11 shows the relationships among sites, domain(s), and OUs.

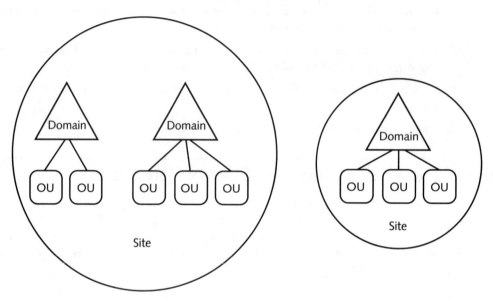

Figure 12-11   Diagram showing relationships

Sites can house one or more domains. On the left, you see a site with two domains. On the right, you see a site with one domain. Policies can be applied to a site. When this occurs, the policies apply to the containers within the site.

You may find it convenient to think of domains as security boundaries. The policy definitions with a domain are unique to the domain. Network administrators nearly always implement Domain policies. A major reason for this implementation is that Password and Account Lockout policies must be applied at the domain level.

If your network administrator requires more granularity in the application of policies, she will choose to implement policy at the OU level. These policies apply to the computers or users positioned within the OU. For example, computers in an open area might be positioned in an OU so that policies can be implemented to restrict access to these computers.

Applying Domain Security Policy

Group Policies are applied at computer startup and when your user logs on. Group Policies stored in Active Directory are refreshed every 90 minutes, when changes occur, or every 16 hours if policy changes have not occurred.

When your user logs on to the computer with a domain user account, Group Policies for Windows XP Professional computers are applied in the following sequence:

1. Any local Group Policies are applied

2. Any site Group Policies are applied

3. Any domain Group Policies are applied

4. Any OU Group Policies are applied

This order of application is important because contradictory settings in the successive policies override the previous policies. For example, if a policy setting appears in both a domain and an OU, with the default behavior, the policy setting in the OU will be used. When processing of all the four levels is completed, the cumulative result is known as the effective policy. If you are resolving a problem with security policies for a computer that is a member of a domain, it is highly likely that the policies in the effective policy are Site, Domain, or OU policies.

When your user logs on to their computer with a local user account, only the Local Group Policy applies. This type of logon would most likely occur because the computer is a member of a workgroup, not a domain.

Viewing Domain Security Policy

When picking a tool to view security policies, you have two choices:

- **Local Security Policy:** Display Local Security Settings from the local computer. Restricts the security settings to the same settings as used on workgroup computers.

- **Group Policy Snap-in:** Displays Group Policy Objects in a Microsoft Management Console. Can be linked to sites, domains, or organizational units as well as Local policy stored on the computer.

Because the Group Policy Snap-in is the most comprehensive in that it can display policy settings in sites, domains, or organizational units, you should learn to use this tool to view security policies, as shown in Figure 12-12.

Security policies have two areas of application: those that apply to the computer and those that apply to the user. Computer-related policies are always applied, regardless of the user who has logged on to the computer. User-related policies are specific to the user.

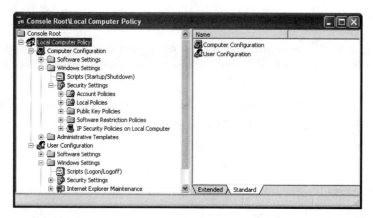

Figure 12-12 Group Policy Snap-in

Computer Configuration Group Policy

Computer-related Group Policies are specific to the computer and apply to all the users of the computer. These policies are applied during the startup phase of Windows XP. When the Windows Logon dialog box appears, the computer-related Group Policies are fully applied.

There are three types of computer-related Group Policy settings:

- **Software Settings:** Enables software to be installed on client computers. Your network administrators use these policy settings to roll out software, for example, to deploy antivirus software to all desktop and laptop computers in the organization.

- **Windows Settings:** Permits a wide range of settings to configure desktop and laptop computers. Your network administrators use Windows Settings to control the appearance and functionality of the desktop.

- **Administrative Templates:** Enables computer-related registry changes to be made. Your network administrators use administrative templates to configure the Windows XP registry.

Here is an overview of the security options that are available in the computer-related Group Policies:

- **Scripts:** Deployed at startup/shutdown. Startup scripts execute before the logon dialog is displayed. Shutdown scripts run after the user has logged off but before services are stopped.

- **Account Policies:** Invoke password policies and account lockout policies. These policies should be in Default Domain Policy.

- **Local Policies:** Set audit policy, user rights assignment, and security options.

- **Public Key Policies:** Create policies related to security key management. Keys for the Encrypting File System are managed here.

- **Software Restriction Policies:** Control which applications can be executed on a computer.
- **IP Security Policies on Local Computer:** Assign IP Security policy for secure communication with other computers.

User Configuration Group Policy

User-related Group Policies are applied to your users. These Group Policies are applied immediately after the log on completes with a successful authentication but before your user gains control of Windows Explorer.

As with the three types of computer-related Group Policy settings, there are the corresponding user-related group settings:

- **Software Settings:** Enables software to be assigned or published to your users' client computers. Your network administrators use these policy settings to roll out software, for example, to deploy Office software to all current users of a previous version of Office.
- **Windows Settings:** Permits settings to configure scripts, folder redirection behavior, and public key policies for your users. Your network administrators use Windows Settings to control the appearance and functionality of the desktop.
- **Administrative Templates:** Enables computer-related registry changes to be made for your users. Your network administrators use administrative templates to configure the Windows XP registry.

Here is an overview of the security options that are available in the user-related Group Policies:

- **Scripts:** Deployed at logon/logoff. Logon scripts execute after the user logs on. Logoff scripts run after the user has logged off.
- **Pubic Key Policies:** Create policies related to security key management
- **Internet Explorer Maintenance:** Administer Internet Explorer settings.

ACTIVITY

Activity 12-8: Placing a Computer in a Domain

Time Required: 15 minutes

Objective: Return a computer to the classroom domain.

Description: In this activity, you will return a computer to the classroom domain from the WORKGROUP workgroup. You will find this activity useful in your career as a DST because, in order to prepare for the viewing of Group Policy in a domain, the computer must be moved from a workgroup to a domain and you will need to have explored the steps to accomplish this task.

1. If necessary, log on to your computer with the user name **student** and password **Password1**.

2. Click **Start**, right-click **My Computer**, click **Properties**, and click the **Computer Name** tab.

3. Click the **Change** button. Under the Member of, click the **Domain** option button, type **classroom** in the Domain text box, and click the **OK** button.

4. Type **admin01** in the User name text box, type **Password1** in the Password text box, and click the **OK** button.

5. Wait for the Welcome to the classroom domain message to be displayed and click the three consecutive **OK** buttons and the **Yes** button.

6. Wait for the computer to restart.

7. In your project log, write a brief explanation for the reason you returned your computer to the classroom domain.

ACTIVITY

Activity 12-9: Viewing Group Policy Settings

Time Required: 15 minutes

Objective: View the Group Policy settings.

Description: In this activity, you will view the Group Policy settings using the Local Security Policy program. You will find this activity useful in your career as a DST because, in order to view the Group Policy Settings using the Local Security Policy program, you will need to have explored the steps to accomplish this task.

1. Log on to your computer with the user name **admin01** and password **Password1** on the **classroom** domain.

2. Click **Start**, point to **Control Panel**, point to **Administrative Tools**, and click **Local Security Policy**.

3. Expand **Account Policies**, Expand **Local Policies**, as shown in Figure 12-13, and view the Account Policies and Local Policies.

4. Click **Password Policy** and view the Password Policy settings.

5. Click **Account Lockout Policy** and view the Account Lockout Policy settings.

6. Click **Security Options**, scroll and locate **Interactive logon: Do not display last user name**, and view the Security Setting.

7. Double-click **Interactive logon: Message title for users attempting to log on**, view the Security Setting, and click the **OK** button.

8. Double-click **Interactive logon: Message text for users attempting to log on**, view the Security Setting, and click the **OK** button.

9. Scroll and locate **Shut down: Allow system to be shut down without having to log on** and view the Security Setting.

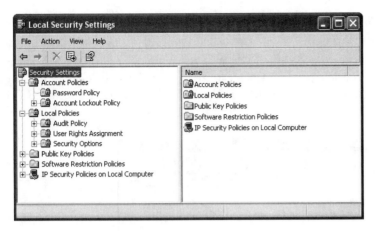

Figure 12-13   Local Security Settings

10. In your project log, write a brief description for the policy settings that you viewed.

11. Close the Local Security Settings window.

Troubleshooting Domain Policy Issues

When policies are applied on multiple levels (for example, site, domain, and organizational unit), the results can be in conflict. If a conflicting policy is set, it can be difficult to track down and resolve. Windows XP provides three tools to assist you as you troubleshoot Group Policy problems.

These three tools are presented in the following sections.

Verifying Policy with Resultant Set of Policy (RSoP)

RSoP can help administrators determine the final set of policies that are applied and track down policy precedence, making troubleshooting easier. **Resultant Set of Policy (RSoP)** is a query engine that polls existing policies and then reports the results of the query. It polls existing policies based on site, domain, and organizational unit.

In addition to checking the policies set by Group Policy, RSoP also checks Software Installation for any applications that are associated with a particular user or computer and reports the results of these queries as well. RSoP details all the policy settings that are configured by a network administrator. This includes Administrative Templates, Folder Redirection, Security, and Scripts.

Administrators can run the Resultant Set of Policy tool in MMC or Gpresult from the command line to see which policies are in effect on any computer. And in the Help and Support Center, you can generate a concise report to see how Group Policy is being applied on a user's computer.

MMC RSoP Snap-in Tool

From the MMC, the RSoP Snap-in lets you verify policies in effect for a given user or computer. You can choose which user you wish to view policy settings for. You can expand the policy tree in the left pane and navigate to any of the policies that are in effect for the target user, as shown in Figure 12-14. You will be learning to use the RSoP tool in Activity 12-10.

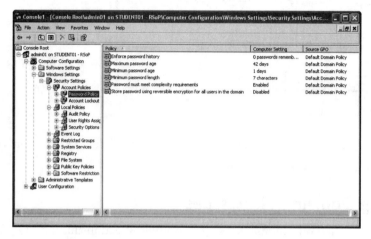

Figure 12-14 RSoP Snap-in results

Activity 12-10: Verifying Group Policy with the RSoP Snap-in

Time Required: 15 minutes

Objective: Verify Group Policy with the RSoP Snap-in.

Description: In this activity, you will verify the Group Policy with the RSoP Snap-in. You will find this activity useful in your career as a DST because, in order to verify the sequence that Group Policies are applied, you will need to have explored the steps to accomplish this task.

1. If necessary, log on to your computer with the user name **admin01** and password **Password1**.

2. Click **Start**, click **Run**, type **MMC** in the Open text box, and click the **OK** button.

3. Click **File**, click **Add/Remove Snap-in**, click the **Add** button, then scroll and click **Resultant Set of Policy**, as shown in Figure 12-15.

4. Click the **Add** button, then click the five consecutive **Next** buttons, the **Finish** button, the **Close** button, and the **OK** button.

5. Expand **admin01 on STUDENT01 – RSoP**, expand **Computer Configuration**, expand **Windows Settings**, expand **Security Settings**, expand **Account Policies**, and click **Password Policy**.

Figure 12-15   RSoP Snap-in selected

12

6. In your project log, write a brief description of the steps to view the Password Policy with the RSoP Snap-in.

7. Close the Console1 window without saving the console.

Command Prompt Gpresult

Gpresult is a command line tool that you run on a computer on which you wish to test Group Policy. Because you can apply overlapping levels of policies to any computer or user, Group Policy generates a resulting set of policies at logon. Gpresult displays the resulting set of policies that were enforced on the computer for the specified user at logon. You will want to redirect the output of Gpresult to a text file. You will learn this technique in Activity 12-11. Figure 12-16 shows the redirected output of Gpresult opened in Notepad.

ACTIVITY

Activity 12-11: Verifying Group Policy Settings with the Gpresult Command

Time Required: 15 minutes

Objective: Verify Group Policy with the Gpresult command.

Description: In this activity, you will verify Group Policy with the Gpresult command. You will find this activity useful in your career as a DST because, in order to verify the sequence that Group Policies are applied, you will need to have explored the steps to accomplish this task.

1. If necessary, log on to your computer with the user name **admin01** and password **Password1**.

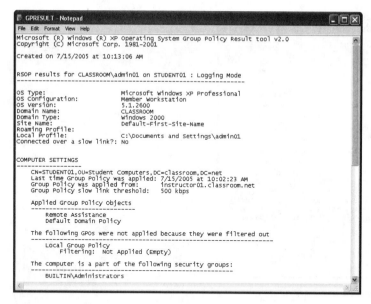

Figure 12-16   Gpresult results displayed with Notepad

2. Click **Start**, point to **All Programs**, point to **Accessories**, and click **Command Prompt**.

3. Type **gpresult > results.txt**, as shown in Figure 12-17, and press **Enter**.

Figure 12-17   Gpresult entered at the Command Prompt window

4. Wait for the result file to be created.

5. Click **Start**, point to **All Programs**, point to **Accessories**, and click **Notepad**.

6. Click the **File** menu, click **Open**, double-click the **My Computer** icon, double-click **Local Disk (C:)**, double-click **Documents and Settings**, double-click **admin01**, click **results**, and click the **Open** button. Again, see Figure 12-16.

7. Under Computer Settings, scroll the text until Applied Group Policy Objects is displayed.

8. In your project log, record the Applied Group Policy Objects for Computer Settings.

9. Under User Settings, scroll the text until Applied Group Policy Objects is displayed.

10. In your project log, record the Applied Group Policy Objects for User Settings.

11. In your project log, write a brief description of the steps to view the Group Policy Objects from Gpresult.

12. Close the Notepad and Command Prompt windows.

Help and Support Center Group Policy

Although less useful, your users can run Help and Support Center RSoP Report on their own computers to verify policy settings. This tool provides a user-friendly report of most policies in effect on the computer on which it is run.

Activity 12-12: Verifying Group Policy Settings with the Help and Support Center

Time Required: 15 minutes

Objective: Verify Group Policy with the Help and Support Center.

Description: In this activity, you will Verify Group Policy with the Help and Support Center. You will find this activity useful in your career as a DST because, in order to verify the sequence that Group Policies are applied, you will need to have explored the steps to accomplish this task.

1. If necessary, log on to your computer with the user name **admin01** and password **Password1**.

2. Click **Start** and click **Help and Support**.

3. Click the **Use Tools to view your computer information and diagnose problems** link.

4. Click the **My Computer Information** link.

5. Click the **View Advanced System Information** link.

6. Click the **View Group Policy settings applied** link.

7. Wait for the information to be collected.

8. Locate and view the **Applied Group Policy Objects**, as shown in Figure 12-18.

9. Scroll to the end of the page.

10. Click the **Run the Resultant Set of Policy tool** link, as shown in Figure 12-19.

11. Wait for the information to be collected.

12

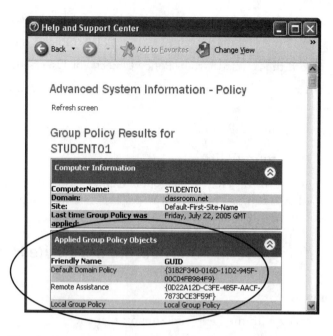

Figure 12-18   Help and Support Center - Applied Group Policy Objects

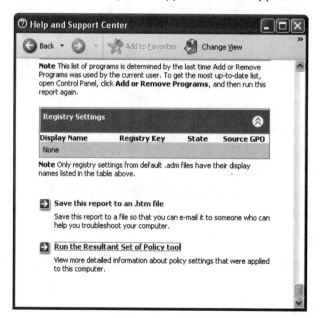

Figure 12-19   Help and Support Center - Run the Resultant Set of Policy tool

12. Notice that the result is the same as the Resultant Set of Policy Snap-in results.

13. In your project log, write a brief description of the steps to view the Group Policy Objects from Help and Support.

14. Close any open windows and log off the computer.

IDENTIFYING AND RESPONDING TO SECURITY INCIDENTS

As a DST, you must be prepared to respond to security incidents. For example, when a worm is present on a networked computer, it can use your user's e-mail address book to send itself to other computers on the network. You should be able to identify that an attack is occurring and be prepared to assist with the resolution to the attack. Of course, prevention would be a better solution. You will be ready to provide your users with answers to their incident-related questions. In the following sections, you will learn how to identify and protect against virus attacks.

Identifying Attacks

Unfortunately, viruses come in many different forms. And new versions arrive almost daily. You can benefit by knowing some general information about the various types of viruses and how they travel.

Three general categories of viruses are presented in the sections that follow.

Viruses

In computers, a virus is a program that replicates itself by being copied by you or your users. However, some viruses can initiate their copying to another program, computer boot sector, or document. Viruses can be transmitted as attachments to an e-mail or in a downloaded file, or be present on a diskette or CD. The receiver of the e-mail note, downloaded file, or diskette is usually unaware that it contains a virus.

Some viruses wreak their effect as soon as their code is executed; other viruses lie dormant until circumstances cause their code to be executed by the computer. Some viruses are benign or playful in intent and effect ("Happy Birthday, Ludwig!") and some can be quite harmful, erasing data or causing your hard disk to require reformatting. A virus that replicates itself by resending itself as an e-mail attachment or as part of a network message is known as a worm.

Worms

A computer **worm** is a self-replicating computer program, similar to a computer virus. A virus attaches itself to, and becomes part of, another executable program; a worm is self-contained and does not need to be part of another program to propagate itself. Worms use the network to replicate. For example, a current technique is to send an e-mail to the addresses in the Outlook Address book. In addition to replication, a worm may be designed to do any number of things, such as delete files on your users' computers or install programs on your users' computers.

More recent worms may carry other executables as a payload. However, even in the absence of such a payload, a worm can wreak havoc just with the network traffic generated by its reproduction. Mydoom, for example, caused a noticeable worldwide Internet slowdown at the peak of its spread.

Trojan Horses

A **Trojan horse** or Trojan is a computer program that pretends to be innocent but instead has a malicious effect—one that the programmer intended and you or your users didn't expect. The term is derived from the classical myth of the Trojan horse.

A Trojan horse differs from a virus in that it is a standalone program—a Trojan does not attach to other programs or files. It differs from a worm in that it does not move from one computer to another on its own. You or your user must transfer and run it deliberately, such as by e-mail or by posting it to a download area where it could be downloaded by a victim.

IN THE WORKPLACE

Here are several Web sites where you can get up-to-date information about the current viruses introduced into the wild:

http://securityresponse.symantec.com/

http://us.mcafee.com/virusInfo/

There are a lot of viruses out there. But some aren't really out there at all. Virus hoaxes are more than mere annoyances, as they may lead your users to routinely ignore all virus warning messages, leaving them vulnerable to a genuine, destructive virus. Next time you receive a suspicious virus warning message, be sure to check the following Web site to authenticate the threat:

http://www.vmyths.com/

Identifying Ways Computers Are Affected

How can you identify affected computers? You or your users may encounter these common signs that a computer is infected:

- Unusual error messages appear
- Applications do not function properly
- A decrease in performance
- Hard drive not accessible
- Unusually high level of disk activity
- New icons appear on the desktop or menus

Protecting Against Attacks

While not all viruses are harmful, you and your users will want to be protected from possible danger. Users expect to be protected from potential attacks. Your information technology organization can take a number of steps to secure computers against attacks:

- Purchase and install antivirus software

- Educate users about viruses

- Isolate the internal network from the Internet

- Install the latest critical security updates

- Use security features in Office products

Using Antivirus Software

Your organization's first action to protect your users should be to purchase and install antivirus software. In today's interconnected networks, antivirus software is more than ever a necessity to protect computers against viruses, worms, and other types of malicious code. Two of the leading antivirus products are: Norton Antivirus and McAfee VirusScan. After antivirus software is installed, it scans your computer and quarantines or deletes any found viruses. Continued protection is achieved as the antivirus software monitors the computer for virus activity. Antivirus software should be configured to scan incoming e-mail messages.

Because new viruses are constantly being released, the makers of antivirus software must constantly update their software with new signatures to detect these new viruses. Out-of-date antivirus software translates to ineffective antivirus software. To keep the virus software effective, your organization must download and deploy these new signatures and the corresponding virus removal tools from the vendor. For computers in a workgroup, you should subscribe each computer to the Web site that automatically provides the signature updates.

IN THE WORKPLACE
I have used the Norton Antivirus on multiple personal computers for years. Two dollars per month per machine is cheap when compared to the alternative! I have turned on the Live Update feature and get updates automatically when I connect to the Internet.

Educating Users

Another way you and your information technology organization can protect the network against virus attacks is to educate your users. This training includes information about how viruses enter the network and how they spread.

Here are some items that should be included in your organization's training sessions:

- **Definitions of terms—(Viruses, Worms, Trojan Horses):** Your users establish a general awareness of computer viruses when they can use the terminology.

- **Methods used by viruses to spread:** Your users are more prone to participate in the spread of viruses when they are unaware of the propagation methods used by viruses.

- **Common signs of viruses:** Your users need to know when they have a virus.

- **Importance of using antivirus software:** The first line of defense on your users' computers is antivirus software.

- **Transporting viruses with floppy diskettes and USB drives:** Your users need to be aware that they can transport viruses in removable media.

- **Replication by e-mail attachments:** E-mail attachments are one of the most frequent methods used by virus programmers to copy the viruses to other computers.

Enabling the Internet Firewall

Before you connect computers in a workgroup to the Internet, you should install a firewall. This is hardware or software that helps to protect your workgroup against hackers. Internet Connection Firewall is Microsoft's firewall for Windows XP; this subject was previously introduced in Chapter 10.

You can enable the firewall component by using these steps:

1. Click **Start**, point to **Control Panel**, and click the **Network Connections applet**.

2. Right-click **Internet connection** and click **Properties**.

3. Select the **Advanced tab**.

4. Under Internet Connection Firewall, check the **Protect my computer...** check box, as shown in Figure 12-20.

I use an Internet router to connect my home network to the Internet. I get all of the features of ICF in a small SOHO router for less than $100.

IN THE WORKPLACE

Managing Critical Updates

After a vendor releases an operating system or application, updates are made available on the vendor's Web site. Frequently, these updates are in response to security issues that have been identified and reported. Windows XP includes the Automatic Updates feature, which can automatically download the latest security updates when your computer is on and connected to the Internet. Information on managing critical updates is located in Chapter 13.

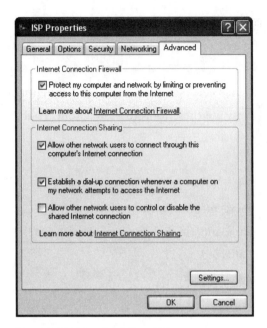

Figure 12-20 Enabling ICF

Using Security Features in Office

As previously mentioned, one of the most common ways viruses spread is by e-mail attachments. Although you may have configured the antivirus software to scan e-mail messages, you should still use the security features in Outlook and Outlook Express. Refer to Chapter 5 for information on securing Outlook Express and Chapter 9 for Microsoft Office 2003 Outlook.

CHAPTER SUMMARY

- By assigning passwords and encrypting files in Office applications, your users can protect files from unauthorized access.
- In Excel, PowerPoint, and Word, your users can configure macro security settings to control against the undesirable effects of macros.
- For computers in workgroups, administrators can:
  - View Local Security Policy settings
  - Establish Password Policy
  - Configure Account Lockout Policy
  - Customize the logon process (disable the username, add a security message, disable the Shutdown button)

❑ To identify and troubleshoot Domain Policy issues, you must know how:

  ❑ Domain security policy is configured

  ❑ Security policy is applied

  ❑ Security policy is viewed (Computer Configuration and User Configuration)

❑ To troubleshoot Group Policy, you must use these tools to view Group Policy:

  ❑ RSoP Snap-in

  ❑ Gpresult command

  ❑ Help and Support RSoP

❑ To identify and respond to security incidents, you must be able to:

  ❑ Identify the sources (viruses, worms, and Trojan horses) of attacks

  ❑ Identify the ways computers are affected

  ❑ Protect your users' computers against attacks.

  ❑ Use antivirus software

  ❑ Educate users

  ❑ Enable Internet Connection Firewall

  ❑ Manage critical updates

  ❑ Use the security features in Office

Key Terms

macro — Executable that can be attached and embedded in a worksheet, presentation, document, or e-mail message.

RC4 — This is a series of encryption routines built on programs first designed by Ron Rivest in 1987. The RC acronym is generally understood to stand for "Ron's Code."

Resultant Set of Policy (RSoP) — Program that polls existing policies and then reports the results of the query.

sandboxing — Programming process that prevents applications from accessing key resources and causing damage.

site — Represents the physical structure of your organization's network.

Trojan horse — Computer program that pretends to be innocent but instead has a malicious effect.

worm — Self-replicating computer program, similar to a computer virus. A worm is self-contained and does not need to be part of another program to propagate itself.

Weak Encryption (XOR) — Retained for use by earlier versions of Word and Microsoft Excel that are still used in Office 2000 when the system locale is France.

REVIEW QUESTIONS

1. Which Office applications can encrypt files to protect the contents? (Choose all that apply.)

   a. Excel

   b. Outlook

   c. PowerPoint

   d. Word

2. The _____ type is not recommended for the encryption of Office data files.

   a. Office 97/2000 Compatible

   b. RC4, Microsoft Base Cryptographic Provider v1.0

   c. RC4, Microsoft DH SChannel Cryptographic Provider

   d. RC4, Microsoft Enhanced Cryptographic Provider v1.0

3. Which option is available to protect Excel workbooks? (Choose all that apply.)

   a. Password to open

   b. Password to modify

   c. Read-only recommended

   d. Access denied

4. A _____ is an executable that can be attached to an e-mail message.

   a. micro

   b. macro

   c. function

   d. subroutine

5. The _____ setting determines the number of unique passwords associated with a user account.

   a. Enforce Password Policy

   b. Maximum Password Age

   c. Minimum Password Age

   d. Minimum Password Length

6. Which of the following is a password policy setting? (Choose all that apply.)

   a. Maximum Password Age

   b. Minimum Password Age

   c. Minimum Password Length

   d. Account Lockout Duration

12

7. Which of the following is an account lockout setting? (Choose all that apply.)

   a. Minimum Password Length

   b. Account Lockout Duration

   c. Account Lockout Threshold

   d. Reset Account Lockout After

8. The _____ setting determines the length of time before an account is unlocked.

   a. Minimum Password Length

   b. Account Lockout Duration

   c. Account Lockout Threshold

   d. Reset Account Lockout After

9. Which action can be taken when customizing the logon process? (Choose all that apply.)

   a. Disabling the default username

   b. Adding a security warning message

   c. Adding a security warning title

   d. Disabling the Shutdown button

10. A _____ represents the physical structure of the network infrastructure.

    a. subnet

    b. site

    c. domain

    d. organizational unit

11. Which of the following represents the logical structure of the network infrastructure? (Choose all that apply.)

    a. subnet

    b. site

    c. domain

    d. organizational unit

12. Which of the following is a type of Group Policies setting? (Choose all that apply.)

    a. Software installation

    b. Windows settings

    c. Administrative templates

    d. Local policy

13. Which of the following is a computer-related Group Policy? (Choose all that apply.)

   a. Scripts

   b. Account policies

   c. Local policy

   d. Public Key policies

14. The _____ tool is a query engine that polls security policies.

   a. RSoP Snap-in

   b. Gpresult command

   c. Help and Support RSoP Report

   d. RSoP viewer

15. The _____ is a tool that can be used by users to view policy settings.

   a. RSoP Snap-in

   b. Gpresult command

   c. Help and Support RSoP Report

   d. RSoP viewer

16. A _____ is a self-replicating computer program.

   a. virus

   b. worm

   c. bug

   d. Trojan horse

17. A _____ is a computer program that appears as a valuable program but contains malicious program code.

   a. virus

   b. worm

   c. bug

   d. Trojan horse

18. Which of the following is a way that a virus might affect a computer? (Choose all that apply.)

   a. Unusual error messages appear

   b. Applications do not function properly

   c. Creates decreases in performance

   d. Unusually high level of disk activity

19. Which of the following is a step to secure computers? (Choose all that apply.)

   a. Install antivirus software

   b. Keep signature files up-to-date

    c. Educate users about viruses

    d. Install latest critical security updates

20. Which of the following is an item that should be completed in training sessions for users? (Choose all that apply.)

    a. Methods used by virus to spread

    b. Common signs of viruses

    c. Transporting viruses

    d. Replication by e-mail attachments

CASE PROJECTS

Case 12-1: Configuring Local Security Settings

You consult as a desktop support technician for a nonprofit organization. Your customer's network consists of five computers configured as a workgroup.

The Volunteer computer is used by the various volunteers of the organization. Each volunteer is provided a user logon ID. The supervisor has been discussing security with one of the volunteers who previously worked at a major corporation.

The supervisor has asked you to "secure" the Volunteer computer. She has asked you to prepare a plan to secure this computer. What security items will be in your plan? What initial settings will you try? Provide an explanation for each security item? Security setting?

Case 12-2: Resolving Group Policy Settings

You are a desktop support technician. Your network consists of a Windows Server 2003 Active Directory domain with 10 servers, including application and database servers and 500 computers running Windows XP Professional.

You are preparing a procedure to be used by the new DST. Include an overview of Group Policy application. Include instructions for the use of three Group Policy resolution tools.

Case 12-3: Preparing for a Presentation on Viruses

You are a desktop support technician. Your network consists of a Windows Server 2003 Active Directory domain with 10 servers, including application and database servers and 850 computers running Windows XP Professional.

Your boss has asked you to assist the corporate training group with a presentation on viruses and their prevention. Prior to meeting with the training group, your boss has asked you to prepare a detailed outline on computer viruses and their prevention by users. It would be helpful if you could include some "candid" explanations of the various terms and techniques.

13

MANAGE OFFICE APPLICATION UPDATES AND UPGRADES

After reading this chapter and completing the exercises, you will be able to:

♦ Track and identify applicable Office Application updates

♦ Manage Office application add-ins and templates

♦ Monitor security vulnerabilities and updates

♦ Distribute updates

As you are aware, the role of the DST requires that you be prepared to assist other members of the Information Technology department with the management of Office updates and upgrades. You must be prepared to answer your users' questions regarding the update process as it affects the users' computers.

On a regular basis, Microsoft provides program updates for the products installed on your users' computers. In this chapter, you will learn how to work within the program update process.

Your users can extend the functionality of Office by using Office **Add-Ins** (supplemental programs that extend the capability of an application) and **templates** (predesigned documents, worksheets, or presentations). You will learn in this chapter how to use these two features to prepare yourself to assist your users.

Security is a big issue! You and other members of the Information Technology department must stay on top of this to prevent security exploits from occurring. You will learn in this chapter how to monitor for security vulnerabilities.

With the volume of updates that occur each year, your organization must be prepared to distribute these updates in an efficient manner. In this chapter, you will learn about the techniques to distribute program updates to your users.

All of the preceding topics will be covered in this chapter.

TRACKING AND IDENTIFYING APPLICABLE OFFICE APPLICATION UPDATES

As a DST, you are aware that software vendors provide updates for the applications that they market. If there are any problems encountered in the marketplace the developer can simply produce a fix in the form of a software update, or patch, and have you download it to update your user's computer. So, when you buy new software off the shelf, chances are the first thing you will need to do when it is installed is to connect to the Internet and check for the latest updates! Microsoft is no exception, and it regularly provides program updates.

In the sections that follow, you will learn about:

- Differences between critical updates and updates
- Types of updates
- Upgrading programs
- Availability of updates
- Assessing the updates
- Obtaining the updates
- Testing the updates
- Deploying the updates

This information is important to the DST because you will be joining the other teams in Information Technology to support updates to the software on your users' computers. Also, you must be prepared to answer your users' questions about updates to the software.

Differences Between Critical Updates and Updates

Many of the updates Microsoft provides correct security problems. Microsoft classifies these updates as critical updates or as updates, as follows:

- **Critical updates** are those that Microsoft highly recommends you implement. A critical update fixes a significant problem. Perhaps, this critical update is in response to a security problem or a potential loss of data. Your users can lose data or have their computer compromised if your organization does not deploy a critical update.

- On the other hand, for a simple **update**, Microsoft recommends only that you apply the update. Following the logic, an update solves a less significant problem. Naturally, the risk is less to your organization for an update.

Types of Updates

Updates come in two basic categories: hot fixes and service packs. These two categories will be presented in the following sections.

Hot Fixes

Microsoft, as well as other vendors, creates program patches or **hot fixes** to solve each immediate problem. Many of the issued hot fixes plug up security vulnerabilities. Because the turnaround between the identification of the problem and the creation of the solution is a matter of days, hot fixes do not get the same testing as service packs. Hot fixes are risky and should be applied only if it is certain that they are needed.

If it's not broke, don't fix it! Your organization should deploy hot fixes only to solve existing problems. Remember, hot fixes receive only limited testing. There have been instances in which a hot fix created a new problem on installation.

Service Packs

Service packs are released by Microsoft from time to time to fix problems, improve performance, and to add new features to the software. Service packs are cumulative; that is, they contain all of the previous service packs and hot fixes since the last service pack. Before a service pack is released, Microsoft tests all of the fixes to make sure that they do not conflict with each other or cause new problems while fixing old problems. This process of testing is called **regression testing**. Prior to release, service packs undergo extensive regression testing. As an additional precaution, service packs can be installed with an option to later uninstall the service pack. This ability to uninstall the service pack might be beneficial when a decision is made to back out the changes of the service pack.

Upgrading Programs

Some of the programs that are installed on your users' computers are upgraded—as opposed to updated—from time-to-time. **Upgrading** simply means that the end user gets a new or enhanced version of the product. Internet Explorer and Outlook Express are good examples of programs that have had numerous free upgrades. Many upgrades are free and available for download from the vendors' Web sites.

On the other hand, your organization can expect to pay for upgrades when a significant number of new features are added to a commercial application. Microsoft Office, which has gone through a number of updates or editions, is currently identified as Office11. The current version offers enhancements that can motivate your organization to make a business decision to purchase this upgrade.

Availability of Updates

As a DST, you need to be aware of the ways to determine the availability of software updates. In the sections that follow, you will learn how to locate updates using the Knowledge Base and the Microsoft Office Online Web site.

Knowledge Base Articles

Supporting Microsoft products is often easier when you feel at home with the Microsoft Knowledge Base, which is accessed on the Microsoft Web site. After navigating to the Search the Knowledge Base page, select the product you are using, type in a few search terms that describe the difficulty—for instance, "can't read file with officeart," as shown in Figure 13-1—and then click the arrow button at the bottom of the screen.

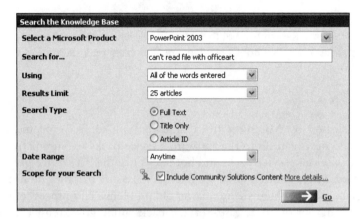

Figure 13-1 Knowledge Base search entry

You can then read the Knowledge base article titles, as shown in Figure 13-2, and select the article that best fits your problem. For example, "Description of the Office critical update..." may have the solution to the problem. Clicking this link will provide the information about this critical update.

 The Knowledge Base can be used to solve less critical problems. I've been able to find advice that I could share with my users. For instance, I once had a user with a Word document that had been assembled from several documents. She called it her "snowflake document," in which almost no two paragraphs looked alike. I searched on the string "Taming unruly formatting" and found tips to solve her formatting problems.

IN THE WORKPLACE

Another way to locate a Knowledge Base article is by the number. This might occur when you are reading a magazine article about a given problem and are given a Knowledge Base number as a reference.

Activity 13-1: Searching Knowledge Base Articles

ACTIVITY

Time Required: 15 minutes

Objective: Search the Knowledge Base for an article.

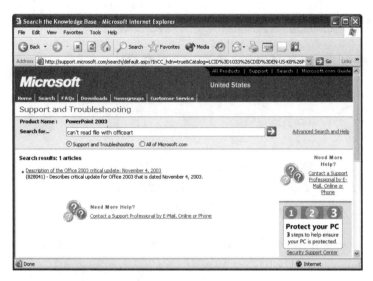

Figure 13-2   Knowledge Base search results

Description: In this activity, you will search for an article in the Knowledge Base by number. Next, you will search for an article by keywords for a problem when using Word. You will find this activity useful in your career as a DST because, in order to answer users' questions about problems in the use of Office, you will need to have explored searching the Knowledge Base in detail.

You must have an Internet connection to complete this activity and the remaining activities in this chapter.

NOTE

1. Log on to your computer with the user name **user01** and password **Password1**.

2. Click **Start** and click **Internet Explorer** from the pinned-items list.

3. Type **support.microsoft.com** in the Address text box and press **Enter**.

4. Click the **Search the Knowledge Base** link.

5. If necessary, click the **Select a Microsoft Product** drop-down list, and scroll and then click **All Microsoft Products**.

6. Type **830000** (or the Article ID suggested by your instructor) in the Search for text box, click the **Article ID** option button, as shown in Figure 13-3, and click the **Go** link.

7. Click the **Description of the update for Word...** (or the link suggested by your instructor) link.

8. Read the article and click the two consecutive **Back** buttons.

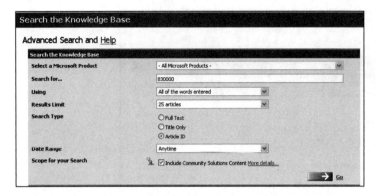

Figure 13-3   Building a search for the Knowledge Base

9. Click the **Select a Microsoft Product** drop-down list, and scroll and then click **Word 2003**.

10. Type **unresponsive when user saves a file** (or the keywords suggested by your instructor) in the Search for text box, click the **Full Text** option button, and click the **Go** link.

11. Verify that you received the same Web page as in Step 5.

12. In your project log, write a brief summary that describes how you could use the Knowledge Base to research a solution to a user's problem.

13. Close any open windows and log off the computer.

Microsoft Office Online

As a DST, you have a responsibility to your users to keep abreast of the changing complexion of Office. One of the best ways to do this is to navigate to the Download page at the *http://office.microsoft.com/* Web site. An easy way to go to this page is to click the Help menu in an Office application and click **Check for Updates**. A representative Office Online Web page is shown in Figure 13-4.

The Microsoft Office Online Web site provides critical updates, updates, and program updates. Also, you will find other useful upgrades that you can install to keep your users' version of Microsoft Office up-to-date with the latest improvements available. Figure 13-5 shows a representative Update Web page.

For more product-specific information, you could click on the Office 2003 link under New Updates. You will then be presented with a list of the critical updates and updates for Office.

Activity 13-2: Checking for Updates

Time Required: 15 minutes

Objective: Check for Updates for Office.

Figure 13-4   Office Online Web page

Figure 13-5   Office Update Web page

Description: In this activity, you will surf to the Office Web site and search for possible critical updates and updates. You will find this activity useful in your career as a DST because, in order to keep the Office software up-to-date, you will need to have explored these steps in detail.

1. Log on to your computer with the user name **admin01** and password **Password1**.

2. Click **Start** and click **Internet Explorer** from the pinned-items list.

3. Type **office.microsoft.com** in the Address text box, and press **Enter**.

4. Click the **Check for Updates** link and click the **Office 2003** link under New updates. Figure 13-6 shows the location of the link.

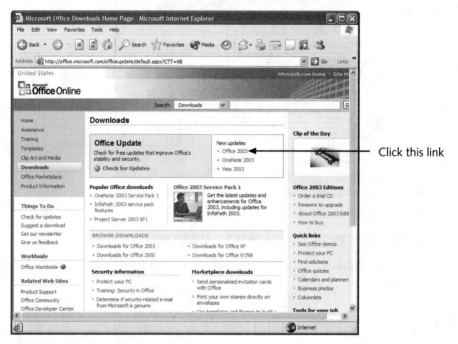

Figure 13-6   Office Update Center

TIP If a security warning appears with the message "Do you want to install and run . . . ," click the **Yes** button.)

5. If the message Wait for Office Update Installing Engine appears, click the **Yes** button.

6. Wait for the Checking for updates scan to complete.

7. Scroll and click the **More Information** link for the first update.

8. In your project log, write down the title of the update, the explanation of the problem, the product(s) affected, and a conclusion regarding the acceptability of the update for your environment.

9. Close the top Internet Explorer window.

10. Repeat Steps 7 and 8 for any remaining updates.

11. Close any open windows.

12. In your project log, write a brief summary that describes the process of locating updates for Office.

Assessing the Updates

Once you identify the release of a critical update or update, you must determine if this affects your organization and whether your users' computers require the patch or update. As mentioned earlier, you can use Microsoft's two-level classification system to assist in this decision. If an update is identified as critical, your organization should consider immediately applying the critical update as soon as testing is completed. If it is not critical, then your organization should determine if the update merits deployment.

IN THE WORKPLACE

Keeping an inventory of the software deployed on the various computers in the organization assists with the assessment activities. This inventory might be as rudimentary as an Excel workbook or as complex as a highly automated system running agents on each computer to monitor software usage. The important issue is that you have a central place where you can locate the information about which software is installed on each desktop computer. When you know where to get your information, you won't get caught in the hallway looking confused and panicked—right when your boss walks by.

Obtaining the Updates

Microsoft provides two methods to obtain updates from the Office Web site:

- **Office Update Center:** Use this center when you want to scan a computer for needed updates, to download and install the update on a single computer.

- **Office Download Center:** Use this center when you know which update you desire and want to install the update on multiple computers. After the download, you can share the download with multiple computers. This cuts download time from the Internet by avoiding multiple downloads for the same file.

Your organization may have established preferences on how to process Office updates. Contact the network administrators to determine the established procedures.

ACTIVITY

Activity 13-3: Obtaining an Update from the Office Update Center

Time Required: 15 minutes

Objective: Obtain and install an Office update.

Description: In this activity, you will scan a computer to determine which Office updates are suggested. After reviewing the list, you will selectively install the needed updates. You will find this activity useful in your career as a DST because, in order to answer your users' questions about updating Office, you will need to have explored these steps in detail.

1. If necessary, log on to your computer with the user name **admin01** and password **Password1**.

2. Click **Start** and click **Internet Explorer** from the pinned–items list.

3. Type **office.microsoft.com** in the Address text box and press **Enter**.

4. Click the **Check for Update**s link and click the **Office 2003** link under New Updates.

5. Wait for the scan to complete. Review the Updates list and uncheck the check box for any unneeded updates.

6. Click the **Start Installation** button. Wait for the Installation wizard to load.

7. Click the three consecutive **Next** buttons.

8. Wait for the download and installation to complete. Click the **Finish** button. If necessary, click the **Yes** button to restart the computer.

9. Close the Internet Explorer window.

10. In your project log, write a brief summary that describes the steps to download and install an update.

ACTIVITY

Activity 13-4: Obtaining an Update from the Office Download Center

Time Required: 15 minutes

Objective: Obtain, save, and optionally, install an Office update.

Description: In this activity, you will obtain a list of Office updates. After reviewing the list, you will selectively install the needed updates. You will find this activity useful in your career as a DST because, in order to answer users' questions about Office updates, you will need to have explored these in detail.

1. If necessary, log on to your computer with the user name **admin01** and password **Password1**.

2. Click **Start** and click **Internet Explorer** from the pinned–items list.

3. Type **office.microsoft.com** in the Address text box and press **Enter**.

4. Click the **Downloads** link under Home.

5. Click the **Downloads for Office 2003** link under BROWSE DOWNLOADS, as shown in Figure 13-7.

6. Click the **Updates** link under Office 2003.

7. Review the Updates for Office 2003 list and click the link for any needed update(s).

8. Read the explanation for the update.

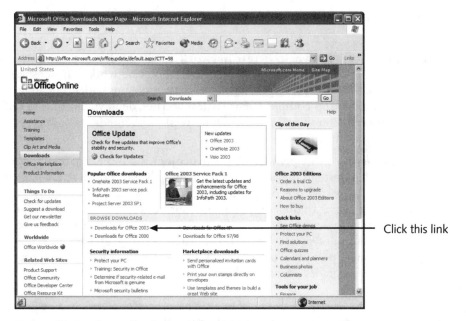

Click this link

Figure 13-7   Downloads for Office 2003

13

9. If necessary, uncheck the **Close this dialog box when download completes** check box. If you decide to apply the update, click the **Download** button (or another appropriate link). Otherwise, skip to Step 14.

10. Click the two consecutive **Save** buttons.

11. To install the update on this computer, click the **Open** button and click the two consecutive **Yes** buttons.

12. Wait for the installation to complete.

13. Click the **OK** button.

14. Close the Internet Explorer window.

15. In your project log, write a brief summary that describes the steps to locate and download an update from the Office Download Center.

16. Log off the computer.

Testing the Updates

Your organization should not place itself at risk by deploying updates and upgrades without testing them in your environment. To do so could result in undesired side effects. For example, a critical user application may not function after the installation of an update, resulting in a loss of sales revenue.

Your organization will want to consider the following measures to ease the testing of updates:

- **Create a test network:** A **test network** contains computers with the standard hardware and software used in the organization's network. This ensures that the hot fix, service pack, or upgrade will not cause problems with other applications on a standard desktop computer. For critical updates, deployment time is critical and your organization should use the test network, which reduces the time to conduct the necessary tests.

- **Implement a pilot project:** A **pilot project** is a project conducted on a small scale to demonstrate the acceptability of an update or upgrade. Users are typically recruited to participate on pilot projects. Service packs and updates should be tested by a subset of the computers on your network. This subset will determine if there are problems that could affect other computers on the network. You will want to use pilot projects only for updates and upgrades because pilot projects require longer periods of time to complete the required activities to ensure that the updates or upgrades are acceptable.

When you are looking for personnel to participate in a pilot project, be sure to include your peers in Information Technology. It is reassuring to the user community that the update is being used by people in IT. Of course, you will want to include representatives from the user community as well. In the end, never forget the following: A successful implementation is almost always preceded by a successful pilot project.

Deploying the Updates

After thorough testing, your organization will be ready to deploy the Office update. Your organization has two choices for deploying the update:

- **Install the update manually:** This will require a trip to each of your users' computers to install the update

- **Install the update using a software deployment system:** For information on automated software deployment, see the information on Installing Office Using Policy-based Installation in Chapter 6.

If your organization is using manual installation for the Office update, then your organization has two locations from which the files required for the update can be obtained:

- **Microsoft Office Update Center:** This will require a greater amount of interaction on your part to process the update. Each computer will be scanned, updates selected, downloaded, and installed on the computer.

■ **Local file server:** The required files will be downloaded once from the Microsoft Download Center and placed in a shared folder on a file server. To update each of your users' computers, connect to the shared folder and run the executable update file. To update multiple desktop computers with the same Office update, this scenario is the most effective.

MANAGING OFFICE APPLICATION ADD-INS AND TEMPLATES

Nearly all of your users will rely on Office to perform many daily tasks. For example, they probably write proposals in Word, give presentations with PowerPoint, and analyze data in Excel. But for all of the bells and whistles Office has to offer, there are still hundreds of Add-Ins—supplemental programs that you install for your users to extend the capabilities of Office by adding custom commands and specialized features—that provide additional tools that extend the capabilities of Office even further.

In addition to Office Add-Ins, you will want to consider Office templates. A template provides a prototype to assist with the creation of an Office document, worksheet, or presentation. For example, a PowerPoint template can provide the basic style or layout to create a presentation. What can a template contain? Templates can store styles, AutoCorrect entries, macros, toolbars, custom menu settings, and shortcut keys.

In the sections that follow you will learn about these two features for which your users expect you to be able to provide assistance.

Managing Add-Ins

Your users have and will want to take advantage of Office Add-Ins. You should be prepared to assist your users with these tasks:

- Loading and unloading existing Add-Ins
- Viewing existing Add-Ins.
- Locating new Add-Ins
- Installing and Testing Add-Ins

Loading and Unloading Existing Add-Ins

Add-Ins are available for the various Office applications. For example, Microsoft Excel ships with a number of Add-Ins. These Add-Ins are representative of the tools that are available to extend the functionality of Excel:

- **Analysis ToolPak:** Adds financial, statistical, and engineering analysis tools and functions.
- **Conditional Sum wizard:** Creates a formula that sums data in a range if the data matches criteria you specify.

- **Euro Currency tools:** Formats values as euros, and provides the EUROCONVERT worksheet function to convert currencies.

- **Lookup wizard:** Creates a formula to look up data in a range by using another known value in the range.

Prior to using an Add-In, your user must load the Add-In. The Add-Ins dialog box, as shown in Figure 13-8, lists the Add-Ins that are available to load into Microsoft Excel. You would check a box to load an Add-In and make its commands and features available in Excel. To unload an Add-In and free up memory, uncheck the box. Unloading the add-in does not remove it from your computer. Loading an Add-In makes the feature available and adds any associated commands to the appropriate menus. For example, after loading the Analysis ToolPak, a new entry, Data Analysis, appears on the Tools menu.

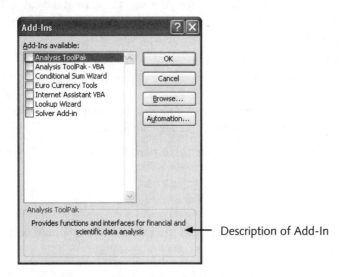

Figure 13-8   Add-Ins dialog box

By default, the Add-Ins dialog box lists Add-Ins installed only in the Program Files\Microsoft Office\Office11\Library folder (including its subfolders) or in the Windows\Profiles\ YourUserName\Application Data\Microsoft\Addins folder. You can click the Browse button to locate an Add-In program installed on your users' computer in locations other than those listed previously in this paragraph.

Activity 13-5: Loading and Unloading an Existing Add-In

Time Required: 15 minutes

Objective: Add or remove an existing Add-In to Excel.

Description: In this activity, you will practice loading and unloading an Add-In. You will find this activity useful in your career as a DST because, in order to answer users' questions about the loading and unloading of Add-Ins, you will need to have explored these in detail.

1. Log on to your computer with the user name **user01** and password **Password1**.

2. Click **Start**, point to **All Programs**, point to **Microsoft Office**, and click **Microsoft Office Excel 2003**.

3. Click the **Tools** menu. If necessary, click the **double chevron (>>)**.

4. Click **Add-Ins**, check the **Analysis ToolPak** check box, and the click the **OK** button.

5. Click the **Yes** button to install the Add-In.

6. Wait for the Installation to complete.

7. Click **Tools**, if necessary, click the **double chevron (>>)**, and click **Data Analysis** which displays the Data Analysis dialog box, as shown in Figure 13-9.

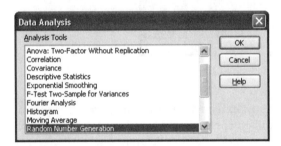

Figure 13-9   Data Analysis dialog box

8. Click the **Cancel** button.

9. Click the **Tools** menu, click **Add-Ins**, uncheck the **Analysis ToolPak** check box, and then click the **OK** button.

10. In your project log, write a brief summary that describes the reasons for loading and unloading an Add-In.

11. Close the Excel window.

Viewing Existing Add-Ins

To see which Add-Ins are installed in Excel, display the Add-Ins in the System Information window. To do this, click the Help menu, click About Microsoft Office Excel, and click System Info. Expand Office 2003 Applications, expand Microsoft Office Excel 2003, and click Add-Ins. A list of the Add-Ins is displayed. The display resembles Figure 13-10.

Locating New Add-Ins

Microsoft provides numerous Add-Ins on their Office Web site for use in Excel, PowerPoint, and Word. In addition to the Microsoft Add-Ins, there are even more Add-Ins available from independent developers. You will want to locate these Add-Ins by searching the Web for "Microsoft Office Add-Ins." With Microsoft's Add-Ins and the ones developed by these

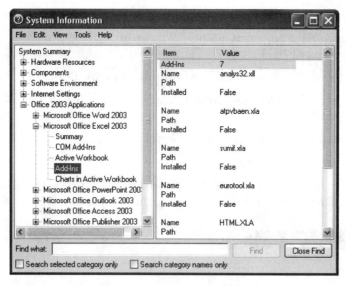

Figure 13-10   Excel Add-Ins listed

independents, your users will be able to extend Office and increase their productivity. Of course, you will want to test the Add-Ins prior to distribution to avoid possible security vulnerabilities, as indicated in the next section of this chapter.

Activity 13-6: Locating Add-Ins for Excel

Time Required: 15 minutes

Objective: Locate the available Add-Ins on the Microsoft Web site.

Description: In this activity, you will go to the Microsoft Office Web site and locate available Add-Ins for Excel. You will find this activity useful in your career as a DST because, in order to answer users' questions about finding Add-Ins, you will need to have explored this in detail.

1. If necessary, log on to your computer with the user name **user01** and password **Password1**.

2. Click **Start** and click **Internet Explorer** from the pinned-items list.

3. Type **office.microsoft.com** in the Address text box and press **Enter**.

4. Click the **Downloads** link under Home.

5. Click the **Downloads for Office 2003** link under BROWSE DOWNLOADS.

6. Click the **Add-ins** link under Excel 2003.

7. Review the Add-Ins for Excel 2003 list and click the link for any desired Add-In.

8. Read the explanation for the Add-In.

9. If you decide to apply the update, click the **Download** button. Otherwise continue with Step 12.

10. If necessary, uncheck the **Close this dialog box when download completes** check box. Click the **Save** button, record the name of the file in the File name text box in your project log, click the **My Documents** icon, and click the **Save** button.

11. When the download is complete, click the Close button.

12. In your project log, write a brief summary that describes the steps to locate and download an Add-In.

13. Close any open windows.

Installing and Testing Add-Ins

Your organization should not place itself at risk by deploying Add-Ins without testing them in your environment. To do so, could result in undesired side effects. For example, one undesired side effect could be that a user-created worksheet does not function—resulting in loss of time to the user.

Check with others in your organization to determine if computers have been set aside to test software prior to installation. If not, you may want to test the Add-In on your computer prior to deployment. Another alternative would be to conduct a pilot test of the Add-In. You would want to select representative users based on job requirements.

13

ACTIVITY

Activity 13-7: Installing and Testing Add-Ins

Time Required: 15 minutes

Objective: Install and test a previously downloaded Add-In.

Description: In this activity, you will install and test a previously downloaded Add-In. You will find this activity useful in your career as a DST because, in order to answer users' questions about working with Add-Ins, you will need to have explored these in detail.

1. If necessary, log on to your computer with the user name **user01** and password **Password1**.

2. Click **Start** and click **My Documents**.

3. Locate the *file name* that matches the file name you recorded in your project log.

4. Double-click the *file name*. Follow the on-screen instructions.

5. Close the **Internet Explorer** window and the **My Documents** folder.

6. In your project log, write a brief summary that describes the steps to install a previously downloaded Add-In.

7. Click **Start**, point to **All Programs**, point to **Microsoft Office**, and click **Microsoft Office Excel 2003**.

8. Complete the steps to test the Add-In installed in Step 4.

9. Close the Microsoft Excel window.

Managing Templates

Your users have and will want to take advantage of Office templates. You should be prepared to assist your users with the management of templates. As with Add-Ins, you will be involved with these tasks: locating, installing, and testing.

As with Add-Ins, templates are available from Microsoft and independent software developers. Searching the Microsoft Office Online Web site for a template is a feature of the Office applications. When your users click the File menu and click New, to create a New Document, New Workbook, or New Presentation, the respective New Document, New Workbook, or New Presentation task pane opens. From this task pane, they can start a search for the template of their dreams. Figure 13-11 shows the New Document task pane for Word.

Figure 13-11   New Document task pane

The top of the Templates section includes a search box named "Search online for:". Your users can start their search by typing keyword(s) into this box to identify templates that might meet the needs of their current project. This search box searches the content at the Microsoft's Office Online Web site and returns a list of templates with descriptions from Office Online.

Your user can select from the templates provided with Office, download one from the Office Download Web site, or use a commercial template that was purchased from an independent developer.

IN THE WORKPLACE Your users can create their own templates. For example, in Human Resources, a generic employment offer letter template could be created. After creating the prototype, it would be saved with the .dot extension. To create an offer letter, the Human Resources staff need only open that template, make the appropriate changes, and then save the file as a .doc file. This final saving stage would create a new document for a specific purpose without changing the content of the original template.

Activity 13-8: Locating and Installing Templates

ACTIVITY

Time Required: 15 minutes

Objective: Locate a template on the Microsoft Web site.

Description: In this activity, you will download and install a template from the Microsoft Web site. You will find this activity useful in your career as a DST because, in order to answer users' questions about templates, you will need to have explored these in detail.

1. Log on to your computer with the user name **user01** and password **Password1**.

2. Click **Start**, point to **All Programs**, point to **Microsoft Office**, and click **Microsoft Office PowerPoint 2003**.

3. Click the **File** menu and click **New**.

4. Type **school** in the Search online for text box, and click the **Go** button.

5. Click on the first template entry.

6. If you like the template, click the **Download** button, otherwise click the **Next** button until you find a template that you could use.

7. Wait for the download to complete.

8. If necessary, click the **No** button.

9. Close any open windows.

10. In your project log, write a brief summary that describes the steps to download and install a template.

11. Log off the computer.

13

Monitoring Security Vulnerabilities and Updates

Microsoft routinely issues security updates for both Windows XP and Office. A failure to apply a security update could compromise a desktop computer. For example, an attacker who successfully exploited vulnerability could take complete control of an affected system.

Now a rhetorical question: What happens if you miss a patch? To help you determine whether computers are vulnerable, Microsoft created the **Microsoft Baseline Security Analyzer (MBSA)** to allow you to check for missing patches and other security vulnerabilities for a wide range of Microsoft products including both Windows XP and Office.

In the sections that follow you will learn more about security bulletins, types of security updates, and the MBSA.

Security Bulletins

Microsoft **security bulletins** contain information about newly discovered security problems with Microsoft products. Each bulletin describes one specific security problem. In most cases each bulletin has an associated hot fix. In many cases there is also an associated Knowledge Base article, but this tends to be very short and merely points to the security bulletin.

Security bulletin numbers are in the form MS*yy-nnn*, where MS stands for Microsoft, *yy* is the last two digits of the year number, and *nnn* is the sequential bulletin number within the year. In 2002, Microsoft published 72 security bulletins. In 2003, they published 51 bulletins. You can receive security bulletins by e-mail. To do so, subscribe to Microsoft's Security Notification Service e-mail newsletter. This is free of charge. There is a link for subscription on this Web page: *www.microsoft.com/technet/security/bulletin/notify.mspx*

NOTE

You will want to surf to this Web site periodically to see if there are security bulletins relative to your environment: *www.microsoft.com/security*

Some security bulletins are released in two versions, a full detailed technical version and a very brief nontechnical version intended for general users. The technical versions of most bulletins are indeed fairly technical and assume familiarity with the subject matter. Some sections of some security bulletins are extremely technical. The brief versions are usually entitled "What You Need to Know About...". The nontechnical versions of most bulletins assume little or no technical knowledge above that of a normal computer user.

IN THE WORKPLACE

Microsoft Security Notification Service e-mails never contain attachments. Any e-mails purporting to originate from Microsoft that contain attachments are hoaxes and should be deleted immediately. Never click open an attachment in an e-mail that purports to originate from Microsoft as it is very likely to be a malicious virus.

For each security bulletin, Microsoft rates the impact that is intended to help your organization decide which patches should be applied and how rapidly your organization needs to take action. The severity rating system provides a single rating for each vulnerability (note that one bulletin can list or describe multiple vulnerabilities). The definitions of the ratings are as follows:

- **Critical:** Could allow the propagation of an Internet worm without user action.

- **Important:** Could result in compromise of the confidentiality, integrity, or availability of users' data, or of the integrity or availability of processing resources.

- **Moderate:** Is mitigated to a significant degree by factors such as default configuration, auditing, or difficulty of exploitation.

- **Low:** Is extremely difficult for it to exploit the desktop computer, or whose impact is minimal.

Microsoft Baseline Security Analyzer

In response to the criticism that Microsoft has received about the security of their products, Microsoft created a free tool to analyze security configurations. The MBSA can be used to detect security vulnerabilities on computers running Windows XP. For Windows XP (both XP Home and XP Professional), the following tests are performed:

- **Hot fix checks:** Scans for missing hot fixes.

- **Password checks:** Checks for blank or weak passwords.

- **Vulnerability checks:** Scans for known security issues and common configuration mistakes.

The MBSA does not work flawlessly. Some Microsoft security bulletins contain workarounds and manual fixes rather than patches to install. For items such as these, MBSA will report yellow Xs, which signifies that it could not tell whether you had applied the patch. Also, there may be discrepancies between what MBSA finds and what Windows Update detects.

Downloading and Installing the MBSA

The current MBSA is available from this Web site: *www.microsoft.com/mbsa*. From this page, you will click on the Download Now link to download the MBSA and install the MBSA. You will want to select the version for the language you want to read.

Activity 13-9: Downloading and Installing the MBSA

Time Required: 25 minutes

Objective: Download and install the MBSA.

Description: In this activity, you will download and install the MBSA. You will find this activity useful in your career as a DST because, in order to use the MBSA to check for security vulnerabilities, you will need to have explored this in detail.

1. Log on to your computer with the user name **admin01** and password **Password1**.

2. Click **Start** and click **Internet Explorer** from the pinned-items list.

3. Type **www.microsoft.com/mbsa** in the Address text box and press **Enter**.

4. Click the **Download Now** link and click the link below English.

5. When the File Download dialog box appears, as shown in Figure 13-12, read the Some files can harm your computer... message, and click the **Open** button.

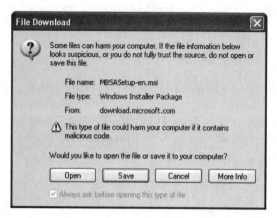

Figure 13-12   File Download message

6. Wait for the File Download to complete and the install to start.

7. Click the **Next** button, click the **I accept the license agreement** option button, click the two consecutive **Next** buttons, and click the **Install** button.

8. After the install completes, click the **OK** button.

9. In your project log, write a description of the steps to download and install the MBSA.

10. Close the Internet Explorer window.

Scanning for Updates with MBSA

Running the MBSA is exceptionally simple as you will see in Activity 13-12. After launching the program, you select the local computer and scan for missing hot fixes, security misconfigurations (see Figure 13-13), and so on.

When the scan completes, an output report appears on screen, as shown in Figure 13-14. The report categorizes vulnerabilities into groupings such as hot fixes, passwords expiration, and so on.

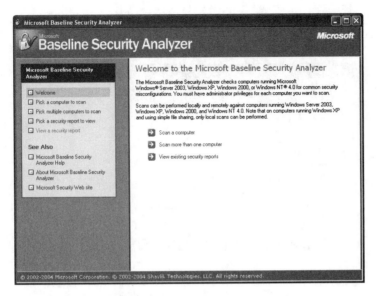

Figure 13-13   MBSA Welcome page

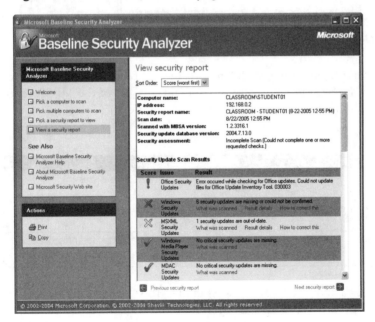

Figure 13-14   MBSA Security report

One area that you will want to pay particular attention to is the Windows Security Updates. In the current example that we are discussing, the report states that 30 security updates are missing or could not be confirmed. Clicking the Result details link provides a list of the missing security hot fixes.

The MBSA checks for security configuration errors. To see these, scroll the MBSA Security Report to the section named Windows Scan Results, as shown in Figure 13-15.

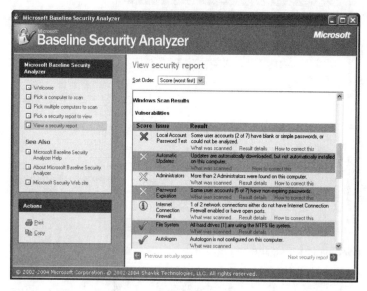

Figure 13-15   Windows Scan Results

What do the icons displayed on the MBSA reports mean? Table 13-1 names the icons used in the Security Update Scan Results section (see Figure 13-14) of the MBSA report. Table 13-2 explains the Windows Scan Results section (see Figure 13-15).

Table 13-1   Security update error icons

Symbol	Description	Example
Red X	Confirms a security update is missing on the scanned machine	A security update is missing
Yellow X	Warning messages	Computer does not have the latest service pack
Blue asterisk	Note messages	Security updates that cannot be confirmed as installed on the machine

You should examine each of the reported issues in the MBSA reports and decide if you need to take corrective actions. For example as reported in this scan, the Local Account Password Test indicates that two user accounts may have blank or simple passwords. Clicking the Result details link indicated that the User02 account and the Guest account had problems. This should be easy to correct. Because this is the Student01 computer and used by User01, you could delete the User02 account. The Guest account is disabled by default and will not be used. In your workplace, you should work through each of these problems and use the skills you developed in the previous chapters to complete the required actions. After reviewing the Security Update Scan Results and Windows Scan Results, you would then work through the remaining sections of the MBSA report. Those remaining sections are Additional System Information and Desktop Application Scan Results.

Table 13-2 Configuration error icons

Symbol	Description	Example
Red X	Critical check failed	A security update is missing, a user has a blank password
Yellow X	Noncritical check failed	An account has a nonexpiring password
Green checkmark	A critical or noncritical check passes	No issue was found for that particular configuration verification
Blue asterisk	Best practice (techniques that are known to provide positive results) checks	Checking if auditing is enabled
Blue I in circle	Information about the machine being scanned	Indicates the operating system version of the scanned machine

ACTIVITY

Activity 13-10: Analyzing Security with the MBSA

Time Required: 30 minutes

13

Objective: Analyze security with the MBSA.

Description: In this activity, you will run an MBSA on a computer to determine if the computer has security vulnerabilities. You will find this activity useful in your career as a DST because, in order to use the MBSA to check for security vulnerabilities, you will need to have explored this in detail.

1. If necessary, log on to your computer with the user name **admin01** and password **Password1**.

2. Click **Start**, point to **All Programs**, and click **Microsoft Baseline Security Analyzer 1.2.1**.

3. Click the **Scan a compute**r link and click the **Start scan** link.

4. Wait for the scan to complete.

NOTE

Depending on the status of previous updates, you may need to install updates before continuing with Step 5.

5. Locate the Vulnerabilities section under Windows Scan Results.

6. For the first entry, click the **What was scanned** link and write a brief explanation in your project log on what was scanned for the Windows Security Updates.

7. Close the top MBSA window. Click **OK** to restart your computer, if necessary.

8. Under Security Update Scan Results, for the Windows Security Updates, click the **Result details** link, then scroll and read over the list of Missing Security Updates.

9. Close the top MBSA window.

10. Click the **How to correct this** link, then scroll and read the solution for this problem.

11. Close the top MBSA window.

12. Scroll and locate the Windows Scan Results section.

13. Locate the **Local Account Password Test** entry, click the **What was scanned** link, and read the information on creating strong passwords.

14. Close the top MBSA window.

15. Click the **Result details** link, then scroll and locate the "weak" passwords.

16. Close the top MBSA window.

17. If available, click the **How to correct this** link, scroll and read the solution for this problem.

18. Close the top MBSA window.

19. Scroll and read the remaining entries in the MBSA report.

20. Close any open windows.

21. In your project log, write a brief explanation of how you would use the information supplied in an MSBA report to secure a desktop computer.

Methods to Distribute Updates

Few things change faster then operating system software, and updating operating system software can be a daunting experience. However, updating your users' operating system software with the latest and greatest can lead to improved security and performance for your users' computers. Microsoft makes the process easier with a number of system update methods for Windows XP:

- **Windows Update:** This online extension of Windows XP connects to the Windows Update Web site for product updates.

- **Automatic Updates:** Updates are downloaded when the computer has an active connection to the Internet.

- **Software Update Services (SUS):** With this method, updates are downloaded to a server on the organization's network for distribution to computers on the network.

These tools will be presented in order in the following sections.

Windows Update

Windows Update is an online extension of Windows XP that provides a central location for updates, such as hot fixes and service packs. New content is added to the Web site regularly. Thus, you will want to contact the Web site frequently to get the most recent updates and hot fixes to protect your computer and keep it running smoothly.

Windows Update scans your computer and provides you with a tailored selection of updates that apply only to the items on your computer. Any update that Microsoft considers critical to the operation of your computer is classified as a "critical update" and is automatically selected for you to install. Critical updates are provided to protect your computer from known security vulnerabilities or help resolve known issues.

ACTIVITY

Activity 13-11: Using Windows Update

Time Required: 30 minutes

Objective: Use Windows Update to scan a computer for needed updates.

Description: In this activity, you will practice using Windows Update to scan a computer for needed updates. You will find this activity useful in your career as a DST because, in order to scan a computer for needed updates, you will need to have explored this in detail.

1. If necessary, log on to your computer with the user name **admin01** and password **Password1**.

2. Click **Start**, click **Help and Support**, and click the **Keep your computer up-to-date with Windows Update** link

3. Click the **Scan for updates** link (or another appropriate link), as shown in Figure 13-16.

4. Wait for the scan to complete.

5. Click the **Review and install updates** link.

6. Review the updates. If you do not want an update, click the **Remove** button next to the update.

7. Click the **Install Now** button. Wait for the download to complete. Progress is indicated by a dialog box similar to Figure 13-17.

8. Close any open windows.

9. In your project log, write a brief summary that describes the steps to scan a computer for updates.

13

Figure 13-16   Using Windows Update

Figure 13-17   Windows Update - Web Page Dialog

Automatic Updates

Windows XP provides automatic updates. With this method, you will not need to check for new features posted to the Windows Update Web site. Because Windows Update downloads files from the Web site during periods of idle network activity, network bandwidth is conserved. However, you must be logged on with administrative privileges for this activity to take place.

To start the configuration of Automatic Updates, click Start, right-click My Computer, click Properties, and click the Automatic Updates tab. Figure 13-18 shows the Automatic Updates tab.

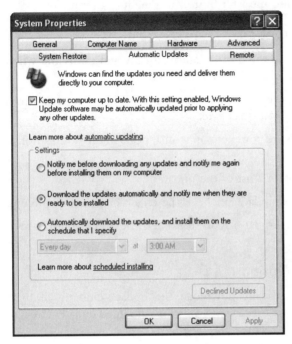

Figure 13-18 Automatic Updates tab

For this feature to work, the Keep my computer up to date check box must be checked. Note that there are three Automatic Update settings, as shown in Figure 13-18. They are discussed in the following sections.

Notify/Notify Update Option

This option appears as "Notify me before downloading any updates and notify me again before installing them on my computer." For this option, there are seven steps:

1. Windows Update uses the Internet connection in the background to search for downloads from the Windows Update Web site.

2. When there are updates, an Automatic Updates icon (globe with Windows logo) appears in the notification area of the taskbar.

3. Click the icon to obtain a list of the updates.

4. If you do not want an update, uncheck the check box next to the update.

5. Click Start Download to download the selected updates.

6. When the download is complete, another message appears in the notification area indicating that the updates downloaded.

7. You click the Automatic updates icon and click the Install button to install the updates or the Remind me later button to schedule a reminder.

Download/Notify Update Option

This option appears as "Download the updates automatically and notify me when they are ready to be installed." For this option, there are five steps:

1. Windows update uses the Internet connection in the background to download from the Windows Update Web site.

2. When the downloads are complete, an icon appears in the notification area of the taskbar.

3. Click the icon to obtain a list of the updates.

4. If you do not want an update, uncheck the check box next to the update.

5. Click the Automatic Updates icon and click the Install button to install the updates.

Download/Install Update Option

This option appears as "Automatically download the updates and install them on the schedule that I specify." You specify the day and time for scheduled updates to occur. For this option, there are six steps:

1. Windows Update uses the Internet connection in the background to search for downloads from the Windows Update Web site.

2. Windows Update uses the Internet connection in the background to download from the Windows Update Web site.

3. An icon appears in the Status area when the download is occurring.

4. When the downloads are complete, another message appears in the Status area, so that you can review the updates that are scheduled for installation.

5. If you do not want an update, uncheck the check box next to the update.

6. If you choose not to install at that time, Windows XP starts the installation on your schedule.

IN THE WORKPLACE

How do you feel about Automatic Update periodically calling home? Whenever Windows XP detects a live Internet connection, the Microsoft Windows Update server is contacted. If you are uncomfortable with this, remember you can turn Automatic Update off.

Activity 13-12: Scheduling Automatic Updates

Time Required: 15 minutes

Objective: Set a schedule for automatic updates.

Description: In this activity, you will establish a schedule for the installation of updates. You will find this activity useful in your career as a DST because, in order to establish a schedule for the installation of updates, you will need to have explored this in detail.

1. Log on to your computer with the user name **admn01** and password **Password1**.

2. Click **Start**, right-click **My Computer**, click **Properties**, and click the **Automatic Updates** tab.

3. Click the **Automatically download the updates and install them on the schedule that I specify** option button.

4. Click the **day** drop-down list arrow, as shown in Figure 13-19, and click **Every day**.

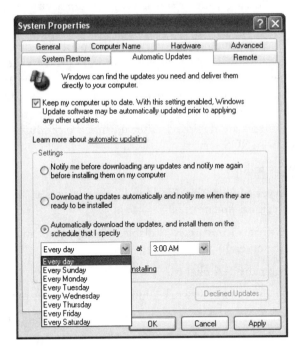

Figure 13-19   Day drop-down list

5. Click the **at** drop-down list arrow, and click the next hour.

6. Click the **OK** button.

7. In your project log, write a brief explanation of the steps to schedule an automatic update.

8. Log off the computer.

IN THE WORKPLACE

If MBSA and Windows Update both scan for missing hot fixes, which should you use? Both! Set up the Windows Update to run automatically. Run the MBSA periodically to audit that all the hot fixes have been applied.

Microsoft Software Update Services (SUS)

The Microsoft Software Update Services (SUS) is the solution to the problem of managing and distributing critical Windows XP updates. As a DST, why is SUS important? If your organization deploys more than a few hundred desktop computers, your organization will be deploying an SUS server. By using SUS, your organization can manage the distribution of Windows updates. SUS works by allowing your organization to set up a virtual Windows Update that can be used to collect and provide the updates in a timely manner.

Figure 13-20 illustrates the SUS environment. Starting at the top of the diagram, the Windows Update server at Microsoft provides the updates. A firewall protects the organization's network from the Internet while permitting communications between the Windows Update server and the SUS server. Within the organization's network, the SUS server manages the update process. Only the SUS server contacts the Windows Update server at Microsoft. To permit testing, test clients are deployed. After testing, the production clients download and install the updates from SUS server.

The steps in the SUS process are as follows:

1. Periodically the SUS server contacts the Windows Update servers at Microsoft to query the existence of critical updates.

2. When it is determined that an update is available, the update is automatically downloaded to the SUS server.

3. The update is tested using the Test clients.

4. When the update passes the tests, a network administrator approves the updates.

5. Periodically the Production Clients contact the SUS server to query the existence of approved updates.

6. The Production clients download and install the updates from the SUS server.

Note the change for the computers running Windows XP. Instead of each desktop computer connecting to the Windows Update servers at Microsoft, they connect to the SUS server located in the organization's network. Only approved updates are available for distribution. Your organization controls the update process!

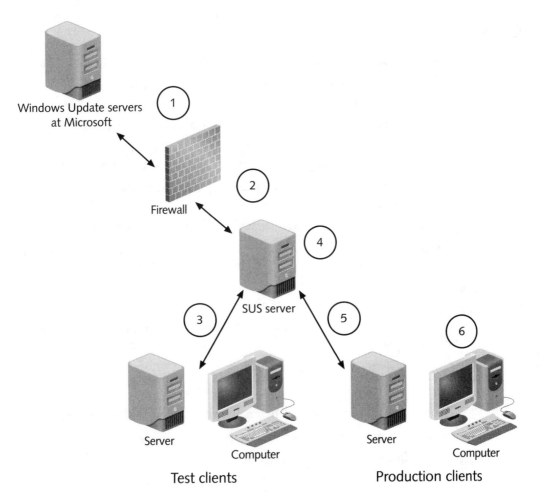

Figure 13-20 SUS environment

IN THE WORKPLACE

The next version of SUS will be called WUS! The Windows Update Services will use the MSI installer on the client. This is the same technology that is used to install Office. In addition, WUS will consolidate a smorgasbord of existing products: Windows Update, MSBA, and SUS 1.x.

CHAPTER SUMMARY

❏ You must be ready to track and identify applicable Office application updates.

  ❏ You learned about the three types of updates: critical updates, updates, and program upgrades.

  ❏ You learned about the differences in hot fixes and service packs.

  ❏ You discovered two ways to find information about updates, particularly critical updates, from Knowledge Base articles and the Microsoft Office Online.

  ❏ You learned the importance of assessing and testing the updates, prior to deployment.

❏ Your users will be using Office Application Add-Ins and templates.

  ❏ So that you can assist your users with Add-Ins, you learned about loading and unloading existing Add-Ins, viewing existing Add-Ins, locating new Add-Ins, and testing Add-Ins.

  ❏ You also learned about managing templates.

❏ As you know, security is a big issue with all organizations. You must be prepared to assist your Information Technology peers with monitoring security vulnerabilities and updates.

  ❏ You learned about security bulletins.

  ❏ You practiced downloading and installing the MBSA.

  ❏ Also, you ran scans on computers with the MBSA and interpreted the results.

❏ You learned three techniques to distribute updates.

  ❏ Windows Update was introduced.

  ❏ Automatic updates including how to schedule updates were discussed.

  ❏ With SUS, your organization can automate the distribution of updates from a server deployed within your organization.

KEY TERMS

Add-Ins — Supplemental programs that extend the capability of an application.

automatic update — Windows XP feature that automatically downloads and optionally installs updates.

critical update — Update that Microsoft deems should be installed promptly.

hot fix — Modification to a software product to address specific critical problems.

Microsoft Baseline Security Analyzer (MBSA) — Security-analysis tool that scans computers in search of security vulnerabilities or missing security updates.

pilot project — Subset of the computers on the network used to test service packs and updates. Used to determine if there are problems that could affect other computers on the network.

regression testing —The process that tests all of the fixes to make sure they do not conflict with each other or cause new problems while fixing old problems.

security bulletin — Bulletin issued by Microsoft indicating that a security vulnerability has been identified. The bulletin provides specific instructions to correct the security problem.

service packs — Updates to software that fix existing problems and, in some cases, deliver product enhancements.

Software Update Services (SUS) — Used to deploy critical updates to computers running Windows XP. A form of the Windows Update that has been configured for deployment in private networks.

templates — Predesigned documents, worksheets, or presentation files.

test network — Network that contains computers with the standard hardware and software used in the organization's network.

update — Software release to add minor new features to a product or to correct errors found in the product.

upgrade — A new or enhanced version of the product.

Windows Update — Online extension of Windows XP that can download and install updates.

13

REVIEW QUESTIONS

1. Microsoft highly recommends that _____ be installed to fix security problems.

   a. program upgrades

   b. program extensions

   c. updates

   d. critical updates

2. Which of the following is a program that has had numerous free upgrades? (Choose all that apply.)

   a. Outlook

   b. Outlook Express

   c. Internet Explorer

   d. Word

3. When searching the Knowledge Base, which search type is available? (Choose all that apply.)

   a. All Words

   b. Full Text

   c. Title Only

   d. Article ID

4. Which one of the following is the Web site for Microsoft Office Online?

   a. *http://online.microsoft.com*

   b. *http://office.microsoft.com*

   c. *http://office.online.microsoft.com*

   d. *http://online.office.microsoft.com*

5. If Microsoft identifies an update as critical, which action should you take?

   a. Install the update immediately on all computers

   b. Test the update

   c. Assess the update and test the update

   d. Assess the update, test the update, and install the update

6. When you want to scan a computer for needed updates and then download and install the update on a single computer, you would use the Office _____ Center.

   a. Online

   b. Update

   c. Upgrade

   d. Download

7. When you know which update you want to install on multiple computers, you would use the Office _____ Center.

   a. Online

   b. Update

   c. Upgrade

   d. Download

8. You will want to test a critical update _____ prior to installing a critical update.

   a. on a user's computer

   b. on your computer

   c. on a test network

   d. with a pilot project

9. _____ are supplemental programs provided by Microsoft that extend the capabilities of Office programs.

   a. Macros

   b. Add–Ins

   c. Templates

   d. Updates

10. Which component can an Office template contain? (Choose all that apply.)

   a. styles

   b. macros

   c. toolbars

   d. custom menu settings

11. Microsoft created the _____ to allow you to check for missing patches and other security vulnerabilities.

   a. Microsoft Border Security Analyzer

   b. Macro Baseline Security Analyzer

   c. Microsoft Baseline Security Assistant

   d. Microsoft Baseline Security Analyzer

13

12. Which of the following is a characteristic of a Microsoft security bulletin? (Choose all that apply.)

   a. describes one specific security problem

   b. usually has an associated hot fix

   c. usually has an associated Knowledge Base article

   d. contains information about a newly discovered security problem

13. An update with a(n) _____ security rating could allow the propagation of an Internet worm without user action.

   a. critical

   b. important

   c. moderate

   d. low

14. An update with a(n) _____ security rating could result in compromise of the confidentiality, integrity, or availability of users' data, or of the integrity or availability of processing resources.

   a. critical

   b. important

   c. moderate

   d. low

15. An update with a(n) _____ security rating is mitigated to a significant degree by factors such as default configuration, auditing, or difficulty of exploitation.

    a. critical

    · b. important

    c. moderate

    d. low

16. For Windows XP, the MBSA performs which of the following tests?

    a. scanning for missing hot fixes

    b. checking for blank or weak passwords

    c. scanning for common configuration mistakes

    d. scanning for known security issues

17. The MBSA displays a _____ icon when a security update is missing.

    a. red exclamation mark

    b. red X

    c. yellow exclamation mark

    d. yellow X

18. Which of the following is a system update tool provided by Microsoft? (Choose all that apply.)

    a. Knowledge Base

    b. Windows Update

    c. Microsoft Baseline Security Analyzer

    d. Software Update Services

19. Which of the following is an option on the Automatic Updates tab? (Choose all that apply.)

    a. Notify me before downloading any updates and notify me again before installing them on my computer.

    b. Download the updates automatically and notify me when they are ready to install.

    c. Automatically download the updates and install them on the schedule that I specify.

    d. Schedule the download for the updates and install them on the schedule that I specify.

20. Which of the following is a characteristic of the SUS environment? (Choose all that apply.)

    a. Obtains updates from the Windows Update servers at Microsoft.

    b. Testing is undertaken on Test clients.